D0034960

Kaua'i

Luci Yamamoto

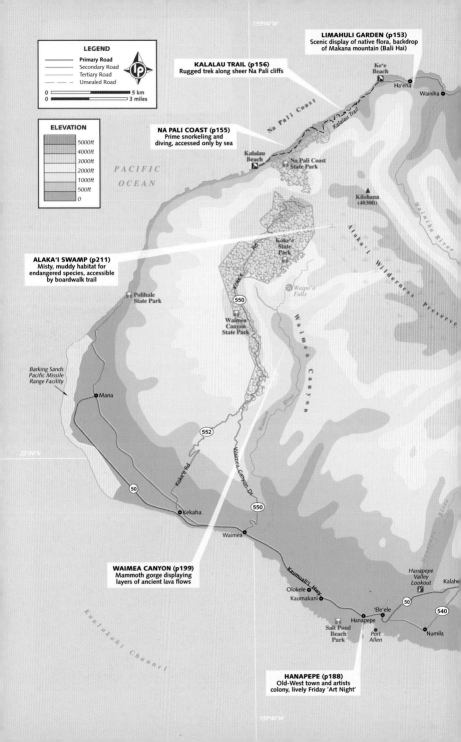

LEGEND

Primary Road
Secondary Road
Tertiary Road
Unsealed Road

0 ————— 5 km
0 ————— 3 miles

ELEVATION

5000ft
4000ft
3000ft
2000ft
1000ft
500ft
0

LIMAHULI GARDEN (p153)
Scenic display of native flora, backdrop
of Makana mountain (Bali Hai)

KALALAU TRAIL (p156)
Rugged trek along sheer Na Pali cliffs

NA PALI COAST (p155)
Prime snorkeling and
diving, accessed only by sea

ALAKA'I SWAMP (p211)
Misty, muddy habitat for
endangered species, accessible
by boardwalk trail

WAIMEA CANYON (p199)
Mammoth gorge displaying
layers of ancient lava flows

HANAPEPE (p188)
Old-West town and artists
colony, lively Friday 'Art Night'

PACIFIC
OCEAN

Na Pali Coast

Ke'e
Beach

Ha'ena

Wainiha

Kalalau
Beach

Na Pali Coast
State Park

Kalalau Trail

Kilohana
(4030ft)

Kōke'e
State
Park

Kōke'e Rd

Alaka'i Wilderness Preserve

Wainiha River

Waipo'o
Falls

Polihale
State Park

550

Waimea
Canyon
State Park

Waimea Canyon

Barking Sands
Pacific Missile
Range Facility

Mana

552

Kōke'e Rd

Waimea River

22°00'N

50

Waimea Canyon Dr

Kekaha

550

Waimea

Kaumuali'i Hwy

Olokele

Kaumakani

'Ele'ele

Hanapepe

Salt Pond
Beach
Park

Port
Allen

Hanapepe
Valley
Lookout

Kalahe

50

540

Numila

Hanapepe River

Kaulakahi Channel

159°40'W

159°40'W

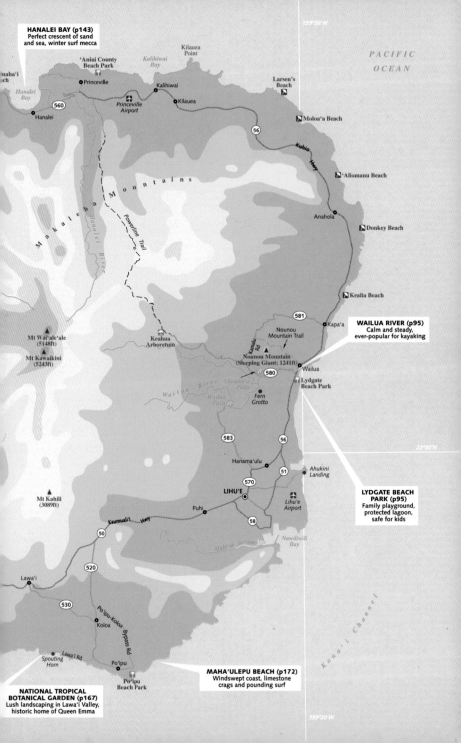

HANALEI BAY (p143)
Perfect crescent of sand and sea, winter surf mecca

PACIFIC
OCEAN

'Anini County Beach Park

Kilauea Point

Kalihiwai Bay

Larsen's Beach

Princeville

Kalihiwai

560

Kilauea

Moloa'a Beach

Princeville Airport

Hanalei

56

Hanalei Bay

Kuhio Hwy

'Aliomanu Beach

M o u n t a i n s

Anahola

Donkey Beach

Hanalei River

M a k a l e h a

Powerline Trail

Kealia Beach

Mt Wai'ale'ale (5148ft)

581

Kapa'a

WAILUA RIVER (p95)
Calm and steady, ever-popular for kayaking

Mt Kawaikini (5243ft)

Keahua Arboretum

Nounou Mountain Trail

Nounou Mountain (Sleeping Giant; 1241ft)

Wailua

580

Wailua River

'Opaeka'a Falls

Lydgate Beach Park

Wailua Falls

Fern Grotto

583

56

Hanama'ulu

Mt Kahili (3089ft)

570

Ahukini Landing

51

LIHU'E

Puhi

58

Lihu'e Airport

LYDGATE BEACH PARK (p95)
Family playground, protected lagoon, safe for kids

Kaumuali'i Hwy

50

Huleia Stream

Nawiliwili Bay

Lawa'i

520

530

Po'ipu-Koloa Bypass Rd

Koloa

K a w a i ' i   C h a n n e l

Spouting Horn

Lawa'i Rd

Po'ipu

Po'ipu Beach Park

MAHA'ULEPU BEACH (p172)
Windswept coast, limestone crags and pounding surf

NATIONAL TROPICAL BOTANICAL GARDEN (p167)
Lush landscaping in Lawa'i Valley, historic home of Queen Emma

159°20'W

22°00'N

159°20'W

Destination Kaua'i

Call it an 'island's island.'

Kaua'i has all the ingredients of a tropical idyll. Look *makai* (toward the sea) and see endless swaths of sand and sea. Look *mauka* (toward the mountain) at towering cliffs, impossibly green and velvety.

Circle the island and marvel at its diversity. The North Shore exudes blooming abundance, a heaven on earth that envelops all who enter. The Westside, with starkly beautiful red-dirt terrain and the vast Waimea Canyon, is just the opposite, exposing one to the elements. The South Shore is a lively gathering place, where the weather and waters are inviting year-round. The Eastside, the island's commercial center, is a down-to-earth mix of locals and tourists, where Mt Wai'ale'ale looms above the Wailua River and plants grow like Jack's beanstalk.

But there's something more, something beyond the Garden Isle's staggering natural beauty.

Locals, who often take for granted their spectacular setting, regard Kaua'i as their own tropical getaway. By far the least-developed major Hawaiian Island, Kaua'i has no skyscrapers and no large towns, only three public high schools and three cinemas – and, among born-and-bred Kaua'ians, little heed for yuppie trappings like luxury cars and designer clothes. Without Honolulu's urban pace, Maui's tourist bustle and the Big Island's sheer vastness, Kaua'i seems more approachable – an island easy to embrace.

The focus on nature is understandable. But the heart of Kaua'i lies in its small-town character – which for now staunchly persists. Kaua'i is an island proud of its island roots.

Opposite: The perfect sandy crescent of Hanalei Bay (p143) lures surfers and sunset-lovers alike.
ANN CECIL

PETER HENDRIE

Nani Ka 'Aina
Beautiful Is the Land

KARL LEHMANN

Featured in the opening credits of the long-running TV show *Fantasy Island*, Wailua Falls (p79) officially plummets 80ft, though some measurements have topped 175ft.

ANN CECIL

Stunning Waimea Canyon (p199), the 'Grand Canyon of the Pacific,' was formed by ancient volcanoes and lava flows. It's now home to Kaua'i's longest river, the Waimea.

ANN CECIL

Kilauea Lighthouse is part of the Kilauea Point National Wildlife Refuge (p128), a sanctuary for nesting seabirds.

ANN CECIL

Tranquil Limahuli Garden (p153) features endangered native plants as well as modern introductions.

8

Helicopter tours (p62) penetrate the otherwise-inaccessible Mt Wai'ale'ale Crater, the wettest place on earth.

Who says Kona is king? Java drinkers from Blair Estate Organic Coffee Farm (p117) sure don't think so.

Emerald-green taro crops abound in lush Hanalei Valley (p140), where the majority of Hawaii's commercially grown poi taro is produced.

KARL LEHMANN

The 11-mile Kalalau Trail (p156) is Hawaii's premier back-packing trail, offering breathtaking scenery and rugged adventure along the island's Na Pali Coast (p155).

ANN CECIL

The enclosed lagoon at Lydgate Beach Park (p95) offers Kaua'i's safest year-round swimming, not to mention excellent snorkeling.

KARL LEHMAN

Hawaii's state bird is the endangered nene (Hawaiian goose; p48). They can be spotted around the island and frequent the Kilauea Point (p128) and Hanalei (p141) National Wildlife Refuges.

Moreton Bay fig tree roots are exposed at Allerton Garden (p167), originated by Hawaii's Queen Emma in the 1870s.

AUSTRALIAN PICTURE LIBRARY / CORBIS / ROBERT HOLM

Nani O Ke Kai
Beautiful Is the Sea

LEE FOSTER

HOLGER LEUE

The Kalalau Trail (p156) rewards hikers with tide pools and snorkeling at Ke'e Beach (p154).

Vast and often luxuriously empty Kekaha Beach Park (p198) is a haven for surfers, swimmers and beachcombers.

Looking for a remote paradise? Visit Polihale State Park (p199) for endless beach, experts-only surf and brilliant sunsets.

KEVIN LEVESQUE

ANN CEC

The virtually inaccessible island of Ni'ihau (p214), a Native Hawaiian preserve, is visible from Kekaha Beach Park (p198).

Drop-dead gorgeous Lumaha'i Beach (p150), one of the world's most frequently photographed beaches, starred alongside Mitzi Gaynor in the 1958 classic film *South Pacific*.

ANN CEC

CASEY & ASTRID WITTE MAHANEY

Surround yourself with schools of colorful fish, like these bluelined snapper, and other diverse marine life while scuba diving (p59) Kaua'i's reef, wall and wreck sites.

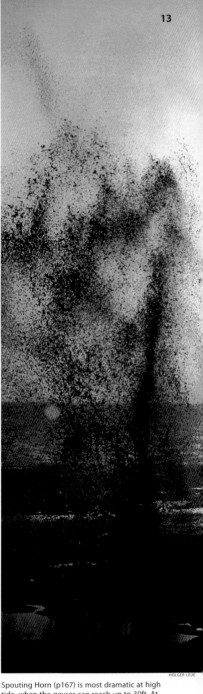

HOLGER LEUE

Spouting Horn (p167) is most dramatic at high tide, when the geyser can reach up to 30ft. At low tide, the gurgling spurt can be unimpressive.

LEE FOSTE

Kaua'i's North Shore boasts some killer waves in winter, but the summer brings surf to the South Shore beaches like Po'ipu Beach (p170).

The top spots for windsurfing (p60) are along the North Shore, especially 'Anini Beach Park (p133).

ANN CECI

AUSTRALIAN PICTURE LIBRARY / CORBIS / JONATHAN BLAIR

As cute and cuddly as Hawaiian monk seals (p170) look, keep your distance – at least 100ft, by law. Monk seals are the most endangered species on Kaua'i, so are well protected.

Kayaking (p55) is all the rage on Kaua'i, especially along the Wailua River (p95).

KARL LEHMANN

Beach-glass lovers rejoice! Multihued Glass Beach (p185) is a collector's mecca.

KARL LEHMANN

Next page:
Spacious Pu'u Poa Beach (p136) offers respite from ritzy Princeville.
ANN CECIL

Contents

Regional Map Contents

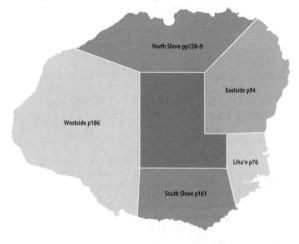

North Shore pp128–9

Eastside p94

Westside p186

Lihu'e p76

South Shore p161

The Authors

LUCI YAMAMOTO

Luci Yamamoto is a fourth-generation native of Hawaii, thus she's not fazed by rain, pidgin or Hawaiian street names. After growing up in Hilo on the Big Island, she left for college in Los Angeles with a simmering case of rock fever. She then moved to Berkeley for law school and spent two summers working in Honolulu, contemplating practicing land-use law while dreaming about a Plan B escape. She ended up joining the California Bar before finally switching careers to pursue writing. Her past work for Lonely Planet includes *Hawaii* 7 and *Hawai'i: the Big Island* 2. Today she is a freelance writer in Vancouver, British Columbia – and she jumps at any chance to return to her native islands.

My Kaua'i

I'm loyal to my Big Island home but Kaua'i is my adopted favorite. The island is small but surprisingly diverse, and each place exudes a distinct vibe. Residential neighborhoods, eg scenic Wailua Homesteads (p106), are great for escaping other tourists, and the surf culture of Hanalei (p142) is palpable and contagious. For ocean fun, I recommend Ke'e Beach (p154) for snorkeling, Hanalei Bay (p143) for surfing and Lydgate Beach Park (p95) for a lazybones day. Koke'e State Park (p206) cannot be beat for hiking in solitude. I savor take-out *poke* from fish markets, and no trip is complete without shave ice (p120). My favorite hangout towns are eclectic Kapa'a (p115) and Wild-West Hanapepe (p188) on Friday 'Art Night.' And I always make time for yoga classes at Yoga Hanalei (p145) and Creative Yoga Kaua'i (p103).

CONTRIBUTING AUTHORS

David Boynton wrote the Environment chapter. David grew up on the beach at Kailua, O'ahu, but his interests turned to the forest environment after college. Twenty years after he moved to Kaua'i, he helped develop the Koke'e Discovery Center, an overnight outdoor-education facility. He has worked in his 'forest classroom' as an environmental resource teacher since 1994. David's writing and photography has been published in numerous local and national magazines; he also has several books to his credit.

Nanette Naioma Napoleon wrote the History chapter. Nanette is a freelance researcher and writer from Kailua, O'ahu, specializing in the history and cultures of Hawaii. She has written a daily history column for the *Honolulu Star-Bulletin* newspaper, and currently writes feature history stories for the *'Oiwi Files News Journal,* a Native Hawaiian newspaper. She is also the state's leading authority on historic graveyards.

Dr David Goldberg wrote the material that formed the basis for the Health chapter. Dr Goldberg completed his training at Columbia-Presbyterian Medical Center in New York City. He is an infectious-disease specialist and the editor-in-chief of www.mdtravelhealth.com.

LONELY PLANET AUTHORS

Why is our travel information the best in the world? It's simple: our authors are independent, dedicated travelers. They don't research using just the Internet or phone, and they don't take freebies in exchange for positive coverage. They travel widely, to all the popular spots and off the beaten track. They personally visit thousands of hotels, restaurants, cafés, bars, galleries, palaces, museums and more – and they take pride in getting all the details right, and telling it how it is. For more, see the authors section on www.lonelyplanet.com.

Getting Started

In a weeklong stay, you can do Kaua'i a modicum of justice. A brief island-hopping trip is also feasible but avoid the temptation to 'circle' the island in a madcap attempt to see everything. Despite its small size, it varies greatly from place to place, so if you have specific expectations, choose wisely and you won't be disappointed.

Kaua'i is a financial splurge only if you cannot live without chichi resorts and restaurants. Touring the island on a budget is possible, if you plan in advance. Avoid paying rack rates by booking accommodations online.

WHEN TO GO

See Directory for more information on climate (p220) and on festivals and events (p223).

Kaua'i's climate is balmy year-round, so there is no off-season in terms of weather. Winter (mid-December through March) is *generally* cooler and rainier than summer (June through August), but both are relatively mild, with consistent tradewinds. Of course, be prepared for unexpected winter downpours. In February 2005, Mt Wai'ale'ale was drenched with over 18in of rain in one 24-hour period – during which Hanalei saw 8in and Wailua and Hanapepe each received 4in.

Depending on your desired outdoor activities, season can really matter: the 17-mile Na Pali Coast kayaking 'challenge' (p144) is possible only in calmer summer waters. Hiking the Kalalau Trail is treacherously slippery during rainy weather, so the drier summertime is typically better. Surf conditions are seasonal: North Shore and Westside waters are typically calm from May to September, with powerfully high surf from October to April. South Shore and Eastside conditions are just the opposite. Of course, weather and waves are unpredictable, so conditions must be assessed on a daily basis.

Another consideration is the tourist season: the winter high season means higher prices for accommodations, plus larger crowds at main attractions. The best times to visit are fall (September through early December) and spring (April through early June), when prices drop and summer vacationers are gone.

DON'T LEAVE HOME WITHOUT...

- Dark clothing (no whites) – red dirt does stain.
- Snorkeling gear if you plan to snorkel often.
- Any specialty items (from maternity swimsuits to Smart Wool socks), as shopping is limited.
- Lightweight rain gear for sudden downpours.
- Broken-in hiking boots or shoes.
- Practicing your 4WD off-roading if you want to explore the backcountry.
- Rashguard (O'Neill can't be beat for perfect fit and cool style).
- ATM card or traveler's checks (small businesses don't accept credit cards).
- Setting your internal clock to 'Hawaiian time' (relaxed pace and hang-loose attitude).
- Sunglasses and sun hat.
- Copy of your travel-insurance policy (see p224).
- Binoculars for whale and bird watching.

Major holidays, including Thanksgiving, Christmas and the New Year week (see p224), create another high-season tier, nudging lodging prices yet higher. A world-famous event is the PGA Grand Slam of Golf (p173) in late November, when all eyes watch the year's top foursome at Po'ipu Bay Golf Course.

COSTS & MONEY

Among the Hawaiian Islands, Kaua'i is one of the pricier destinations. Budget accommodations are limited and, on the North Shore, virtually nonexistent. Basic needs, such as gasoline, are more expensive here. But if you book one of the cheap sleeps early and eat take-out, you can stretch your dollars. Of course, the sky's the limit for a luxury jaunt in Po'ipu or Princeville.

Airfares vary greatly, particularly from the US mainland, where you can expect to pay about $400 round-trip from the west coast and $600 from the east coast. Interisland flights generally cost between $75 and $105 one way, but specials can drop fares to $39. Book by Internet, not by phone, for the lowest fares. The arrival of go!, a discount air carrier, in 2006 and the Hawaii SuperFerry (p233) in 2007 promise to reduce interisland travel costs.

Kaua'i's bus system is quite limited and, frankly, you can't see the island properly without a car. Renting a compact car typically costs between $160 and $250 per week, plus taxes and fees. Rates fluctuate wildly and vary widely among different agencies; obtain Internet quotes and lock in the best rate.

Accommodations run the gamut, with the cheapest motel or inn rooms starting from $40 to $45 nightly. Most prevalent are midrange options, which start between $80 to $100 but typically run closer to $150. To hear soothing waves outside your window, expect to pay $200 nightly, while you're out $350 for the cheapest room at top-end hotels and condos.

To cut costs, weekly and monthly condo or vacation-home rates are unbeatable. Most include full kitchen and washer/dryer. If you prefer the amenities of hotels or the personal touch of B&Bs, inquire about discounts for multiple-night stays.

Grocery items imported from the mainland typically cost 25% higher on Kaua'i. Local produce is also surprisingly pricey, especially if it's organic. Still, eating in is always cheaper than eating out. Enjoy bargains at fish markets (p67), farmers markets (p88) and roadside fruit stands.

Many sights and activities are discounted for children and seniors (see p222).

TRAVEL LITERATURE

Learn about Kaua'i's unique relationship to the other Hawaiian Islands in Edward Joesting's classic *Kaua'i: The Separate Kingdom* (1988). Chuck Blay and Robert Siemers cover everything geological about Kaua'i, from its volcanic origins to the cathedral cliffs of Na Pali, in their colorfully illustrated *Kauai's Geologic History: A Simplified Guide* (2004) – not quite 'simple' but ever fascinating.

Environmentalist David Boynton captures the island's scenic splendor in *Kaua'i Days* (2005), a classy photographic collection. Identify the island locations of your favorite movie scenes in *The Kaua'i Movie Book* (1996), by Chris Cook, with photography by David Boynton.

A good primer on Hawaiian history, Gavan Daws' *Shoal of Time: A History of the Hawaiian Islands* is almost required reading (and certainly so for local high-school students). It covers the period from Captain

HOW MUCH?

Wailua River kayak tour $40-90

Camping per night $0-10

Hawaii Regional Cuisine dinner per person $40

View of 'Bali Hai' sunset $0

1hr helicopter tour $200

TOP TENS

Festivals & Events

Locals sure know how to throw a party. Visit during one of Kaua'i's main attractions and you're bound for an unforgettable experience. For more listings, see p223.

- Kaua'ian Days (islandwide, January; p223)
- E Pili Kakou I Ho'okahi Lahui (Lihu'e, January; p84)
- Koloa Plantation Days Celebration (Koloa, July; p164)
- Aloha Festival (islandwide, August; p223)
- Kaua'i Composer's Contest and Concert (Lihu'e, September; p85)
- Kaua'i Mokihana Festival Hula Competition (Po'ipu, September; p173)
- Annual Eo e Emalani I Alaka'i (Koke'e State Park, October; p212)
- 'Kaua'i Style' Hawaiian Slack Key Guitar Festival (Lihu'e, November; p85)
- PGA Grand Slam of Golf (Po'ipu, November; p173)
- Lights on Rice Parade (Lihu'e, December; p85)

Hidden Adventures

To understand Kaua'i you must veer off the beaten path and see places yet to be developed, and locals in their own backyards.

- Handmade chips at Taro Ko Chips Factory in Hanapepe (p191).
- Backcountry trails around Koke'e State Park (p208).
- The Maha'ulelpu Coast along the island's undeveloped southeast shore (p172).
- Touring the Hanalei National Wildlife Refuge on the Ho'opulapula Haraguchi Rice Mill Tour (p145).
- The Waimea Rock Cabin in rugged, red-dirt country (p195).
- Secluded beaches in Kekaha and beyond (p197).
- Genuine Hawaiian bodywork at Angeline's Mu'olaulani (p123).
- Challenging backpacking trek to Kalalau Valley (p156).
- Peaceful picnic site at Keahua Arboretum (p100).
- Kayaking smaller tributaries, such as Hanalei River (p144) and Kalihiwai Stream (p132).

Activities on a Shoestring

Kaua'i is not exactly a budget destination, but if you appreciate simple pleasures, you won't miss out. For a list of top noncondo budget rooms, see p106.

- Hike for free on trails across the island (p61).
- Play golf at Kukuiolono Golf Course (p182) for $8, or after noon, for lower rates, at world-class resort courses (p63).
- Rent a place with a kitchen and eat in.
- Buy take-out poke (p67) and farmers-market produce (p88).
- Fill your gas tank on the Eastside (and never at the Princeville Chevron!).
- Watch a sunset from the lawn outside the Princeville Hotel (p135).
- Entertain the kids at Lydgate Beach Park's giant playgrounds (p95).
- Rent a kayak and go solo on the manageable Hanalei River (p144).
- Visit Limahuli Garden (p153), a $10 stroll through thriving native flora.
- Whale watch (p187) from the shore during winter (binoculars help).

Cook's arrival to statehood. More approachable is *Yesterday in Hawaii: A Voyage Through Time* by Scott CS Stone, with compelling photos and drawings.

Hawaii literature, written by locals, hit the national radar in the 1990s. Introduce yourself to the genre with *Growing Up Local: An Anthology of Poetry and Prose from Hawai'i*, a compendium that captures both the pidgin vernacular and local perspectives. For more on Hawaii literature, see p45.

Introduce children to island culture with *Hide & Seek in Hawaii: A Picture Game for Keiki*, a stunningly photographed series of 'find-the-object' books by Jane Hopkins and Ian Gillespie. If phrases like *da kine* and *stink eye* perplex you, must-reads are Douglas Simonson's *Pidgin to da Max* and its sequel, *Pidgin to da Max Hana Hou*, illustrated pidgin dictionaries guaranteed to make you laugh until you hurt.

INTERNET RESOURCES

County of Kaua'i (www.kauai.gov) Basic county information, eg bus schedules, farmers markets and camping permits.

Kaua'i Festivals (www.kauaifestivals.com) Handy list of festivals for the entire year.

Kaua'i Visitors Bureau (www.kauaidiscovery.com) Attractive, user-friendly introduction to Kaua'i.

LonelyPlanet.com (www.lonelyplanet.com) Travel news and nifty Thorn Tree bulletin board, where you can get the lowdown from recent Kaua'i visitors.

Ulukau: The Hawaiian Electronic Library (www.ulukau.org) Online Hawaiian-to-English (and vice versa) dictionaries and key Hawaiian texts.

Itineraries

CLASSIC ROUTES

SHORT, SWEET SAMPLER   Four to Five Days

A weekend might seem enough for a 555-sq-mile island, but Kaua'i deserves more. In five days, you can enjoy a sampler tour.

Get your bearings on day one by kayaking up **Wailua River** (p95), fed by Mt Wai'ale'ale. Drive up scenic **Kuamo'o Rd** (p98), stopping at the sights and enjoying a picnic at **Keahua Arboretum** (p100). Relax at **Lydgate Beach Park** (p95), with a sheltered lagoon and playground. On day two, head to the North Shore and hike the first leg of the **Kalalau Trail** (p156). Recover by snorkeling at **Ke'e Beach** (p154), and catch the sunset from **Hanalei Bay** (p143).

The next day, drive to **Waimea Canyon** (p199), stopping at the **Waimea Canyon Lookout** (p200) and the **Kalalau** and **Pu'u o Kila Lookouts** (p207); choose from a range of **hiking trails** (p202 and p208).

On day four, relax in sunny **Po'ipu** (p166) and enjoy some swimming, snorkeling, surfing, boogie boarding or scuba diving. Stroll through the lush **National Tropical Botanical Garden** (p167). Stop in **Koloa** (p162) for souvenir shopping and a taste of *poke* (cubed, marinated raw fish) from the **Koloa Fish Market** (p165). Spend your last day trying an activity on your to-try list or simply enjoying a leisurely day.

Short on time? You can still explore the entire island, from Ke'e Beach to Koke'e State Park (82 miles), and appreciate its natural wonders. Establish a home base and go day-tripping.

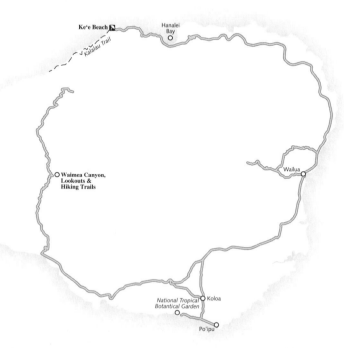

CIRCLE TOUR
Eight to Nine Days

Exploring Kaua'i properly requires at least a week, plus a car. The main hubs are Po'ipu, Princeville and the Coconut Coast – and here we'll start on the North Shore. Before hitting the road, see p235 and check www .kauaiworld.com/gasprices for current gas prices.

On the first day, shake off jet lag with an invigorating snorkel at **Ke'e Beach** (p154) or by hiking the first leg of the **Kalalau Trail** (p156). Eat, drink and be merry in **Hanalei** (p142). The next day, take a **surfing lesson** (p145) and visit **Limahuli Garden** (p153) in Ha'ena. Stop by the **Princeville Hotel** (p135) to watch the sun set behind Makana mountain, commonly known as 'Bali Hai.'

On day three go bird watching at **Kilauea Point** (p128) and hang out in lively, nouveau-hippie **Kapa'a** (p115). Browse at shops and galleries, and don't miss a shave ice from **Hawaiian Blizzard** (p120). Paddle the **Hule'ia River** (p82) or try **ziplining** (p82) or **tubing** (p82). Find a picnic spot at **Keahua Arboretum** (p100) or hike the **Eastside trails** (p103).

Head to the South Shore on day five: tour the verdant **National Tropical Botanical Garden** (p167) and sail to the **Na Pali Coast** (p185) to snorkel. On day six, visit awesome **Waimea Canyon** (p199) and hike in Koke'e State Park's unique **Alaka'i Swamp** (p211).

After touring the island for a week, splurge on a **helicopter ride** (p190) to identify your favorite places and see otherwise-inaccessible spots like famous Mt Wai'ale'ale. Visit quaint **Hanapepe** (p188) on a Friday 'Art Night.' On day eight, walk to **Maha'ulepu Beach** (p172) or play a round of **golf** (p63). End your trip by repeating a favorite activity or just put your feet up and relax.

With over a week, you can immerse yourself in local culture, which is surprisingly varied across the island. Along the 82-mile journey, try the gamut of outdoor adventures, including outstanding hiking, kayaking and surfing. You'll surely marvel at compact Kaua'i's amazing diversity.

TAILORED TRIPS

EXTREME ADVENTURE

Fit, outdoorsy types will relish the plethora of adventures on Kaua'i. Generally summer is the best time. The grueling 17-mile **Na Pali Coast kayaking trip** (p144), feasible only during summer, is a must. Novices, try sea kayaking off **Po'ipu** (p171) as training. River kayaking is another option, especially **Wailua River** (p100) and **Hanalei River** (p144).

South Shore waters offer decent scuba diving, but advanced divers should head to **Ni'ihau** (p171 and p185). Snorkeling is best offshore along the **Na Pali Coast** (p185), where catamarans and rafts sail year-round. Surfing is great all year, at **Hanalei Bay** (p143) and **Tunnels Beach** (p151) in winter and at **Kalapaki Beach** (p79) and **Po'ipu** (p171) in summer.

Windsurfing is excellent at **'Anini Beach** (p133) and, for experienced folks, the **Maha'ulepu Coast** (p172). The signature backpacking experience is the **Kalalau Trail** (p156), which traverses sheer Na Pali cliffsides. There's also a myriad of trails crossing **Koke'e State Park** (p206) and **Waimea Canyon State Park** (p199). Scenic hiking is also available on the **Eastside** (p103). Rugged mountain bikers can use almost any hiking trail or dirt paths (there are countless old cane-haul roads) across the island. For more information on outdoor activities in Kaua'i see p54.

THE LAND & THE PEOPLE

Tourism is Kaua'i's main industry today, but historically agriculture drove the island's economy. Take a cultural ecotour to appreciate the island's colorful past. First bone up on Hawaiian history at **Kaua'i Museum** (p78) in the heart of Lihu'e. Stop by **Grove Farm Homestead** (p81) and **Wai'oli Hui'ia Church & Mission House** (p142) to witness missionary plantation life. Learn about Kaua'i's geological origins at **Koke'e Natural History Museum** (p207).

Next head to **Limahuli Garden** (p153) to view native and Polynesian-introduced flora. Check out heiau (ancient Hawaiian religious sites) and other ancient sites across the island.

Commercial agriculture might miss sugarcane, but it's still a major industry on Kaua'i. Tour the Gay & Robinson **sugar plantation** (p191), the last on Kaua'i. As owners of Ni'ihau island, the Robinsons play a key role here; their Ni'ihau **helicopter tour** (p215) is a unique experience. In Hanalei the **Ho'opulapula Haraguchi Rice Mill tour** (p145) allows you to view the otherwise off-limits Hanalei National Wildlife Refuge, a historic rice mill and a working taro farm. Sample coffee at **Kaua'i Coffee** (p185) and **Blair Estate Organic Coffee Farm** (p117), and stop at **Guava Kai Plantation** (p129) to see rows of neatly planted guava trees. Take home a live orchid plant from **Yamada's Orchid Nursery** (p121).

GARDENS GALORE

It ain't called the 'Garden Isle' for nothing. Plenty of sun and rain means anything green thrives here. Just driving around residential neighborhoods you'll see backyard gardens bursting with fruits and flowers. On the South Shore, the biggie is the **National Tropical Botanical Garden** (NTBG; p167), which comprises the Allerton and McBryde Gardens, deep in the Lawa'i Valley. A modest but impressive cactus and succulents garden, **Moir Gardens** (p169), sits prettily on the grounds of the Kiahuna Plantation.

On the North Shore, don't miss NTBG's **Limahuli Garden** (p153), a scenic display of native Hawaiian flora. Learn to distinguish between native species and plants introduced by Polynesians or by modern Westerners. For a stark contrast, also visit the sprawling, sculpture-filled, meticulously landscaped gardens at **Na 'Aina Kai Botanical Gardens** (p127), near Kilauea.

On the Eastside, the grounds of **Smith's Tropical Paradise** (p96) resemble Disneyland more than untouched Kaua'i, but they provide a pleasant setting for the on-site luau. The 458-acre site at **Kaua'i's Hindu Monastery** (p100), perched above Wailua River, is stunningly green, featuring both natural foliage along a stream and hundreds of flourishing trees planted by resident monks. Viewing is allowed only during tours. If you're a garden fan, consider staying in the **Wailua Homesteads** (p106), an upland neighborhood where rainfall is a given and houses are surrounded by luxuriant leafiness.

Snapshot

Anyone who beholds Kaua'i immediately deems it 'paradise.' But behind the island's natural splendor and laid-back lifestyle, change is rampant. Perhaps more apt than the word 'paradise' are Joni Mitchell's unforgettable lyrics: 'They paved paradise, and put up a parking lot.'

For years sugar was Kaua'i's largest agricultural industry, but today only one plantation is left (see p191), and diversified agriculture is a goal. Coffee, taro and guava are profitable but they hardly fill the gap.

Tourism is the overwhelming base of Kaua'i's economy, for better or for worse. Remarkably Kaua'i's tourist industry is a post-WWII phenomenon: Lihu'e Airport's modern site was built in 1950 and the first famous resort, Coco Palms, in 1953. By 1970 tourism jobs outnumbered agriculture jobs, causing simmering opposition to resort development. By 1987 luxury resorts emerged in Po'ipu and Princeville. Today one million visitors arrive annually.

The biggest local complaint is traffic. Weekday commute gridlock is guaranteed into Lihu'e from the Westside and especially from the Eastside. Road distances might be short, but Kaua'i is 100% dependent on the automobile. Residential neighborhoods are typically far from commercial centers – and locals *never* take the bus!

The county is allowing massive new resort development across the island. Underway in both Po'ipu and Princeville are 2000 to 3000 new condo units. Developers are also gentrifying average-income neighborhoods such as Hanama'ulu, just outside Lihu'e, which is slated for a 1500-unit development. Many worry about Kaua'i's already-strained highway, water and sewage infrastructure.

The housing market is rapidly shifting from owner-occupied homes to vacation rentals. Especially since 9/11, real-estate sales have skyrocketed – a boom often attributed to spooked citydwellers' desires for secluded island hideaways. To US mainlanders, Kaua'i land prices are relative bargains, and their buying power has shoved locals out of contention. In 2000 the median home price was a mere $250,000; in 2005 it became the state's highest at $700,000 (of course, that North Shore beach house of your dreams probably runs above $3 million). In 2006 the market softened slightly, but clearly Kaua'i has been 'discovered' and there's no turning back. In places like Po'ipu, Princeville and Hanalei, where second-home vacation rentals are the norm, locals lament the disintegration of 'community,' when neighbors are tourists with no long-term stake in the neighborhood.

Another issue is reduced access to natural areas: tourists often seek off-the-beaten-path adventures nowadays, entering wilderness previously used only by locals intimately familiar with the land (eg surfers and hunters intimately familiar with the land). When they go off-trail or jump into ponds and get injured, the state or county sometimes prohibits all entry to the place (to avoid legal liability), ultimately encroaching on locals' traditional stomping grounds (and ticking off groups like the Sierra Club).

Since the mid-1990s, big-box retailers, including Wal-Mart, Kmart and Home Depot, have mushroomed in Lihu'e. Chains such as Starbucks and Jamba Juice in 2004 joined the longstanding Pizza Hut and McDonald's branches, which locals unabashedly frequent. A much-contested Costco will likely open in fall 2006 – to the chagrin of those seeking to prevent further Californization and suburbanization of the island.

FAST FACTS

Population: 62,000

Land area: 555 sq miles

Maximum building height: 40ft (height of a coconut tree)

Total number of resident-owned vehicles: 36,800

Median household income: $45,000

Unemployment rate: 5.3%

Residents born in Hawaii: 62%

Princeville residents born in Hawaii: 23%

Anahola residents born in Hawaii 85%

Average commute time: 21.5 min

History Nanette Naioma Napoleon

MYTH, MIGRATION & FOREIGN INVASION

In one version of Hawaiian creation, the islands of the Hawaiian archipelago were born from the gods, with Kaua'i being *hiapo* (firstborn), a status that came with attendant privileges and responsibilities. Some say this is why Kaua'i was favored with Mt Wai'ale'ale (literally, 'overflowing water'), the 5514ft precipice on central Kaua'i that is the wettest place on earth, with an average rainfall of more than 400in per year (see p220).

The Hawaiian word for wealth is *waiwai*, with *wai* being fresh water, the basic element of all life. Kaua'i was blessed with a great wealth of fresh water to make the island grow into an abundant and beautiful place. And indeed, such is the case. The island's nickname, the Garden Island, is a testament to this.

Most archaeologists now believe that the first settlers of the Hawaiian Islands came from Marquesas Islands via Southeast Asia around 2000 years ago. Why they came is still a subject of debate. Some speculate it was because of famine or overpopulation, while others believe that the migration was led by chiefs who wanted new lands to rule without competition from other chiefs. Still others believe that these first settlers were much like the astronauts of today: adventurers out on voyages of discovery to the unknown.

Whatever the reason, travel they did across the biggest body of water on the planet, across 2000 miles of open ocean in two great migration waves over a period of 200 years. Over time, all of the eight major islands were settled and a new 'Hawaiian' culture emerged that was similar to other Polynesian cultures, yet unique in many ways.

However, because the island of Kaua'i (and Ni'ihau its closest neighbor) was located relatively far from the islands of O'ahu, Maui, Moloka'i and the Big Island of Hawai'i, which are clustered close together, Kaua'i evolved more slowly culturally, socially and politically.

In his book *Kaua'i: The Separate Kingdom*, Edward Joesting says that 'Kaua'i was a place distinct from the other islands…an independent and isolated place…whose isolation prevented it from invasion by chiefs from the other islands.' And thus it remained for over a thousand years until one fateful day in 1778.

The Rise & Fall of Captain Cook

When esteemed British naval captain James Cook inadvertently sighted the uncharted island of O'ahu on January 18, 1778, during his third great voyage of discovery to the Pacific, he became the first Westerner to do so. While this find would later make Cook a hero of legendary proportions in Europe, it would also be, quite literally, the death of him, and would change the course of Hawaiian history and culture in many unalterable ways.

Strong westerly winds on that fateful day forced Cook to abandon landing on O'ahu. Instead he rode the winds and came upon the island

The Kaua'i Historical Society website, www.kauaihistoricalsociety.org, highlights many of the island's historic and cultural sites, and lists current historical and cultural community events.

Kauai Ancient Place-Names and Their Stories (1998), by Frederick B Wichman, is recommended for visitors who want more in-depth information about sites on the island and the colorful stories behind them.

TIMELINE	1770s	1835
	Captain Cook makes landfall at Waimea Bay on Kaua'i, explores the Big Island, and is killed at Kealakekua Bay	Ladd & Company establishes the first large-scale sugar plantation in the Hawaiian Islands, at Koloa, Kaua'i

of Kaua'i, where he made landfall on January 20 at Waimea Bay (p192). Cook promptly named the islands the 'Sandwich Islands,' after his patron, the Earl of Sandwich.

Cook and his men were enthralled with Kaua'i and its inhabitants, considering them to be 'robust and handsome' in physical appearance, and 'friendly and generous' in trade dealings. The Hawaiians, on the other hand – who had not seen people from outside the islands for hundreds of years – found Cook and his men to be quite astounding.

Most historians believe that, to the Hawaiians, Cook was the earthly manifestation of the great god Lono, who left the islands with the promise that he would return with an abundance of food and other resources for the people. Islanders thronged to the bay to witness this great event and to trade goods. (See the boxed text, p35.)

After two weeks on the islands, Cook continued north on his mission to find the elusive Northwest Passage across North America. For eight months Cook searched in vain, and when the frigid north winds approached, he reluctantly headed south to winter in Hawaii.

On November 26, 1778, Cook sighted Maui for the first time, but did not land, choosing instead to head farther south to explore the nearby island of Hawai'i with its towering volcanic mountains, the likes of which he had never seen before. After cruising the eastern coast of the Big Island for 47 days in search of a suitable landing, Cook came across the picturesque Kealakekua Bay on January 17, 1779, where he landed.

After a leisurely stay of two weeks at Kealakekua, which nearly depleted the local supply of food and other resources, Cook departed for a second attempt at the Northwest Passage. But only two days later, while still near the Big Island, his ships ran into a powerful storm that severely damaged the main mast of the *Resolution*. Reluctantly, Cook limped back to Kealakekua to make the needed repairs.

However, when Cook arrived this time he was not greeted as a returning god, but rather as a houseguest who had stayed too long. The high chief of the area, Kalaniopu'u, was reluctant to take the now-limited resources from his people to pay tribute to Cook, who had lost some of his status as a god. Events that occurred over the next few days led to feelings of animosity on both sides, culminating in a tense confrontation between Cook and Kalaniopu'u. The result was an armed skirmish and the death of Cook, several of his men and many Hawaiians. The exact circumstances of Captain Cook's death still generates debate among Cook scholars.

The Captain Cook statue in Waimea is one of six Cook memorials on the islands, and one of more than 80 worldwide.

The Captain James Cook Society has a comprehensive website, www .captaincooksociety.com, containing a plethora of information on the intrepid traveler.

The Floodgates Open

When the news of Cook's discovery of the Hawaiian Islands reached Europe, it opened a floodgate of other Western explorers, traders, farmers and merchants eager to exploit this new Pacific resource. Whalers came by the thousands and villages such as Honolulu (O'ahu) and Lahaina (Maui) quickly became the main whaling ports of the Pacific. Traders ravaged the countryside on all islands in search of the aromatic sandalwood, a commodity that brought high revenues in China. Sugar planters established some of the most productive plantations in the world, making them wealthy and politically powerful.

1860	1898
First hotel on Kaua'i opens, the Fairview Hotel in Lihu'e. New Hawaii census shows a total population of only 69,800 across the islands	First automobile appears on the islands

THE KINGDOM OF HAWAII

Among the Hawaiian warriors in the battle that felled Captain Cook was a young, exceedingly tall and physically strong man named Paiea. Over a period of 30 years this charismatic leader, who became known as Kamehameha the Great, would accomplish what no other chief had ever done before: rise through military conquests to be the *mo'i* (king) of the islands of Hawai'i, Maui, Moloka'i and O'ahu.

The Kauai Papers (1991), by the Kaua'i Historical Society, gives the reader a glimpse of life on Kaua'i during the 19th and early 20th centuries through personal accounts and stories that bring the people of the island to life.

To make his domain complete, Kamehameha tried to conquer the island of Kaua'i, but was thwarted by the formidable island chief Kaumuali'i. Kamehameha did, however, manage to negotiate a diplomatic agreement with the chief, which put the island under Kamehameha's new kingdom, but gave Kaumuali'i the right to rule the island somewhat independently.

Kamehameha is credited with unifying all of the islands, bringing an end to the interisland rivalries and wars, and establishing a peaceful and solidified kingdom. He was widely acknowledged as being a benevolent and just ruler, much loved by his people until his death in 1819.

Upheaval: Missionaries Replace Tradition

Upon the death of King Kamehameha the Great, and at the urging of some foreigners, the young King Kamehameha II (Liholiho), in concert with the Queen Regent Ka'ahumanu, ordered that the ancient religious *kapu* system be abolished. The *kapu* was a strict set of religious and social laws that governed every aspect of Hawaiian life, such as what people could eat, how they should live and whom they should worship. Consequences for breaking the *kapu* could range from minor beating or banishment to immediate death. The fall of the *kapu* system proved to be the beginning of the end of hundreds of years of tradition and stability.

The first missionary station in Hawaii was established at Waimea in 1820.

When the Boston-based brig *Thaddeus* arrived in Kona on the Big Island on April 4, 1820, with the first group of foreign missionaries to the islands, they just happened to arrive during the early tumultuous months of the abolishment of the *kapu* system, when Hawaiian society

---

HAWAII'S RULING MONARCHS

All of Hawaii's monarchs died in office except for Queen Lili'uokalani, who was overthrown in 1893 (p33). She died in 1919. Kamehameha I came to power through conquest; his sons, Kamehameha II and III, and grandsons, Kamehameha IV and V, succeeded him. Because Kamehameha V died in office without any children and without naming an heir, an election was held among eligible Hawaiian nobles, resulting in a victory for Lunalilo. Under similar circumstances, Kalakaua was also elected, and Lili'uokalani inherited the throne from Kalakaua, her brother.

The following table lists Kaua'i's ruling monarchs in chronological order:

Ruler	Reign	Ruler	Reign
Kamehameha I	1795-1819	Kamehameha V	1863-72
Kamehameha II	1819-24	Lunalilo	1873-74
Kamehameha III	1824-54	Kalakaua	1874-91
Kamehameha IV	1854-63	Lili'uokalani	1891-93

1900

Hawaii becomes a US territory. Census report puts the population of Hawaii at 154,000, with Caucasians only 6% of the total

1925

First attempted mainland-to-Hawaii airplane flight ends 25 hours and 300 miles short of landfall

was in great social and political upheaval. Subsequently many of the people, particularly the *ali'i* (chiefs), found the foreigner's Protestant faith an appealing replacement. Ka'ahumanu, in particular, embraced this new religion with great enthusiasm, encouraging her people to do the same. And many did just that, not wanting to live without any kind of religious structure.

For the next 50 years, more missionaries of different faiths came to the islands and jostled with each other for dominance in the rabid soul-saving atmosphere that ensued. These missionaries are credited with setting up many schools and teaching Hawaiians how to read and write, which helped them to communicate with the increasing numbers of foreigners on the islands. Most of the religious doctrines they preached, however, required the abolishment of some of the most fundamental social and religious practices of the Hawaiians, such as hula dancing (see p43), which was seen as 'licentious and vulgar,' and surfing, which was seen, as one missionary put it, as a 'wanton waste of precious time that could be better used to serve God in spiritual pursuits.'

Kaua'i has a number of historic churches, such as the Wai'oli Hui'ia Church (p142) in Hanalei, which date back to this time and have become popular wedding venues.

The word *waita*, as in Waita Reservoir in Koloa, is a combination of the Hawaiian word *wai* (water) and the Japanese word *ta* (rice paddy). The Hawaiian language has no letter *t*.

On the Brink of Extinction

In addition to bringing new religious, social and political doctrines, the foreigners also brought a slew of new diseases – such as smallpox, diphtheria, typhoid fever and tuberculosis – to which the Hawaiians, being so isolated from the rest of the world, had no immunity.

When Captain Cook arrived, he found a thriving population of between 500,000 and 800,000 people. By the time the first missionaries arrived, fewer than 25 years later, that population had dwindled to 130,000. By the turn of the 20th century that number had dropped to 39,000. Today the total number of pure Hawaiians is less than 1% of the total population, while the total number of part-Hawaiians is about 19% of the population.

King Sugar

Ko (sugarcane) arrived in Hawaii with the early Polynesian settlers. While Hawaiians enjoyed chewing the cane for its juices, they never refined it into sugar. The first known attempt to produce sugar in Hawaii was in 1802, when a Chinese immigrant on the island of Lana'i boiled crushed sugarcane stalks in iron pots. In 1835 a young Bostonian named William Hooper founded Hawaii's first large-scale sugar farm, Koloa Plantation (p162), which operated for 113 years. By 1850 the number of plantations on the islands had grown to seven, and the industry was beginning to take off. Fewer than four decades later, there were 80 plantations and 'King Sugar' was the backbone of the Hawaiian economy.

Because the Hawaiian population was declining at an alarming rate, the planters had to import cheap labor from outside Hawaii. The Chinese were the first group of contract laborers to be imported in 1851, followed by the Japanese in 1868 and the Portuguese in 1878. These laborers made as little as $1 per day and lived in plantation 'camps', divided by

1936	1946
First commercial airplane service from the mainland to Hawaii started by Pan American Airways	The largest tsunami to hit Hawaii in recorded history devastates Hilo on Hawai'i, killing 165 and causing $26 million in damages

ethnicity in order to keep the races from mingling and possibly teaming up to form unions. Life was harsh on the plantation for these workers, and most left the fields after their two-to-three-year contracts expired. This added greatly to the diverse ethnic population that has made Hawaii such a cosmopolitan state.

The website www .hawaiiweb.com/kauai /html/sites/koloa_town .html describes the color and charm of Old Koloa Town, one of the few intact historic towns on the islands.

Because of the economic dominance of sugar, virtually all of the sugar barons became highly influential in the business community as well as in government and politics. These planters, most of whom were American, made concerted efforts to bring the kingdom of Hawaii into the political and economic sphere of the United States, in order to have sugar import taxes reduced or waived altogether. In 1876 they successfully lobbied Congress to ratify a reciprocity treaty, which allowed sugar from Hawaii to enter the United States duty-free. This not only increased the planter's economic standing, but also solidified their political influence.

End of a Kingdom

In 1893 a small group of visiting American marines, urged by the sugar planters and the US American Consul on the islands, stormed 'Iolani Palace, the royal residence and capitol in Honolulu, and successfully overthrew the ruling monarch, Queen Lili'uokalani, in a bloodless coup d'etat.

A few years earlier the Queen had witnessed the forced signing of a new constitution by her brother, King Kalakaua. This 'Bayonet Constitution,' as the Hawaiians called it, effectively took away many of the constitutional and traditional powers of the monarch, and placed them in the hands of an oligarchy of foreigners in high government positions.

When the Queen came to power upon the death of King Kalakaua, she made it publicly known that she would restore the old constitution, which subsequently launched a secret plot by the Committee of Safety (whose members were mostly missionary descendants) to overthrow her and abolish the kingdom. On January 17, 1893, they did just that, despite the fact that there was a treaty with the US that acknowledged the sovereignty of the kingdom. Also unusual, the citizens of the independent nation had never been asked, through a referendum vote, if they approved of annexation, which had been required of all other territories seeking statehood.

THE ANTIANNEXATION PETITION

After the overthrow of the monarchy in 1893, both the revolutionists and the royalists lobbied hard in Congress for their respective causes. Hawaiians staged mass rallies and formed two protest groups: Hui Aloha 'Aina, also known as the Hawaiian Patriotic League, and Hui Aloha 'Aina o Na Wahine. In 1897 the groups launched an all-island antiannexation petition drive that garnered more than 21,000 signatures, which was more than two-thirds of the entire population.

A delegation of Hawaiians hand-delivered this petition to Congress with an emotional plea to reinstate the sovereign Kingdom of Hawaii, which was illegally overthrown, but their appeal was denied. Despite ongoing protests by the majority of the citizens, annexation was granted in 1898 – an action that was unprecedented in the history of the United States.

1967	1969
The first year during which there are a million visitors to the islands	The *Hawaii Five-O* TV series makes its debut and runs for 12 years

When word of the illegal overthrow reached President Grover Cleveland, he immediately sent an envoy, Congressman James Blount, to the islands to conduct an investigation. Despite Blount's scathing 1400-page report, which in the end condemned the overthrow and recommended the restoration of the crown, and in spite of President Cleveland's urgings, Congress refused to restore the kingdom.

THE LONG ROAD TO STATEHOOD

After the overthrow of the kingdom, the monarchy was first replaced by a provisional government; a republic was declared 18 months later. The primary goal of the leaders of the republic, none of whom was Hawaiian, was to obtain annexation to the United States. Even though most Hawaiians were fervently against annexation and signed an antiannexation petition to make their view known, their cry went unheeded with the new government leaders (see p33). Heavy lobbying in Congress on the part of the sugar planters and other foreigners finally paid off when, on July 7, 1898, Hawaii was annexed to the US, and on April 30, 1900, was declared a territory through the Organic Act.

'On July 7, 1898, Hawaii was annexed to the US, and on April 30, 1900, was declared a territory through the Organic Act'

But the road to statehood would not be an easy one. In the early part of the 20th century, members of Congress, particularly those from the south, did not like the fact that the majority of the population on the islands was made up of non-whites: primarily Hawaiians, Japanese, and Chinese. The fact that Hawaii was not a contiguous part of the US was another factor against statehood.

As the early years of the 20th century went by and Hawaii sugar and dock workers began to form powerful unions, 'Red Scare' and 'Yellow Peril' sentiments swept the country, resulting in a harsh and misinformed conclusion that these unions were in control of the islands and that most of their members were communists.

It was not until WWII (1941–45), when so many Hawaii residents of Japanese descent served loyally and valiantly in the all-Japanese 442nd Infantry Battalion and the 100th Combat Regiments, did the tide turn in Hawaii's favor with regard to statehood.

Finally, in August 1959, both houses of Congress voted to approve statehood, President Dwight D Eisenhower signed the statehood bill, and Hawaii residents approved statehood in a voter plebiscite. Hawaii had finally become a state.

STATEHOOD AT LAST!

When the US House of Representatives voted 323 to 89 in favor of statehood for Hawaii on March 12, 1959, the citizens of the territory celebrated almost continually for two days. Businesses, government offices and schools were shut down, and big commemorative events where held at 'Iolani Palace, Honolulu Hale (City Hall), Kawaiaha'o Church and the Honolulu Stadium. Church bells rang throughout the islands, streets were closed off, people attended parades in the day and danced at night until dawn. Large bonfires were lit, the Navy shot flares into the sky from ships offshore and fireworks displays were seen everywhere. It was a time of wild jubilation and excitement shared by the majority of citizens on the islands. Antistatehood proponents, however, mostly kept to themselves during those days, and wept silently.

Early 1970s	1975
Protect Kaho'olawe 'Ohana begins to protest the use of the island of Kaho'olawe as a practice bombing site by the US Navy	*Hokule'a* makes its maiden voyage from Hawaii to Tahiti

---

THE HAWAIIAN SEASONS

The traditional Hawaiian calendar consists of only two seasons: the wet season, from November to April; and the dry season, from May to October. The calendar is based on the nightly phases of the moon instead of the coming and going of the sun.

Fishing and farming were conducted according to specific phases of the moon, each of which had a name (a moon chant made the names easier to memorize). On the first night of the new moon, for example, reef fish hid in caves; therefore it was best to go deep-sea fishing. For farming, the 18th to 21st moon phases were best for gathering medicinal herbs. Certain moon phases were dedicated to specific gods, and carried certain *kapu* (restrictions on what could be fished or farmed, and what could or could not be eaten).

TOURISM & THE JET AGE

After WWII tourism began to grow rapidly, largely fueled by returning GIs who had been stationed on the islands during the war. Almost overnight, the laidback rural resort area of Waikiki experienced a boom in hotel development. In 1959, the same year as statehood, the first commercial jetliner landed in Honolulu, bringing with it the first of millions of visitors from across the globe.

Over the next 40 years tourism would continue to grow while the sugar industry waned, mostly due to the decline in the price of sugar produced outside the US, where the labor costs were much lower. The last of the major sugar plantations were forced to close in the 1990s. Since then, diversified agriculture and high-tech industries have been pushing hard to fill the economic gap left by the loss of the sugar industry.

Kaumuali'i Hwy in south Kaua'i is named for the last island king who ruled here before King Kamehameha the Great unified all of the islands.

THE HAWAIIAN RENAISSANCE

One of the most profound social changes to affect Hawaii during the last 30 years has been the birth of the 'Hawaiian Renaissance' movement.

Throughout most of the 19th and 20th centuries, Hawaiians were increasingly colonized and marginalized by Western social, political and economic influences. The Hawaiian language had nearly died out, land was impossible for most Hawaiians to buy, and most of the traditional ways of life, which supported a self-sustaining and independent people for over 2000 years, were lost. Without these, Hawaiians lost much of their own identity and became alienated within their own homeland. As a sad result, Hawaiians have experienced the highest incidences of crime rates, life-threatening health problems and a host of other social problems.

In the early 1970s this began to change when the **Protect Kaho'olawe 'Ohana** (PKO; www.kahoolawe.org), a small group of native Hawaiians on the island of Moloka'i, began to protest the use of the tiny island of Kaho'olawe as a practice bombing site by the US Navy. The Hawaiian community rallied strongly around this cause, and even though it was a long and painful struggle, it instilled a new political awareness that prompted many Hawaiians into taking more active social and political measures to help to improve the conditions of the Hawaiian people. (In 2003 the Navy released the island from practice bombings.)

In 1975 another event would also dramatically alter modern Hawaiian culture: the **Polynesian Voyaging Society** (PVS; www.pvs-hawaii.com) was formed.

1982	1986
Hurricane 'Iwa causes one death and $234 million in damages, $150 million on Kaua'i	The first Hawaii-born astronaut, Major Ellison Onizuka, dies aboard the space shuttle Challenger when it explodes shortly after take off

This group's goal was to build a long-distance voyaging canoe, in the manner of the ancients, to prove that the first settlers to the islands were capable of navigating the Pacific without the use of Western technology such as sextants and compasses.

The Kauai Album (1981), by Carol Wilcox, John Wehrheim and TK Kunichika, tells the story of the island's grassroots community through beautiful black-and-white photos and insightful essays.

When the *Hokule'a* made its maiden voyage from Hawaii to Tahiti in 1975, it instantly became a symbol of rebirth for Hawaiians, prompting a cultural revival unparalleled in Hawaiian history. Hula, which had largely been stripped of its traditional roots, began to emerge once again as thousands of Hawaiians and non-Hawaiians enrolled in hula schools across the state. Many Hawaiians became dedicated students in the nearly lost arts of feather-lei making, *lua* (a form of martial art), and many other traditional crafts and activities. Hawaiian language–immersion schools were established, and more than just a handful of Hawaiians began attending college and earning degrees.

1992	1999
Hurricane 'Iniki kills six, causes more than $3 billion in damages and strands some *Jurassic Park* film-crew members on Kaua'i	Largest aloha shirt ever made, with a chest measurement of 14ft and a neck measurement of 5ft, is created by Hilo Hattie

The Culture

REGIONAL IDENTITY

At first glance, being 'local' in Hawaii means talking pidgin and wearing a T-shirt and *rubbah slippah* (rubber flip-flops). But underneath it's a mindset that comes from living 2500 miles from the nearest continent, in communities where everyone knows everyone. Here family background and connections are important – not to be snooty, but to find common bonds.

Among the major Hawaiian Islands, Kaua'i is the most rural, where no town population reaches 10,000 and circling the island takes less than three hours. All the Neighbor Islands are considered 'country,' if not *da boonies* (the boondocks), compared to Honolulu – and Kaua'i remains the most countrified of the major islands. If locals themselves crave a tropical hideaway, especially for honeymoons, they head to Kaua'i.

Kaua'ians tend to be easygoing and low-key. Rarely will locals voice their opinions in public or 'make waves.' Most avoid embarrassing confrontations and prefer to 'save face' by keeping quiet. Public conversations, both among friends and strangers, are typically kept to casual topics; if you hear an intense discussion on international politics, Greek philosophy or sex and relationships, it's likely the speakers are mainland transplants or tourists. That said, locals do have opinions – they just don't broadcast them.

On Kaua'i one sees only minimal mainland influences. Sure, kids watch the same TV and listen to the same music as mainlanders. Sure, small pockets of highly educated and upper-income residents also fall outside the usual definition of 'local-ness,' as they speak no pidgin and aspire to professional careers. But overall Kaua'i people are less striving and competitive. They take pride in being local – and despite the spate of moneyed newcomers, they remain smug that local-insider status cannot be bought.

WHO'S WHO

- Hawaiian: people of Native Hawaiian ancestry. It's a faux pas to call any Hawaii resident 'Hawaiian' (as you would a Californian or Texan), thus ignoring the existence of an indigenous people.

- Local: people who grew up in Hawaii. Locals who move away retain their local 'cred,' at least in part. But longtime transplants (see below) never become local. To call a transplant 'almost local' is a welcome compliment, despite its emphasis on the insider-outsider mentality.

- *Kama'aina*: literally defined as 'child of the land,' *kama'aina* are people native to a particular place. A Hanalei native is a *kama'aina* of Hanalei and not of Hanapepe, for example. It assumes a deep knowledge of and connection to the place.

- Haole: a Caucasian person. Often further defined as 'mainland haole' or 'local haole.'

- Transplant: person who moved to the islands as an adult.

- Neighbor Island resident: person who lives on the Hawaiian Islands other than O'ahu.

Note: in this book, Hawai'i (with the *'okina* punctuation mark) refers to the island of Hawai'i (Big Island), while Hawaii (without the *'okina*) refers to the state. We use this distinction to avoid confusion between the island and the state, but locally the *'okina* spelling is official and ubiquitous for both.

Luxury cars, designer shoes and Ivy League degrees really have little clout on Kaua'i. One can spend weeks here and never see a Mercedes or BMW (nor the enviro-bourgeois car of choice, the Prius). Instead one sees countless monster trucks, Kaua'i's status vehicle – for good reason, as the prime recreational activities are hunting and surfing, which often take folks off-road – with a dog or two roaming in the back. It's a place for functional, not fancy: no Prada suit can substitute for a suntanned, ripped surfer's finesse on the waves.

Learn about Native Hawaiian issues and current events at www.oha .org, the Office of Hawaiian Affairs website.

Of course, Kaua'i residents include a sizable contingent of transplants, especially gypsy types from the US mainland and abroad. Chat with residents and you're sure to find folks who came to visit and ended up staying for a year, then five, then 10 or more. They might be post-college wanderers, surfer dudes, middle-aged folks in transition or retirees seeking idyllic seclusion. Many hail from California and the Pacific Northwest – outdoorsy types who discover a superior outdoors here.

One might assume that Kaua'i's geographical compactness means locals circumnavigate the island often, but residents tend to stick to their regions. A Waimea resident might drive to Lihu'e once a quarter to stock up at Wal-Mart; a Hanalei resident might drive to the Coconut Marketplace for an occasional movie. Indeed, each town has a distinct vibe. Lihu'e, the county seat, is a functional town where people go to work, not to play. Hanapepe is a sleepy plantation-town-cum–artists colony. Hanalei is an iconic surf town. And locals rarely visit the luxury, planned community of Princeville (unless to splurge on a round of golf).

LIFESTYLE

'Ohana (family) and the outdoors are the predominant forces. 'Ohana is central to the islanders' interactions with each other and with outsiders. Weekends are generally reserved for school sporting events, all-day picnics at public parks and evening cookouts with massive amounts of food. You need not be related by blood or marriage to be considered 'ohana, and lots of 'uncles' and 'aunties' are not relatives at all.

The ocean is the primary playground, and families often own their own fishing boats. Surfing, especially in Hanalei and Po'ipu, is the sport of choice. Local Asians tend to give it up once they're adults, while

---

NATIVE SONS & DAUGHTERS

Underlying local consciousness are longstanding Native Hawaiian issues. The 1970s Hawaiian cultural renaissance initiated changes, such as the reestablishment of Hawaiian as an official language, hailed by all locals (see p35). But contentious issues remain.

Regarding sovereignty, the proposed Native Hawaiian Government Reorganization Act (better known as the 'Akaka Bill,' crediting its sponsor, Senator Daniel Akaka) might finally receive a full congressional hearing. If passed it would formally acknowledge Native Hawaiians' status as indigenous people and extend official federal recognition of a future Native Hawaiian governing body.

Recent lawsuits have undermined the Office of Hawaiian Affairs (OHA) programs designed to benefit Native Hawaiians. In 2000 the US Supreme Court ruled that OHA elections cannot be limited only to Hawaiian voters, and in 2002 the 9th US Circuit Court of Appeals upheld a decision allowing non-Hawaiians to become OHA trustees. In 2005 the 9th Circuit ruled that Kamehameha Schools' Hawaiian-preference admissions policy violates federal civil rights law.

Even among Native Hawaiians, divisiveness exists. In 2005 five Hawaiians filed a lawsuit claiming that the OHA is illegally spending trust funds on all Hawaiians, not just those with at least 50% Hawaiian blood. Most Hawaiians disagree with any blood quantum requirement.

CHANCE 'EM!

When locals go on vacation, they go to…Las Vegas. Perhaps blasé about tropical scenery, a surprising number enjoy the artificial glitz, theme-park casinos, nearby golf courses, all-you-can-eat buffets and the chance to win big. (Gambling is illegal only in two states: Utah and Hawaii. Over the years Hawaii has considered ending its gambling ban, but opposition abounds from a bipartisan coalition of politicians, religious groups and the general public. Despite the state's financial woes and the local penchant for playing the slots, island gambling remains taboo.)

Mostly, however, Hawaii people go to Vegas to hang out with other locals. On any given trip, locals are bound to spot folks they recognize from home. While the Vegas habit crosses ethnic and age lines, seniors are particularly frequent returnees.

The Honolulu–Vegas circuit is a well-oiled machine, and outfits such as Sam Boyd's Vacations-Hawaii offer discount packages that keep locals coming back – often multiple times a year. Most stay downtown at the California Hotel, rather than at the upscale resorts on the Strip.

A sizable community of Hawaii expatriates lives in Vegas (dubbed the 'Ninth Hawaiian Island'), largely due to the low cost of living. But most locals shake their heads in disbelief. Vegas is fun, but there's no place like Hawaii.

Hawaiians and haole transplants keep riding until old age. Hunting for wild pigs and deer is a major weekend pastime, and hunters know the island terrain better than anyone else on Kaua'i.

The workday starts and ends early, and most find a comfortable work-home balance. Childcare is shared with grandparents and relatives, typically eager babysitters. Retirees often congregate in friendly gangs for morning golf or coffee, and virtually all homeowners grow fruits and vegetables in their backyards.

But you might be surprised at how much Lihu'e and the Eastside resemble a mini version of mainland suburbia, with strip malls and guaranteed commute traffic. Despite Kaua'i's compact size, the island is entirely auto-dependent. Public bus transit is negligible, sidewalks are rare, and residential neighborhoods are miles from commercial centers. The cost of living, including gas, groceries and electricity, is sky-high here (not to mention the stratospheric real-estate market).

City pursuits – shopping, theater, cinema and museums – are minimal. The sole major shopping mall is Kukui Grove Shopping Center in Lihu'e, but it's no comparison to Honolulu or the mainland and offers just the basics, sans upscale designer or department stores. With only three public high schools on the island, education remains a weak point. Parents, especially if they're mainland transplants, often send their kids to private schools.

Locals tend to travel to Neighbor Islands to visit relatives, to Honolulu to shop and dine out, to mainstream US attractions like Disneyland and to Asia if they go abroad (it's closer and cheaper). Among the Hawaiian Islands, Kaua'ians prefer the Big Island, its kindred sibling, which shares a similar small-town character.

Not surprisingly, Kaua'i locals tend to follow traditional lifestyle patterns (which parallel the standard 'American dream'). They tend to marry early and stick to traditional male and female domestic roles (it's still odd for a wife not to take her husband's surname). The easy lifestyle, especially in surf towns like Hanalei, seems to squelch ambitions to travel the world or attend mainland schools; a number of mainland-transplant parents say they have to cajole their kids to leave!

In Hawaii, *pakalolo* (marijuana) remains a billion-dollar underground industry (and the state's most profitable crop) and the use of 'ice' (crystal

Spot a Union Jack lookalike in the Hawaii state flag? You're right. It symbolizes the friendship between the British and King Kamehameha I, who commissioned the flag in 1816.

methamphetamine) has become rampant since the 1990s. But Kaua'i remains a relatively low-crime place, with only one murder in 2005. Residents tend not to lock their cars or even their front doors, but of course tourists and rental cars are commonly targeted.

POPULATION

The state's population, approaching 1.3 million, is heavily concentrated on O'ahu, where Honolulu is the state's only true city. According to a July 2004 US Census report, the population of Kaua'i County was just under 62,000, up from just over 58,500 in 2000. The largest town is Kapa'a with almost 9500 people, followed by Lihu'e with 5675, Wailua Homesteads with 4600 and Kalaheo with almost 4000.

The Kauaian Institute (www.kauaian.net) offers intriguing demographic data on Kaua'i, from population to tourism to traffic.

Of the total population, about 48,600 are single-race residents and a sizeable contingent of about 13,300 are mixed-race. Statewide, Hawaii's mixed-race population is the highest nationwide at 20.1% in July 2004 (compared with 1.5% for the whole nation). Half of all marriages in Hawaii are mixed-race.

On Kaua'i, whites constitute almost 33.5% of the population, followed by full or part Native Hawaiians at just over 24%, Filipinos at almost 22% and Japanese at around 14%. The seemingly high number of Native Hawaiians is rather misleading because only a tiny percentage are predominantly Hawaiian. The number of 'pure' Hawaiians has dropped steadily ever since Captain Cook's arrival; experts estimate their number to be under 5000 nationwide.

Paralleling trends across the USA and other developed countries, Kaua'i's median age increased from 36.7 years in 2000 to 38.2 years in 2004 – the highest median age among the Hawaiian Islands. Likewise its senior (55 years and older) population saw an 18% increase between 2000 and 2004 (Maui saw a nearly 20% increase) – reflecting Hawaii's growing status among retirees.

Kaua'i's daytime and nighttime populations highlight why Eastside highway traffic is a nightmare: during the day, county capital Lihu'e's population of almost 5675 practically doubles due to commuting workers.

SPORTS

Kaua'i isn't populous enough to support big-ticket pro or college sports. Instead, the main spectator sports on Kaua'i are high-school varsity games and youth Pop Warner and PONY leagues. In 2005 the Lihu'e Patriots Pee Wee team won the Division II Pop Warner National Championship in Orlando, Florida – and returned to a downtown parade in their honor. Also in 2005, 10-year-old Pono Tokioka, who is deaf, made national headlines when the youth baseball organization PONY denied him a sign-language interpreter in the dugout during games. Among Tokioka's supporters are Hawaii's two US senators, local government officials, advocacy groups and even Cal Ripken Jr, who personally wrote him an encouraging letter. A complaint filed with the US Department of Justice remains pending.

Water sports are big draws, especially surfing competitions such as the Pine Trees Longboard Classic in April and the Pine Trees Classic in February; see www.hanaleisurf.com for photos and past winners. Famous Kaua'i surfers include big-wave legend Titus Kinimaka, three-time ASP World Champion Andy Irons and 2004 Eddie Aikau Champion Bruce Irons, plus teen stars Alana Blanchard, Bethany Hamilton (see p151) and Kyle Ramey. Boogie boarding (officially called bodyboarding) is not just a side sport but has its own pro tour, and Kaua'i's own Jeff Hubbard, native of Lihu'e, is a top-ranked pro, known for radical aerial maneuvers. Lifeguarding competitions are big events for youths (many who strive to become professional lifeguards); the Kaua'i Jr Lifeguard Program won a second straight state title in 2005 at Kalapaki Beach.

The most-celebrated sports event on Kaua'i is the PGA Grand Slam of Golf (p173), hosted by the Po'ipu Bay Golf Course since 1994. The season-ending event features winners of the year's Masters, US Open, British Open and PGA Championship.

MULTICULTURALISM

It's a common misconception that Hawaii is a 'melting pot' of races and ethnicities. Certainly all the islands' populations are diverse, with no ethnic majority, and locals are generally tolerant of differences. But lines do exist. The old plantation stereotypes and hierarchies continue to influence social interaction in Hawaii. Caucasians have historically held the most power and remain the predominant private landowners on Kaua'i. But early immigrant groups, particularly the Chinese, Japanese and Portuguese, have proven upwardly mobile. Later immigrants, including Filipinos, Southeast Asians and other Polynesians, have had less time to advance and often hold service jobs.

Lihu'e has the largest concentration of Japanese (almost 30%), while its surrounding communities of Puhi and Hanama'ulu are both 50% Filipino. Kalaheo is known as 'Portuguese town.' The North Shore is predominantly Caucasian, from Kilauea (at 45%) to Hanalei (at 56%) to Princeville (at a whopping 80%). Eastside towns Wailua and Kapa'a show the most even distribution among ethnicities, while Anahola is over 70% Native Hawaiian.

Among themselves, locals joke good-naturedly about what are admittedly island stereotypes: Portuguese talk too much, Chinese are tight with money, Japanese are uptight do-gooders, haole act like know-it-alls, Hawaiians are huge and lazy, Filipinos eat dog and so forth. Hawaii's much-loved comedians of the 1970s and 1980s – Andy Bumatai, Frank DeLima and Rap Reiplinger – used such stereotypes to comic effect appreciated by all. Locals seem slightly perplexed at the emphasis on 'political correctness' on the mainland. But such humor is also an insider phenomenon; it's generally unwise to banter as an outsider.

Captain Cook wrote Hawai'i as Owy-hee, Maui as Mowee, O'ahu as O-ahoo, Kaua'i as Atowai and Ni'ihau as Neehau.

Translate your name into Hawaiian at www.aloha friends.com/names.html.

ANCIENT PANTHEON

Ancient Hawaii was a polytheistic society. The four major gods were Ku, god of war and male generating power; Kane, god of fresh water, sunlight and procreation; Kanaloa, god of the ocean and ocean winds; and Lono, god of peace and agriculture.

Dozens of demigods and deities reigned over the natural and supernatural worlds. Among those still worshipped today are Pele, goddess of volcanoes; Laka, goddess of hula; and Hina, goddess of the moon.

Most deities had *kinolau* (earthly counterparts), which could be animate or inanimate objects, such as rocks, animals and trees, or other natural elements, such as wind and rain. Virtually everything in the earthly world were the *kinolau* of a deity, therefore all things were considered to have mana (spiritual essence).

Ancient Hawaiians believed that when humans die, their spirits live on in the form of 'aumakua (guardian spirits) that protect living family members. 'Aumakua adopt earthly forms such as sharks, geckos, birds or fish. A reciprocal relationship existed: 'aumakua would provide guidance and protection to the living, who in turn were duty-bound to revere and protect their guardian spirits on earth.

Interestingly, while locals recognize the different Asian ethnicities, they lump all whites into one group: haole. If someone calls you haole, don't worry; there's usually no negative subtext. But depending on the tone of voice (and any accompanying adjectives), it can be an insult or a threat. Generally prejudice against haole depends on personal factors, such as whether they are local or longtime residents and, above all, whether they respect island ways.

RELIGION

Ancient Hawaiian society followed a strict *kapu* (taboo) system of religious laws that governed all behavior. Breaking a rule often meant immediate death. With the influx of foreigners, natives saw that rules could be violated without any consequences. The system inevitably eroded, thus when King Liholiho symbolically broke a major *kapu* by dining with Queen Ka'ahumanu (and suffered no divine punishment), many Hawaiians rejected the entire tradition and were willing converts to Christianity (see p31). But others took the Hawaiian religion underground. While the traditional beliefs never regained their former command, the philosophy endured, often expressed as aloha *'aina* (reverence for the land's sanctity). In part the Hawaiian sovereignty movement is rooted in aloha *'aina*, to reclaim the land regarded as abused by outsiders.

For such a small island, Kaua'i has dozens of churches and temples, especially on the Westside. The predominant religion is Christianity, with Roman Catholics constituting the largest denomination. Mainstream Protestant Christianity is struggling with declining membership, while evangelical churches are burgeoning. A handful of Buddhist temples reflect the immigration of Japanese laborers, while the spectacular Kaua'i Aadheenam, a 458-acre Saivite Hindu monastery in the Wailua Homesteads area, belies the miniscule number of Hindus here.

Across the island, ruins of heiau (ancient Hawaiian religious sites) exist as partial stone structures and walls. Most are modest, and if one is unfamiliar with their significance, they will resemble a mere pile of rocks. Hawaiians located heiau on particular, spiritually powerful sites; to understand a heiau requires appreciation of stark, untouched nature.

ARTS
Music

Slack-key guitar fans: www.dancingcat.com is a good introduction to the genre and includes a schedule of US performances. Geared toward guitarists, with reviews of instructional materials and online discussion boards, is www.taropatch.net.

Integral to Hawaiian music is the guitar, first introduced to the islands by Spanish cowboys in the 1830s. The Hawaiians made the guitar their own during the 19th century by adopting steel strings and the slack-key method (*ki ho'alu,* which means 'loosen the key'). For *ki ho'alu,* the six strings are slackened from their standard tuning to facilitate a full sound on a single guitar – the thumb plays the bass and rhythm chords, while the fingers play the melody and improvisations, in a picked style.

The most influential slack-key artist was Gabby Pahinui (1921–80), who launched the modern slack-key era with his first recording in 1946. Over the years he played with the legendary Sons of Hawaii and later formed the Gabby Pahinui Hawaiian Band with four of his sons; his home in Waimanalo on O'ahu was a mecca for backyard jam sessions. Current masters, including Raymond Kane and Ledward Ka'apana, have perpetuated the tradition and introduced it to wider audiences.

The instrument most commonly associated with Hawaii is the ukulele, though it's derived from the *braguinha,* a Portuguese instrument introduced to Hawaii in the late 19th century. Ukulele means 'jumping flea' in Hawaiian, referring to the way the players' deft fingers would swiftly

---

KAUA'I'S SLACK-KEY GUITARISTS

Tune in to Kaua'i's own, at a range of venues islandwide.

- Cindy Combs (www.slackkeylady.com): a Kaua'i resident since 1985, Combs first learned the slack-key method from Keola Beamer. Check out *Slack Key Lady*, her first CD for George Winston's slack-key label, Dancing Cat. She performs on Friday nights at Hanapepe Café (p191).

- Ken Emerson (www.kenemerson.com): award-winning slack-key and steel guitarist Emerson, currently living on the North Shore, contributed a track to the album that won the first-ever 2005 Grammy for Hawaiian music. His CD *Hawaiian Tangos, Hulas & Blues* is an excellent introduction to classic sounds. Catch him at Princeville's Living Room and La Cascata (p140) when he's not touring.

- Hal Kinnaman (www.halkinnaman.com): a longtime teacher, composer and performer based in Hanapepe, Kinnaman is well-known islandwide. He has mentored many students (including Togioka, below) in guitar and ukulele, and he invites visiting musicians to take a lesson or two. He is available to perform at island weddings.

- Doug and Sandy McMaster (www.hawaiianslackkeyguitar.com): this prolific and community-oriented couple performs affordable ($10) concerts on Sunday and Friday afternoons year-round in Hanalei (p150).

- Paul Togioka (www.paultogioka.com): recently bursting into the spotlight, Togioka is a local boy whose 2004 release *Ki ho'alu Inn* garnered great reviews. Originally from Kekaha, he now lives in Wailua Homesteads. He frequently gigs at special functions and tours with the Hawaiian Slack Key Guitar Festivals (p85).

Other respected guitarists include Allan Thomas, Ernest Palmeira, Norman K Soloman and Mike Young.

'jump' around the strings. Hawaii's ukulele masters include Eddie Kamae, Herb Ohta and Jake Shimabukuro.

Over the years Hawaiian music has progressed from the lighthearted, novelty music of the 1930s to '50s, such as 'Lovely Hula Hands' and 'Sweet Leilani,' to a more sophisticated sound. In the 1970s Hawaiian music enjoyed a rebirth, and artists such as the Sunday Manoa, Cecilio & Kapono, Hui 'Ohana and the Beamer Brothers remain icons in Hawaii. Perhaps the most famous island musician is the late Israel Kamakawiwo'ole (informally known as 'Bruddah Iz'), whose *Facing Future* is Hawaii's all-time best-selling album. Bruddah Iz died in 1997 at age 38, due to morbid obesity, but he remains a driving force in putting Hawaiian music on the map.

A new Grammy Award for Best Hawaiian Music Album was established in 2005. Its first winner was the multiartist instrumental CD **Slack Key Guitar, Volume 2** (www.palmrecords.com/cd_slack_key_2.html). All but one of the 2006 nominees were also instrumental compilations, which disappointed those who had hoped Hawaiian lyrics and vocals would garner the spotlight. The 2006 winner, **Masters of Hawaiian Slack Key Guitar, Volume 1** (www.slackkey .com/CD2004.htm), comprises live recordings from performances at Maui's Ritz-Carlton Kapalua.

In 1874 King David Kalakaua wrote *Hawai'i Pono'i*, which in 1967 became Hawaii's state song (and the only state song not in English).

Hula

In ancient Hawaii, hula was not entertainment, but religious expression. Hula dances and chants also helped perpetuate oral history because Hawaiians had no written language. Dancers' rhythmic movements, facial expressions and hand gestures convey Hawaiian genealogy, history and mythology, as well as reverence to Hawaiian deities, such as the volcano goddess, Pele. They wore *kapa* (bark cloth), never the stereotypical grass skirts. When the Christian missionaries arrived, they viewed hula dancing as too licentious and suppressed it. The hula might have been lost forever if the 'Merrie Monarch' King Kalakaua, the last king of Hawaii, had not revived it in the late 19th century.

Today's commercial hula shows, which emphasize swaying hips and nonstop smiling, might be compelling but they're not 'real' hula. Serious students join a *halau* (school), where they undergo rigorous training and adopt hula as a life practice. They learn both *kahiko* (ancient) and *'auana* (modern) styles.

One of the best venues to view serious hula is the Kaua'i Mokihana Festival Hula Competition (p173) in Po'ipu.

Holo Mai Pele, a mesmerizing performance of ancient hula, premiered on *Great Performances* in 2001. For a video or book, go to www.pbs.org /holomaipele, which also features excellent photo clips and background information.

Hawaiian Arts & Crafts

Ancient Hawaiians relied on manual handiwork for everything, from clothing to canoes. Thus almost all traditional objects are aesthetic specimens, handmade according to exacting detail. Nowadays a small group of artisans and craftspeople perpetuate the old traditions, such as woodworking, which uses prized koa and other hardwoods to create hand-turned wooden bowls and furniture, impossibly smooth and polished. *Lauhala* weaving crafts the *lau* (leaves) of the *hala* (pandanus) tree into mats, floor coverings, hats, placemats and baskets.

Christian missionaries introduced patchwork quilting to Hawaiians, who at the time lacked a surplus of cloth scraps and thus eschewed chopping up fabric simply to reunite them in small squares. Instead they created their own elegant style, which features a single piece of stylized tropical flora on a contrasting background.

Lei-making remains a popular craft, as people continue to wear lei on a regular basis. Today's popular tourist lei feature flashy or fragrant flowers,

---

NO TALK LI' DAT

The Hawaii educational system has traditionally pushed local kids to use standard English and not pidgin in the classroom. State department of education leaders (and many parents) often blame low scores on standardized tests on local kids' speaking, thinking and writing in pidgin. But a movement to legitimize pidgin as a language is afoot. Da Pidgin Coup, a group of University of Hawai'i faculty and graduate students, asserts that pidgin can coexist with standard English and should not be forbidden if its use facilitates the learning process. As the argument goes, *what* you say is more important than *how* you say it.

The most well-known champion for pidgin use is Lee Tonouchi, a lecturer in the English Department at Kapiolani Community College on O'ahu, who was hired with an application written entirely in pidgin. A prolific writer and playwright, he makes an intriguing, subversive argument for legitimizing pidgin. His books include *Da Word* (short stories), *Living Pidgin: Contemplations on Pidgin Culture* (essays) and, most recently, *Da Kine Dictionary* (pictorial dictionary).

This debate parallels the 1996 debate over Ebonics (black English) in Oakland, California, where the local school board recognized Ebonics, a term derived from ebony and phonics, as a separate language. The board concluded that most African-American children come to school fluent in their vernacular, and to condemn it would be counterproductive.

Granted, pidgin use is not universal among locals and is determined by socioeconomic class. But all locals clearly understand it – and they regard pidgin as social glue, bonding them to a shared identity and sense of humor. Most locals straddle the two languages, using either pidgin or standard English when it's most appropriate.

Advice to tourists: don't try to talk pidgin. Few nonlocals can do it, and most attempts come across as insulting.

such as plumeria or dendrobium orchids. In fact, many orchid lei originate in Thailand and are not Hawaiian at all. Traditionally lei were more subtle in their beauty, made of *mokihana* berries, *maile* leaves and other greenery.

In a category of its own is the Ni'ihau shell lei, which is actually fine jewelry. Rare white, yellow, blue and gold shells must be collected, sorted, finely drilled and intricately strung into necklaces and chokers. Only shells from Ni'ihau are considered of museum quality and can receive a certificate of authenticity.

Literature

For years 'Hawaii literature' referred to fiction set in Hawaii, typically by nonlocal writers. Oft-cited examples include *Hawaii,* James Michener's ambitious saga of Hawaii's history, and *Hotel Honolulu,* Paul Theroux's novel about a washed-up writer who becomes the manager of a run-down Waikiki hotel. Also widely read is Isabella Bird, the 19th-century British adventurer, who captures the exoticism of the islands for outsiders. Today, however, a growing body of local writers is redefining the meaning of Hawaii literature.

Local literature doesn't consciously highlight Hawaii as an exotic setting but instead focuses on the lives and attitudes of universal characters. **Bamboo Ridge Press** (www.bambooridge.com), which publishes contemporary local fiction and poetry in a biannual journal, *Bamboo Ridge,* has launched the careers of many local writers including prolific, award-winning novelist Lois-Ann Yamanaka. Her novels, from her debut *Wild Meat and the Bully Burgers* to her 2005 *Behold the Many,* portray an impoverished, rather squalid side of island life that is not exactly the norm; but they introduce readers to pidgin dialogue and pack an emotional punch. Playwright Lee Cataluna is another notable, and her anthology *Folks You Meet in Longs and Other Stories* is a humorous, spot-on introduction to local sensibilities. A well-known Kaua'i writer is Frederick B Wichman, whose series of Hawaiian legends include *Kaua'i Tales* and *Pele Ma: Legends of Pele From Kaua'i.*

Cinema & Television

Kaua'i's most famous Hollywood star is easy to spot: just look around. The spectacular beaches, jungles and cliffs have starred in dozens of movies and TV shows. Filmmakers often use Kaua'i to replicate other locales, including Central and South America, Africa, Southeast Asia and the South Pacific. It all started in 1933 when director Lois Weber brought a film crew to shoot *White Heat.* Most oft-cited nowadays is the blockbuster 1993 film *Jurassic Park,* which was filmed islandwide in locations from Allerton Garden (p167) to the backcountry above Wailua Homesteads (p101). For a list of other movie locations, see p113. Also visit the Kaua'i Film Commission website at www.filmkauai.com.

Many movie stars have second homes on Kaua'i, but one who actually lives here is Cary Hiroyuki Tagawa, who starred in *The Last Emperor* (1987), and then landed dozens of roles including Commander Mirou Genda in *Pearl Harbor* (2001) and Krull in *Planet of the Apes* (2001). Most recently he played 'The Baron' in *Memoirs of a Geisha* (2005). He lives in Kilauea with his wife, artist Sally Phillips.

Koloa-born Sanoe Lake debuted on the big screen in the 2002 surfer-chick flick *Blue Crush.* She learned to swim at age six and, as a teen in the mid 1990s, became the face of Roxy, Quiksilver's women's surf-apparel line. In 2005 at age 26 she had already penned a memoir: **Surfer Girl: A Guide to the Surfing Life** (www.surfergirlthebook.com).

For children's books with a Hawaii twist, *Ten Days in Hawaii: A Counting Book* and its sequels are both educational and brilliantly illustrated. The author is Kaua'i pediatrician 'Dr Carolan' and the illustrator, Joanna Carolan (see p190).

A Kaua'i Reader (1995), edited by Chris Cook, is an assorted introduction that covers Hawaiian history, legends and personal accounts. Writers range from King David Kalakaua to surfers Titus Kinimaka and Terry Chung.

Environment David Boynton

Maika'i Kaua'i
Hemolele i ka malie
Beautiful is Kaua'i
Perfect in the stillness

Hawaiian chant

Beaches of Kaua'i and Ni'ihau (1990) is an authoritative account of Kaua'i's shoreline, fourth in a statewide series, with maps, history, anecdotes and detailed descriptions.

Against the vastness of the Pacific Ocean, Kaua'i is a tiny speck that has engendered fame far beyond its size. It is the oldest and fourth largest of the main inhabited Hawaiian Islands. Known as the Garden Island, Kaua'i's volcanic origins are mostly hidden by a carpet of forests, ferns and shrublands that spread across a mountainous interior. Five million years have left their mark, with deeply wrinkled valleys radiating outward from a central plateau and basaltic rock, transformed into rust-colored hues of soil, lending its color to the ubiquitous 'red dirt T-shirts' (p91) sold around the island.

THE LAND

Altogether, the Hawaiian archipelago consists of more than 100 distinct volcanoes. The oldest and most distant, Meiji Seamount, is around 80 million years old. The chain is literally inching northwestward, as if on a geo–conveyor belt, at an average rate of 3.4in per year by steady shifting of the Pacific tectonic plate. Given many millions of years, Kaua'i will follow its brethren in gradual subsidence and erosion, shrinking and sinking until it too becomes an atoll and seamount.

Kaua'i's volcanic history is not as clear-cut as once assumed. For decades scientists have stated that Kaua'i was created by a single large volcano (unlike the Big Island, which incorporates seven volcanoes, and Maui, which, about a million years ago, was united with Moloka'i, Lana'i, and Kaho'olawe as a super-island known as 'Maui Nui'). The central crater of the Kaua'i volcano was estimated to have been 11 miles across, largest of any known caldera in the Hawaiian chain. The caldera gradually filled with successive flows of ponded lavas that cooled slowly, forming a central plateau of more dense, fine-grained lavas upon which the Alaka'i Swamp now sits. Geologists believed the thick horizontal strata that you see directly across the canyon from Waimea Canyon Lookout were the caldera-filling lavas. Flows of the island's original dome can be seen sloping downward toward the ocean on the west side of the canyon.

Evidence collected during the past two decades has brought forth new hypotheses about Kaua'i's origins, indicating the presence of at least two 'shield' volcanoes, the second one (Lihu'e Shield) originating about a million years after the first. Scientists believe that a 'catastrophic' slumping of the entire eastern side of Kaua'i beyond Waimea Canyon occurred, leaving a steep *pali* (cliff) along what is now the Canyon's western edge. The supposed ponded lavas of the original caldera (horizontal strata) are instead thought to have their source in eruptions from the four-million-year-old Lihu'e Shield that flowed westward to the *pali*. Erosion of the canyon was caused by water from 'captured' streams all flowing together into Waimea River, which runs southward some 2500ft below the state park overlooks along Waimea Canyon Drive.

Kaua'i has shrunk with age and is slowly subsiding into the ocean floor at a rate of less than an inch per century. Those inches have added up to a loss of 3000ft in elevation, culminating in today's high point of 5243ft at Kawaikini.

Erosion has tremendously altered Kaua'i's original volcanic form, creating deep valleys that fan out like spokes of a wheel from the island's central plateau. Some are very narrow, others broadly expansive, but all have a stream flowing down the center. Almost all residential development on the island occurs on coastal plains and broad valley floors.

Among the most visually spectacular valleys is Kalalau, which drops 4000ft below the two lookouts at the end of the road in Koke'e State Park (p206). Kalalau is your archetypal amphitheater-headed valley, carved from the basalt by several million years of streams and waterfalls flowing down paths of geological weakness to create the curtain-like folds and knife-edge ridges that encompass the valley. To the north and west of Kalalau, numerous other steep-sided valleys pierce the magnificent sea cliffs of Na Pali Coast, which extend for 14 miles around the northwestern side of Kaua'i. Views of Na Pali are spectacular from the deck of a boat or windows of a helicopter, from Nu'alolo-Awa'awapuhi Trail in Koke'e, and from the challenging trek of the 11-mile Kalalau Trail.

Kaua'i's coastline also features more extensive reef formations than the younger islands, but they're not really 'coral' reefs. Instead, various forms of stony coralline algae predominate, although most visitor bureau publications refrain from revealing this true nature of the island's reefs. Regardless of their composition, the reefs provide an excellent habitat for colorful fish and invertebrates, enjoyed by snorkelers and divers around the island. One of the most popular scuba dive spots is Sheraton Caverns off Po'ipu (p166) on Kaua'i's South Shore, a series of partially collapsed lava tubes 10ft or more in height, with shafts of glowing sunlight illuminating their dim interior.

Kaua'i has over 40 miles of sandy beaches, more per mile of shoreline than any of the other main Hawaiian Islands.

In 1986 geoscientist Chuck Blay circumnavigated Kaua'i on foot examining its geologic history. Ten years later he founded The Edge of Kaua'i Investigations (TEOK), which offers compelling scientific insights at www .teok.com.

WILDLIFE
Animals
With no native amphibians or reptiles, and only one native land mammal – the endangered Hawaiian bat – the islands offer no great treasure trove for wildlife enthusiasts unless, of course, they have a fondness for birds or ocean wildlife. Whale watching is very popular off Kaua'i's South Shore, with most boats departing from Port Allen Harbor (p185)

THE NORTHWESTERN HAWAIIAN ISLANDS
The main Hawaiian Islands stretch northwest for over 500 miles from the Big Island to Kaua'i. This is just a portion of the entire archipelago, which extends another 1500 miles beyond Kaua'i in the form of islets and atolls of the Northwestern Hawaiian Islands. These tips of ancient, sinking volcanoes were designated in 1909 by President Theodore Roosevelt as the country's first national wildlife refuge.

Closest to Kaua'i, at a distance of 130 miles, is 900ft Nihoa, which encompasses an area of just 160 acres. Next in line is 10-million-year-old Mokumanamana (Necker), hardly an island with less than 64 acres of land. Continuing northwest are the barely-above-sea-level bumps of French Frigate Shoals, Gardner Pinnacles, Maro Reef, and an assortment of progressively older atolls terminating with Midway and 30-million-year-old Kure. Beyond this outpost, another 2000-mile chain of sunken islands known as guyots or seamounts dot the ocean floor all the way past the Aleutian Islands to Kamchatka Peninsula (Russia). Here, ancient islands are sunken below the Eurasian continental plate, with deep oceanic trenches marking the boundary.

near Hanapepe. The endangered humpback whales winter in Hawaii, with first arrivals usually appearing in November and most departing by May (see p187). Pods of spinner dolphins, with their famed spiraling leaps, regularly approach boats cruising in Kaua'i waters, and can also be seen from the shoreline in areas such as Kalihiwai Bay (p132) and off Kilauea Point (p128) on the North Shore. Threatened green sea turtles, often seen feeding on seaweed along rocky coastlines, are a great attraction for snorkelers. Endangered Hawaiian monk seals (see p170) haul up on shore occasionally, a thrill for beachgoers, and by law must be observed only from a distance. Federal and state laws help protect all four of these species from harassment.

Just a few introduced mammals have become established, including feral goats and wild boar, and black-tailed deer from Oregon, which were first introduced in 1961. Goats prefer open slopes and can be seen along Na Pali Coast and Waimea Canyon, while feral pigs inhabit forested areas around the island, often ranging into rural neighborhoods. The deer were released on leeward slopes west of Waimea Canyon, and mostly inhabit shrublands and montane forests on Kaua'i's west side, preferring drier habitats over rainforest. Along with cattle, these animals have caused extensive damage to native ecosystems.

BIRDS

Like the smorgasbord of plant life, birds seen around Kaua'i's inhabited lowlands are mostly species introduced from around the world, as reflected in their common names: Japanese white-eye, Chinese thrush, Indian myna, California quail, Northern mockingbird, Western meadowlark, Brazilian (red-crested) cardinal, and Java sparrow, to name a few. In the evenings, barn owls introduced from the mainland in 1959 are sometimes seen along roadways and over open fields. Kaua'i's native short-eared owl or pueo may also be seen soaring over grasslands and mountain slopes, hunting for rats and mice during both day and night.

The Birds of Kaua'i (1999), written and photographed by Westside resident Jim Denny, is an excellent guide to the feathered fauna of the island.

Water Birds

Lowland wetlands feature four endangered waterbirds that are cousins of mainland species: the Hawaiian duck, coot, moorhen, and stilt. The best place to view these is the Hanalei National Wildlife Refuge (p141) on the North Shore; an overlook near Princeville Shopping Center provides an interpretive sign along with a great view of the habitat consisting of shallow ponds and cultivated taro fields.

Migratory birds that spend warm winters on Kaua'i but breed in western Alaska and Canada also frequent the wetlands, but prefer shoreline habitats. Among these are golden plover, wandering tattler, ruddy turnstone and sanderling. Hawaii's state bird, the nene or Hawaiian goose, is an endangered species that can often be seen in Hanalei wetlands, but also ranges around golf courses and open fields throughout the island. Nene were reintroduced to Kaua'i in 1991 within the predator-proof fence on Crater Hill at Kilauea Point National Wildlife Refuge (p128). Since then, they have thrived and expanded in numbers to become the state's healthiest population. Part of the reason that Kaua'i's population has done so well is that mongoose, predators of ground-nesting birds, never became established here.

Forest Birds

Native forest birds are more challenging to observe, but still abound in Koke'e State Park (p206) and the Alaka'i Wilderness Preserve (p211).

'*Apapane* is the most abundant, a bright-red bird the same color as the lehua flowers from which it takes nectar. It is one of six honeycreepers that may be seen in forests above 3000ft in elevation.

Honeycreepers are a uniquely Hawaiian sub-family (Drepanidinae) with more than 50 species that evolved over millions of years from a finch-like ancestor, a world-renowned example of the evolutionary process known as adaptive radiation. Three other fairly common honeycreepers seen in Koke'e – '*amakihi*, '*anianiau*, and '*akeke'e* – are varying shades of green and yellow, camouflage coloring to hide from now-extinct eagles, hawks, and long-legged predatory owls that once patrolled Kaua'i's skies. Considered the most beautiful of Kaua'i's honeycreepers is the orangey-red '*i'iwi*, with a decurved salmon-colored bill that fits perfectly into the flowers of native lobelia relatives.

A native member of the flycatcher family, the '*elepaio* is a small brownish grey insect-eater with a perky tail, the most approachable of Kaua'i's native forest birds. Best access to see this avian menagerie is the Pihea-Alaka'i Swamp Trail that begins where the paved road ends at the second lookout (Pu'u o Kila) over Kalalau Valley in Koke'e State Park (p211).

Unique footage delves into the lifestyles and survival challenges of native forest birds in *Birds of the Rainforest: Kaua'i* (2001), distributed through www .kauaibirds.com.

Plants

Kaua'i truly lives up to its nickname the 'Garden Island,' its mountainous terrain lushly carpeted by hundreds of native plant species. However, the island's ancient inhabitants would not recognize most of the flora that now abounds throughout the populated regions of the island. Exotic tropical flowers that beautify roadways, resorts and residential neighborhoods represent a transported landscape, brought to the islands from around the world. Likewise, delicious Hawaiian fruits sampled along trails, blended into smoothies, or added to tasty fruit salads are not truly Hawaiian: guavas, papayas, avocados, passion fruit and pineapples were introduced from tropical America; lychee and mango from Asia; 'Hawaiian' macadamia nuts from Australia; and good old 'Kaua'i Coffee' from Africa. Just as Hawaii has become a melting pot of diverse ethnic groups, the inhabited landscape consists largely of plants used and valued by the immigrants, or collected by early horticulturists seeking to provide for people's needs.

POLYNESIAN INTRODUCTIONS (CANOE PLANTS)

It's difficult to imagine Kaua'i without coconut trees, but when the first Polynesians arrived here over 1500 years ago in their great double-hulled sailing canoes, there apparently were none. About two dozen useful plants – including the coconut – were introduced by voyagers from the Marquesas islands and Tahiti, along with a few weeds. Some of these early imports have become important agricultural crops, including taro, bananas and sugar cane. Taro, for example, is still grown in much the same way that it was centuries ago, and today's view of flooded taro fields in Hanalei Valley has changed little over the past several hundred years. Sugar cane ruled as king of the Hawaiian economy for a century (p32), although today only one plantation, the Gay & Robinson Sugar Company on the Westside, has survived the challenges of economic globalization.

NATIVE PLANTS

Despite all the changes, native forest still flourishes throughout much of the island's mountainous interior in Koke'e State Park (p206) and the 10,000-acre Alaka'i Wilderness Preserve (p211). Hawaii's native flora is very unique, with over 90% of the more than 1000 flowering plant species being endemic to the islands (occurring naturally nowhere else on earth).

Coastal Plants

Oddly enough, the coastal shoreline, with all its development, is also a good place to find native plants on Kaua'i. This is a harsh environment (windblown and salt-sprayed, often arid, with nutrient-poor sandy soil) and special adaptations are required for survival. Several of the plant species have a waxy coating on their leaves to help prevent drying out, while others have a silvery reflective color, are succulent, or grow flat on the ground. One of the best places to learn about native coastal plants is at Kilauea Point National Wildlife Refuge (p128), Kaua'i's northernmost point, where interpretive signs describe some of the species.

The character of Kaua'i's native flora is greatly influenced by climatic conditions, which vary according to both elevation and exposure to the trade winds that blow in from the northeast during much of the year. The windward side of the islands are much more moist and cool compared with the arid leeward side. Rainfall at Hanalei Beach, for example, averages 100in per year compared with desert-like conditions at Polihale, where the average is about 20in. At one time, leeward portions of Kaua'i were covered by native shrubland and dryland forest, but human habitation has not been kind to this now-rare flora. Over 90% of the state's dryland forest habitat has been destroyed; what remains, including small patches in Waimea Canyon and along Na Pali Coast, is highly threatened.

> A record rainfall occurred at Kilauea in 1956 when a storm dumped 38in in one day, including 11in during a one-hour period.

Mesic Forest

Along the rim of Waimea Canyon, koa trees abound. Koa, an endemic hardwood, is Hawaii's most commercially valuable tree, with its fine woodworking qualities, rich color and swirling grain. Prices of the finest 'curly' koa range up to as much as $70 per board foot. Some of the tallest koa trees in Koke'e State Park (p206), planted in the 1930s, are found along the dirt roads below Koke'e Museum, and on the Water Tank-Berry Flat Trail. Koa trees disappear as conditions become wetter in the area of Kalalau Lookout at 4000ft. Here the rainforest begins, with an annual average of 100in per year.

Rainforest

From Pu'u o Kila Lookout (p207) at the road's end, the Pihea-Alaka'i Swamp Trail (p211) provides the best access to native rainforest. The most abundant rainforest tree is 'ohi'a lehua, a hardwood with bright orange or red pompomlike flowers that are a source of nectar for forest birds. Another dominant is 'olapa or lapalapa, a member of the ginseng family, with long-stemmed leaves that flutter in the slightest breeze. Hula dancers are also referred to as 'olapa, perhaps a reference to their constant motion. These and other trees are enveloped by a cloak of moss and ferns on their trunks and branches, holding moisture like a wet sponge even through sunny days.

Alaka'i Swamp Trail does not really pass through a swamp, but there are openings in the rainforest known as bogs with small ponds of orangey 'sun-tea' water and dwarfed vegetation. Trees that might be 30ft or 40ft high in the surrounding forest are just 1ft or 2ft high in the bogs. Among bog inhabitants are sundews: tiny 2in insectivorous herbs that absorb nutrients from miniature insect prey entrapped on the plant's glue-tipped hairs.

STATE PARKS & RESERVES

In the 1960s, more than 100 sq miles of northwestern Kaua'i was proposed for national park status. It is an amazing area. From the arid dunes of Polihale, the state's longest beach, the park would have included 14 miles of spectacular sea cliffs and the remote valleys of Na Pali Coast; lush windward coastline fronting rich nearshore reefs at Ha'ena on the North Shore; the varied forests and hiking trails of Koke'e; the 2500ft-deep chasm of Waimea Canyon; and thousands of acres of rainforest of the Alaka'i Swamp, extending to the bogs of Mt Wai'ale'ale, one of the world's rainiest places with an average of about 430in per year.

Yet in the face of local opposition – families afraid of losing their mountain cabins, their hunting and gathering traditions, and local control over park use – the proposals to create a national park on Kaua'i failed to garner the necessary support. The proposed area, nearly one-fifth of the northwest side of the island, is instead under control of the understaffed, underfunded State Department of Land & Natural Resources. Kaua'i's 'crown jewel,' as Secretary of the Interior Stewart Udall once called it, has been divided into a checkerboard of management zones including five state parks, two forest reserves, two game management areas, two natural area reserves and the Alaka'i Wilderness Preserve.

Hanalei provided Hawaii's first coffee exports totaling 245 pounds in 1845; today Kaua'i is the state's largest producer, with over 3 million pounds per year.

State Parks

Kaua'i's five state parks offer a wonderful variety of recreational opportunities. Miles of white sandy beach at Polihale provide room to roam away from crowds, but visitors must be aware of potentially hazardous ocean conditions, especially during winter months. Polihale and Hanakapi'ai Beach on Na Pali Coast have claimed more lives by drowning than almost any other beach in Hawaii.

Polihale, the arid western end of Na Pali Coast, is accessible via a 5-mile bumpy gravel road through agricultural fields. The trail to Hanakapi'ai, one of the most-hiked trails in the state, begins at Ke'e Beach, a favorite snorkeling spot in Ha'ena State Park (p154) where the road ends on the North Shore. Hanakapi'ai's beautiful, wide, sandy beach of summer disappears in big winter surf each year. The trail continues another 9 miles to the amazing fluted cliffs of Kalalau, a world-class hiking destination where camping is allowed for a few days by permit, obtainable online.

Koke'e features a dozen easy-to-moderate hiking trails through a diversity of forest zones, while a 6-mile hiking trail leads to several campsites in the canyon. For more on camping, see p217.

There are several other small state parks and numerous county parks around Kaua'i available for recreational and picnic use, including a few that allow camping by permit. Among the most popular are Po'ipu Beach Park (p170), on the sunny South Shore; 'Anini Beach Park (p133), on the North Shore; and Lydgate Beach Park (p95), next to the mouth of the Wailua River.

For images and information on the flora, wildlife and history of Kauai's three national wildlife refuges at Kilauea Point, Hanalei, and Huleia see www.kilaueapoint.com.

Wildlife Refuges

There may be no national park on the island, but a federal presence is here with three refuges in the Kaua'i National Wildlife Refuge (NWR) Complex. Headquarters are at Kilauea Point National Wildlife Refuge (p128), which features a historic lighthouse on a bluff 200ft above the ocean at the northernmost tip of the island. It's a great place to view ocean wildlife and huge winter surf, and has the only diverse seabird colony on the main Hawaiian Islands. Six species nest in the refuge (two tropicbirds, two shearwaters, albatross and boobies) and two

KAUA'I NATURE AREAS

Nature area	Area (acres)	Features	Activities	Page
Alaka'i Wilderness Preserve	9939	rainforest, bogs, forest birds, boardwalk, classic view of North Shore	hiking, walking, bird watching, sunset watching	p211
Ha'ena State Park	7	archaeological features, nearshore reefs, green sea turtles	swimming, snorkeling	p154
Hanalei National Wildlife Refuge	917	endangered waterbirds, scenic viewpoints, taro fields, great photo opportunities	bird watching (limited access)	p141
Hule'ia National Wildlife Refuge	241	endangered waterbirds	bird watching (limited access)	p80
Kilauea Point National Wildlife Refuge	203	seabirds, coastal plants, nene, sightseeing interpretive center, historic lighthouse	bird watching, whale watching,	p128
Koke'e State Park*	4345	waterfall hikes, forest birds and plants, interpretive center	camping, hiking, bird watching	p206
Na Pali Coast State Park	6175	unbeatable trails, coastal flora, seabirds, archaeological features, photographer's paradise	camping, hiking, swimming (dangerous currents)	p155
Polihale State Park	138	coastal dune flora, state's longest beach	camping, walking, swimming (dangerous currents), sunset watching	p199
Waimea Canyon State Park	1866	remnant dryland and mesic forest, unbeatable views of 'Grand Canyon of the Pacific'	camping, hiking, mountain biking	p199

*Koke'e was a pre-statehood territorial park.

others roost here (frigatebird and brown booby). Small flocks of nene (Hawaiian goose) thrive within the protected sanctuary of the refuge's predator-proof fence. Nene also frequent Hanalei and Huleia National Wildlife Refuges, which were established for protection of Hawaii's four endangered waterbird species.

ENVIRONMENTAL ISSUES

Since the 1970s, resort development has been a central issue on the Garden Island. Compared to the full-speed-ahead proclivities toward tourist sprawl on O'ahu, Maui and the Big Island's Kona Coast, Kaua'ians have been content to leave it in low gear. Where else, except perhaps among the coconut trees of Moloka'i, could you find a planning credo that restricts building heights to 'no taller than a coconut tree'? The Kaua'i General Plan sets the tone by limiting resorts to Visitor Destination Areas in Princeville, Wailua-Kapa'a, Lihu'e, Po'ipu, and lightly in Waimea. Yet cumulative impacts from the ceaseless trickle of development are being felt, as every last 'hidden' spot is discovered and favorite beaches begin to feel like Waikiki.

On an island where (except for a few spots) a single-lane highway in both directions is the only option, traffic gridlock is on everyone's mind. A Kapa'a–Wailua bypass road has been under discussion for decades, but inertia prevails. An early morning contra-flow lane and mini-bypass

Three special sanctuaries for native birds and flora come to life in *Kilauea Point and Kaua'i's National Wildlife Refuges* by David Boynton (2004).

road through Kapa'a have helped, but four resort developments in the
first decade of the 21st century will add hundreds of additional vehicles
to the already vexing traffic stall.

A relatively recent issue that concerns many islanders, especially organic farmers, is the use of agricultural lands for experimentation with,
and production of, genetically modified (GMO) crops. Major multi-
national corporations such as Monsanto, Syngenta Seeds, and Pioneer
Hi-Bred International have found Kaua'i's climate and resources perfect
for production of up to three crops per year, on lands once primarily used
for growing sugar cane. GMO corn is the major crop. A veil of secrecy
surrounds GMO experimentation, but it appears that soybeans, cotton,
sorghum, tobacco and sunflowers are part of the mix here. This is an issue
fraught with misconceptions – problems however have indeed surfaced,
such as genetic contamination of non-GMO papaya varieties.

The green movement simmers on Kaua'i, with a rather small entou-
rage of dedicated activists and single-issue advocates. The challenges are
many and unrelenting: Hawaiian sovereignty, affordable housing, vacation rentals in residential neighborhoods, gated communities, watershed
management, invasive species, roadside herbicides, beach and mountain
access.

The organization **Malama Maha'ulepu** (www.malama-mahaulepu.org) has been a
model of excellence for grassroots activism. It has stimulated widespread
community interest through educational outreach about the unique
Maha'ulepu Coast, a wildland area east of Po'ipu, once proposed for
massive resort development (see p172). Another group with a successful
public participation program is the **Koke'e Resource Conservation Program**
(p228) which involves student groups, interns, visitors and the general
public in efforts to control invasive species in native forest areas.

'A relatively
recent issue
that con-
cerns many
islanders...
is the use of
agricultural
lands for
experimen-
tation with...
genetically
modified
crops'

Kaua'i Outdoors

Sure, Kaua'i boasts its share of top resorts and restaurants – but people flock here not for the manmade, but for the outdoors. Whether you are a water baby or a landlubber, a panoply of sports and activities await you. The surf and terrain are diverse, thus accommodating buff athletes, weekend gym-goers and tiny tots.

Bear in mind, you might hear about exotic island adventures that have folks trailblazing to reach waterfalls, swimming in freshwater pools (stagnant water be damned!) or sloshing through dark caves or tunnels. While they might make for memorable experiences, heed the threats of injury or death – whether by leptospirosis or by tumbling over a sheer cliff. Locals, especially parks and forestry officials, have little patience for tourists who take risks, only to require expensive rescue missions that jeopardize others' safety.

WATER SPORTS

Of Kaua'i's 111 miles of coastline, sandy beaches constitute almost 50%. You need not drive far to find another – and yet another! – gorgeous beach. Water conditions are changeable, however, so don't underestimate their lethal force. Note the seasonal changes in surf conditions: North Shore and Westside beaches are most hazardous around winter (October to April), when South Shore and Eastside beaches are quite calm. The pattern reverses in summer. Of course, conditions change daily and exceptions are the rule. While easy to ignore, drowning is not uncommon: January 2006 saw two deaths, on the Wailua River and in high surf at Donkey Beach. A tempting water thrill is not worth your life.

Kaua'i's circular shape and lack of nearby islands produces extremely high wave energy on all shorelines.

Before jumping in, get a free copy of the informative (and potentially life-saving) brochure *Kaua'i Beach Safety Guide* from the **Kaua'i Visitors Bureau** (Map p78; ☎ 245-3971, 800-262-1400; www.kauaidiscovery.com; 4334 Rice St, Suite 101, Lihu'e). **Franko's Dive Map of Kaua'i** ($7) is an excellent resource, and identifies all the top diving, snorkeling, surfing and kayaking sites.

TOP 10 BEACHES

- Ke'e Beach (p154) for a picturesque setting and spectacular snorkeling.
- Po'ipu Beach Park (p170) for gentle waters and throngs of happy families.
- 'Anini Beach Park (p133) for placid waters and beginner windsurfing.
- Lydgate Beach Park (p95) for kid-friendly waters and a jumbo playground.
- Maha'ulepu Beach (p172) for trekking windswept cliffs above pounding surf.
- Hanalei Bay (p143) for sandy, crescent-shaped perfection.
- Kalapaki Beach (p79) for convenient swimming and boogie boarding.
- Salt Pond Beach Park (p189) for a beach both untouristy *and* accessible without a precarious hike.
- Shipwreck Beach (p171) for advanced surfing, boogie boarding and bodysurfing.
- Tunnels Beach (p151) for an outstanding shore dive and killer surf break.

OCEAN SAFETY

Drowning is the leading cause of accidental death for visitors. If you're not familiar with water conditions, ask around. Don't swim alone in unfamiliar waters. Some common dangers:

Rip currents Rips, or rip currents, are fast-flowing ocean currents that can drag swimmers out into deeper water. Anyone caught in one should either go with the flow until the rip loses power or swim parallel to shore to slip out of it.

Rogue waves Never turn your back on the ocean. Waves don't all come in with equal height or strength, and sometimes one can sweep over a shoreline ledge and drag sunbathers from the beach into the ocean.

Shorebreaks If waves that are breaking close to the shore are only a couple of feet high, they're generally fine for novice bodysurfers. But large shorebreaks can hit hard with a slamming downward force.

Undertows Common along steeply sloped beaches, undertows occur where large waves wash back directly into incoming surf. Swimmers caught up in one can be pulled underwater. Don't panic; go with the current until you get beyond the wave.

KAYAKING
River Kayaking

With seven rivers, including the only navigable one statewide, river kayaking is the rage here. The Wailua River paddle and hike, ending at a 130ft waterfall, is by far the most popular. The river is strictly monitored against overuse, and guided kayaking tours (p100) are encouraged. Only four outfitters have permits to rent a limited number of individual kayaks for the Wailua – going on your own is recommended only for experienced kayakers. Find outfitters in Wailua (p100), Hanalei (p144), Lihu'e (p82) and Po'ipu (p171). Generally single kayaks rent for $25 to $45 per day, double kayaks are $50 to $75 per day, and guided Wailua River tours cost around $40 without lunch and around $95 with lunch.

Kaua'i's other rivers are much less regulated, and you can enjoy them at your leisure. Hanalei River (p144) and Kalihiwai Stream (p132) are highly recommended. A handful of good tours (p82) paddle the Hule'ia River, which passes through the off-limits Hule'ia National Wildlife Refuge.

Sea Kayaking

Officially all sea kayaking off Kaua'i must be done on tour because of rough surf. Beginners can learn in Po'ipu (p171) and Hanalei (p144), while fit athletes should sign up for the unforgettable 17-mile Na Pali endurance paddle (p144), possible only in summer.

SURFING

In the 1970s surf bums flocked to the North Shore, where fierce winter waves challenged even the die-hards. Today Hanalei remains a surf town, and now it's no secret: Kaua'i is great for surfing. Granted, Kaua'i's breaks are limited compared to O'ahu's, but surfers will not lack for action – and the vibe is relatively mellow (as long as visitors show respect for locals' turf).

Generally waves are best on the North Shore in winter, especially at Hanalei Bay (p143) and Tunnels Beach (p151), where winter waves average 6ft to 8ft (with 20ft or higher surf possible at any time). The South Shore is best in summer, where hugely popular Po'ipu (Sheraton) Beach (p170) crowds up, while Shipwreck Beach (p171) and Maha'ulepu Beach (p172) draw daredevils. Pakalas (p195), near Waimea, is the Westside's hottest break, but the unprotected western waters mean winter breaks are often

For a down-to-earth account of renowned Native Hawaiian surfer and waterman Titus Kinimaka (plus shots of epic waves that'll give you chills), see *Nihi*, an indie documentary that's available at www .alohafilms.com.

KAUA'I WATER SPORTS

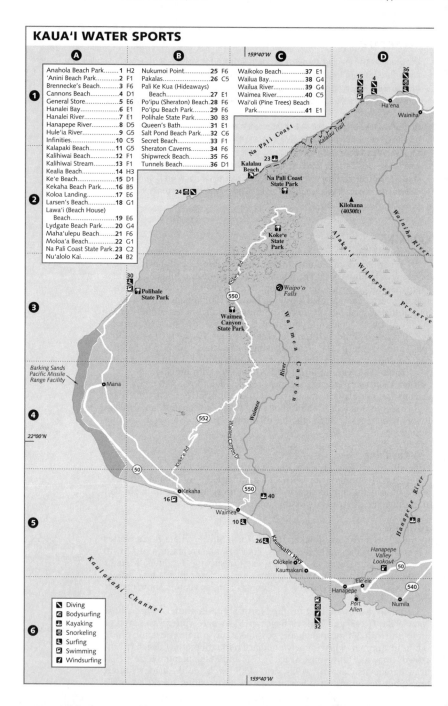

Ⓐ

Anahola Beach Park.......**1** H2	
'Anini Beach Park..........**2** F1	
Brennecke's Beach..........**3** F6	
Cannons Beach..............**4** D1	
General Store................**5** E6	
Hanalei Bay..................**6** E1	
Hanalei River...............**7** E1	
Hanapepe River............**8** D5	
Hule'ia River.................**9** G5	
Infinities.....................**10** C5	
Kalapaki Beach.............**11** G5	
Kalihiwai Beach............**12** F1	
Kalihiwai Stream............**13** F1	
Kealia Beach................**14** H3	
Ke'e Beach..................**15** D1	
Kekaha Beach Park........**16** B5	
Koloa Landing..............**17** E6	
Larsen's Beach.............**18** G1	
Lawa'i (Beach House)	
Beach....................**19** E6	
Lydgate Beach Park........**20** G4	
Maha'ulepu Beach........**21** F6	
Moloa'a Beach.............**22** G1	
Na Pali Coast State Park..**23** C2	
Nu'alolo Kai...............**24** B2	

Ⓑ

Nukumoi Point..............**25** F6	
Pakalas......................**26** C5	
Pali Ke Kua (Hideaways)	
Beach....................**27** E1	
Po'ipu (Sheraton) Beach..**28** F6	
Po'ipu Beach Park..........**29** F6	
Polihale State Park.........**30** B3	
Queen's Bath................**31** E1	
Salt Pond Beach Park......**32** C6	
Secret Beach................**33** F1	
Sheraton Caverns..........**34** F6	
Shipwreck Beach............**35** F6	
Tunnels Beach..............**36** D1	

159°40'W **Ⓒ**

Waikoko Beach.............**37** E1	
Wailua Bay...................**38** G4	
Wailua River..................**39** G4	
Waimea River...............**40** C5	
Wai'oli (Pine Trees) Beach	
Park........................**41** E1	

Ⓓ

Ha'ena

Wainiha

Na Pali Coast

Kalalau Trail

Kalalau Beach **23**

Na Pali Coast State Park

Kilohana (4030ft)

Weiniha River

24

Koke'e State Park

Alaka'i Wilderness Preserve

30 Polihale State Park

Koke'e Rd

550

Waipo'o Falls

Waimea Canyon State Park

Waimea Canyon

River

Barking Sands Pacific Missile Range Facility

Mana

22°00'N

552

Koke'e Rd

Waimea Canyon Dr

Waimea

50

Kekaha

16

550 **40**

Waimea

10

26

Kaumuali'i Hwy

Olokele

Kaumakani

Kaulakahi Channel

Hanapepe River

8

Hanapepe Valley Lookout

50

Ele'ele

Hanapepe

Port Allen

Numila

540

32

Legend:
- **Ⓝ** Diving
- **Ⓖ** Bodysurfing
- **Ⓚ** Kayaking
- **Ⓢ** Snorkeling
- **Ⓢ** Surfing
- **Ⓢ** Swimming
- **Ⓦ** Windsurfing

159°40'W

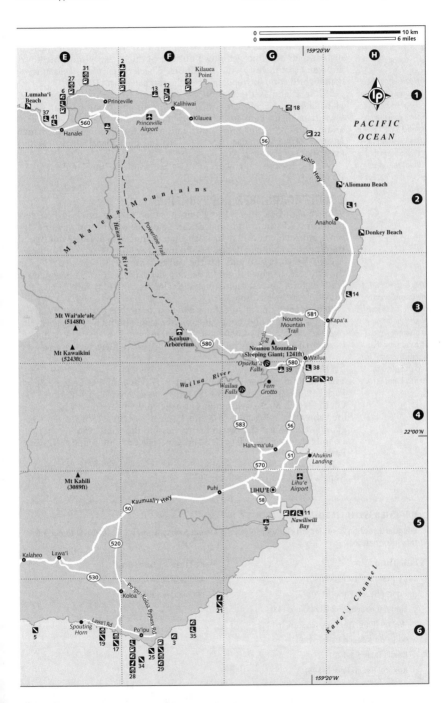

0 _____ 10 km
0 _____ 6 miles

159°20'W

E F G H

PACIFIC
OCEAN

Kilauea
Point

Lumaha'i
Beach

Princeville
Princeville
Airport
Kalihiwai

Kilauea

Hanalei

560

Kuhio Hwy

Aliomanu Beach

Makaleha Mountains

Hanalei River

Powerline Trail

Anahola

Donkey Beach

Mt Wai'ale'ale
(5148ft)

Nounou
Mountain
Trail

Kapa'a

Mt Kawaikini
(5243ft)

Keahua
Arboretum

Nounou Mountain
(Sleeping Giant; 1241ft)

Wailua

'Opaeka'a
Falls

Wailua River

Wailua
Falls

Fern
Grotto

22°00'N

Hanama'ulu

Mt Kahili
(3089ft)

Puhi

LIHU'E

Lihu'e
Airport

Ahukini
Landing

Kaumuali'i Hwy

Kalaheo Lawa'i

Nawiliwili
Bay

Koloa

Po'ipu-Koloa Bypass Rd

Spouting
Horn

Lawa'i Rd

Po'ipu

Kaua'i Channel

159°20'W

treacherous. Transitional swells happen on the Eastside, when surfers hit Kealia Beach (p122) or Wailua Bay (p95). Eastside swells often break on distant reefs and thus get blown out except during early-morning hours and *kona* (southwest) wind conditions. Check on current swells at www .kauaiworld.com/surfreport or call the **surf hotline** (☎ 335-3720).

While O'ahu is the site of the state's major surfing competitions, Hanalei is an ideal place to watch amazing, up-and-coming talent. Check www.hanaleisurf.com for photos of the all-blond Hanalei Surf Team and recent events; for more information, see the websites for the **Hawaii Amateur Surfing Association** (www.hasasurf.org) and the **National Scholastic Surfing Association** (www.nssa.org). Also see p40.

Surfing lessons and board rentals are available in Hanalei (p145), Po'ipu (p171) and Waipouli (p113).

BOOGIE BOARDING & BODYSURFING

While boogie boarding is less glamorous than surfing, pro bodyboarders perform wild stunts and novices can enjoy the sport from day one. It's more affordable and easy to learn than surfing and also provides good training for catching a wave. Try Po'ipu (Sheraton) Beach (p170), Brennecke's Beach (p170) and, for the skilled, Shipwreck Beach (p171). On the Eastside, newbies should start at Kalapaki Beach (p79) near Lihu'e, while experts can test themselves at Kealia Beach (p122) and Hanalei Bay (p143) near the pavilion.

Rentals are found at surf shops and cost around $5 per day and $20 per week. Or just buy one; boogie boards (the iconic brand is Morey) are relatively affordable and you can quite easily transport them home. A rashguard is essential (raw, prickly rashburn is no fun), as are fins to catch waves.

SWIMMING

You can find protected swimming lagoons year-round at Lydgate Beach Park (p95), Salt Pond Beach Park (p189) and 'Anini Beach Park (p133). On the North Shore, swimming is feasible only in summer, when waters are calm at Ke'e Beach (p154) and Hanalei Bay (p143). In winter, when giant swells pound the North Shore, head to the South Shore, especially Po'ipu (Sheraton) Beach (p170) and, especially for children, Po'ipu Beach Park (p170).

If you're totally ocean-phobic, there are two public pools on Kaua'i, in Kapa'a (p117) and Waimea (p195).

Too old to surf? In the truly inspirational *Surfing For Life* (www.surfingfor life.com), documentary filmmaker David L Brown profiles 10 lifelong surfers, champions in their youth and still catching waves in their 70s, 80s and 90s.

Andrea Gabbard's *Girl in the Curl: A Century of Women in Surfing* gives long-overdue recognition to *wahine* (female) surfers, including the celebrated Rell Sunn and Kaua'i champion and instructor Margo Oberg.

BEACHES WITH LIFEGUARDS ON DUTY

Lifeguard staffing is subject to change, so call the **Ocean Safety Bureau** (☎ 241-6506) to confirm this information.

Full-Time
- Lydgate Beach Park (p95)
- Po'ipu Beach Park (p170)
- Hanalei Beach Park Pavilion (p143)
- Wai'oli (Pine Trees) Beach Park (p144)
- Salt Pond Beach Park (p189)
- Kealia Beach (p122)
- Kekaha Beach Park (p198)

Part-Time or Seasonal
- Anahola Beach Park (p122)
- Wailua Bay (p95)

SNORKELING

Snorkeling is an everyman sport, giving everyone, young and old, the chance to explore Kaua'i's underwater world. The most convenient snorkeling is found right offshore: the best spots include Po'ipu Beach Park (p170), with dense fish populations and frequent turtle spottings, on the South Shore; Salt Pond Beach Park (p189), with shallow waters, on the Westside; Lydgate Beach Park (p95), for a protected lagoon perfect for kids, on the Eastside; and Ke'e Beach (p154) and Tunnels Beach (p151), for the most spectacular setting (both above and below water), on the North Shore.

Your snorkeling options multiply if you take a cruise. The scenic Na Pali Coast circuit is the star; tours leave from Port Allen (p185), Kikialoha Small Boat Harbor (p198) and Hanalei Bay (p145), which is recommended (as departing from the North Shore means you see the whole Na Pali Coast). The best tours stop for snorkeling at Nu'alolo Kai. Morning trips generally have calmer seas and lots of dolphins. Book as early in your trip as possible, as high surf or foul weather can cancel tours (or at least the snorkeling part). Seasickness is common: take remedies 24 hours before departure.

The major difference in tours is the type of boat: catamaran (sailing or motorized) or rafts. Certainly rafts are the most exhilarating, bouncing along the water and entering caves (in mellower weather), but most lack any shade, restroom or comfy seating, so they're not for everyone (folks with bad backs should beware). The best rafts are rigid-hull inflatables, with hard bottoms that allow smoother rides; and note that large rafts might include a restroom and canopy. Sit in back for less jostling.

Catamarans are cushier, with smooth rides, ample shade, restrooms and crowd-pleasing amenities, like trampolines for sunning and water slides. Some catamarans sport sails (and actually use them), while others are entirely motorized.

Shops all over Kaua'i sell 'snorkel food' to whip fish into a feeding frenzy for your viewing pleasure. This is not only harmful to the fish, but soils the water. Shops renting snorkel gear are ubiquitous (corrective masks are available, too).

SCUBA DIVING

While Kaua'i might not compare to the calm, clear waters off the Big Island's Kona Coast, it still boasts remarkably good diving. While South Shore waters see the most diving activity, the North Shore reefs at Tunnels and Cannons are local favorites. The top shore-diving site is Koloa Landing (p169), a great beginner spot that is conveniently located and allows easy entry. Others are Po'ipu Beach Park (p170), Ke'e Beach (p154) and Tunnels Beach (p151).

Boat dives widen your options, but again the majority of sites run along the South Shore, such as Sheraton Caverns, with three lava tubes, a coral wall and diverse marine life; Nukumoi Point, a shallow site and habitat for green sea turtles; and General Store, with sharks, octopuses, eels and the remains of an 1892 shipwreck. The hottest dive site for experienced divers, perhaps statewide, is Ni'ihau (p214), which features deep wall dives, lava formations, caves, plentiful marine life (including pelagics such as sharks) and crystal-clear waters. The often-choppy crossing between Kaua'i and Ni'ihau takes about 2½ hours and is doable only in summer.

Two-tank shore dives with equipment cost around $85, boat dives $100 to $135, night dives around $80, introductory dives from $100 and certification courses between $400 and $500. Most shops allow you to do certification coursework at home, then come to Kaua'i for open-water

Divers Alert Network (www.diversalertnetwork.org), based at Duke University Medical Center, is an excellent resource on diving safety, insurance and training.

RESPONSIBLE DIVING

The popularity of diving is placing immense pressure on many sites. Please consider the following tips when diving, to help preserve the ecology and beauty of reefs.

- Do not use reef anchors and take care not to ground boats on coral. Encourage dive operators to establish permanent moorings at popular sites.

- Avoid touching living marine organisms with your body or dragging equipment across the reef. Polyps can be damaged by even the gentlest contact. Never stand on coral. If you must hold on to the reef, touch only exposed rock or dead coral.

- Be conscious of your fins. Even without contact, the surge from heavy fin strokes near the reef can damage delicate organisms. When treading water in shallow reef areas, take care not to kick up clouds of sand. Settling sand can easily smother the delicate organisms of the reef.

- Practice and maintain proper buoyancy control. Major damage can be done by divers descending too fast and colliding with the reef. Make sure you are correctly weighted and that your weight belt is positioned so that you stay horizontal. Be aware that buoyancy can change over the period of an extended trip: initially you may breathe harder and need more weight; a few days later you may breathe more easily and need less weight.

- Take care in underwater caves. Spend as little time within them as possible, as your air bubbles may be caught within the roof and thereby leave previously submerged organisms high and dry.

- Resist the temptation to collect or buy coral or shells. Aside from the ecological damage, taking home marine souvenirs depletes the beauty of a site and spoils others' enjoyment.

- Ensure that you take home all your rubbish and any litter you may find as well. Plastics in particular are a serious threat to marine life. Turtles can mistake plastic for jellyfish and eat it.

- Resist the temptation to feed fish. You may disturb their normal eating habits, encourage aggressive behavior or feed them food that is detrimental to their health.

- Minimize your disturbance of marine animals. It is illegal to approach endangered marine species too closely; these include many whales, dolphins, sea turtles and the Hawaiian monk seal. In particular, do not ride on the backs of turtles, as this causes them great anxiety.

dives. Recommended outfits offering certification courses and all types of dives include those listed in the Kapa'a (p117), Koloa (p162) and Po'ipu (p171) sections.

Note that the closest hyperbaric chambers for recompression therapy are located in Honolulu. If you encounter trouble, call ☎ 911 and the **Coast Guard Rescue Center** (☎ on O'ahu 808-536-4336).

WINDSURFING & KITESURFING

The main site for windsurfing is 'Anini Beach Park (p133), with calm, shallow waters protected by a reef. This spot is ideal for beginners, who use specialized equipment – jumbo boards that offer stability and small, lightweight sails. More experienced folks can handle Salt Pond Beach Park (p189), Tunnels Beach (p151) and Maha'ulepu Beach (p172).

Kitesurfing (available at the windsurfing beaches mentioned previously) is a related sport that ramps it up a notch. Picture yourself with feet strapped on a board (like a short surfboard), towed by a huge kite.

WATERSKIING & WAKEBOARDING

While not a major sport like surfing, waterskiing on the Wailua River has its fans. There's just one outfitter that offers waterskiing tours: Water Ski, Surf & Kayak Company (p102), in Wailua. You can also try wakeboarding, the water equivalent of snowboarding, in which you're towed behind a boat on a single board.

FISHING

Fishing is a mainstay sport among locals. If you're an avid fisherman at home, you'll enjoy deep-sea fishing off Kaua'i, where you can sail to depths over 6000ft within an hour at trolling speed. The day's offshore catch varies among giant marlin and tuna, and midweight fish such as mahimahi and *ono* (wahoo). Inshore catches include *uku* (gray snapper), *ulua* (jack), *kaku* (barracuda) and *kamanu* (rainbow runner).

Charter fishing boats depart mainly from Nawiliwili Small Boat Harbor (p83), Port Allen (p188) and 'Anini (p133). Ask about sharing the catch if you keep what you hook – not all charters spread the wealth. Seasickness is common, so take medication before you depart; try to plan a charter when seas are calm (although this is hard to predict).

Freshwater bass fishing is possible in man-made reservoirs; also rainbow trout fishing is an annual summer event at Pu'u Lua Reservoir (p202) – a guaranteed catch. To cast independently you'll need a freshwater license from the **Division of Aquatic Resources** (☎ 274-3344; www.hawaii .gov/dlnr/dar; 7-day tourist license adult/child $10/4) or consider using the established guides at **Cast & Catch** (☎ 332-9707; half-day charter for half-anglers $250).

LAND ACTIVITIES

Would you rather keep your feet dry and planted on solid ground? No problem! Kaua'i offers the gamut of terrestrial pursuits, from world-renowned hiking to golf, mountain biking and horseback riding. Exhilarating soft adventures include ziplining, where you're strapped into a harness and zoom via gravity and a pulley mechanism high above the ground, amid rain forest splendor.

HIKING

With just a pair of trusty shoes and an intrepid spirit, hikers can spend their whole trip on foot, yet never run out of trails to explore. Hiking runs the gamut, from easy walks to precarious treks, and each trail displays a different 'face' of Kaua'i. The greatest concentration of Kaua'i trails is on state forest-reserve land around Waimea Canyon State Park (p202) and Koke'e State Park (p208). Hike the Pihea Trail to the Alaka'i Swamp Trail for a look at pristine native forestland, or brave the steep Awa'awapuhi Trail for breathtaking views of the Na Pali Coast.

'With just a pair of trusty shoes and an intrepid spirit, hikers can spend their whole trip on foot'

TREAD WITH CARE

Kaua'i hikers can forget about poison ivy or oak, snakes, bears and volcanic eruptions. But hiking here poses unique challenges. Trails are often muddy and slippery, adjacent to rocky drop-offs. Flash floods are always a threat in the many narrow valleys that require stream crossings. Darkness falls quickly in deep gorges like Waimea Canyon, and cell phones are useless outside main towns. Here are a few items hikers should carry:

- compass
- signal mirror
- flashlight
- walking stick
- first-aid kit
- plastic bag to carry out any trash
- map
- mosquito repellent
- water
- sunscreen
- jacket and hat

BIRD'S-EYE VIEW OF KAUA'I

On the ground, the omnipresent droning of commercial helicopters can be annoying. Even along the remote Na Pali Coast or in the depths of Waimea Canyon, you're not alone but fully visible from rapt eyes far above. But, don't knock 'em till you've tried 'em. While wilderness aficionados resent the intrusion of helicopters into otherwise-serene areas, almost anyone with a deep appreciation of nature secretly relishes the bird's-eye view.

Helicopter rides can swoop around Kaua'i's otherwise inaccessible cliffs, valleys and mountains, giving you a unique, encompassing perspective. The view of Mt Wai'ale'ale from inside the mysterious crater, all misty and ringed by waterfalls, is nearly impossible to describe adequately – and you'll marvel at seeing double rainbows and the perfect curve of Hanalei Bay. Helicopters provide those with mobility problems their only way to see the Na Pali Coast.

If you're keen to do a chopper tour, arrange it early in your trip in case yours is cancelled due to bad weather. While outfits do take walk-ins (and you can thus wait until a sunny day with the best visibility), bear in mind that tours do book up. Choose a company that uses noise-canceling headphones and helicopters with large windows; passengers in middle seats often feel cheated due to lower visibility.

Most companies fly A-Star helicopters, which fit four passengers in back and two with the pilot in front (needless to say, these are primo seats). Highly recommended are the open-door rides offered only by **Inter-Island Helicopter** (☎ 335-5009, 800-335-5567; http://hawaiian.net/~interisland/; 1-3410 Kaumuali'i Hwy; flights regular/waterfall $185/250), which flies Hughes 500 helicopters, seating two in back and two in front. In back, the right seat is superior to the left because the route is clockwise and thus passes the Na Pali Coast on the right side. Seating is arranged to balance all the passengers' body weights, so it's hard to argue for that coveted front seat.

While overall these outfits have outstanding safety records, accidents do happen: in 2003 a helicopter crashed over Mt Wai'ale'ale, killing the pilot and all four passengers. In September 2005 a chopper crashed into North Shore waters near Ke'e Beach during a heavy rainstorm, killing three passengers. Two other passengers survived, along with the pilot who was indicted on manslaughter and reckless endangering charges in December 2005. Of course, during clear weather over 1000 tours fly every week without incident, so odds of landing safely are well in your favor.

The going rate is around $200 for an hour's flight; shorter 45-minute 'circle-island tours' zoom by the main sights and feel rushed. Ask about discounts and peruse the freebie tourist magazines for coupons (but note that discounters don't necessary represent the best companies). The following operators depart from Lihu'e airport except where noted:

Air Kauai (p84)
Heli USA Airways (p137) Flies from Princeville Airport.
Inter-Island Helicopter (p190) Flies from Hanapepe's Burns Field.
Jack Harter Helicopters (p84)
Safari Helicopters (p84)
Will Squyres (p84)

On the North Shore, the Kalalau Trail (p156) has become such an icon that visitors from tots (in slings) to geezers hike at least the first leg. The Eastside also boasts numerous mountainous trails (p103), including the scenic Kuilau Ridge and Moalepe trails, and three trails across Nounou Mountain. In addition to designated trails, Kaua'i's vast coastal miles also make pleasant beachfront walks.

The majority of Kaua'i's trails are managed by **Na Ala Hele** (☎ 274-3442; www.hawaiitrails.org; Department of Land & Natural Resources, Division of Forestry & Wildlife, 3060 Eiwa St, Room 306, Lihu'e, HI 96766; map $6), a statewide program under the Division of Forestry and Wildlife. In addition to trail management, they maintain campsites, roads and hunting areas. Generally the forest-reserve trails are better maintained – graded every few months and marked with distance markers every quarter mile. Contact Na Ala Hele for a detailed topographic map and invaluable firsthand information from those on the frontline (who know the trails in and out).

The remainder of public trails – which essentially means the Kalalau Trail and the Koke'e State Park trails nearest Waimea Canyon Dr (ie Cliff Trail, Canyon Trail and Halemanu-Koke'e Trails; see p208) – are managed by the **Division of State Parks** (☎ 274-3444; www.hawaii.gov/dlnr/dsp; Department of Land & Natural Resources, Division of State Parks, 3060 Eiwa St, Room 306, Lihu'e, HI 96766).

Hiking Tours

The Kaua'i branch of the **Sierra Club** (☎ 651-0682; www.hi.sierraclub.org/kauai/kauai .html) leads guided hikes (suggested donation $3) ranging from beach clean-up walks to rigorous overnighters. Advance registration might be required; check the website in advance. Koke'e Natural History Museum also offers guided hikes for a nominal donation during summer months.

For the ultimate learning experience, hike with geologist Chuck Blay's company, **Kaua'i Nature Tours** (☎ 742-8305; 888-233-8365; www.kauainaturetours.com; PO Box 549, Koloa, HI 96756; tours adult $82-97, child under 13 $45-64). He offers a variety of hikes across the island, from Waimea Canyon to the Maha'ulepu Coast to the Na Pali Coast. Tours include lunch and transportation.

For detailed directions to dozens of Kaua'i hikes, see Kathy Morey's *Kaua'i Trails*.

GOLF

While Kaua'i has only nine courses (see below), five of them rank in the state's top 15 – meaning this is one primo place for golf. In 2004 *Golf Digest* ranked Princeville's Prince Course as the state's best; also Kaua'i Lagoons' Kiele Course at number four, Princeville's Makai Course at number 10, Wailua Municipal Golf Course at number 12 and Po'ipu Bay Golf Course at number 14.

While golfing between emerald mountains and azure seas at Princeville is a visual treat, the one drawback is the frequency of rain on the North Shore. Plan accordingly.

To save on resort course fees, golf during 'twilight hours,' generally from noon; fees drop further later in the afternoon. Another option is to book at tee time at www.teetimeshawaii.com, which also provides detailed information about 50 courses statewide. For even bigger savings, buy an annual membership card for $39.95.

KAUA'I GOLF COURSES

Golf course	Features	Page
Kaua'i Lagoons Kiele Course	stunning oceanside setting, highly challenging and rewarding	p82
Kaua'i Lagoons Mokihana Course	gentler, better-value option for beginners, less spectacular than Kiele	p82
Kiahuna Golf Club	decent quality, dry weather, bargain for Po'ipu	p173
Kukuiolono Golf Course	modest, originally private, 9-hole course, $8 all-day fee	p182
Po'ipu Bay Golf Course	site of the PGA Grand Slam, sprawling green near Maha'ulepu Beach, less difficult than Prince Course	p173
Princeville Golf Club Makai Course	sprawling 27-hole course, scenic 'economy' option at Princeville	p136
Princeville Golf Club Prince Course	state's top-ranked course, visual treat, challenging (not for novices) and exclusive	p136
Puakea Golf Course	views of Ha'upu mountain range, windy, well-kept, moderately difficult course	p82
Wailua Municipal Golf Course	outstanding municipal course, conveniently located, popular among locals	p105

BUZZ OFF

The biggest annoyance on Kaua'i comes in a tiny package: mosquitoes! With the island's wet climate, it's no surprise that the mosquito population thrives. The Hawaiian Islands are home to four types of pest mosquitoes. One species, the Asia tiger mosquito, a daytime biter that arrived in Hawaii 100 years ago, was introduced to the US mainland in 1985 but is not found in the west. Thus people from California and other western states might never have encountered this aggressive species and, when bitten, developed those unsightly (and irritating) red welts. Locals often seem unbothered despite bare arms and legs.

Mosquitoes are most prevalent in rainy areas with lots of standing water (breeding sites). When hiking on the Kalalau Trail, any of the Eastside trails or any forested area, be sure to wear repellent. Along windswept coasts, eg Maha'ulepu Beach, and at high elevations, eg Koke'e State Park, you'll find few or no mosquitoes.

DEET is the most widely used and effective repellent for mosquitoes. Use the lowest effective percentage, such as 20% (up to 35%). If you're allergic to DEET, you could treat your clothing or try a natural repellent, such as Burt's Bees or Avon Skin So Soft, but they're not as effective. If you are dining at an outdoor restaurant, ask for a mosquito coil. For additional information, see p240.

MOUNTAIN BIKING & CYCLING

Kaua'i is better for mountain biking than for cycling, although it is possible to ride along the belt highway throughout the Westside, South Shore and Eastside. The North Shore, past Princeville, is impossible, as the highway narrows and curves over steep cliffs. Cyclists can look forward to the Kaua'i Coastal Path, a 16-mile coastal path currently under construction, which will run from Nawiliwili (in Lihu'e) to Anahola. Already completed is a 2.5-mile path in Lydgate Beach Park, and a 4.3-mile stretch from Kapa'a to Donkey Beach. To be completed in 2008, the path will be 12ft wide in places, and it will serve not only bikes and pedestrians but also horses.

Hawaii's Sports Hall of Fame (www.alohafame .org) honors the state's champion athletes and outstanding coaches.

For mountain bikers, countless dirt roads and trails are available islandwide. On the Eastside, the Powerline Trail (p105) from Wailua to Hanalei is a good option (you need not ride the whole way), as are the Kuilau Ridge and Moalepe Trails (p103). Near the coast, the cane-haul road between Anahola and Kealia Beach offers a scenic but jaw-jarring ride. The dirt roads near Po'ipu, above Maha'ulepu Beach, are good, especially since it's less likely to rain here. For a solitary ride, your best bets are the hunter roads at Waimea Canyon State Park (p199). Outfitters Kaua'i leads an easy downhill tour (p202) on Waimea Canyon Dr between the 12-mile marker and Kekaha.

For more information see the Na Ala Hele website, www.hawaiitrails .org, which indicates which trails are open for mountain biking.

ZIPLINING

Since the 2000s, zipline 'rides' have become the latest outdoor adventure. The zipline trend, which emerged in Costa Rica canopy parks, is proliferating across the US mainland. But the appeal of 'flying' or swinging like Tarzan is certainly heightened by the location – and Kaua'i's lush rainforests are memorable. This outdoor adventure takes no skill or training, but participants must fit the standard harness (body weight minimum 80lb to 100lb, maximum 250lb).

Near Lihu'e, Kaua'i Backcountry Adventures (p82) offers a tour devoted to zipping on seven ziplines. Outfitters Kaua'i has a single zipline (although they are currently building more), which is included in an all-day adventure tour including kayaking, hiking, swimming and much more. On the North Shore, Princeville Ranch Adventures (p137) offers a tour that includes eight ziplines.

HORSEBACK RIDING

Vast pastureland stretches from open coastal cliffs to jungly rainforests – providing ample terrain for horseback riding. A handful of stables offer tours, mainly for beginners. On the South Shore, CJM Country Stables (p172) rides along the Maha'ulepu Coast, while on the North Shore, Princeville Ranch Stables (p136) and Silver Falls Ranch (p132) traverse green pastures, streams and waterfalls. In Kapa'a, Esprit De Corps Riding Academy (p117) offers the most varied selection of rides, making it the best option for advanced riders.

Food & Drink

Locals don't eat for survival – they eat for pure pleasure. Indeed, the sheer variety of island food will tempt any palate. You can go highbrow at fine-dining restaurants serving Hawaii Regional Cuisine, which bursts with Pacific Rim flavors and island-fresh ingredients. Or you can sample everyday *local kine grinds* – hearty, flavorful and, most important, plenty! Local street food is often fried, salty, gravy-laden and meaty. But a trend toward healthy cooking is afoot, and you can find plate lunches featuring grilled fish and brown rice. Vegetarians will find lots of options: luscious fresh papaya and pineapple, organic greens, tofu mains and more. No one on Kaua'i goes hungry.

In The Best of the Best from Hawaii Cookbook, Gwen McKee and Barbara Moseley compile 300 recipes from Hawaii's most-popular community cookbooks into a plastic-spiral-bound, neo-retro masterpiece.

STAPLES & SPECIALTIES

Nowadays you can find haute cuisine and imported haole (Caucasian) supplies (like olive oil, artisan bread and balsamic vinegar) anywhere in the islands. But at heart, Hawaii is a 'beer and rice' type of place – the 'wine and cheese' crowd has a long way to go. A meal is incomplete without the foremost local staple: sticky, medium-grain, white rice. The rice pot accompanies even pasta or potato meals, and 20lb bags of rice are typical raffle prizes. While ketchup and salsa might be the mainland's top condiments, the local essential is soy sauce, always called by its Japanese name, shoyu.

Restaurants that top pizzas with pineapple and call it 'Hawaiian' are way off. The pineapple was introduced to Hawaii in 1813 and grown commercially only after 1900.

Native Hawaiian

Before Hawaii's first human settlers arrived, the only indigenous edibles were ferns, *'ohelo* berries and other barely sustaining plants. Thus the Polynesians created Hawaii's modern-day cornucopia when they brought *kalo* (taro), *'ulu* (breadfruit), *'uala* (sweet potato), *mai'a* (banana), *ko* (sugarcane), *niu* (coconut) and mountain apple, plus chickens, pigs and dogs for meat – and also discovered an abundance of seafood.

The centerpiece of a native Hawaiian meal is *kalua* pig, baked underground in an *imu* (a pit of red-hot stones). To cook the pig, layers of

---

EDIBLE SOUVENIRS

When Neighbor Islanders visit Kaua'i, they always return home laden with *omiyage* (Japanese word for gift or souvenir). Unique edibles include the following, which are sold at island retailers such as Longs Drugs and grocers (unless otherwise noted):

- Aunty Lilikoi condiments
- Taro Ko chips (p191)
- Hamura Saimin fresh noodles (p86)
- Anahola Granola
- Kilauea honey
- dried fruit by **Uncle Mikey's** (☎ 645-1928; www.unclemikeyshawaiianfoods.com)
- cookies (Popo's, Kauai Kookie Kompany and Hanalima Baking)
- coffee (Kaua'i Coffee and Blair Estate Organic Coffee Farm)
- *malasada* (Portugese fried dough) and other pastries (Kaua'i Bakery & Cinnamons, p86)

TOP FIVE TAKE-OUT POKE

Fish markets sell their homemade fresh *poke* (cubed, marinated raw fish) reasonably priced by the pound. Go for the classic *'ahi* recipes, or try the smoked salmon or marlin for a change.

- Koloa Fish Market (p165)
- Fish Express (p87)
- Pono Market (p119)
- Kaua'i Pupu Factory (p190)
- Kilauea Fish Market (p131)

---

crushed banana trunks and ti (common native plant) leaves are placed over the stones. The pig, stuffed with hot stones, is laid atop the bed, along with other foods wrapped in ti and banana leaves. Everything receives another covering of ti leaves, a layer of mats and dirt to seal in the hot steam. To *kalua* means to cook using this method. Cooking time is four to eight hours, depending on the quantity of food. Traditional *kalua* cooking is rather rare nowadays, as resorts perform the *imu* ceremony only for show, and few folks are willing to sacrifice their home backyards for a cooking pit that scorches surrounding vegetation.

Wetland taro was the Hawaiians' primary starch, usually eaten as poi, a paste pounded from cooked taro. The paste is thinned to a desired consistency by adding water. You might hear locals describe poi texture by the number of fingers needed to scoop it into the mouth: one-, two- and three-finger poi. Poi is highly nutritious, easily digestible and a perfect complement to strongly flavored foods. But many nonlocals find poi bland and describe the texture as akin to 'wallpaper paste,' which strikes locals as not only absurd but also insulting. Taro is a sacred food, considered the root of all life. Traditional Hawaiian households always show respect for taro: when the poi bowl sits on the table, one is expected to refrain from arguing or speaking in anger.

Other commonly eaten Hawaiian foods are *laulau* (bundle of pork, chicken or butterfish, wrapped in taro leaf, which cooks to a soft texture similar to spinach, and steamed in a covering of ti leaf); *lomilomi* salmon (a dish of minced, salted salmon, diced tomato and green onion); baked *'ulu*; raw *opihi* (limpets picked off the reef at low tide); *pipikaula* (beef jerky); *haupia* (a stiff pudding made of coconut cream and arrowroot); and raw *'a'ama* (black crab).

Local Food

While 'destination' restaurants might show off Hawaii's finest flavors, the soul of island food resides in cheap everyday eats, including the following:

Bento A remnant of plantation days, this prepackaged Japanese-style box lunch includes rice and your choice of meat or fish, along with pickles, *kamaboko* (a cake of puréed, steamed fish) and cooked vegetables.

Crack seed A Chinese snack food made with dried fruit, often plums or lemon. Crack seed can be sweet, sour, salty or a combination of all. The most popular – and most overwhelming to the uninitiated – is *li hing mui*. Today locals use *li hing* flavoring to spice up everything from fresh apples to margaritas!

Loco moco For an only-in-Hawaii experience, try this amalgamation of rice, fried egg and hamburger patty topped with gravy and a dash of shoyu. It's surprisingly appetizing, and meatless versions are available.

In 2002 the University of Hawai'i (UH) received US patents on three lines of disease-resistant taro, enraging farmers and activists who argue that the UH cannot invent or 'own' taro.

Locals have insatiable sweet teeth. To try their favorites, a good starter is *Hawaii's Best Local Desserts*, by Jean Watanabe Hee, while fancier recipes are found in *101 Great Desserts From Hawaii's Favorite Restaurants*, by Cheryl Chee Tsutsumi.

Okazu-ya If you want to cobble together your own meal, Japanese 'fast food' is sold individually (by the piece) at *okazu-ya* (lunch counters). There are dozens of options, including *musubi* (rice ball), *maki* (hand-rolled) sushi, tofu patties, shrimp tempura, *nishime* (stew of root vegetables) and Japanese-style fried chicken.

Plate lunch This fixed-plate meal (akin to a 'blue-plate special') comprises 'two scoop rice,' a scoop of macaroni salad and a main, such as beef stew, *tonkatsu* (pork cutlets), grilled mahimahi or teriyaki chicken.

Pupu *Anykine* (any kind) snacks or appetizers. An irresistibly savory favorite is *poke* (*poh*-kay), which contains cubed raw fish (often *'ahi*) typically marinated in shoyu, sesame oil, salt, green onion and chili pepper. Traditional *poke* includes *ogo* (seaweed) and *inamona*, a flavoring made of roasted and ground *kukui* (candlenut), while countless current renditions might use oysters, tofu or fruit. Also worth trying are boiled peanuts in the shell, which are similar to the *edamame* (boiled soybeans) popular at sushi bars, and taste fresher than the usual dry-roasted nuts.

Saimin Found only in Hawaii, this noodle soup is garnished with your choice of toppings, such as green onion, dried nori (seaweed), slices of *kamaboko* (steamed fish cake), egg roll and *char siu* (Chinese roast pork).

Shave ice Called 'ice shave' on the Big Island, this is a mainland 'snow cone' taken to the next level: the ice is shaved fine like powdered snow, packed into a paper cup and drenched with syrups in eye-popping hues. For a change, try sweet azuki-bean paste or ice cream underneath. Also see p120.

Hawaii Regional Cuisine

For Spam trivia, history, events, recipes and more, go to www.hormel .com and search the site for Spam.

Less than two decades ago, Hawaii was not exactly a foodie destination. Sure, locals savored their Spam *musubi* and enjoyed decent ethnic fare, but fine dining typically meant imitation 'continental' fare that ignored the bounty of locally grown produce, seafood and meat.

In the late 1980s and early 1990s top island chefs finally showed off local ingredients and multicultural influences – and quickly hit the gourmet radar. The movement was dubbed 'Hawaii Regional Cuisine' and the pioneering chefs became celebrities. Roy Yamaguchi is the fore-runner who opened his original Roy's restaurant in Honolulu in 1988. Today's culinary connoisseurs seem rather jaded by his ever-growing empire of 30 restaurants across the US, but you can judge for yourself at his outpost in Po'ipu: annoying ambience, top-quality food. Kaua'i's fine-dining restaurants all offer a variation of Hawaii Regional Cuisine, whether influenced by Mediterranean, Italian, Asian or California cuisine. Don't assume the ritzy resort restaurants are always best; many are

COMFORT FOOD IN A CAN

Hawaii is the Spam capital of the US, and locals consume a whopping four million cans per year, or 10,958 cans per day (which is 3½ times more than any other state!). While US food maker Hormel's Spam, a pork-based luncheon meat, is the butt of jokes almost everywhere, there's very little stigma in Hawaii. Rather, Spam is seen as a comfort food – always eaten cooked, not straight from the can.

Why Spam? No one knows exactly. Some people say it simply goes well with rice, Hawaii's ubiquitous starch. Others claim it's a legacy of plantation cookery, when fresh meat wasn't always available. Even today, whenever the islands are threatened by a hurricane or dock-workers' strike, locals stock up on water, batteries, toilet paper, 20lb bags of rice and…Spam.

A local favorite is Spam *musubi*: a block of rice with a slice of fried Spam on top (or in the middle), wrapped with a strip of black sushi nori. Created in the 1960s or '70s, it has become a classic, and thousands of *musubi* are sold daily at grocers, lunch counters and convenience stores. The Spam *musubi* phenomenon has even reached Hormel, which in 2004 released a collector's-edition can called 'Hawaiian Spam' with a recipe for you know what on the back.

excellent, but so are indies like Postcards Café in Hanalei and Hanapepe Café in Hanapepe.

DRINKS
Nonalcoholic
The best-known drink in Hawaii is world-renowned Kona coffee, which typically costs $20 per pound. But actually Kaua'i is the state's main producer of coffee, the largest producer being Kaua'i Coffee (see p185). While locals are regular coffee drinkers, café 'culture' – master baristas, potent espresso, intense chitchat or novel writing – remains nascent and more of a mainland thing. Kaua'i's handful of cafés close by dinnertime and exude a hippie, not hipster, vibe.

While fruit smoothies are sold everywhere in Hawaii, they are more prevalent on Kaua'i, where roadside fruit stands feature delicious combinations of locally grown fruit. An offshoot of the smoothie is the frosty, an icy dessert with the texture of ice cream, made by puréeing frozen fruit in a food processor. Banana Joe's Fruitstand (p131) is the best place to try both fruity treats.

Traditionally, Hawaiians had no alcoholic drinks, but whalers introduced them to liquor and taught them to make their own, 'okolehao, distilled from the ti root. Instead they drank an 'awa (kava) concoction as a mild intoxicant, as medicine and for rituals. For a health tonic they drank *noni* (Indian mulberry) juice, which is touted to reduce inflammation, boost energy and help cure everything from arthritis to cancer. Sold commercially, the pungent (to put it mildly) fruit is usually mixed with other juices.

Alcoholic
In general, drinking is a social pastime more than daily habit. The drinking age in Hawaii is 21, and shopkeepers will card baby faces.

Beer is the drink of choice, due to habit and cost (it's cheap). There are two microbreweries on Kaua'i: Waimea Brewing Company (p196) offers both beer and food at its plantation-style restaurant-pub in Waimea; and **Keoki Brewing Company** (☎ 245-8884; www.keokibrewing.com; 2976 Aukele, Lihu'e) sells two popular brews available at restaurants and stores island-wide, plus proprietary brews for the Shack Sports Bar (p121), Pizzetta (p121 and p165) and Hanalei Bay Resort (p138), to name a few. Wine is gaining in popularity among the upper-income classes and all top-end restaurants offer a decent selection. Roy's Po'ipu Bar & Grill (p177) boasts one of the island's most-extensive lists, while Longs Drugs (p90) in Lihu'e and the **Wine Garden** (☎ 245-5766; 4495 Puhi Rd, Puhi; ⏰ 10am-6:30pm Tue-Sat) are your best bets for retail bottles.

As for the kitschy 'umbrella' drinks often associated with Hawaii, be forewarned that no self-respecting local would ever order a Chi Chi or, worse, any blue beverage.

CELEBRATIONS
All local celebrations call for feasting. Year-round, you're bound to see large gatherings at beaches and parks, where groups often reserve a pavilion for all-day potlucks, where numerous tables are literally covered with piles of food. Public festivals feature booths selling inexpensive street food, from Japanese specialties at the Obon Celebration (p223) to coconut concoctions at the Kapa'a Coconut Festival (p118). More extravagant (with $75 price tags) are the Spring Gourmet Gala (p84) and Annual Taste of Hawaii (p106). Milestone events invariably involve

Kaua'i Coffee Company's average annual production is 3.5 million pounds, which is 60% of all coffee produced in Hawaii (including Maui and the Big Island's world-renowned Kona Coast).

County law prohibits retail sales of alcohol past 11pm. If you're too late, bars are your only option for midnight drinking.

a massive spread, and locals celebrate the standard American holidays much as mainlanders do, with elaborate birthday and wedding cakes, Easter egg hunts, Super Bowl beer parties and Thanksgiving turkey dinners. The difference lies in the nontraditional variety of food served. Sure, you'll see a whole turkey on the table for Thanksgiving, but you'll also see rice (never mashed potatoes), teriyaki-barbecued meat, fried whole shrimp, *maki* sushi and much more.

Homesick locals living on the mainland share their recipe collections online at www.alohaworld .com/ono.

WHERE TO EAT & DRINK

No need to bring a tie or heels to Kaua'i, as even fine dining is island-style casual. For eating on the run, head to takeout counters and hole-in-the-wall fish markets. The selection of prepared dishes and fresh fish is excellent – and you're often welcome to sample a bite.

For an online restaurant-review blog by a local in the know (complete with photos!), click on http://onokinegrindz .typepad.com.

Diner-style restaurants abound, and if the modest decor is acceptable, you'll enjoy the hearty servings of pancakes, omelettes, sandwiches and plate-lunch meals. While neither fancy nor especially healthful, they serve decent food at decent prices. For brunch or dinner, folks with eclectic tastes or bottomless-pit stomachs should try the all-you-can-eat buffets offered at hotels. Gaylord's (p89) offers a scrumptious daily breakfast buffet, plus an elaborate Sunday brunch.

For formal dining, Kaua'i's top-end restaurants can hold their own among their peers statewide. Don't expect the smooth, sophisticated service or clientele you might find in New York or San Francisco. Kaua'i is not a white-tablecloth-and-silver type of place, so relax and go with the flow.

For groceries, Kaua'i's Big Save supermarket chain, with locations around the island, is convenient but mundane. Smaller indie supermarkets offer the best selection of local produce, meat and fish. Tourists tend to flock to Safeway, the island's largest supermarket, which caters to middle-America tastes (don't forget your Safeway discount card). Universally, while you'll find bargains on sashimi-grade 'ahi, packaged items (eg a box of cereal) shipped from the mainland are woefully pricey. Surprisingly, island-grown produce is expensive except at fruit stands and farmers markets.

HAWAIIAN FEASTS

The best-known local celebration is the luau, the native Hawaiian feast that's become a household word across the USA. Early Hawaiians celebrated auspicious occasions – such as a child's birth, war victory or successful harvest – with a feast to honor the gods and share their bounty. Called *'aha'aina* (gathering for a meal) in ancient times, the term luau became common much later; it also refers to the young edible taro leaves that traditionally were used to wrap food cooked in the underground *imu*.

Today there are two types of luau: private and commercial. Private luau are family affairs, thrown for a Hawaiian wedding or a baby's first birthday, sans fire-eaters and Tahitian dancers and the rousing 'Alooooooooooha!' greeting. Guests feast on raw shellfish delicacies never served at commercial luau, and the entertainment is a lively local band, which might spur the *tutu* (grandmothers) to get up and dance hula with their grandchildren.

But unless you have connections, your only option is a commercial luau performance. These are well-choreographed, Vegas-style shows that include an all-you-can-eat buffet and flashy Polynesian performances. The food tends to be mediocre, featuring the Hawaiian standards like poi and *kalua* pig – plus roast beef, teriyaki beef, fried rice and motley options designed to please all. On Kaua'i, the most local luau are offered at Smith's Tropical Paradise (p110) and Kilohana Plantation (p89).

KAUA'I TOP FIVE EATS

Budget

- Hamura Saimin (p86)
- Mermaids Café (p121)
- Kilauea Bakery and Pau Hana Pizza (p131)
- Hanalei Taro & Juice Company (p148)
- Kalaheo Coffee Co & Café (p182)

Midrange

- Polynesia Café (p149)
- Kintaro (p109)
- Caffé Coco (p109)
- Blossoming Lotus (p120)
- Hanapepe Café (p191)

Top End

- Beach House Restaurant (p178)
- Hukilau Lanai (p109)
- Postcards Café (p149)
- Café Hanalei (p139)
- Roy's Po'ipu Bar & Grill (p177)

Grocers

- Ishihara Market (p196)
- Sueoka Store (p166)
- Farmers Markets (p88)
- Papaya's Natural Foods (Kapa'a, p114, and Hanalei, p149)
- Banana Joe's Fruitstand (p131)

VEGETARIANS & VEGANS

While most locals are omnivores, vegetarians and vegans luck out on Kaua'i. Perhaps due to the North Shore hippie influence, numerous eateries on the island cater to vegetarian, vegan, fish-only or healthful diets. Asian culinary influences also guarantee plenty of vegetable and tofu options. Notable venues include the vegan Blossoming Lotus (p120) and its Lotus Root Juice Bar & Bakery (p120); Postcards Café (p149); Hanapepe Café (p191) for meatless fine-dining; eb's EATS (p87) for healthful deli mains, salads and sandwiches; and Mema (p109) for Thai cuisine. Another option is to cobble together your own meals from farmers markets and health-food stores.

While vegetarians aren't the target market (a plate lunch without meat or fish is not quite a plate lunch), the trend toward meatless diets is growing, mostly among young women and transplants (hippie or otherwise). Most locals eat everything in moderation, view vegetarianism as rather extreme and would probably consider you over-the-top if you admonish them about the evils of meat eating. As you'd expect, the most ardent supporters of meatless diets and organic, local and sustainable farming are haole newcomers.

If you think vegan cuisine is bland, think again. *Vegan World Fusion Cuisine* is an elegant cookbook coauthored by Mark Reinfeld (executive chef of Blossoming Lotus).

EATING WITH KIDS

Restaurants are usually quick to accommodate children with high chairs and booster seats, though too much noise or unruliness is inappropriate for the upscale establishments (locals are courteous to the nth degree and might not complain, but why stick out like a tourist?).

Families should enjoy the daily opportunity to eat outdoors, from impromptu plate lunches at the beach to fresh fruit at a roadside stand. Mimic the locals: buy a *goza* (inexpensive roll-up straw mat), pack a picnic and head to the nearest park.

Kids will find lots of treats, such as premium ice cream, shave ice, pizza and taro chips. As for main dishes, the local palate tends toward the sweet and straightforward side, without too much garlic, bitter greens, pungent cheeses and strong spices – which typically agrees with kids' tastes.

HABITS & CUSTOMS

Locals eat three square meals early and on the dot: typically 6am breakfast, noon lunch and 6pm dinner. Restaurants are jammed around these mealtimes, but they clear out an hour or two later, as locals are not lingerers. If you dine at 8:30pm you might not have to wait at all! But bear in mind that most places shut down by 10pm. In general, locals tip slightly less than mainlanders, but still up to 20% for good service and at least 15% for the basics.

Home entertainment always revolves around food, usually served potluck style with all guests adding to the anything-goes smorgasbord. Throwaway paper plates and wooden chopsticks make cleanup easy, and the rule is 'all you can eat' (and they really mean it). If you're invited to someone's home, show up on time and bring a dish, preferably homemade (but a bakery cake or pie is always appreciated). Remove your shoes at the door. And don't be surprised if you're forced to take home a plate or two of leftovers.

Cook 'em Up Kaua'i is a user-friendly, spiral-bound classic produced by the Kaua'i Historical Society, a nonprofit organization founded in 1914. Contributors' recipes feature local favorites, including an easy *liliko'i* cheesecake recipe.

EAT YOUR WORDS

If someone offered you a *broke da mout malasada* or *'ono kine poke*, would you try it? Don't miss out because you're stumped by the lingo, whether Hawaiian, Japanese or purely pidgin. For pronunciation tips, see p243.

Food Glossary

'a'ama	black crab
'ahi	yellowfin tuna
aku	bonito (skipjack tuna)
'ama'ama	mullet
a'u	swordfish, marlin
awa	milkfish
'awa	kava, a native plant used to make an intoxicating drink
'awapuhi	wild ginger
azuki bean	used as a sweetened paste in Japanese desserts; also added as a topping to shave ice
bento	Japanese-style box lunch
broke da mout	delicious
crack seed	Chinese preserved fruit; a salty, sweet or sour snack
donburi	large bowl of rice and main dish
grind	to eat
grinds	food; *'ono kine grinds* is good food
gyoza	grilled dumpling usually containing minced pork or shrimp
haupia	coconut pudding
he'e	octopus; also called *tako* in Japanese
humuhumunukunukuapua'a	triggerfish; Hawaii's unofficial state fish
imu	underground earthen oven used to cook kalua pig and other luau food
inamona	ground and roasted kukui (candlenut), used to flavor dishes such as poke
kalua	traditional method of cooking in an underground pit
kamaboko	a block of puréed, steamed fish
kaukau	food
laulau	a bundle made of pork or chicken and salted butterfish, wrapped in taro and ti leaves and steamed
li hing mui	sweet-sour crack seed
liliko'i	passion fruit
loco moco	dish of rice topped with a hamburger, a fried egg and gravy; nonmeat options available

lomilomi salmon	minced, salted salmon, diced tomato and green onion
luau	Hawaiian feast
mahimahi	also called 'dolphin,' but actually a type of fish unrelated to the marine mammal
mai'a	banana
mai tai	alcoholic drink made from rum, grenadine, and lemon and pineapple juices
malasada	Portuguese fried dough, served warm and sugar-coated
manju	Japanese bun filled with sweet bean paste
mochi	Japanese sticky rice, pounded and shaped into a dumpling
nishime	stew of root vegetables and seaweed
noni	Indian mulberry; a small tree with yellow, smelly fruit that is used medicinally
nori	Japanese seaweed, usually dried
ogo	seaweed
ohelo	shrub with edible red berries similar in tartness and size to cranberries
onaga	mild-tasting red snapper
ono	wahoo fish
'ono	delicious
'ono kine grinds	good food
'opae	shrimp
'opakapaka	blue snapper
'opelu	pan-sized mackerel scad
'opihi	edible limpet
pad thai	rice noodles stir-fried with tofu, vegetables, egg and peanuts
pho	a Vietnamese soup of beef broth, noodles and fresh herbs
pipi kaula	salted, dried beef that is served broiled; Hawaiian-style beef jerky
poha	gooseberry
poi	staple Hawaiian starch made of steamed, mashed taro
poka	a fruit in the passion fruit family
poke	cubed raw fish mixed with shoyu, sesame oil, salt, green onion, chili pepper, inamona and other condiments
pupu	snack or appetizer; also Hawaiian word for shell
saimin	a Hawaiian version of Japanese noodle soup
shoyu	soy sauce
soba	buckwheat noodles
star fruit	translucent yellow-green fruit with five ribs like the points of a star and sweet, juicy pulp
taro	plant with edible corm used to make poi and with edible leaves eaten in laulau; *kalo* in Hawaiian
teppanyaki	Japanese style of cooking with an iron grill
tonkatsu	breaded and fried pork cutlets, also prepared as chicken katsu
tsukemono	pickled vegetables
'uala	sweet potato
'ulu	breadfruit
ume	Japanese pickled plum
unagi	eel
wana	sea urchin

LIHU'E

Lihu'e

Whether you arrive by air or by sea, your gateway to Kaua'i is Lihu'e – home to state and county offices, retail chains from Borders to Wal-Mart and the island's only major hospital. For most visitors, Lihu'e is a necessary stop, not a destination.

While Lihu'e makes a ho-hum first impression, it might surprise you upon a second look. Tucked away on nondescript side streets or behind simple facades are eateries you'll find nowhere else, and Kaua'i Museum is a worthwhile diversion. Lihu'e's modest resort strip near Nawiliwili Harbor cannot compete with the cachet of Po'ipu or Princeville, but the central location might be convenient – and Kalapaki Beach and Kaua'i Lagoons Golf Club are top-notch.

Perhaps the best thing about Lihu'e is its down-to-earth vibe: at lunch counters you'll mingle with locals on their breaks and at supermarkets you'll queue up with folks *pau hana* (after work). The ethnic makeup of Lihu'e and its vicinity also reflects the island's plantation history: here, the largest ethnic group are the Japanese at just under 30%, followed by Caucasian and mixed-race individuals, each at about 20%. The virtually contiguous communities of Puhi (population 1186) and Hanama'ulu (population 3272) both comprise majority Filipino populations. Multiculturalism is palpable here.

To the south, the stately Ha'upu mountain range looms in the distance, and miles of wild sugarcane and forest land sprawl toward the Pacific Ocean. Adventure tours traverse these pristine, private lands.

In Lihu'e, ordinary people lead ordinary lives. It puts things in perspective.

HIGHLIGHTS

- Kayaking or canoeing the **Hule'ia River** (p82)
- Learning about ancient Hawaii at **Kaua'i Museum** (p78)
- Splashing at **Kalapaki Beach** (p79)
- **Zipping** (p82) and **tubing** (p82) in the backcountry
- Slurping noodles at **Hamura Saimin** (p86)
- Golfing at the seaside **Kaua'i Lagoons Golf Club** (p82)

WHAT'S THAT FUNNY-LOOKING APOSTROPHE?

If you're stumped by the spelling of Kaua'i as Kaua'i, relax. That upside-down, backward apostrophe is the *'okina*, a diacritic that signals a glottal stop in the pronunciation of Hawaiian words. Another diacritic is the *kahako*, which signifies a macron for long vowels (and which we do not use in this book).

The *'okina* (and *kahako*) can dramatically change a word's meaning. For example, lanai (with no *'okina*) means porch or balcony, while Lana'i refers to a Hawaiian island. The vast majority of people pronounce island names incorrectly, but it's simple if you just observe the *'okina* placement. Thus Kaua'i is kau-a-i, not ka-*waaee*.

Since the late 1990s and early 2000s, state and county governments have advocated including the diacritics in all place and street names. Thus you will see them, especially the *'okina*, in newspapers, advertisements, street signs, government websites and so forth. The switch has been patchy but it's very clear which way the islands are headed. But ironically, a contingent of elderly Native Hawaiians actually prefer spelling Hawaiian words without the diacritics because they learned to read and write using the Hawaiian Bible, which was written without the marks.

As for the official spelling of Hawaii, the US government recognizes Hawaii to be the official state name under the Admission Act of 1959. Thus, while state and county governments have embraced the *'okina*, the federal spelling is used for interstate and international dealings.

Non-native speakers sometimes get too eager to use the *'okina*, which inevitably appears where it does not belong. Before you an 'okina willy-nilly plop in any Hawaiian word, check the online **Hawaiian dictionary** (www.wehewehe.org).

In this book, we use Hawaii (without the *'okina*) to indicate all the major Hawaiian Islands as a group, whether pre- or post-statehood. We use Hawai'i (with the *'okina*) to indicate the Big Island.

See p44 for more on the Hawaiian language.

HISTORY

Lihu'e arose as a plantation town back in the day when sugar was king and the massive Lihu'e Plantation sugar mill (still standing south of town along Kaumuali'i Hwy) was Kaua'i's largest. The plantation relied solely on rainwater during its early years, but then William Harrison Rice, who bought the company in the early 1860s, became the first planter in Hawaii to irrigate sugarcane fields. The plantation closed in 2001, ending more than a century of operation.

Lihu'e (population 5674) is a blink-and-you'll-miss-it capital seat. Designed in the 1920s, the town layout features wide streets centered around the government buildings, notably constructed of concrete, stone and other durable materials rather than typical plantation-era wood. Lihu'e Airport, first opened in 1950, remains the only point of arrival and departure for major airlines and the primary base for helicopter tours.

Without a town center or pedestrian boulevard, Lihu'e is a drive-in, drive-out town and traffic is jammed during rush hour. The county is pushing major retail here, and Kukui Grove Shopping Center is teeming with the usual suspects, including Home Depot, Kmart and, soon, Costco.

ORIENTATION

Lihu'e is surrounded on all sides by highways: the Kuhio Hwy (Hwy 56) to the west and the Kapule Hwy (Hwy 51) to the east, while Ahukini Rd (Hwy 570) and Nawiliwili Rd (Hwy 58) roughly represent north and south borders respectively. The town's main drag, Rice Street, runs east–west through the heart of town. Here you'll find the post offices, government buildings and business services. Kukui Grove Shopping Center is slightly south of town – you can't miss it. Restaurants and sights are scattered, so don't expect to park only once.

Maps

For drivers, the **Ready Mapbook of Kaua'i** ($11) is an invaluable road atlas, sold online at www.geckofarms.com and at island bookstores. See p225 for other excellent maps.

LIHU'E AREA

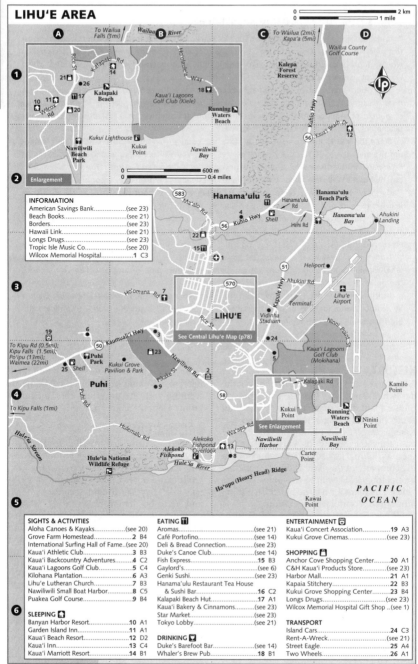

INFORMATION
American Savings Bank.................(see 23)
Beach Books.................................(see 21)
Borders.......................................(see 23)
Hawaii Link.................................(see 21)
Longs Drugs................................(see 23)
Tropic Isle Music Co.....................(see 20)
Wilcox Memorial Hospital................1 C3

SIGHTS & ACTIVITIES
Aloha Canoes & Kayaks...............(see 20)
Grove Farm Homestead....................2 B4
International Surfing Hall of Fame..(see 20)
Kaua'i Athletic Club..........................3 B3
Kaua'i Backcountry Adventures........4 C2
Kaua'i Lagoons Golf Club..................5 C4
Kilohana Plantation...........................6 A3
Lihu'e Lutheran Church......................7 B3
Nawiliwili Small Boat Harbor.............8 C5
Puakea Golf Course...........................9 B4

SLEEPING
Banyan Harbor Resort.....................10 A1
Garden Island Inn............................11 A1
Kaua'i Beach Resort.........................12 D2
Kaua'i Inn.......................................13 C4
Kaua'i Marriott Resort......................14 B1

EATING
Aromas..(see 21)
Café Portofino...............................(see 14)
Deli & Bread Connection................(see 23)
Duke's Canoe Club.........................(see 14)
Fish Express....................................15 B3
Gaylord's...(see 6)
Genki Sushi...................................(see 23)
Hanama'ulu Restaurant Tea House
  & Sushi Bar..................................16 C2
Kalapaki Beach Hut.........................17 A1
Kaua'i Bakery & Cinnamons...........(see 23)
Star Market...................................(see 23)
Tokyo Lobby.................................(see 21)

DRINKING
Duke's Barefoot Bar.......................(see 14)
Whaler's Brew Pub.........................18 B1

ENTERTAINMENT
Kaua'i Concert Association..............19 A3
Kukui Grove Cinemas....................(see 23)

SHOPPING
Anchor Cove Shopping Center........20 A1
C&H Kaua'i Products Store.............(see 23)
Harbor Mall....................................21 A1
Kapaia Stitchery...............................22 B3
Kukui Grove Shopping Center........23 B4
Longs Drugs..................................(see 23)
Wilcox Memorial Hospital Gift Shop ..(see 1)

TRANSPORT
Island Cars......................................24 C3
Rent-A-Wreck................................(see 21)
Street Eagle.....................................25 A4
Two Wheels......................................26 A1

INFORMATION

Bookstores

Beach Books (Map p76; Harbor Mall, 3501 Rice St; 8:30am-7:30pm Mon-Sat) Cheap new and used beach reading.

Borders (Map p76; ☎ 246-0862; Kukui Grove Shopping Center, 4303 Nawiliwili Rd; 9am-10pm Mon-Thu, to 11pm Fri & Sat, to 8pm Sun) Large chain with wide range of books, CDs and DVDs; lots of local selections unavailable on the mainland. In-store Starbucks café.

Tropic Isle Music Co (Map p76; ☎ 245-8700; www .tropicislemusic.com; Anchor Cove Shopping Center, 3416 Rice St; 9am-9pm) Impressive stock of Hawaii- and Kaua'i-specific books, CDs and videos.

Emergency

Police (Map p78; ☎ 241-1771; 3060 Umi St) For non-emergencies, incident reporting and information.
Police, Fire & Ambulance (☎ 911)
Sexual Assault Crisis Line (☎ 245-4144)

Internet Access

Beach Books (Map p76; Harbor Mall, 3501 Rice St; per 15min $3; 8:30am-7:30pm Mon-Sat) One computer for Internet access.

Hawaii Link (Map p76; ☎ 246-9300; Harbor Mall, 3501 Rice St; per hr $12; 9am-6pm Mon-Fri)

Laundry

Lihu'e Laundromat (Map p78; ☎ 332-8356; Rice Shopping Center, 4303 Rice St; 6am-9pm)

Media

NEWSPAPERS

Essential Kaua'i (www.essentialkauai.com) Offshoot of *The Garden Island*, this bimonthly publication packs useful news, local profiles and reviews in a slim package.

The Garden Island (www.kauaiworld.com) Kaua'i's daily newspaper is a lean, 'just the basics,' small-town paper, but it's a good source of local events and issues.

RADIO

KITH 98.9FM Contemporary island music, including Hawaiian and reggae (bet you'll hear Israel Kamakawiwo'ole and Bob Marley), plus local-favorite covers of American pop classics. Upbeat choice for island cruising.

KKCR 91.9FM Community radio at its best, broadcasting local events and a range of music, including blues, reggae, salsa and lots of Hawaiian. On North Shore, frequency is 90.9FM.

KONG 570AM News, sports, and talk, including syndicated shows by Rush Limbaugh, Dr Dean Edell, Mitch Albom and Al Franken.

KONG 93.5FM (www.kongradio.com) Mainstream US pop and contemporary island music. Excellent DJs Ron Wiley (mornings) and Marc Valentine (afternoons). On North Shore, frequency is 94.5FM.

KTOH 99.9FM Oldies, classic hits from the 1960s to 1990s.

KUAI 720AM The best station for news, every hour on the hour, plus extended coverage at 7am, noon and 5pm on weekdays. Catch the early-morning show with longtime DJ Reggie DeRoos.

TELEVISION

KVIC A televised loop of Kaua'i tourist information on channel 3.

Medical Services

Longs Drugs (Map p76; ☎ 245-7771; Kukui Grove Shopping Center, 3-2600 Kaumuali'i Hwy; store 7am-10pm Mon-Sat, 8am-8pm Sun, pharmacy 8am-9pm Mon-Sat, 9am-6pm Sun)

Wilcox Memorial Hospital (Map p76; ☎ 245-1010, TTY 245-1133; 3420 Kuhio Hwy) Kaua'i's only major hospital. Emergency services 24 hours.

ON THE ROAD

If you ask Kaua'i locals for driving directions, be prepared for island-style lingo:

- Instead of giving standard north/east/south/west directions, locals simply refer to *mauka* (toward the mountains; inland) and *makai* (toward the ocean; seaward).

- Highways are known by their Hawaiian common names, not by number. See p237 for a key.

- Locals invariably refer to landmarks ('turn right at the Shell station' or 'go past Longs Drugs') rather than cross streets or driving mileage, so be eagle-eyed when checking out your surroundings.

- Mainlanders generally talk *much* faster than locals, who take their time getting to the point. If you find yourself growing impatient when trying to eke out simple directions, take a deep breath and keep your mouth shut. Relaaaax, you're on vacation.

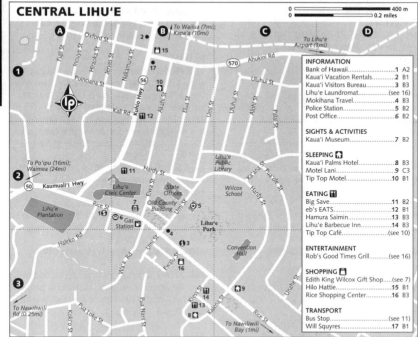

CENTRAL LIHU'E

INFORMATION	
Bank of Hawaii	1 A2
Kaua'i Vacation Rentals	2 B1
Kaua'i Visitors Bureau	3 B3
Lihu'e Laundromat	(see 16)
Mokihana Travel	4 B3
Police Station	5 B2
Post Office	6 B2

SIGHTS & ACTIVITIES	
Kaua'i Museum	7 B2

SLEEPING	
Kaua'i Palms Hotel	8 B3
Motel Lani	9 C3
Tip Top Motel	10 B1

EATING	
Big Save	11 B2
eb's EATS	12 B1
Hamura Saimin	13 B3
Lihu'e Barbecue Inn	14 B3
Tip Top Café	(see 10)

ENTERTAINMENT	
Rob's Good Times Grill	(see 16)

SHOPPING	
Edith King Wilcox Gift Shop	(see 7)
Hilo Hattie	15 B1
Rice Shopping Center	16 B3

TRANSPORT	
Bus Stop	(see 11)
Will Squyres	17 B1

Money

Banks with 24-hour ATMs:
American Savings Bank (Map p76; ☎ 246-8844; Kukui Grove Shopping Center, 3-2600 Kaumuali'i Hwy)
Bank of Hawaii (Map p78; ☎ 245-6761; 4455 Rice St)

Post

Longs Drugs (Map p76; ☎ 245-7771; Kukui Grove Shopping Center, 3-2600 Kaumuali'i Hwy; 🕑 7am-10pm Mon-Sat, 8am-8pm Sun) In-store postal center offers photocopying, FedEx and UPS, and US Postal Service (at a slightly higher cost than at a post office).
Post office (Map p78; ☎ 800-275-8777; 4441 Rice St, Lihu'e, HI 96766; 🕑 8am-4:30pm Mon-Fri, 9am-1pm Sat) Main post office holds poste restante (general delivery) mail for a maximum 30 days. Service here is generally faster than at the jammed Kapa'a branch.

Tourist Information

See p227 and visit the websites listed on p23) for pretrip planning.
Kaua'i Visitors Bureau (Map p78; ☎ 245-3971, 800-262-1400; www.kauaidiscovery.com; 4334 Rice St, Suite 101) Offers monthly calendar of events, bus schedules and list of Sunshine Markets. Visit the attractive website for pretrip planning and order a free 'vacation planning kit'

online (or by calling the 800 number). For brochures and other printed tourist information, the airport has a better selection.

Travel Agencies

Unless you need a human touch, the Internet can't be beat for finding lodging and flights. If you want personal help, however, **Mokihana Travel** (Map p78; ☎ 245-5338; 3016 Umi St, Suite 3; 🕑 8am-5pm Mon-Fri, to noon Sat) is a reliable agency.

SIGHTS
Kaua'i Museum

A quick hour spent in this modest but interesting **museum** (Map p78; ☎ 245-6931; www.kauaimuseum.org; 4428 Rice St; adult/child 6-12/youth 13-17/senior $7/1/3/5, 1st Sat of month free; 🕑 9am-4pm Mon-Fri, 10am-4pm Sat) will give you a solid grounding in Kaua'i's history. For a more in-depth experience, make reservations for a **guided tour** (tour $10; 🕑 10am Mon, Wed & Thu). Free **Hawaiian quilting demonstrations** (🕑 9am-noon Wed & Thu) and **lauhala-hat weaving demonstrations** (🕑 1pm Mon & Wed) are given year-round.

Straightforward, well-written displays explain the Hawaiian Islands' volcanic genesis and the formation of the island chain from the ocean floor, as well as Kaua'i's unique ecosystems. They all focus on native flora and fauna. Early Hawaiian artifacts – tapa (bark cloth), wooden bowls, ceremonial lei etc – are also in the collection here.

Upstairs the collection is Kaua'i-specific, covering the arrival of missionaries, sugar and the waves of immigrants who came to work the fields. In a socioeconomic commentary that still rings true, a replica of a plantation worker's spartan shack sits opposite the spacious bedroom of an early missionary's house, furnished with a koa four-poster bed and Hawaiian quilts. Hawaii's multiethnic roots and vastly unequal distribution of land are clearly the result of Hawaii's sugar and pineapple empires. Anyone interested in the so-called Forbidden Island, Ni'ihau, shouldn't miss the photographs which give outsiders a rare peek into the inaccessible, privately owned isle.

If you run out of time before seeing the entire museum, ask for a free re-entry pass when you leave. An adjacent gallery shows rotating exhibits of contemporary art.

Wailua Falls

Best known for its appearance in the opening credits of the *Fantasy Island* TV series, this waterfall keeps drawing daily sightseers. Located just north of Lihu'e, it's officially listed as 80ft but repeatedly measures between 125ft to 175ft. Indeed, this gushing double waterfall (Wailua means 'two waters') misting the surrounding tropical foliage is a fantastic photo op, especially when the falls merge into one wide cascade after downpours. Sometimes you can watch fish literally flung outside the pounding falls for a flying dive into the pool below.

At the lookout spot, a sign at the parking lot near a closed path reads: 'Slippery rocks at top of falls. People have been killed.' Of course, folks inevitably scramble down the unmaintained path to swim at the base of the falls. The path is steep and slippery, and people do slide off the rocks (the lucky ones miraculously grab roots and get rescued). Another eroded trail exists a third of a mile before the road's end, at a large dirt shoulder. While not quite as steep as the other path, it's also closed to the public.

The falls plummet into a deep pool, spurring the truly intrepid to dive from the top, as ancient Hawaiians did to prove their manhood. The display was often fatal then – and it remains so today. In 1995 a man died after leaping for the thrill of it. In 2000 two 22-year-old men from California leaped, and a local 22-year-old man slipped, from the top, all in the same week. Each rescue cost the county about $1500 in helicopter and personnel time. From 2000 the county stated that future jumpers would receive a ticket and a bill for rescue costs.

To get here from Lihu'e, follow Kuhio Hwy north and turn left onto Ma'alo Rd (Hwy 583), a narrow paved road that weaves through sugarcane fields and ends at the falls after 4 miles.

Lihu'e Lutheran Church

Atop a curvy country lane just off Kaumuali'i Hwy (Hwy 50) is Hawaii's oldest Lutheran **church** (Map p76; ☎ 245-2145; 4602 Ho'omana Rd; ☒ services 8am & 10:30am Sun), a quaint, clapboard house of worship, with a few surprises. Crossing the threshold, you step in and...wait a minute. As soon as you enter the church proper, its slanted floor suddenly resembles a ship's deck and its balcony, a captain's bridge. These and other architectural details are thanks to the German immigrants who built this church, styling it after the boat that brought them over in the late 19th century. Completed in 1983, this building is actually a faithful reconstruction of the 1885 original, which was leveled in Hurricane 'Iwa in 1982.

Fancying an afterlife with a view, the immigrants themselves now lie at rest in the church cemetery on a knoll overlooking the cane fields in which they toiled. Visitors are welcome to stroll amid the graves and take pictures inside and out, except during Sunday service.

Kalapaki Beach

Surfers and boogie boarders trot toward the swells, while mainlanders bask on the sands of Lihu'e's best beach (Map p76). Sheltered by points and breakwaters at Nawiliwili Bay and lined with coconut palms, this beach off Kapule Hwy lies in front of the Kaua'i Marriott Resort. While it might appear to be the resort's beach, it's open to the public (free parking is close to the water at the hotel's north side). Swimming is usually good, even in winter. A beach hut here rents snorkel gear, surfboards and kayaks, and a variety of restaurants, from casual to 'dis betta be worth it,' lines the beach. Chill out here before catching your flight out.

Fronting the beach is the **International Surfing Hall of Fame** (Map p76; ☎ 632-2270; adult/child under 12 $10/free; ☺ 9am-9pm). In existence since the '60s, but without a bricks-and-mortar home, this long-overdue tribute to the world's greatest surfers exhibits boards, memorabilia and original art in cool digs replete with thatched roof and piped-in surfing tunes. The museum screening room shows classic surf movies.

Nawiliwili Beach Park

A footbridge from Kalapaki Beach crosses Nawiliwili Stream to Nawiliwili Beach Park (Map p76), from where you can see the light beacon on Kukui Point. At the far end of the parking lot, you can also see, in the distance, the lighthouse on Ninini Point. Right at the mouth of the stream under ironwood trees sits a simple shelter with a wooden sign reading 'Pine Tree Uptown' – an impromptu neighborhood open-air bar, you might call it. Old-timers gather here with beers during the day to talk story and play music.

Gargantuan cruise ships dock at Nawiliwili Harbor and smaller boats, including deep-sea fishing charters and kayak tours, leave from nearby Nawiliwili Small Boat Harbor. See p83 for suggested charters.

Alekoko (Menehune) Fishpond

A tranquil oasis surrounded by vast forestland, the 39-acre Alekoko (Menehune) Fishpond (Map p76) is an ancient *loko wai* (freshwater pond). It was in great condition until 1824, when Kaua'i's leader Kaumuali'i died and *ali'i* (chiefs) from O'ahu and Maui ruled the island as absentee landlords. With no *ali'i* to feed and maintain the pond, it sorely declined. Later the surrounding area was planted with taro and rice. Today the US Fish & Wildlife Service owns the lands surrounding the fishpond (238 acres of river basin and steep forested slopes along the north side of Hule'ia River). In 1973 the area was designated the **Hule'ia National Wildlife Refuge** (http://pacificislands.fws.gov/wnwr/khuleianwr .html) and now provides breeding and feeding grounds for endemic water birds. To get to the overlook, drive up Hulemanu Rd for 0.5 miles.

According to legend, the fishpond, created by a stone wall that runs along a bend in Hule'ia River, was built overnight by Kaua'i's legendary *menehune* (little people). The stone wall is now covered by a thick green line of mangrove trees. To avoid the afternoon sun in your eyes, visit in the morning.

The refuge is closed to the public, but kayak tours (p82) along Hule'ia River drift through it; actually the views from above are more scenic, but the mana (spiritual essence) is more powerful at eye level.

If you continue along Hulemalu Rd, you'll eventually hook up with Kipu Rd;

DETOUR: KIPU FALLS

Admit it. You fantasize about those ol' Mountain Dew commercials, where sunshine peeks through leafy trees and you can splash into a swimming hole from a rope swing. Guess what? You can taste that life at Kipu Falls, a short drive and hike from Lihu'e. This waterfall, swimming hole and 20ft rope jump have long been a low-key favorite (you'll still see 'Locals Only!' and 'No Haole!' graffiti around). Now that the word is out, locals are ticked. To minimize tourist impact, come early or late on weekdays (leave the weekends for residents) and keep it clean.

Note that Kipu Falls is private property. People have been injured here, and too many accidents might prompt the landowner to close it to trespassers. Don't take undue risks and ruin the fun, not only for yourself but also for local kids.

To get here, take Kipu Rd off Kaumuali'i Hwy at the 3-mile marker. A dirt path leading to the falls is just under a mile, starting before the one-lane bridge. You can walk to the site in five minutes. Don't leave anything of value in your car. Returning to Lihu'e, you can take pastoral Hulemalu Rd (turn right off Kipu Rd 0.75 miles from the dirt path), which takes you past the Alekoko Fishpond and hooks up with Wa'apa Rd near Nawiliwili.

a left turn will take you to the dirt path to Kipu Falls (see opposite).

Ninini Point

Hardly any tourists venture here, but this point allows 360-degree vistas: jets directly above swoop in for landing and waves crash against the rocks below. Looking east, soaring cliffs cut off rainbows and, closer in, golfers tee off near a beckoning scoop of beach. These terrific views from Ninini Point are made more so by its 100ft **lighthouse** marking the northern entrance to Nawiliwili Bay. Here, Hawaiians still fish, pick *opihi* (edible limpet) and gather *limu* (edible seaweed).

The road to the lighthouse begins off Kapule Hwy, just over 0.5 miles south of the intersection with Ahukini Rd and marked with two concrete slabs. You'll pass a guard gate (usually empty) and through Hole 12 of the Mokihana Golf Course, for a total of just over 2 miles, most of it rutted dirt road, before you reach the short spur to the lighthouse.

To get to **Running Waters Beach** (the little slice of sand visible from Ninini Point) return to Hole 12 and park in the lot just before it, then follow the signs for Shore Access. Turn right at Whaler's Brew Pub and descend to its parking lot, where you'll see another Shore Access sign to your left. It's a steep, quick walk to the beach below, where the sand is golden and the surf runs in and out of naturally carved channels in the volcanic rock. You'll probably have the beach to yourself, and it makes a wonderful picnic spot. Wading beyond ankle depth is not advisable here. You can also reach this beach (but not the lighthouse) by driving through Kaua'i Marriott Resort and following the signs to Whaler's Brew Pub.

Grove Farm Homestead

If you're a history buff, this **plantation museum** (Map p76; ☎ 245-3202; Nawiliwili Rd; 2hr tour adult/child under 12 $5/2; ☼ tours 10am & 1pm Mon, Wed & Thu), open only for tours, is worth a look-see – otherwise it's not a must. Grove Farm was among the most productive sugar companies on Kaua'i, and George Wilcox, the son of missionaries Abner and Lucy Wilcox, built this well-preserved farmhouse in 1864. It feels suspended in time, with rocking chairs sitting dormant on a

covered porch and untouched books lining the shelves of the musty library. Call first as reservations are required.

Note that Grove Farm Museum is today run by George Wilcox's niece, Mabel, and operates independently of Grove Farm Company, the largest developer in eastern Kaua'i. You might have heard about Grove Farm Company in the news, as AOL founder Steve Case bought the company's 21,600 acres in 2000 for $26 million. The holdings then included Kukui Grove Shopping Center, Puakea golf course, and the coastal land surrounding Maha'ulepu Beach – and made Case the second-largest private landowner on Kaua'i. In 2005, former Grove Farm owners and shareholders sued Case, claiming that the property was actually worth $152 million and they did not receive fair market value for it.

Kilohana Plantation

With acres of vivid lawn and neatly manicured gardens, this **plantation** (Map p76; ☎ 245-9593; www.kilohanakauai.com; Kaumuali'i Hwy; admission free; ☼ 9:30am-9:30pm Mon-Sat, to 5pm Sun) looks like the rich man's estate that it is. Sugar baron Gaylord Parke Wilcox, once the head honcho of Grove Farm Homestead, built the house in 1935. Today it is a tourist magnet thanks to its famous luau, Gaylord's restaurant and one-stop upscale shopping. Trivia buffs take note: the Wilcox family was the model for James Michener's famous epic, *Hawaii*.

The 15,000-sq-ft Tudor-style mansion has been painstakingly restored and its legacy as one of Kaua'i's distinguished historic houses is unquestioned. Antique-filled rooms and Oriental carpets laid over hardwood floors lead you past cases of poi pounders, koa bowls and other Hawaiiana to a row of gallery shops. Behind the main house is **Kilohana Clayworks** pottery shop, where you can watch potters at work.

Carriages pulled by Clydesdale horses **tour** (adult/child $12/6; ☼ 11am-5pm) the 35-acre grounds, including gardens and livestock barns – a bit hokey but fun for kids.

At the time of research, the museum was preparing a new attraction featuring vintage locomotives used to haul cane from the late 1890s to the late 1950s. A 2.3-mile recreational railway system will take visitors past a train station, plantation cottage, sugar and coffee fields and an agricultural display of local crops from bananas to hardwood trees.

Kilohana Plantation is 1.5 miles west of Lihu'e.

ACTIVITIES
Golf
The two Jack Nicklaus–designed 18-hole par-72 courses at **Kaua'i Lagoons Golf Club** (Map p76; ☎ 241-6000, 800-634-6400; www.kauaila goonsgolf.com; Kaua'i Marriott, 3351 Ho'olaule'a Way; Kiele green fees morning nonguest/guest $170/125, afternoon nonguest/guest $115/105, Mokihana morning nonguest/guest $120/75, afternoon nonguest/guest $65/59, club rental $35) include the highly regarded and challenging Kiele Course, surrounded by crashing waves, with each hole named for an animal (note the marble statues at each tee), the last being an aptly named golden bear. The adjacent Mokihana Course is less dramatic but gentler and better for higher handicaps.

The lush cliffs of Mt Ha'upu serve as a backdrop to the Robin Nelson–designed **Puakea Golf Course** (Map p76; ☎ 245-8756, 866-773-5554; www.puakeagolf.com; 4315 Kalepa Rd; green fees incl cart before/after 1pm $125/65, club rental $30/20), which first opened in 1997 (with an odd 10 holes) and became an 18-hole course in 2003. Located near Kukui Grove Shopping Center.

Kayaking & Canoeing
While Wailua Falls is Kaua'i's main kayaking spot, other waterways are also scenic and much less crowded, including the Hule'ia River near Lihu'e. Tours depart from Nawiliwili Harbor.

Outfitters Kaua'i (☎ 742-9667, 888-742-9887; www.outfitterskauai.com; Po'ipu Plaza, 2827-A Po'ipu Rd; tour per adult/child 3-14 with lunch $99/75, without lunch $90/70; ☑ check-in 8am or 9:30am Mon-Sat) offers a pleasant kayaking and hiking tour in the Hule'ia National Wildlife Refuge. The kayak trip is only two miles, downwind, and instead of paddling back against the wind, you ride on a motorized canoe. The hike is 0.75 miles one way. The company also runs a 'mega adventure tour' (see opposite), which includes kayaking.

Island Adventures (☎ 245-9662, 888-245-1707; www.kauaifun.com; Nawiliwili Small Boat Harbor; adult/child 8-12 $89/69; ☑ check-in 8am Mon-Sat) offers an 4.5-hour tour in the Hule'ia National Wild-life Refuge, where you'll paddle 2.5 miles, walk along a forest trail, ride a van, then hike to two private waterfalls. At the 50ft Jungle Falls, you can swim for 30 minutes before refueling with a deli picnic lunch. A shorter afternoon tour (sans waterfalls) is also offered (adult/child aged two to 12 $59/49).

Owned and operated by Hawaiians, **Aloha Canoes & Kayaks** (Map p76; ☎ 246-6804, 877-473-5446; www.hawaiikayaks.com; Anchor Cove Shopping Center, 3416 Rice St, Lihu'e; double hull canoe adult/child 3-11 $82/70; ☑ check-in 9am Tue, Thu & Sat) offers a 3.5-hour tour that allows you to paddle a 12-person canoe (probably with the *Hawaii Five-O* theme ringing in your ears) in the Hule'ia River, swim and rope jump; lunch is included. Kayaking tours are offered, too.

Tubing
Folks of all ages can climb atop a tube and float down old irrigation ditches and tunnels amid pristine greenery with **Kaua'i Backcountry Adventures** (Map p76; ☎ 245-2506, 888-270-0555; www.kauaibackcountry.com; tour including lunch per person $92; ☑ departures 9am, 10:30am, 1pm & 2:30pm Mon-Sat, 9am & 1pm Sun). The three-hour tour ends with lunch at a swimming hole. If too much spinning makes you dizzy, ask the guide to check your tube, as some are more prone to rotating when afloat. Great for the whole family (including kids as young as five). Call to reserve because cruise-ship passengers often fill entire tours when they dock twice a week.

Ziplining & Multiactivity Adventures
The latest outdoor thrill on Kaua'i is 'ziplining,' meaning soaring across a forest canopy, high above the ground. Well, actually you're attached to a cable. But you go as fast as 35mph. You cannot get any closer to flying or playing Tarzan. Another zipline park, with eight lines, exists near Princeville.

The only tour dedicated to zipping is run by **Kaua'i Backcountry Adventures** (Map p76; ☎ 245-2506, 888-270-0555; www.kauaibackcountry.com; Kuhio Hwy; tour incl lunch per person $110; ☑ departures 9:30am & 2pm Mon-Sat). It lets you scream and shout on seven ziplines (the largest zipline park in the state) elevated as high as 200ft above the ground and running as far as 900ft (three football fields). This 3.5-hour tour also ends with a picnic and swim. Note that the age and weight minimums are 15 years and 100lb. Small groups of 11 maximum, with two guides.

Ziplining is one of many activities offered by **Outfitters Kaua'i** (☎ 742-9667, 888-742-9887; www.outfitterskauai.com; Po'ipu Plaza, 2827-A Po'ipu Rd; tour incl lunch per adult/child 3-14 $145/105; ☺ check-in 7:30-8:15am). Its action-packed tours are run on private property adjacent to the Hule'ia National Wildlife Refuge. The six-hour (whew) adventure includes kayaking, hiking, riding a covered-wagon tractor and a motorized canoe, swimming, rope-swinging and 20ft cliff-jumping (both optional!) and ziplining 50ft above the ground. There is no age minimum, but the general rule is that 'zippers' must be at least 10 years old and 80lb (exceptions made at guide's discretion). A three-hour tour without lunch (per adult/child aged 10 to 14 $94/75; check-in 8am and 1pm) is also offered. If you want a tour dedicated to zipping, opt for Kaua'i Backcountry Adventures.

ATVs

Driving an obnoxious ATV across the pristine 3000-acre Kipu Ranch sounds destructive, but accessing a hiking trail in a 4WD is no less questionable. The two tours offered by **Kipu Ranch Adventures** (☎ 246-9288; www.kiputours.com; waterfall tour adult/child/senior $140/90/120) are actually considered eco-tours because they introduce visitors to diverse landscapes and their history. The tours cross private land and are highly regulated so any damage is minimized. The backdrop of the Ha'upu mountain range and Kipu Kai coast are gorgeous and otherwise inaccessible. You're also likely to see cattle, wild pigs, pheasants, peacocks and wild turkeys. The four-hour waterfall tour is superior, as it includes two waterfalls, a swimming hole, a more challenging ride and lunch. You can choose between a single-rider Honda (the minimum age is 16) or a double-passenger Yamaha (the minimum age is 21), or you can ride in a guide-drive four-passenger Kawasaki.

Fishing

Kaua'i waters are well-stocked with fish, from deep-sea biggies like marlin and tuna to more manageable inshore species like gray snapper. See p61 for more on fishing. Recommended outfitters departing from Nawiliwili Small Boat Harbor include the following:

Kai Bear (☎ 652-4556; 4hr shared charter per person $139-179)

True Blue Charters (☎ 246-6333, 888-245-1707; www.truebluecharters.com; charter 4hr shared per person $139-239, private per 6 anglers $850) Shared charters include standard (maximum 10 anglers) and deluxe (maximum four anglers). Spectators can ride for half price.

Wild Bill's (☎ 822-5963; 4hr shared charter per person $115)

Tennis

You can play tennis for free at county tennis courts in central Lihu'e at Lihu'e Park (Map p78), and across from Kaua'i Community College in Puhi Park (Map p76).

Fitness

Kaua'i's main nonresort fitness center is **Kaua'i Athletic Club** (Map p76; ☎ 245-5381;

WHAT'S THE CATCH?

Locals usually use the Hawaiian or Japanese names of fish:

- *'ahi* – yellowfin tuna
- *aku* – skipjack tuna; *katsuo* in Japanese
- *akule* – big-eyed scad
- *a'u* – swordfish, marlin
- *mahimahi* – white-fleshed fish also called 'dolphin' (not the mammal)
- *mano* – shark
- *onaga* – mild-tasting red snapper
- *ono* – white-fleshed wahoo
- *opah* – moonfish
- *'opakapaka* – pink snapper
- *'opelu* – pan-sized mackeral scad
- *papio* or *ulua* – jack fish
- *tako* – octopus
- *uhu* – parrotfish
- *uku* – strongly flavored gray snapper
- *ula* – Hawaiian lobster
- *wana* – sea urchin

DETOUR: HANAMA'ULU

Hanama'ulu is a low-key residential town between Lihu'e and Wailua along Kuhio Hwy. It's significant in Hawaiian folklore as the birthplace of Kaua'i's legendary hero Kawelo, depicted in folktales as a skillful warrior and champion spear thrower.

Three-quarters of a mile from the village, **Hanama'ulu Beach Park** (Map p76) lies inside Hanama'ulu Bay, a deep, protected bay with a partial boulder breakwater. The park has campgrounds with full facilities, but it's a rather sketchy local hangout and not recommended for solo women travelers. The waters are occasionally off-limits because of pollution. To get here from Kuhio Hwy, turn makai (seaward) at the 7-Eleven onto Hanama'ulu Rd. After a quarter mile, turn right onto Hehi Rd. As you enter the park, you'll first go under the highway bridge and then the picturesque arched trestle of an abandoned railroad bridge.

Locals flock to the crossroads of Kuhio Hwy and Hanama'ulu Rd for generous servings of Japanese food at the longstanding **Hanama'ulu Restaurant Tea House & Sushi Bar** (Map p76; ☎ 245-2511, 245-3225; 3-4291 Kuhio Hwy; mains $7-10, special platters $17-20; ✆ 11:30am-9:30pm Tue-Sun). The main dining room might seem unfashionably retro, so head to the Japanese-style rooms overlooking the garden in back. The menu, which oddly also includes Chinese dishes, is mainstream, but well worth the price. It specializes in crispy fried dishes, from Chinese ginger chicken to Japanese tempura and pork or chicken tonkatsu (breaded and fried cutlets). The all-you-can-eat Sunday dinner buffet (adult/child aged seven to 12 $22/16, for each year of age of a child under seven $1) is a real crowd-pleaser. And only at such an old-fashioned local restaurant would you find Jell-O on the dessert menu.

Drivers, take note: the Hanama'ulu **Shell** (Map p76; ✆ 5:30am-10pm Mon-Sat, 7am-10pm Sun & holidays) gas station, across from the Hanama'ulu Restaurant, sells consistently low-priced gas and a 4¢ discount on Tuesdays. And they even do full-serve for free.

4370 Kukui Grove St; per day/week/month $12/40/80; ✆ 5:30am-9pm Mon-Fri, 8am-5pm Sat & Sun), which features aerobic and resistance machines, free weights, outdoor swimming pool (48ft long), classes and courts. The locker rooms include saunas.

TOURS

Most helicopter tours fly from Lihu'e Airport. The going rate for a 60-minute flight is about $200; see p62 for more on helicopter tours. The following companies are recommended:

Air Kaua'i (☎ 246-4666, 800-972-4666; www.airkauai .com) Cushy A-Star helicopters with large windows, air-con and excellent narration.

Jack Harter Helicopters (☎ 245-3774, 888-245-2001; www.helicopters-kauai.com)

Safari Helicopters (☎ 246-0136, 800-326-3356; www .safariair.com)

Will Squyres (☎ 245-8881, 245-7541, 888-245-4354; www.helicopters-hawaii.com; cnr Kuhio Hwy & Ahikini Rd)

Consider flying with Inter-Island Helicopters (p190), which flies open-door copters from Burns Field in Hanapepe. You start closer to the hot destination sites so less time is 'wasted' flying over Lihu'e and pastureland. Another suggestion, albeit lukewarm, is **Heli USA Airways** (p137), which flies from Princeville Airport.

FESTIVALS & EVENTS

Kaua'ian Days Parade and Ho'olaule'a (☎ 634-5352; www.kauaiandays.org; ✆ parade 10am) Held in mid- to late January. Parade begins at Kukui Grove Pavilion and ends at Kaua'i Community College. Ho'olaule'a (celebration) follows with ethnic food booths, Hawaiian arts and crafts exhibits, demonstrations and entertainment.

E Pili Kakou I Ho'okahi Lahui (☎ 246-4752; www .epilikakou.org) Popular annual two-day hula retreat in late January at the Kaua'i Marriott Resort, where you can participate in classes or just watch.

Spring Gourmet Gala (☎ 245-8359; Kaua'i Community College; admission $75; ✆ 6pm) Famous local chefs, such as Alan Wong, Chai Chaowasaree, and Beth-Ann Nishijima headline this food and wine fundraiser in early April for Kaua'i Community College's culinary arts program.

Kaua'i Polynesian Festival (☎ 335-6466; www .kauai-polyfest.com) This four-day event in late May featuring loads of food, cultural workshops, and hula exhibits and competitions is held at picturesque Kukui Grove Pavilion & Park.

Fourth of July Concert in the Sky (☎ 246-2440) Feast on island foods and enjoy live entertainment all day before the grand finale fireworks show set to music; held at Lihu'e's Vidinha Stadium.

Kaua'i County Farm Bureau Fair (☎ 828-2120; admission adult/child $3/2) Old-fashioned family fun in late August, with carnival rides and games, livestock show, petting zoo, hula performances, eating contests and demonstrations on bonsai, orchids and cooking. Lots of local-food booths; held at Vidinha Stadium.

Aloha Festival Ho'olaule'a & Parade (☎ 245-8508; www.alohafestivals.com; admission free) This statewide event in early September is launched on Kaua'i with a parade from Vidinha Stadium to the historic county building lawn. The *ho'olaule'a* features music, hula, crafts and an appearance by Kaua'i's royal court.

Kaua'i Composer's Contest & Concert (☎ 822-2166; www.mokihana.kauai.net; Kaua'i Community College; admission $10-15; ☽ 7pm) The signature event of the Kaua'i Mokihana Festival, this contest in mid- to late September showcases local composing talent in five categories: Hawaiian, contemporary Hawaiian, open, youth and professional.

'Kaua'i Style' Hawaiian Slack Key Guitar Festival (☎ 239-4336; www.hawaiianslackkeyguitarfestivals.com, www.livefromkauai.org; Kaua'i Beach Resort; admission free; ☽ noon-6pm) Hear top slack-key musicians in the Kaua'i venue of an annual series of slack-key guitar festivals across the Hawaiian Islands. An opportunity to see masters like Ledward Ka'apana, Mike Ka'awa and Dennis Kamakahi for free is not to be missed!

Lights on Rice Parade (☎ 246-1004; admission free; ☽ 6:30pm) A dazzling array of floats bedecked with lights parade along Rice St in early December during this popular event.

SLEEPING

While Lihu'e is centrally located, its utilitarian atmosphere might disappoint visitors seeking a charming setting. But if all you want is a place to crash, you will find the island's two cheapest hotels in 'downtown' Lihu'e – along with highly recommended newcomer Kaua'i Palms Hotel, which definitely gives you the most for your money. Near Nawiliwili Harbor and Kalapaki Bay, you'll find a mini strip of hotels, including the upscale Kaua'i Marriott Resort. But compared with the lively Po'ipu or Coconut Coast, Lihu'e's resort stretch feels, oddly, both subdued and touristy. **Kaua'i Vacation Rentals** (Map p76; ☎ 245-8841, 800-367-5025; www.kauaivacationrentals.com; 3-3311 Kuhio Hwy, Lihu'e, HI 96766), an established vacation-rental agency, is located right on Kuhio Hwy in

Lihu'e. You probably won't need an agency for Lihu'e, but their rental list covers the entire island.

Budget

Motel Lani (Map p78; ☎ 245-2965; 4240 Rice St; r $34-36; ☒) You can't miss the salmon-pink Motel Lani, hiding behind tropical foliage along Lihu'e's Rice St thoroughfare. While the busy location might be off-putting, this family-run motel is Kaua'i's cheapest. Don't expect much. The six rooms are tiny and well worn, if not shabby, although they are clean and come with a small refrigerator (no TV or phone). During the work week, the motel is often booked by Neighbor Island construction workers.

Tip Top Motel (Map p78; ☎ 245-2333; tiptop@ aloha.net; 3173 Akahi St; r $50; ☒) As a last resort only, try the historic Tip Top, where you can at least wake to yummy pancakes at the café. The 34 rooms are depressingly institutional, with white cinder-block walls, linoleum floors, iron-gated windows, fluorescent bathroom lighting and an antiseptic odor. Rooms do include TV and window-box air-con. At the time of visiting, there was no help in the charm department from the brusque staff.

Kaua'i Palms Hotel (Map p78; ☎ 246-0908; www .kauaipalmshotel.com; 2931 Kalena St; r $65; ☽ office hours 7am-8pm) No doubt about it: fresh paint, new furniture and squeaky-clean rooms are not the norm among Lihu'e's budget hotels. Thus Kaua'i Palms, totally remodeled in November 2005, is a gem. The two-story, open-air main building houses 15 compact rooms with refrigerator and flat-screen cable TV. Windows on opposite walls allow a cooling cross breeze. The best rooms are upstairs, with king beds (the smaller downstairs rooms have queen beds). Also available are two larger rooms that sleep four, including one with kitchenette ($95). Coin-operated laundry available.

Midrange

Kaua'i Inn (Map p76; ☎ 245-9000, 800-808-2330; www .kauai-inn.com; 2430 Hulemalu Rd; r with kitchenette incl breakfast $80-110; ☒) Off the beaten track, this peaceful property en route to the Alekoko Fishpond Overlook is Kaua'i's oldest hotel. Originally the Fairview Hotel (founded in 1890 and located near the Ace Hardware on Rice St), it hosted such luminaries as Lee

Marvin and John Wayne. After Hurricane 'Iniki destroyed virtually the entire hotel, the McKnight family bought the property around 1995 and spent nearly a decade restoring the 48 rooms. While not fancy, rooms are clean and quite spacious, with sliding doors leading to back porches. The cheapest rooms are serviceable, but dark; upstairs units are better.

Garden Island Inn (Map p76; ☎ 245-7227, 800-648-0154; www.gardenislandinn.com; 3445 Wilcox Rd; r with kitchenette $95-105, ste with kitchenette $135; ⊠) With colorful door murals and friendly staff, this inn exudes aloha. Ground-floor units are nicely appointed with overhead fans, quality double beds, rattan furniture and kitchenettes. Rooms on the 2nd and 3rd floors are more inviting still, with bigger living space and lanai. The best 3rd-floor suites are No 20 (largest) and No 21 (primo view). Available downstairs is a well-equipped wheelchair-accessible room, complete with small adjoining quarters for an attendant. Kalapaki Beach is just up the street and, while the immediate commercial area is rather touristy, you can easily walk to shops and restaurants from here.

Banyan Harbor Resort (Map p76; ☎ 245-7333, 800-422-6926; www.vacation-kauai.com; 3411 Wilcox Rd; 1-/2-bedroom unit $115/145; ⊠) Families might consider this 148-unit condo complex for its spacious rooms and convenient amenities, such as a full kitchen and a washer and dryer. But quality is extremely variable and you might end up in a unit that had clearly housed a cigarette smoker. Up to four people can squeeze into a one-bedroom unit, up to six in a two-bedroom unit.

Top End

The rates listed for these top-end establishments are rack rates, which are charged only during periods of full occupancy. Go online for the best rates.

Kaua'i Beach Resort (Map p76; ☎ 245-1955, 888-805-3843; www.kauaibeachhotelandresort.com; 4331 Kaua'i Beach Dr; r $250-360; ⊠ ⊇) This former Radisson used to be a last-resort option, with rooms nondescript in their beigeness, small sitting areas and teeny lanai. At the time of research, however, the resort was under major renovation and conversion to a four-star condo-hotel. It could go either way.

Kaua'i Marriott Resort (Map p76; ☎ 245-5050, 800-220-2925; www.marriotthotels.com; Kalapaki Beach;

r $330-445; ⊠ ⊇) Driving toward the Marriott under the thick canopy of monkey-pod trees feels like an escape to another world. And the feeling continues when you descend the escalator to the lobby…and behold the spectacular 26,000-sq-ft, four-part swimming pool and Kalapaki Beach beyond. This resort is the best of the East-side biggies, with a tropical grandeur sure to impress: nene (Hawaiian geese) wander around koi-stocked ponds, the koa canoe *Princess* gleams in the lobby and room decor features island-style orchid bedspreads and botanical prints. The resort is part time-share (232 units) and part hotel (356 units), a combination that is becoming common.

EATING
Budget

Kaua'i Bakery and Cinnamons (Map p76; 246-4765; www.kauaibakery.com; Kukui Grove Shopping Center; 3-2600 Kaumuali'i Hwy; pastries 49¢-$1.75, cakes & pies $8-16; ⌚ 7am-7pm Mon-Thu & Sat, to 9pm Fri, to 6pm Sun) Don't miss stopping here – as soon as you walk inside, you'll blast to the past with old-fashioned cinnamon rolls, apple turnovers, bread pudding and *malasada* (Portuguese doughnuts without a hole). Tantalize your tastebuds with local flavors, including a light-as-air guava chiffon cake or soothing banana cream pie.

Genki Sushi (Map p76; ☎ 632-2450; Kukui Grove Shopping Center, 3-2600 Kaumuali'i Hwy; à la carte nigiri & rolled sushi from $1.60, bento from $8.50; ⌚ 11am-8pm Sun-Thu, to 10pm Fri, to 9pm Sat) Affordable sushi? Sure! In a no-frills diner setting, you order from a set menu of individual items topping out at $4.60. Where else can you find *tekka* (tuna) maki for $2 and *hamachi* (yellowtail) nigiri for $2.60? Round out your meal with vegetable croquettes, miso soup and ice cream. Only takeout sushi is available from 3pm to 5pm Monday to Thursday. Party platters are a bargain for large groups.

Hamura Saimin (Map p78; ☎ 245-3271; 2956 Kress St; noodles $3.75-4.50; ⌚ 10am-11:30pm Mon-Thu, to late Fri & Sat, to 9:30pm Sun) Tucked in a side street, behind a broken sign and rickety screen that slams behind you, family-run Hamura Saimin epitomizes the hole-in-the-wall classic. In the past, obvious tourists were given *da stink eye* (dirty look or cold shoulder); today Hamura's is on the map, and you'll find the gamut of diners, slurping noodles elbow-to-elbow at orange U-shaped counters. The famous homemade saimin noodles are peerless (Neighbor Islanders buy fresh bundles of noodles by the dozen as gifts). Another specialty is the *liliko'i* (passion fruit) chiffon pie (slice/whole $2/10.75). The boiling vats and lack of air-con makes it stifling inside, but you can cool off with a decent shave ice from the in-store Holo Holo Shave Ice (open 1pm to 4pm Monday to Friday).

Deli & Bread Connection (Map p76; ☎ 245-7115; Kukui Grove Shopping Center; 3-2600 Kaumuali'i Hwy; sandwiches $4.50-6.50; ⏰ 9:30am-7pm Mon-Thu & Sat, to 9pm Fri, 10am-6pm Sun) When all you want is a good, old-fashioned sandwich, hightail it here. Classics feature the whole range of deli meats, all on freshly baked breads, available by the loaf. Herbivore options include a generous veg burger with mushrooms and cheese.

Tip Top Café (Map p78; ☎ 245-2333; 3173 Akahi St; breakfast mains $4.50-7, lunch mains $4.50-8.25; ⏰ 6:30am-2pm, Sushi Katsu 11am-2pm & 5:30-9pm Tue-Sun) The white, cinder-block building is lacking in atmosphere, but the main draws are the famous pancakes ($4 to $4.50) and oxtail soup ($8.25). Meat eaters can try local favorites like *loco moco* (two fried eggs, hamburger patty, rice and gravy) for $6.75, saimin, and beef stew. The café is open only for breakfast and lunch, while the restaurant's Sushi Katsu offers value-priced sushi for lunch and dinner.

Kalapaki Beach Hut (Map p76; ☎ 246-6330; 3474 Rice St; breakfast & burgers $4-7; ⏰ 7am-7pm) This archetypal beachside café faces Kalapaki Beach and features big breakfasts, from egg-and-cheese sandwiches ideal to go to tasty omelettes sautéed with fresh *ono* (wahoo). The fast-food lunch menu exemplifies the island's multiculturalism, including items such as the 'local boy' burger with Portuguese sausage, green onion and kimchi (Korean hot pickled cabbage). Perhaps the main selling point is the upstairs dining lanai, with an unobstructed ocean view – delicious and zero calories.

eb's EATS (Map p78; ☎ 632-0320; 3-3142 Kuhio Hwy; salads & sandwiches $5-8; ⏰ 7am-6pm Mon-Fri, 9am-3:30pm Sat) If you're a gourmet foodie hankering for a healthy yet tasty meal, eb's is ideal. Founded in 2005 by a youthful Californian (along with her mom and aunty), this cheery eatery offers hearty sandwiches,

from old-fashioned country meatloaf to roasted veggie and goat cheese drizzled with olive oil and basil pesto. Or cobble together three 'showcase salads,' from savory salmon salad to grains like couscous, wheat berry or wild rice, into a filling meal ($8). Save room for the homemade cakes and cookies.

Fish Express (Map p76; ☎ 245-9918; 3343 Kuhio Hwy; lunch $6-7.50; ⏰ 10am-7pm Mon-Sat, to 5pm Sun, lunch served to 3pm daily) At first glance, all you'll see is glass cases of fresh fish. But this ain't just any fish market. The takeout menu includes mouth-watering fish preparations, such as grilled *ono* with orange-tarragon sauce or macadamia-crusted *'ahi* (yellowfin tuna) in *liliko'i*-dill sauce, which come with rice and salad ($7.50). Japanese box lunches and sushi rolls are perfect, packable meals to go. Outside of lunch hours, snag something from the deli case, perhaps a sample of *poke* (marinated raw fish) or fresh fish, sold reasonably by the pound.

For groceries, the two major supermarkets are **Big Save** (Map p78; ☎ 245-6571; 4444 Rice St; ⏰ 7am-11pm), near the government buildings in the heart of town (enter on Hardy St), and **Star Market** (Map p76; ☎ 245-7777; Kukui Grove Shopping Center; ⏰ 6am-11pm).

Midrange & Top End

Tokyo Lobby (Map p76; ☎ 245-8989; Harbor Mall, 3501 Rice St, Suite 103; mains $12-15; ⏰ 11am-2pm Mon-Fri, 4:30-9:30pm daily) With its generic name and standard interior design, it's hard to tell if Tokyo Lobby is the real deal or just a tourist trap. Lucky for you, the former is generally true, and for reasonable Japanese cuisine you can't go wrong here. The varied menu features the usual suspects: *'ahi* or *hamachi* (yellowtail) sashimi, crispy seafood and veg tempura, broiled *unagi* (eel) and lots of combination plates. For lunch the generous *donburi* (rice and hot main dish) and steaming bowls of *udon* (thick wheat noodles) are deliciously satisfying.

Café Portofino (Map p76; ☎ 245-2121; www .cafeportofino.com; Kaua'i Marriott Resort, Kalapaki Beach; appetizers $8-12, mains $16-29; ⏰ dinner) If you cringe at white tablecloths, low lighting and live harpists, keep looking. Otherwise, transport yourself to the Italian Riviera at this award-winning, oceanfront restaurant, headed by charming chef Giuseppe Avocadi.

LIHU'E

FRESH FROM THE FARM

For farm-fresh fruits and vegetables, find a farmers market. You can find seasonal fruit like sugar-sweet lychee and the gamut of citrus, from local oranges (the rough rind belies the bursting flavor inside) to gigantic pomelo. Try the stubby apple-bananas, with tart-sweet taste and amazing shelf life. Lettuces and herbs are perky fresh, and baseball-size avocados are a steal.

Arrive early because once the whistle blows people rush in, scooping things up quickly. Depending on the location, it can all wrap up within an hour or so. Sellers typically offer $1 or $2 bundles so bring lots of dollar bills. Most of the markets listed below are the county-managed Sunshine Markets. The Wednesday market in Kapa'a is the largest and the most congested, as the town already suffers from daily traffic jams and the market time of 3pm only exacerbates the after-school rush.

Monday

- Noon at Knudsen Park, Maluhia Rd, Koloa (Map p164)
- 3pm at Kukui Grove Shopping Center, Kaumuali'i Hwy, Lihu'e (Map p76)

Tuesday

- 2pm in Waipa (slightly west of Hanalei), Kuhio Hwy
- 3pm at Kalaheo Neighborhood Center, Papalina Rd, Kalaheo (Map p181)
- 3pm at Wailua Homesteads Park, Malu Rd

Wednesday

- 3pm at Kapa'a New Park, Kahau St, Kapa'a (Map p116)

Thursday

- 3:30pm at Hanapepe Town Park, behind the fire station
- 4:30pm at Kilauea Neighborhood Center, Keneke St, Kilauea (Map p130)

Friday

- 3pm at Vidinha Stadium, Ho'olako Rd and Kapule Hwy, Lihu'e (Map p76)

Saturday

- 9am at Kekaha Neighborhood Center, Elepaio Rd, Kekaha
- 9am at Christ Memorial Episcopal Church, Kolo Rd, Kilauea (Map p130)

The menu is traditional, featuring lots of veal, such as house specialty osso buco (veal shank). Vegetarians won't go hungry with varied meatless options, such as the ultrahealthy penne with broccoli and spinach. Joining the homemade gelato and tiramisu are profiteroles (decadent cream puffs filled with vanilla ice cream).

Duke's Canoe Club (Map p76; ☎ 246-9599; Kaua'i Marriott Resort; appetizers $7-9, mains $17-29; ❤ dinner) You can't top Duke's for sheer beach-bopping ambience. The open-air setting overlooking Kalapaki Beach is the spitting cliché of tropical-island dining – enjoy it! The flavorful food won't disappoint. Start with savory appetizers like spicy sugarcane shrimp or crab wontons and don't miss the seven-spiced 'ahi with papaya-mustard vinaigrette. Live music happens nightly from 6:45pm. Convenient parking is behind the Kalapaki Beach Hut, where a footbridge crosses the stream to Duke's.

Aroma's (Map p76; ☎ 245-9192; Harbor Mall, 3501 Rice St, Suite 207; breakfast mains $7.25-8.50, lunch mains $10.50-12.50, dinner mains $18-27; ❤ 7am-9:30pm Tue-Fri, 8am-9:30pm Sat & Sun) Don't be fooled by the tourist-strip mall. Head upstairs and enter the warm, inviting dining room of Aroma's, a Pacific-Mediterranean bistro that bridges 'local' and 'gourmet' cuisine. Lunch salads, like the papaya and cashew-chicken salad, make a meal. For dinner start with the 'Poketian,' layered 'ahi poke, crab, shrimp and rice in a martini glass. The veg mains are sumptuous and not token offerings.

Lihu'e Barbecue Inn (Map p78; ☎ 245-2921; 2982 Kress St; lunch $5-12, dinner $19-24; ❤ 10:30am-1:30pm & 5-8:30pm Mon-Thu, 10:30am-1:30pm & 4:30-9pm Fri & Sat) From the outside, this plain ol' family-style diner might not impress. But looks are deceiving. The food and friendly service here keeps everyone coming back. The menu is almost a book, with a wide selection (but inexplicably no real barbecue). The fish dishes are particularly good, especially the seared 'ahi salad (with the fish cooked to whatever 'doneness' you desire). Unless you expect nouveau cuisine and a stunning view, you'll leave satisfied.

Gaylord's (Map p76; ☎ 245-9593; www.kilohana kauai.com/gaylords.htm; Kilohana Plantation, Kaumuali'i Hwy; lunch $8-14, dinner $20-35; ☺ 7:45-10am, 11am-2pm & 5:30-9pm Mon-Sat, 7:45am-2pm & 5:30-9pm Sun) Outside, the manicured lawn and horse-drawn carriage suggest a country club. Inside, the club tone continues with white tablecloths and a menu starring old-school meats (with an island touch). The filet mignon ($30) is bathed in *liliko'i* sauce and peppercorns, while the shiitake and prime rib salad ($14) features Maui onions and Kamuela tomatoes. Despite the seemingly formal setting, the staff is local-style friendly. Big breakfast eaters, try the generous daily buffet (adult/child $12/7) or Sunday brunch ($18). Be patient exiting the grounds into the relentless traffic along the Kaumuali'i Hwy heading toward Lihu'e.

DRINKING & ENTERTAINMENT
Bars & Nightclubs

Duke's Barefoot Bar (Map p76; ☎ 246-9599; Kaua'i Marriott Resort, Kalapaki Beach; ☺ 11am-midnight) Leave your shoes at the door at this chill-out place right on Kalapaki Beach. A good mix of Hawaiian, rock and pop music livens things up nightly, and there's a casual burgers-and-sandwiches bar menu served until 11pm.

Whaler's Brew Pub (Map p76; ☎ 245-2000; 3132 Ninini Point; ☺ 11:30am-2am Mon-Sat, DJs from 10pm Thu-Sat) You can sample a handful of beers brewed on-site at this pub overlooking Nawiliwili Harbor and the lighthouse on Ninini Point. By day there's a simple bar menu; by night, dancing and DJs.

Rob's Good Times Grill (Map p78; ☎ 246-0311; Rice Shopping Center, 4303 Rice St; ☺ 9pm-2am) The atmosphere might be a little hokey, but a young, energetic crowd comes out to boogie to a live DJ Thursday through Saturday (Friday is the hottest). Sunday through Tuesday is karaoke and Wednesday is country line dancing (yeehaw!). There are typically whopping drink specials, like $3 Coronas.

Cinemas

Kukui Grove Cinemas (Map p76; ☎ 245-5055; Kukui Grove Shopping Center, 3-2600 Kaumuali'i Hwy; adult/child $6/4, before 5pm $4) Catch a movie at this four-plex. This is one of the venues for the Hawaii International Film Festival: www.hiff.org.

Concerts

Kaua'i Concert Association (☎ 245-7464; www .kauai-concert.org; Kaua'i Community College Performing Arts Center; admission $20-30; ☺ 7pm) Classical, jazz and dance concerts. Past performers have included Poncho Sanchez, Kronos Quartet and Ernie Watts.

Luau

Luau extravaganzas might not be authentically Hawaiian, but they've become a 'must-see' for first-time visitors. The all-you-can-eat buffet and open bar are selling points, but the main draw is the action-packed show, featuring hula, chanting and, most of all, the Samoan fire dance. Performances typically draw from all Polynesian cultures rather than only Hawaiian.

Kilohana Plantation (Map p76; ☎ 245-9593; www .kilohanakauai.com/luau.htm; Kaumuali'i Hwy; adult/child 4-12/senior & teen 13-18 $65/35/61; ☺ 5:30pm Tue & Thu) You'll find the best dining experience here, as the luau food is prepared by Gaylord's restaurant onsite. Not only is *kalua* pig cooked in the *imu* (underground earthen oven) but also *ono* (wahoo) and mahimahi (white-fleshed fish). The historic plantation setting transports you to the grand, early-1900s plantation days. Featured in the show are Hawaiian, Tahitian, Maori and Samoan dances.

Kaua'i Beach Resort (Map p76; ☎ 335-5828; www .luau-hawaii.com; 4331 Kaua'i Beach Dr; adult/child/teen $57/27/37; ☺ 5:15pm Thu & Sun) Presented by the famous Punua hula *halau* (troupe), this luau is both flashy and family-oriented, as performers include the whole range, from *keiki* (children) to *tutu* (grandparents). Wallis and Shana Punua, who direct the show, follow in the footsteps of Kumu Hula Ku'ulei Punua, one of the most senior hula teachers on Kaua'i. The dinner might satisfy big appetites, but it's your standard open bar, all-you-can-eat buffet. The same hula *halau* performs at the luau at the Aloha Beach Resort.

SHOPPING
MALLS

Memorize the names of Kaua'i's shopping centers. Many useful services and recommended restaurants are located at shopping centers, so they also serve as landmarks in locals' street directions. You'll so often hear 'turn right at Big Save,' it's worth knowing where they are located.

Kukui Grove Shopping Center (Map p76; ☎ 245-7784; 3-2600 Kaumuali'i Hwy) Far and away the largest shopping center on Kaua'i, this is the only true 'mall' that includes major department and big-box stores including Macy's, Sears, Longs Drugs, Borders, Kmart, Star Market, Radio Shack and banks. It's a basic mall (don't expect designer boutiques or fancy restaurants), and is functional rather than fun. Borders offers the best selection of island-music CDs – and with blasting air-con and hangout café, it's a perfect respite from heat or rain.

Smaller malls include the following:

Anchor Cove Shopping Center (Map p76; ☎ 246-0634; 3416 Rice St) Near Nawiliwili Harbor.

Harbor Mall (Map p76; ☎ 245-6255; 3501 Rice St) Near Nawiliwili Harbor.

Rice Shopping Center (Map p78; 4303 Rice St) In central Lihu'e.

STORES

Lihu'e is not quite a shopper's paradise, but a few notables are reviewed following.

C&H Kaua'i Products Store (Map p76; ☎ 246-6753; Kukui Grove Shopping Center, 3-2600 Kaumuali'i Hwy, Suite D8; 🕑 9:30am-7pm Mon-Thu & Sat, to 9pm Fri, 10am-6pm Sun) Browsers and gift hunters, this is a convenient one-stop shop for any price point. The downside is the odd combination of quality items (eg pricey genuine koa bowls) and cheesy knickknacks not made in Hawaii. The name refers not to C&H Sugar but to the owners' first names, Cindy and Herb Schoenhardt.

Edith King Wilcox Gift Shop (Map p78; Kaua'i Museum, 4428 Rice St) Based at the Kaua'i Museum,

this is a shopping treat, with a broad selection of Hawaiiana books, and a small collection of koa bowls and other handicrafts. You can enter the shop, free of charge, through the museum lobby.

Hilo Hattie (Map p78; ☎ 245.3404; www.hilohattie .com; 3-3252 Kuhio Hwy; 🕑 8:30am-6:30pm) Located right off Ahukini Rd toward the airport, this ubiquitous statewide tourist chain makes sure it gets you coming and going. While it's a one-stop shop, beware of over-priced edibles or mediocre souvenirs made in China or the Philippines.

Longs Drugs (Map p76; ☎ 245-7771; Kukui Grove Shopping Center, 3-2600 Kaumuali'i Hwy; 🕑 7am-10pm Mon-Sat, 8am-8pm Sun) Yes, it's just a drugstore. But throughout the islands, Longs is everyone's favorite catchall store. People here assume Longs is a local store! Find a wide range of gifts – from chocolate-covered macs to locally published children's books – plus snorkeling gear, boogie boards and cheap *rubbah slippah* (rubber flip-flops).

Kapaia Stitchery (Map p76; ☎ 245-2281; 3-3551 Kuhio Hwy; 🕑 9am-5pm Mon-Sat) Nirvana for folks who sew, with a wide selection of tropical fabrics, Hawaiian quilt and pillow kits and needlepoint designs. Custom-made aloha shirts and other handmade items on sale for those who can't thread a needle.

Kilohana Plantation (Map p76; www.kilohana kauai.com/shopping.htm; Kaumuali'i Hwy) For sheer variety, quality and presentation, this classy collection of shops is a cut above. Here you can browse through one of Kaua'i's widest collections of arts and crafts. Finely strung Ni'ihau shell lei, scrimshaw, dolls, woodcarvings and contemporary paintings by local artists are crammed into every room in the house, including the closets and bathrooms. The aloha shirts at Kilohana

---

TOP SHOPS FOR ALOHA SHIRTS

Read all about Hawaii's iconic shirts in *The Hawaiian Shirt* (1984), by H Thomas Steele, and *The Art of the Aloha Shirt* (2002), by DeSoto Brown and Linda Arthur. The top spots to buy them:

- Hilo Hattie (Lihu'e, above) for an only-on-vacation shirt (loud and cheap).
- Hula Girl (Kapa'a, p121) for an upscale, vintage selection.
- Kapaia Stitchery (Lihu'e, above) for custom-made shirts.
- Kilohana Clothing (Lihu'e, above) for tasteful local creations.
- Pohaku T's (Koloa, p166) for shirts handmade by a well-known Kaua'i seamstress.
- Reyn Spooner (Po'ipu, p180) for the Honolulu businessman's shirt of choice.

WEAR A DIRTY SHIRT

Locals always warn: 'Don't wear white because Kaua'i's red dirt can't wash out!' And yet the most-popular souvenir is...a red-dirt T-shirt.

Across the island (and state), you cannot miss the unique rust-red T-shirts with local screened prints. The craze started in the early 1990s and while minds differ on who 'invented' the first *purposely stained* shirt, the iconic brand is **Original Red Dirt Shirt** (☎ 335-5670, 800-717-3478; www.dirtshirt.com; 4350 Waialo Rd, 'Ele'ele; T-shirts $20-22; ☯ 8am-5pm Mon-Fri, 9am-5pm Sat & Sun), which has by far the largest line. Its story began after Hurricane 'Iniki hit in 1992 and destroyed Robert Hedin's screen-printing business in Kalaheo. He then relocated to 'Ele'ele and started anew in December 1993. In 1994 a big windstorm blew red dirt from nearby sugarcane fields into his shop's machines and shirt inventory. He was ready to chuck it all when a friend suggested he make red-dirt shirts. The Kaua'i Product Council promoted his shirts in November 1994 and ultimately his company hit the bonanza, becoming a multimillion-dollar company with over 10 retail stores by 1999. Hedin sold his shares of the business in 2001. On Kaua'i, two branch stores are located in Lihu'e and one in Kapa'a.

Another top brand is **Red Earth Hawaii** (☎ 245-5123, 800-799-5834; www.redearthhawaii.com; Kaua'i Screen Prints, 3116 Ho'olako St; T-shirts adult/child from $17/10), created by Steven Hirano, a longtime clothing manufacturer and screen printer who studied chemistry and worked two years to develop a special dyeing technique to keep the process 100% natural. He uses high-quality shirts that are individually hand-dyed twice and feature either screen-printed or embroidered designs. Hirano doesn't care to grow huge but focuses on his custom screen-printing work and his handful of red-shirt retailer accounts across the island, including Hilo Hattie (opposite).

Since the red-dirt shirt boom, specialty dyed shirts have proliferated. Industry giant Crazy Shirts started with coffee-dyed shirts in 1996 and followed with chocolate and beer. And a Google search reveals scads of 'original' dirt shirts featuring soil from Oklahoma to New Mexico to Prince Edward Island.

Note: while a red-dirt shirt is itself dirt-proof, it's liable to stain everything else in your laundry. Thus, when new, wash separately and don't wear in the rain!

Clothing Company feature fine fabrics and precise finishing.

Wilcox Memorial Hospital Gift Shop (Map p76; ☎ 245-1010, TTY 245-1133; 3420 Kuhio Hwy; ☯ 9am-4pm Mon-Fri, 10am-2pm Sat) While you probably hope to avoid the hospital, the gift shop here sells an irresistible array of toys, including a bunch of under-$5 retro items. Remember those drawing boards with faces covered by magnet shavings? Find 'em here. Also carries a wide selection of the popular Crocs rubber clogs (worn by doctors and nurses).

GETTING THERE & AWAY

For more on transportation to and from Lihu'e, see p230.

Air

The vast majority of flights arrive at **Lihu'e Airport** (LIH; ☎ 246-1448; www.hawaii.gov/dot/airports/kauai/lih; ☯ visitor hotline 6:30am-9pm), the only airport serving major commercial airlines. The airport is located 1.5 miles east of Lihu'e, with vehicular access on Ahukini Road, which crosses Kapule Highway.

The small airport is simple to negotiate, and the only problem you might encounter is rush-hour traffic as you exit Lihu'e. Try to avoid arriving in the late afternoon, as traffic will be crawling in either direction.

Boat

While a handful of seafaring options exist, by far the most popular are the **Norwegian Cruise Line** (☎ 800-327-7030; www.ncl.com) cruises between the Hawaiian Islands that start and end in Hawaii, launching either in Honolulu or on Maui. Seven-day trips (starting in Honolulu and stopping on Maui and Kaua'i, and in Hilo and Kona) are offered. On Kaua'i, ships dock at Nawiliwili Harbor for one night: the *Pride of Aloha* on Mondays and the *Pride of America* on Thursdays.

Some might find the cruise concept appealing (à la *The Love Boat*) but the drawbacks are myriad, including the ridiculously brief one-night stop and the lack of independent transportation on the island. Cruise directors arrange for passengers to join kayak tours and attend luau shows, but this quickie option is strictly for the circle-island-tour types.

Car & Motorcycle

The main roads into Lihu'e are Kaumuali'i Hwy (Hwy 50) heading west, Kuhio Hwy (Hwy 56) heading north and Kapule Hwy (Hwy 51) or Ahukini Rd (Hwy 570) to the airport. Unlike the other major Hawaiian Islands, Kaua'i is amazingly rural, with no highways with over two lanes (one in each direction). Few will find it difficult to drive here, except during the rush hour, when commuters flock into Lihu'e in the morning and dash out in the late afternoon.

GETTING AROUND
To/From the Airport

Most tourists rent cars from rental booths right outside the baggage-claim area. Vans transport you to the nearby rental-car lots, and access to the highways is clearly marked.

Bus

The **Kaua'i Bus** (☎ 241-6410; www.kauai.gov; 3220 Ho'olako St; per trip adult/senior & youth 7-18 $1.50/75¢; ⏱ 7:45am-4:30pm Mon-Fri) serves Lihu'e with two main routes: routes 100, 100E, 200 and 200E stop at Wal-Mart, Wilcox Memorial Hospital, Big Save, Kukui Grove Shopping Center and Lihu'e Airport. These stops run along the Kaua'i Bus service from Lihu'e to Koloa, Po'ipu and the Westside. Service is limited, with frequency ranging from 40 minutes to two hours. Buses run from Monday to Saturday.

Within Lihu'e, route 700 offers more stops within town, running hourly buses with stops including Kukui Grove Shopping Center, Garden Island Inn (Kalapaki Beach), Big Save, Wal-Mart and Wilcox Memorial Hospital from 8am to 3pm Monday to Friday.

Car & Motorcycle

Kaua'i is a driving town, so most businesses have parking lots and street parking is relatively easy to find. Metered parking in Lihu'e costs 25¢ for 30 minutes. For information about car and motorcycle rentals, see p236.

Taxi

Taxicabs (or phones to call one) are available curbside of the baggage-claim area. The following table shows average fares to popular destinations from Lihu'e airport.

Destination	Cost
Ha'ena	$95
Kapa'a	$20
Lihu'e	$10
Po'ipu	$35-40
Princeville	$72
Wailua	$17

Eastside

Reduced to its parts, the Eastside is impressive. It boasts a majestic river, thundering waterfalls, miles of beaches, coconut trees galore and the island's greatest concentration of lodging, dining and shopping. But the sum – a long stretch between Wailua and Kapa'a dubbed the 'Coconut Coast' – can assault the senses. Too many same-old shopping centers and resorts, separated way too far for pleasant walking. The biggest local complaint: too much traffic.

Still, the Eastside will ultimately win you over. It manages to juxtapose tourists and locals, as the bulk of Kaua'i's population lives around here. You are bound to mingle with locals, grocery shopping or eating out or killing time in traffic. Here you experience the 'real life' less evident at Kaua'i's swankier resort strongholds.

The Eastside offers a centrally located home base. Budget travelers, especially, will find the best selection of lodging. The *mauka* (inland) residential neighborhoods amid jungly rainforests or rolling pastureland offer a scenic alternative to the standard beach setting.

We separate this chapter by town: Wailua, Waipouli and Kapa'a. But on the ground, their boundaries are fuzzy. To further complicate matters, the US Postal Service groups all addresses from the Wailua River to Kawaihau Rd, at the north end of Kapa'a, as 'Kapa'a.'

On the cusp of both the Eastside and the North Shore is Anahola, where Native Hawaiians constitute 70% of the population. We cover Kaua'i's northeast coast in this chapter, but it's a rustic world all its own.

HIGHLIGHTS

- Kayaking the **Wailua River** (p95), hardly novel but still a treat
- Hiking atop the **Sleeping Giant** (p104) or **Kuilau Ridge** (p103)
- Rejuvenating yourself at **Angeline's Mu'olaulani** (p123)
- Hanging out in lively **Kapa'a** (p115)
- Visiting a magnificent **Hindu Monastery** (p100)
- Frolicking at **Lydgate Beach Park** (p95)

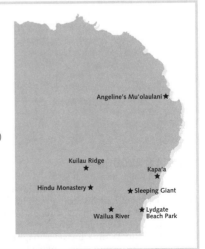

EASTSIDE

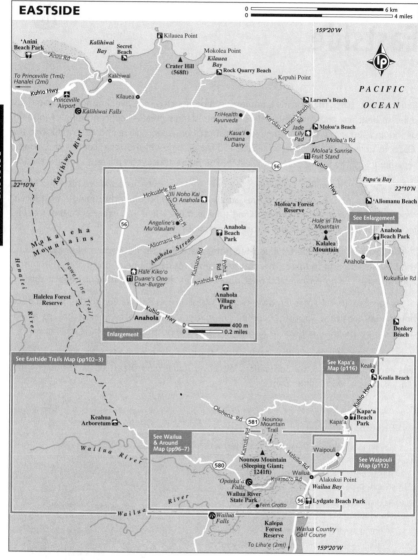

WAILUA & AROUND

pop Wailua & Wailua Homesteads 6650

As soon as you cross the Wailua Bridge, you hit the first leg of Kaua'i's strip – mini malls and condos ad nauseam on the 3-mile stretch of Kuhio Hwy (Hwy 56) between Wailua and Kapa'a. But Wailua boasts a magnificent river, the island's best playground

and an absolutely lovely upland residential neighborhood.

The Wailua Homesteads neighborhood (population 4567) sits to the west of Nounou Mountain, the unmistakable (to most) Sleeping Giant. Looking west, the Makaleha mountain range rises dramatically, a seemingly eternal chain of verdant slopes; its

Hawaiian name means 'eyes looking about as in wonder and admiration,' which you'll most certainly do.

Here you can also view stone relics known as the 'Seven Sacred Heiau,' running from the mouth of the Wailua River up to the top of Mt Wai'ale'ale. Six of these heiau sites (ancient Hawaii religious site) are located within a mile of the river mouth. Five are visible, while the sixth is abandoned in a field on the northern side of the Wailua River. All date to the early period of Tahitian settlement.

Orientation

The main roads in Wailua are Kuhio Hwy and Kuamo'o Rd (Hwy 580), which leads both to residences and to a handful of notable sights. If you are headed to Kapa'a or beyond, take the Kapa'a By-Pass Rd, which cuts northeast at Coconut Plantation and, after winding through pastureland, leads you onto Olohena Rd (Hwy 581) then back to Kuhio Hwy at the north end of Kapa'a town.

Sights

WAILUA RIVER STATE PARK

Majestic and calm, the Wailua River stands in vivid contrast to the capricious Pacific Ocean into which it feeds. At 12 miles long, it is the only navigable river in Hawaii. It's formed by the convergence of two large streams, known as its north and south forks, both fed by Wai'ale'ale. From a distance its mysterious emerald surface gleams under a jungly canopy, inviting onlookers to come closer.

By far the most popular river activity is kayaking, as it is relatively easy and tours are ubiquitous. But kayakers do share the waterway with riverboat barges, waterskiers and wakeboarders. See p102 for details.

The state park also includes most of the Seven Sacred Heiau, the Fern Grotto, a riverboat basin (see p105 for tours) and a public boat-ramp. For a distant view of the river, head to the lookout opposite 'Opaeka'a Falls.

WAILUA BAY

The Wailua River empties into a sweeping bay of golden sand, where swimming is possible along the edges. As always, avoid the river's mouth because currents and water depth here is unpredictable. Toward the south, a summer surf break draws locals and also surf students. The long stretch of sand is ideal for walking, and since the bay is so centrally located, it makes a convenient stop for a quick jog or stroll.

LYDGATE BEACH PARK

Perfect for families, **Lydgate Beach Park** (www .kamalani.org), on Kuhio Hwy between the 5- and 6-mile markers, offers protected swimming in a large seawater pool created with stone walls. Here you'll find Kaua'i's safest year-round swimming. Despite a lack of coral, this is an excellent beginner snorkeling site, with a decent variety of colorful fish, including large unicorn tangs. Beware of the open ocean beyond the pool, where currents are strong; many drownings have occurred on both sides of the Wailua River mouth, just north of Lydgate. Amenities here include changing rooms, rest rooms, showers, drinking water and picnic pavilions, and there's a lifeguard.

In 1994 thousands of local volunteers helped build the enchanting **Kamalani Playground** at the northern end of the park. This massive 16,000 sq ft wooden castle has swings, slides, mirror mazes, a suspension bridge and other kid-pleasing contraptions. At the southern end of the park, the **Kamalani Kai Bridge**, is reason alone to stop here. Another community-built, giant wooden labyrinth with spiral slides, confounding ramps and stairs to nowhere, plus kid art strewn throughout, this fanciful bridge fosters serious playtime. Adults will dig it, too: go early before the munchkin crowds arrive, and clamber up for unobstructed sea views. Future projects here include campsites and soccer fields.

If you look straight out across Wailua Bay, you can see the remains of **Kukui Heiau** on Alakukui Point. Only its foundation stones are discernible. In ancient times torches were lit on the point at night to help guide outrigger canoes. If you walk straight down to the beach while looking toward Alakukui Point, you may find ancient stones with petroglyphs carved into the rock, but they're usually hidden under shifting sands.

Hikina Akala Heiau

One of the remnants of Wailua's royal heyday, Hikina Akala Heiau (meaning 'Rising of the Sun'), is here, too. This long, narrow

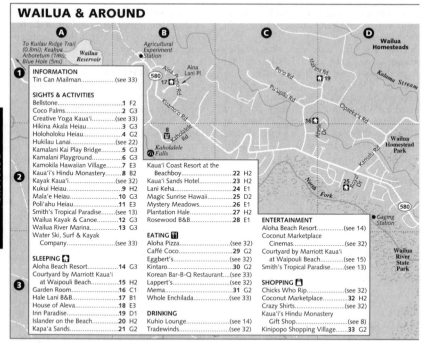

WAILUA & AROUND

INFORMATION
Tin Can Mailman.................(see 33)

SIGHTS & ACTIVITIES
Bellstone......................................1 F2
Coco Palms..................................2 G3
Creative Yoga Kaua'i...........(see 33)
Hikina Akala Heiau.....................3 G3
Holoholoku Heiau......................4 G2
Hukilau Lanai.........................(see 22)
Kamalani Kai Play Bridge..........5 G3
Kamalani Playground.................6 G3
Kamokila Hawaiian Village........7 E3
Kaua'i's Hindu Monastery..........8 B2
Kayak Kaua'i..........................(see 32)
Kukui Heiau.................................9 H2
Mala'e Heiau............................10 G3
Poli'ahu Heiau..........................11 E3
Smith's Tropical Paradise.....(see 13)
Wailua Kayak & Canoe............12 G3
Wailua River Marina.................13 G3
Water Ski, Surf & Kayak
   Company...........................(see 33)

SLEEPING
Aloha Beach Resort..................14 G3
Courtyard by Marriott Kaua'i
   at Waipouli Beach.................15 H2
Garden Room............................16 C1
Hale Lani B&B...........................17 B1
House of Aleva..........................18 E3
Inn Paradise..............................19 D1
Islander on the Beach...............20 H2
Kapa'a Sands.............................21 G2

Kaua'i Coast Resort at the
   Beachboy.............................22 H2
Kaua'i Sands Hotel...................23 H2
Lani Keha..................................24 E1
Magic Sunrise Hawaii...............25 D2
Mystery Meadows.....................26 E1
Plantation Hale.........................27 H2
Rosewood B&B.........................28 E1

EATING
Aloha Pizza..........................(see 32)
Caffé Coco.............................29 G2
Eggbert's..............................(see 32)
Kintaro.................................30 G2
Korean Bar-B-Q Restaurant...(see 33)
Lappert's..............................(see 32)
Mema....................................31 G2
Whole Enchilada....................(see 33)

DRINKING
Kuhio Lounge.......................(see 14)
Tradewinds............................(see 32)

ENTERTAINMENT
Aloha Beach Resort..............(see 14)
Coconut Marketplace
   Cinemas............................(see 32)
Courtyard by Marriott Kaua'i
   at Waipouli Beach.............(see 15)
Smith's Tropical Paradise.......(see 13)

SHOPPING
Chicks Who Rip....................(see 32)
Coconut Marketplace............32 H2
Crazy Shirts.........................(see 32)
Kaua'i's Hindu Monastery
   Gift Shop...........................(see 8)
Kinipopo Shopping Village......33 G2

temple is aligned directly north to south at the northern end of the Lydgate Beach parking lot. The heiau is thought to have been built around AD 1200. Boulders still outline the shape, so you get a sense of its original size, though most of the stones are long gone. Walk around the heiau, and you'll see a bronze plaque reading: 'Hauola, City of Refuge.' The mounded grassy area behind the plaque is all that remains of this former refuge for *kapu* (taboo) breakers. About 10ft left of the plaque, the stone that has the bowl-shaped depressions is an adze grinding stone. The stone hasn't always been in this upright position; to grind a correct edge, it would have been laid flat. Flat stone salt pans can also be found on the grounds.

MALA'E HEIAU

All heiau require a leap of imagination, but the ruins of this ancient Hawaiian temple in particular are lost in the thicket at the edge of an abandoned cane field, just 40ft inland of Kuhio Hwy, across Aloha Beach Resort. This was once Kaua'i's larg-est heiau, perhaps 275ft by 325ft, covering 2 acres, but today it's choked with grasses and Java plum trees, and almost impossible to explore. Plans to incorporate it into Wailua River State Park, hopefully accompanied by a restoration effort, are in the offing.

Little is known about Mala'e Heiau, but it is known that human sacrifices were made here. In the 1830s Christian missionaries converted Deborah Kapule, the last queen of Kaua'i, and she transformed the interior of Mala'e Heiau into a cattle pen. Despite this alteration, the site is relatively well preserved, thanks largely to its impenetrable overgrowth. The stone walls, which encompass an altar, reach up to 10ft high and extend 8ft wide.

SMITH'S TROPICAL PARADISE

Make no mistake: it's hokey. But the hour-long loop trail through theme gardens at **Smith's Tropical Paradise** (☎ 821-6895/6; www .smithskauai.com/paradise.html; adult/child under 12 $5.25/2.50; Wailua Marina; ☽ 8:30am-4pm) offers the cheapest landscaped flora experience on the

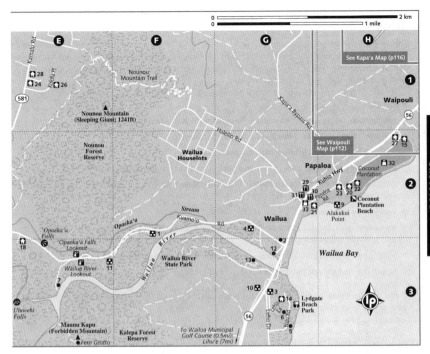

Eastside. You can ride a Disney-esque tram or walk through gardens like 'Bamboo Rain Forest,' 'Japanese Garden Island' and even a cartoony replica of Easter Island. The Allerton and McBryde Gardens (p167) in Po'ipu and Limahuli Garden (p153) in Ha'ena are far superior. If you're planning to catch the luau (p110) here, forgo a separate trip, as you'll have ample time to tour the grounds before dinner.

COCO PALMS

Coco Palms is iconic as Kaua'i's first resort, and a Hollywood landmark. Built in 1953 on the site of Kaua'i's ancient royal court in a historic 45-acre coconut grove, the tropical-theme hotel epitomized a tropical movie set, with lagoons, lush gardens, thatched cottages, torch-lit paths and, of course, coconut groves galore. In fact, the hotel's outdoor chapel was built in 1954 for the movie *Sadie Thompson* with Rita Hayworth.

The highest-profile onscreen wedding here was when Elvis Presley wed Joan Blackman in the 1961 film *Blue Hawaii*. At

its height, the Coco Palms was the place for mainland couples to get hitched, as well as a playground for Hollywood leading males and their ingenues. It was the type of old-Hawaii place where guests knew hotel staff on a first-name basis and returned year after year.

In 1992 the then-396-room hotel was demolished by Hurricane 'Iniki. After years of benign neglect, the defunct Coco Palms is now headed toward resurrection: by winter 2008, 200 condo units, 48 resort bungalows, a lobby identical to the original and its former tropical-paradise atmosphere are scheduled to be restored. On sale since fall 2005, the $1.5 million to $2.5 million condos are a hot commodity.

Today, all you see are palm trees swaying majestically at the corner of Kuhio Hwy and Kuamo'o Rd. But weddings are performed on the grounds by iconic Kaua'i musician, composer and wedding coordinator **Larry Rivera** (☎ 822-3868; http://homepages.hawaiian.net /zx/larry). Rivera, a Kapa'a High School alumnus, has mingled with Hollywood legends from Elvis Presley to Bing Crosby, and in

---

KIDDIE KAUA'I

Family trips can often cause a dilemma, as places tend to be geared toward either adults or children. No such problem on Kaua'i. The whole family can find their pleasure here, and the casual atmosphere means kids are welcome almost everywhere. Even a day just picnicking at a park and doing 'nothing' is great family fun.

In addition to the obvious outdoor activities, Kaua'i's kid-friendly attractions include the following:

- gargantuan jungle gym at **Kamalani Playground & Kamalani Play Bridge** (p95)
- children's Garden at **Na 'Aina Kai Botanical Gardens** (p127)
- indoor fun at **Kaua'i Children's Discovery Museum** (p112)
- video games at **Fun Factory** (p112) and computer games at **ComputerWeb** (p111)
- gentle waters at **Po'ipu Beach Park** (p170), **Baby Beach** (p167), **Salt Pond Beach Park** (p189) and **Lydgate Beach Park** (p95)
- **snorkeling cruises** (p185) off the Na Pali Coast
- icy sweet treats, including frosties at **Banana Joe's** (p131) ice cream at **Lappert's** (p160, p110 and p191) or **shave ice** (p120)
- a trip down the old Lihu'e sugarcane irrigation ditch on floating **tubes** (p82)
- hiking the first mile or two of the **Kalalau Trail** (p156).

If you need a break, babysitting services are available (see p176). For more information about traveling with children, see p219.

1999 he was named a 'Living Treasure of Kaua'i' by the Kaua'i Museum.

COCONUT PLANTATION BEACH

The Eastside's main resort development is Coconut Plantation on Kuhio Hwy, between the 6- and 7-mile markers, with four hotels, a condo and a shopping center. It fronts a half-mile-long beach, but water activities are restricted due to the low lava shelf that runs along most of the beach and the strong currents that prevail beyond. The best section for swimming and surfing fronts the Kaua'i Sands Hotel, where there's a break in the shelf. You can occasionally spot monk seals basking on the shore. The large field between the resorts here is popular with golden plovers and other migratory birds.

KUAMO'O RD (HWY 580)

No, the winding highway itself isn't a destination, but it leads to a string of lookout points and sights. The road starts at the traffic light on Kuhio Hwy at Coco Palms. After passing heiau, historical sites, towering 'Opaeka'a Falls and Wailua Homesteads it ends at Keahua Arboretum, the starting

place for a couple of worthwhile hiking trails (p103).

Note that the stoplight at the intersection of Kuamo'o Rd and Kuhio Hwy is exceptionally long (three minutes) but only for drivers trying to enter the highway.

About halfway up the hill, you'll pass Kamalu Rd, which connects with Kuamo'o Rd at its southern end and with Olohena Rd at its northern end. Together, Kamalu Rd and Olohena Rd form Hwy 581.

The residential area along Kuamo'o Rd is called the Wailua Homesteads. It sprang up when early homesteaders, taking advantage of multiacre parcels courtesy of the government, used the land to graze cattle. The Dole Company once grew pineapples up here, like almost everywhere in Hawaii. Today pastoral Wailua Homesteads is a peaceful, scenic neighborhood, where you can find upscale inns and B&Bs mixed with longtime residents who breed fighting cocks and hunt for deer on weekends.

Holoholoku Heiau

This *luakini* (temple of human sacrifice) is 0.25 miles up Kuamo'o Rd on the left. Like all of the Wailua heiau, this one was an enclosure-type construction, with its stone walls built directly on the ground rather than on terraced platforms. This whole area used to be royal property; on the west side of the grounds, against the flat-backed birthstone, queens gave birth to future kings. This stone is marked by a plaque that reads 'Pohaku Ho'ohanau' (royal birthstone). Only a male child born here could become king of Kaua'i.

Another stone a few yards away, marked 'Pohaku Piko,' was where the *piko* (umbilical cords) of the babies were left. Above the temple where Hawaiian royals were born, steps lead to a hilltop cemetery where latter-day Japanese laborers lie at rest.

Poli'ahu Heiau

Perched high on a hill overlooking the meandering Wailua River, this temple is named after the snow goddess Poli'ahu, one of Pele's sisters. The relatively well-preserved heiau is also believed to have been a *luakini*. Poli'ahu Heiau is immediately before the 'Opaeka'a Falls lookout, on the opposite side of the road.

Immediately south of Poli'ahu Heiau, on the same side of Hwy 580, look for a 'Falling Rocks' sign that marks a short and rutted dirt drive leading to a **bellstone**. If struck with another stone, the bellstone resonates at a distinctive low frequency audible up to a mile away. It is believed that ancient Hawaiians used the bellstone to ward off commoners approaching too close to *kapu* (forbidden) areas, to announce impending naval attacks and to ring out royal birth announcements.

Because of the road's angle, it's easiest to approach coming downhill from Poli'ahu.

There are actually two stones at the end of the drive, one with an all-too-perfect petroglyph whose age is suspect. Archaeologists question just which stone may have been the bellstone. Although you can find depressions in them, they may be the result of modern-day poundings by people trying to check out the resonance for themselves.

'Opaeka'a Falls

While neither the highest nor the prettiest, this waterfall became a major tourist attraction because it's visible from a major road. Just head up on Kuamo'o Rd for 1.5 miles and turn right into the lookout parking lot. This is a guaranteed stop on the tour-bus circuit, so you're likely to encounter a herd of stop-and-go sightseers (all raptly capturing exactly the same shot) during daylight hours.

The high, broad 40ft waterfall usually flows as a double cascade, though after a heavy rain the two sides often merge. The peaks of the Makaleha Mountains form a scenic backdrop; look for white-tailed tropical birds soaring in the valley below the falls.

For the best viewing angle, walk up the sidewalk past the parking lot toward the bridge. Also cross the road for an overhead view of the Wailua River (check out the groovy pedestrian-crossing sign). To locals, 'Opaeka'a Falls is an afterthought, just part of the roadside scenery, so they zoom up and down Kuamo'o Rd, the main thoroughfare for Wailua Homesteads. But they're well aware of the back-to-back lookout points and someone always stops.

THE LAST BIG ONE

September 11 has proved inauspicious more than once: in the 1973 coup of Chile's Allende and in the 2001 World Trade Center attacks. Likewise, Kaua'i suffered its own 9/11 in 1992, when Hurricane 'Iniki made a direct hit on the island. The most powerful storm to hit the state in a century, 'Iniki blew in with sustained winds of 145mph and gusts of 165mph; a weather-station meter in mountainous Koke'e broke off at 227mph. The hurricane snapped trees by the thousands, ruined 5000 utility poles and affected an estimated 50% of buildings on Kaua'i, damaging 5000 and totally demolishing over 1300 of them. Thirty-foot waves washed away entire wings of beachfront hotels – Po'ipu and Princeville were particularly hard hit.

Miraculously, only four people died, but the total value of the damage to the island was $1.6 billion. The tourist industry bounced back by the late 1990s and today is thriving. While locals notice the changed landscape, newcomers would never realize the havoc wreaked 15 years ago. Unfortunately a couple of Kaua'i's native bird species have not been spotted since 'Iniki.

Kamokila Hawaiian Village

Kamokila means 'stronghold' in Hawaiian, and indeed this re-created **Hawaiian village** (☎ 823-0559; www.kamokila.com; self-guided tour adult/ child $5/3; ☯ 9am-5pm) perched on the bank of the Wailua River is a survivor. The modest operation, run by a Hawaiian family, includes grass huts, an assembly house, a shaman's house and other structures, and approximates a traditional indigenous settlement. A small map gives you the gist of each building's purpose. As you walk around, you might recognize the village as that used in the movie *Outbreak*.

While the village is not a must-see, the **outrigger canoe tours** (adult/child $30/20; ☯ departures hourly 9:30am-2:30pm) on the Wailua River are personalized and unique. Tours, which include a paddle, hike and waterfall swim, offer an interesting variation on the regular Wailua River kayak trip (right), as it leaves from the village and guarantees a Hawaiian guide. Canoes can hold about seven.

Kamokila is on the south side of Kuamo'o Rd, opposite 'Opaeka'a Falls, at the end of a steep, narrow 0.5-mile paved road.

Keahua Arboretum

Amid towering trees, a gurgling stream and cool misty rain, this arboretum is an excellent place to picnic or just enjoy the island greenery. Here and there you'll see mini groves of mature teak, eucalyptus and shower trees. The Department of Land and Natural Resources planted them in the 1940s to create an outdoor nature classroom, showcasing the benefits of forest management. They planted a variety of native and introduced species to see which would thrive – and by their soaring heights today, it seems they all did. When the stream is calm and ponds are deep, kids can swim in 'swimming holes.' But be careful on slippery rocks, and never enter if the current is strong.

Avoid the area at night, when it becomes the scene for rave parties. While the county tries to maintain the property, Kaua'i struggles with the same 'urban' problems as anywhere else, and you might see litter or abandoned vehicles in the parking lot.

KAUA'I'S HINDU MONASTERY

On an island virtually devoid of Hinduism, the splendid Kaua'i Aadheenam, commonly called simply **Kaua'i's Hindu Monastery**
(☎ 822-3012; www.himalayanacademy.com/ssc/hawaii; 107 Kaholalele Rd), is both serious monastery and growing tourist attraction. Located on 458 acres of lush rainforest above the Wailua River, the traditional South-Indian Saivite (Shiva-worshipping) monastery is a sprawling garden oasis, with a meditation hall and Ganesha statues sitting amid wildly tropical landscaping.

About 20 monks live on-site, so access is limited to **tours** (tours free, donations welcome; ☯ 9am, 3 or 4 per month), which provide a background on the monastery's late founder and on Hinduism. Led by a charming, articulate monk, the tours are well worth the time – and they typically draw 80 or more visitors each time. Check the website for tour dates, as they change monthly.

Plants thrive in the upland rainforest and include 300 types of ti (native plant whose leaves are used for cooking and weaving) and native fruit like *noni* (type of mulberry). In **Kadavul Temple** (☯ 9am-noon), guests can see the world's largest single-pointed quartz crystal, a 50-million-year-old, six-sided wonder that weighs 700 pounds and stands over 3ft tall. In the temple, meditating monks have been rotating in three-hour vigils round the clock since the temple was established in 1973. Hindu pilgrims may attend the daily Siva *puja* (worship ceremony) at 9am.

The highlight of the tour is the Chola-style **Iraivan Temple**, a monumental work-in-progress that is being entirely hand carved from white granite by a village of artisans founded in Bangalore, India, specifically for this project. The scale is tremendous: the dome alone weighs 8.5 tons and took three people four years carving full-time to complete. The crafting, shipping and assembling of this structure will be particularly interesting for artists, architects and engineers. The monumental crystal will move here when the temple is completed around 2012.

Guests can also visit the **Sacred Rudraksna Forest** (7345 Kuamo'o Rd; admission free; ☯ 6am-6pm).

Parking is limited in the small gravel lot, but there's additional street parking in the surrounding residential neighborhood.

Activities
KAYAKING

Among the must-do activities on Kaua'i is kayaking the Wailua River. No surprise: the 5-mile round-trip is doable by most folks.

DETOUR: BLUE HOLE

Beyond Keahua Arboretum at the end of Kuamo'o Rd, you can trek out on the Powerline Trail (p105) or you can head back...or you can continue on. This detour will lead you across a bumpy ride and muddy walk to 'Blue Hole,' a scenic site with a pretty stream beside a water-diversion ditch that's as close as you'll get to Mt Wai'ale'ale on the ground.

You definitely need a 4WD for the head-jarringly rough, unpaved road. To get here, once past Keahua Arboretum, veer left onto Wailua Forest Management Rd. After less than 1.5 miles, you'll reach a junction; turn right (a gate blocks the left direction). Go straight for about 2 miles. Along the way, you'll pass an otherworldy forest of false staghorn, guava, eucalyptus and native *mamane* and *ohia*. The dense foliage introduces you to a rainbow of greens, from deep evergreen to eye-popping chartreuse.

This setting substituted for Costa Rica in *Dragonfly* and for the prehistoric era in *Jurassic Park*. As you drive in, look to your left at a wide clearing, which served as the trailer camp during filming. When Kevin Costner drove down this dirt road while filming *Dragonfly*, the weather was dry, so sprinklers were installed alongside to simulate rain.

You will then reach a locked yellow gate; it is meant to keep out cars but the state allows foot traffic (the mud actually deters most people from willingly hiking here). This gate is where the entrance gate to *Jurassic Park* stood. From here you must slosh 0.75 miles till you reach the dammed stream, which is the north fork of Wailua River.

The stream rises and falls depending on the season and rainfall. Occasionally it is deep enough for kids to swim. You cannot actually see the interior of Mt Wai'ale'ale, which is visible only by helicopter.

Blue Hole is a quiet, secluded spot, not a tourist destination by a long shot. But it makes for a mini adventure. Hawaii Movie Tours (p113) comes here during their 4WD tour. Hunters use the area to hunt pigs on the weekend and Monday.

EASTSIDE

The centrally located launch site is convenient, and kayak rentals are available right at the boat ramp.

The route typically doesn't pass the Fern Grotto and instead takes a fork in the river leading to a mile-long side hike through dense forest to Uluwehi Falls (aka Secret Falls), a 130ft waterfall. An alternate tour takes you past the Fern Grotto to a swimming hole.

Note that while the river flows downstream, it is easier to paddle upstream (against the current) because of the wind direction. While the return trip is harder than the first leg, most find the whole experience to be easier than it looks. Kayakers must stay on the north side of the river, while the Smith's boats cruise in the center.

The county strictly regulates commercial kayak use of the river, due to congestion. Only 15 tour companies are allowed to lead groups of 12 people (typically in six double kayaks) twice per day. Most tours include lunch and leave around 7am or noon; call for exact check-in times. As for individual kayak rentals, the county is even more prohibitive, allowing only four companies to rent them (with a maximum of six in the river at any time). No kayak tours or rentals are allowed on Sundays.

If you're trying to decide whether to join a tour or explore on your own, consider your comfort level on the water. If you're an adept kayaker and obtain clear directions of where to find the falls or swimming hole, there's no real advantage to a costly tour. Allow about three hours for a round-trip. Rental rates usually include paddles, life vests and a car-rack setup. But guided tours, which widely vary in price, are definitely better for solo travelers and all novice paddlers. While the river looks glassily calm, paddlers must contend with wake from boats and the current can move rapidly.

The following companies offer both kayak tours and individual rentals for the Wailua River. Prices tend to reflect high commissions that outfits must pay to middlemen. While the larger two companies, Kayak Kaua'i and Outfitters Kaua'i, are excellent and recommended for their other, more adventurous tours, consider saving a buck on the easy Wailua River with the smaller two companies' cheaper deals.

EASTSIDE TRAILS

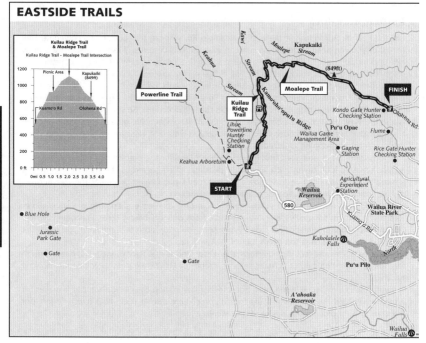

Kayak Kaua'i (☎ 826-9844; 800-437-3507; www .kayakkauai.com; Coconut Marketplace, Wailua; single/ double kayak per day $45/75, tour per adult/child $85/60; ☸ check-in 7:45am & 12:15pm), with shop locations both in Wailua and in Hanalei, offers river and sea kayaking tours, including the Na Pali trip. Japanese- and Spanish-speaking guides are available.

At **Outfitters Kaua'i** (Map pp168-9; ☎ 742-9667, 888-742-9887; www.outfitterskauai.com; Po'ipu Plaza, 2827-A Poipu Rd, Po'ipu; kayak per person per day $40, tour adult/child 5-14 $94/72; ☸ check-in 7:45am) you can pick up kayaks from Wailua Kayak & Canoe so there's no need to transport them from Po'ipu.

Wailua Kayak Adventures (Map p112; ☎ 822-5795, 639-6332; www.kauaiwailuakayak.com; Kuhio Hwy, Waipouli; single/double kayaks $25/50, tour per couple $85; ☸ check-in 7am & 1pm) has a choice of three Wailua River tours, often discounted. Call for times, as they vary slightly for each tour. It's located behind Coconuts restaurant.

In business since the mid-1990s, the Hawaiian-owned **Wailua Kayak & Canoe** (☎ 821-1188; wkc@aloha.net; Wailua River State Park; single/double kayak per 5hr $45/75, tour per person $40) is friendly,

honest and the only rental outfit right at the boat ramp. Its tour is 'bring your own lunch' (it provides coolers). Check well-worn equipment carefully. Direct bookings only.

Other recommended tour companies (but with no individual kayak rentals for the Wailua River):

Ali'i Kayaks (Map p76; ☎ 241-7700, 877-426-2544; www.aliikayaks.com; Harbor Mall, 3501 Rice St, Lihu'e) Wailua River tour with lunch adult/child $90/70; Kalapaki Bay tour per person $20.

Kamokila Hawaiian Village (p100) Small-group canoe tours to Uluwehi Falls.

Kayak Wailua (☎ 822-3388; www.kayakwailua.com; tour per person $39.95) Small, family-run company offers cheap, casual tours but staff can be 'immature.' Only outfitter on Kaua'i with adult triple kayak. Meet tour guide at Shell gas station in Wailua. No lunch.

WATERSKIING AND WAKEBOARDING
The only non-ocean waterskiing in the state is found here on the Wailua River, only from the Wailua Bridge to the first big bend in the river.

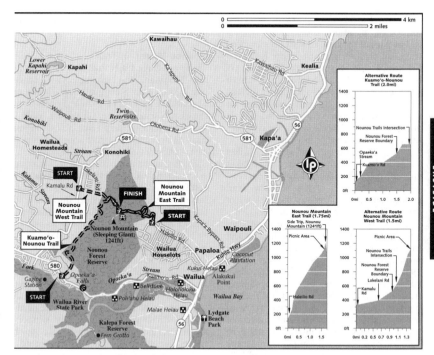

Try waterskiing or wakeboarding with a tow by **Water Ski, Surf & Kayak Company** (☎ 822-3574; Kinipopo Shopping Village, 4-356 Kuhio Hwy; per 30/60min $65/120). The company also rents water equipment, including surfboards (per day/week $10/50, $200 deposit), boogie boards (per day/week $5/20, $75 deposit) and snorkel gear (per day/week $5/15, $75 deposit). Conveniently located near the Wailua River marina; there's also a surf shop on-site.

YOGA & MASSAGE

All comers will feel welcome at the low-key **Creative Yoga Kaua'i** (☎ 822-1881; www.creativeyogacenter.com; Kinipopo Shopping Village, 356 Kuhio Hwy; drop-in class $15, massage per hr from $80), founded by Brenda Winston, an experienced yoga teacher and massage therapist. Her diverse background lies in Sivananda, Ashtanga and Jivamukti yoga, plus Iyengar influences. A variety of bodywork is available; Winston's deep-tissue work is excruciatingly satisfying. As a gift to the community, Winston offers free 6am Mysore (self-led Ashtanga) practice sessions by appointment.

HIKING

While less popular than the North Shore's Kalalau Trail and less diverse than the myriad paths traversing Koke'e State Park, the Eastside offers outstanding hiking. The trails can be quite steep and allow stupendous views. Best of all, they are centrally located and thus easy to fit into a day's activities.

Be aware that hunting is allowed in this area on weekends, holidays and Monday. One-way mileage distances are given in the following sections.

Kuilau Ridge & Moalepe Trails

While they are indeed independent trails, the Kuilau Ridge Trail (2.1 miles) and Moalepe Trail (2.25 miles) are often mentioned together because they connect and can be hiked in sequence. Both are moderate hikes and, for the effort, they are among the most visually rewarding on Kaua'i. Together they make an easy 9-mile hike or bike, with sweeping views of lush valleys, mist-covered mountains and the sparkling ocean beyond. Both are out-and-back trails, however, so you will need either to hike the entire two trails back or persuade someone to pick you up at one end.

The Kuilau Ridge Trail starts at a marked trailhead on the right just before Kuamo'o Rd crosses the stream at the Keahua Arboretum, 4 miles above the junction of Kuamo'o Rd and Kamalu Rd. The Moalepe Trail trailhead is at the end of Olohena Rd where it bends into Waipouli Rd. While you can park at either spot, as always don't leave anything of value in your car.

While both are interesting, the Kuilau Ridge Trail is recommended because it takes you immediately into the forest wilderness, while the first mile of the Moalepe Trail crosses the simple, treeless pastureland of the Wailua Game Management Area.

The Kuilau Ridge Trail commences up a wide dirt path also used by horses and the occasional renegade dirt biker. Like most Eastside trails, this path began in the 1930s as a road to haul in hunting materials. Along the way, birdsong emanates from the dense native vegetation, including koa trees, 'ohi'a lehua (native tree with red pom-pom-like flowers) and thickets of ti. The sheaths of peeling eucalyptus bark here look and feel like human skin. In the upper reaches, the lush, fern-covered hillsides provide broad vistas of the mountains. Guava trees and wild thimbleberries grow along the path.

The hike climbs up Kamo'oho'opulu Ridge ('Wet Ridge,' in Hawaiian), which allows stunning views into patchwork valleys clear down to the coast. You can see Kapa'a to the east and the island's uninhabited central region to the west. It takes about 40 minutes to walk the 1.25 miles up to a clearing on the ridge top, where a rustic picnic shelter lets you sit and enjoy the view of Mt Wai'ale'ale in peaceful solitude.

Beyond the clearing, to the right past the picnic area, the Kuilau Ridge Trail continues as a narrow footpath with even more spectacular views. It ends in about a mile at the Moalepe Trail. If you don't want to go that far, at least walk a little of it, as some of the best views, including cliffs cleaved by waterfalls, are along the next half mile.

If you go left at the connection with the Moalepe Trail, you'll come to a viewpoint after about 10 minutes. If you go right on Moalepe, you'll come out on Olohena Rd in Wailua Homesteads after about 2.25

miles. Both trails are well maintained and signposted.

Nounou Mountain Trails

There are three trails that trek along Nounou Mountain, the famous Eastside landmark known as Sleeping Giant: Nounou Mountain East Trail (1.75 miles) starts from the east, Nounou Mountain West Trail (1.5 miles) from the west, and Kuamo'o-Nounou Trail (2 miles) climbs from south to northeast – and they all meet near the center.

Each trail has its benefits, but mainland visitors tend to prefer the **Nounou Mountain East Trail** because it is most exposed and offers ocean views. The well-maintained trail takes 1½ to two hours round-trip and provides a hardy workout thanks to its pitch.

The east trail begins at a parking lot a mile up Haleilio Rd in the Wailua Houselots neighborhood. The trail is steep, with switchbacks almost to the ridge. This is a wonderful trail to do early in the morning, when it's relatively cool and you can watch the light spread across the valley. The hardpacked dirt trail is exceedingly slippery when wet; look for a walking stick, which hikers sometimes leave near the trailhead.

The eucalyptus trees at the trailhead soon give way to a tall, thick forest of Norfolk pines. About five minutes into the woods, right after the Norfolk pines begin, there's a fork. Veer left up the path with the large rock beside it. The trail then passes through thick strawberry guava bushes that can grow up to 15ft high, creating a canopied, tunnellike effect. Strawberry guava is considered the sweetest of any guava; pop the small red fruits whole. But the bountiful trees also litter the ground in gooey blobs and splashes.

A few minutes' walk below the summit, the eastern and western trails merge on the ridge. Continue up to the right past some *hala* (pandanus) trees. The trail ends at a picnic-table shelter at the summit, perfect to escape the frequent passing showers that can create vivid valley rainbows. The east trail joins the west trail near the 1½-mile post.

If you go south across the picnic area, the trail vaguely continues for about five minutes to another good viewpoint. It's unwise to try climbing the ridge farther up the giant's chin – it's precariously steep, with loose rocks and slides.

The **Nounou Mountain West Trail** is perhaps steeper but equally pleasant and even better if you prefer a cooler, shaded forest trail, with tall trees and moss-covered stones. There are two ways to access the trailhead: from Kamalu Rd, near telephone pole No 11, or from the end of Lokelani Rd, off Kamalu Rd. Walk through a metal gate marked as a forestry right-of-way.

The **Kuamo'o-Nounou Trail** runs through groves of trees planted in the 1930s by the Civilian Conservation Corps; it connects with the west trail. The trailhead is right on Kuamo'o Rd, near a grassy field between the 2- and 3-mile markers.

Powerline Trail

The **Powerline Trail** (13 miles) is actually a former maintenance road for the electric powerlines running along the mountains between Wailua and the North Shore. When the powerlines were established back in the 1930s, county officials used land vehicles to access them. Today, helicopters are the mode of choice, so the road has fallen into disuse.

While hiking is definitely possible on the road, the trek is long, exposed and, especially toward the north, rather monotonous. The Powerline Trail is perhaps a better setting for all-terrain vehicles (ATVs) and mountain bikes – but still jarringly rough. If you decide to hoof it anyway, note that the hike takes a full day and is recommended only in dry weather. Beware of steep drop-offs, hidden by dense foliage alongside the trail. Never drive a conventional vehicle on this trail: you'll probably require an expensive tow out.

The south end of the trail begins across the stream at the Keahua Arboretum, at the end of Kuamo'o Rd. (During rainy spells, the stream will be too high to cross.) After fording the stream, look for the trailhead on your right after cresting the hill. Dark and steep at first, the trail passes into sunlight, providing views of the Makaleha Mountains and Mt Kawaikini. Alternating ocean, mountain and valley views dominate for the next several miles. After about two hours of hiking, you'll come to a steep ascent and a lookout, at the trail's highest point. The remaining 6 miles to Princeville make for mostly dull, flat walking, in land shared with hunters and their hounds; we suggest you turn around here.

GOLF

Ranked among the finest municipal golf courses nationally, the **Wailua Municipal Golf Course** (☎ 241-6666; green fees weekday/weekend & holidays $32/44, optional cart rental $16,/club rental from $15) is an 18-hole, par-72 course off Kuhio Hwy north of Lihu'e. Plan ahead because morning tee times are reserved up to a week in advance at this popular course, designed by former head pro Toyo Shirai. After 2pm the green fees drop by half and play is on a first-come, first-served basis.

Tours

Every bus tour itinerary includes the 2-mile riverboat tour up the Wailua River to the Fern Grotto, making it Kaua'i's best-known tourist attraction. The scenic

---

GREENING THE GROTTO

The Fern Grotto was not quite so lush from the mid-1990s to early 2000s, during a decade of localized drought starting in 1994. This happened because cane fields above the cliffs had gone out of production and irrigation stopped, leaving no water to seep through crevices into the natural amphitheater. In 2003 the Hawai'i Tourism Authority provided $245,000, and Kaua'i County added $50,000, to remedy the problem.

Today, water is restored into the plantation reservoir sitting on the plateau above the grotto, and a siphon system runs water to the cliff edge. This allows water to flow over the side in a waterfall, resembling the one that existed during cane cultivation. The groundwater then hits underground rock formations and finds its way to the cliff face.

The striking grotto is not only the backdrop to the Smith's featured music show, but also provides ideal acoustics. Every tour includes a rendition of 'Ke Kali Nei Au,' better known as the 'Hawaiian Wedding Song' after Elvis Presley sang it in English in *Blue Hawaii*. Actually, it is not a wedding song, but its fate seems set – and couples from around the world come to marry at the Fern Grotto to the Elvis version.

grotto is an overhanging cliff at the base of Maunu Kapu (Forbidden Mountain), which looms from the river, dripping with yard-long sword ferns and delicate maidenhair. The riverboats are open-air, covered barges with wide, flat bottoms, and tourists are herded on and off all day. During the leisurely 1½-hour round-trip, guides provide interesting historical commentary and hula dancers cajole passengers to let loose and learn a few moves. At the grotto, musicians serenade with favorites, including the mandatory 'Hawaiian Wedding Song,' dedicating it to all the newlyweds and newlyweds-at-heart. It's the type of corniness that will either please or force a smile. Regardless, this is the site of countless weddings, for which Smith's can arrange a private tour.

Since 1946, **Smith's Motor Boat Service** (☎ 821-6892; www.smithskauai.com; adult/child 2-12 $20/10; ☷ 9-11:30am, 12:30-3:30pm) has been the foremost boat tour on the Wailua River. Boats leave the marina, on the south side of the river, every 30 minutes. Smith's also has a ticket booth on the north bank of the river.

Festivals & Events

Annual Taste of Hawaii (☎ 822-7449; Smith's Tropical Paradise; admission $75-80; ☷ 11:30am-4pm) The Rotary Club of Kapa'a hosts an 'Ultimate Sunday Brunch' in early June, featuring culinary creations by over 40 of Hawaii's distinguished chefs. Additional booths provide wines, microbrews, ice cream, desserts and live entertainment.

Aloha Festivals Royal Court Investiture (☎ 245-8508; www.alohafestivals.com; admission incl lunch $15) The statewide Aloha Festivals in late August is launched on each island with presentation of a royal court. Held at Kamokila Hawaiian Village, the event includes special ceremonies of traditional chanting and hula. The admission fee includes lunch.

Sleeping

If your heart is set on the sound of waves lulling you to sleep, choose an oceanfront room. Indeed, you'll find an excellent selection of midrange options just a stroll away from the beach. But in the residential neighborhood Wailua Homesteads, about 3 miles from the coast, B&Bs and inns lie quietly as best-kept secrets. Listed as follows are excellent lodging options (especially for budget travelers). All of these are within a couple of miles of the intersection of Kuamo'o Rd and Kamalu Rd. Remember, many require two- or three-night minimums.

For more options, contact Rosemary Smith of **Rosewood Kaua'i** (☎ 822-5216; www.rosewoodkauai.com).

Bear in mind that Wailua, Waipouli and Kapa'a are practically the same town. Consider options in all three towns when planning Eastside lodging.

BUDGET

Bunk House at Rosewood B&B (☎ 822-5216; www.rosewoodkauai.com; 872 Kamalu Rd; r with shared bathroom $45-55) Backpackers will feel right at home in Bunk House, a trio of cheerful, private rooms that share a bathroom and outdoor shower. Each compact room sleeps two and includes sink, toaster, refrigerator, coffee maker, microwave, dinnerware and the use of the gas Weber grill on the patio. When booking, indicate whether you prefer two twins, a king, or a king plus queen futon.

House of Aleva (☎ 822-4606; 5509 Kuamo'o Rd; r with shared bathroom incl tax & breakfast $50-55) Remember spending the night at Grandma's?

TOP 10 BUDGET SLEEPS

Budget travelers, especially singles, stick to the Eastside. You can also snag deals on basic digs in Po'ipu and across the island, but the North Shore is pricey unless you're traveling as a family or group.

Simple upstairs bedrooms. Living room plastered with family photos. Shared bathroom down the hall. Well, you can relive such a memory at Anita Perry's home, which has welcomed budget travelers since 1992. The two bedrooms (which share a bathroom) include a small fridge. Bonuses include use of washer/dryer and a full, cooked breakfast. One drawback: the location on busy Kuamo'o Rd, near Opaeka'a Falls, means speeding cars, especially at rush hour.

Magic Sunrise Hawaii (☎ 821-9847; www.magic sunrisehawaii.com; 139 Royal Dr; r with shared bathroom $55-85, apt from $99, cottages from $111; ☐ ☒) A friendly Swiss native runs this communal inn with a New Age, nouveau-hippie vibe, on a pastoral property overlooking the Wailua River. It's a favorite among solo travelers (especially Europeans) who don't mind sharing space with the hosts and pet dogs. In the main house you'll find three stylishly appointed rooms (with shared bathroom) with Indonesian-type bamboo beds, hardwood floor and exotic decor. For more space and privacy, book the classily designed adjacent cottage with full kitchen and washer/dryer. French, Italian and Swiss German spoken here.

Lani Keha (☎ 822-1605; www.lanikeha.com; 848 Kamalu Rd; s/d $55/65) If you're the communal, 'gather around the kitchen' type traveler, Lani Keha provides a low-key setting, where you can meet others yet retreat to a private room. Nothing fancy, the two rooms feature *lauhala* (pandanus leaf) mat flooring, king beds and well-worn but clean furnishings. Guests share the kitchen, living room, dining room and lanai (porch) with the occupants.

Garden Room (☎ 822-5216, 822-3817; 6430 Ahele Dr; r $65) No doubt, this aptly named studio overlooking a pretty koi pond is the best budget room in town. First, the location, in a cul de sac off Kuamo'o Rd is quiet and safe, with easy parking. Second, the room features a private entrance and fully equipped kitchenette (that second sink sure comes in handy). Third, from your glass sliding door you behold a lovely backyard. The pond, topped with blooming waterlilies and a favorite spot for birds, adds a calming touch. Honeymooners, call ☎ 822-3817 to ask about the one-week package including guided tours of the island, or visit www .hawaiianhoneymoonadventure.com.

MIDRANGE

You'll enjoy an outstanding selection of midrange lodging in Wailua Homesteads, where it's now commonplace for homeowners to rent a room (or whole cottage) to vacationers. Remember, the following reviews are listed by price and not by preference – all are excellent.

B&Bs & Inns

Inn Paradise (☎ 822-2542; www.affordable-paradise .com/kauai87_e.html; 6381 Makana Rd; r $75, ste $90-95) Longtime innkeepers Major and Connie Inch have perfected the art of hosting discerning visitors. From the classy rooms to the bonuses like washer/dryer and ice machine, it's hard to imagine any dissatisfaction here. In a bungalow overlooking spectacular pastureland, the three spacious units each have a private entrance, hardwood floors, Persian carpets and a shared backyard lanai. The most expensive King Kaumuali'i suite ($95) resembles a small house, with full kitchen and spacious living room. The Prince Kuhio studio ($75) is perfect for one or two (no kitchen). When you arrive, you're greeted with a huge fruit basket, yummy banana muffins and all the breakfast basics.

Rosewood B&B (☎ 822-5216; www.rosewoodkauai .com; 872 Kamalu Rd; r $85, 1-bedroom cottages $115, 2-bedroom cottages $135; ☐) Storybook yellow houses surrounded by a white picket fence on Kaua'i? Welcome to Rosewood, with lodging options for all pocketbooks. In addition to the budget Bunk House option singles can stay in a classy B&B bedroom in the main house, complete with heated floor (to steam out that perennial Wailua dampness!). The 'Thatched Cottage,' with kitchenette, tucked behind a romantic garden, is perfect for one or two. For just $20 more, the comfortable 'Victorian Cottage' (a replica of the main house) includes full kitchen, master bedroom and 'attic' bedroom with twin beds (best for kids or petite people), washer/dryer and computer with high-speed Internet access. Hosts Rosemary and Norbert are longtime Kaua'i residents and gracious B&B hosts with a sixth sense for welcoming visitors warmly while respecting their privacy. Internet available in two-bedroom cottage only.

Hale Lani B&B (☎ 823-6434, 877-423-6434; www .halelani.com; 283 Aina Lani Pl; studios $105-115, 2-bedroom ste $140, cottages $150, all incl breakfast) Hale

Lani was designed to be a B&B. And it shows. The four units, which make terrific use of space, feature not only fresh (if occasionally country-cute) furnishings, kitchenettes/kitchens and private hot tubs, but also thoughtful touches like hand-painted murals and blooming orchid plants. Picky about cleanliness? Rest assured: here, not only are linens washed when guests depart, but also bedspreads and rugs – and the hot tub is drained and cleaned for every new guest. The most-economical 'garden' studio is particularly cheery. Breakfast is served take-out style, in a cooler.

Mystery Meadows (☎ 822-5216; 5767 Kololia Pl; r $120) Modern and sophisticated, with a stunning view of the Makeleha mountain range, Mystery Meadows is one class act. From the glossy black range and refrigerator to the wall-to-wall picture windows, the recently built property feels like an urban apartment smack in the middle of a bucolic village. Guests enjoy lots of privacy since all windows face away from the main part of the house. A wraparound lanai adds to the airy atmosphere.

Hotels

Kaua'i Sands Hotel (☎ 822 4951, 800-560-5553; www .kauaisandshotel.com; 420 Papaloa Rd; r $88-128; ⚥ ⚲) The good news? You can see and hear the ocean. The bad news? Rooms are rather dim and small at this basic 200-room hotel. Still, it's a bargain, as guests can simply stroll across a lawn, past the pool, to the best stretch of Coconut Plantation Beach. This hotel belongs to a local, family-owned chain of dependable, affordable hotels on the Big Island, Maui and here on Kaua'i. Coconut Marketplace is right next door.

Islander on the Beach (☎ 822-7417, 877-997-6667; www.resortquesthawaii.com; 440 Aleka Pl; r Internet/rack from $111/156; ⚥ ⚲) Midrange hotels tend to blur together in a 'seen one, seen 'em all' haze. But the best-value Islander will jolt you awake. The open-air grounds feature a pleasant pool just yards from the beach. All 198 rooms were renovated in fall 2005 and, with classy tiled foyers and granite countertops, plush beds, teak furnishings and lanai, they feel more upscale than their peers. Kids under 18 stay free. Buildings are named after the Hawaiian Islands, and rooms in the Kaua'i and Ni'ihau

buildings enjoy the best ocean views. Most units include a queen bed plus a sofa bed; if you need two queen beds, choose the Maui, Moloka'i or main buildings.

Courtyard by Marriott Kaua'i at Waipouli Beach (☎ 822-3455, 800-760-8555; www.courtyard marriottkauai.com; 4-484 Kuhio Hwy; r Internet/rack from $139/229; ⚥ ⚲) With a sweeping lobby and prime setting overlooking the beach, the Courtyard would satisfy the most discerning eye. Formerly the Kaua'i Coconut Beach Resort, the 311-room hotel was totally renovated and reopened as a Marriott property in February 2005. Rooms are tastefully appointed with rich colors, dark woods and upscale touches like black marble counters. Business travelers might appreciate the desk with rolling, padded chair, and free wi-fi throughout the hotel, including the airy lobby which is full of plush seating. Parking costs are valet/self $6/7.

Aloha Beach Resort (☎ 823-6000, 888-823-5111; www.abrkauai.com; 3-5920 Kuhio Hwy; r Internet/rack from $110/219, cottages Internet/rack $220/359) More spacious than comparable hotels; rooms include two double beds, living area with sofa, wide-screen TV, dining table and chairs. The hotel, just south of the Wailua River mouth, feels quite secluded and abuts the kid-friendly Lydgate Beach Park, so the location is convenient for families to access the beach and playground. The one-bedroom cottages are worth the splurge, for more privacy. Bear in mind, the published rack rates are double the Internet rates, so the hotel is much more affordable than you might think.

Condos

Plantation Hale (☎ 822-4941, 800-775-4253; www .plantation-hale.com; 4-484 Kuhio Hwy; 1-bedroom units Internet/rack from $89/165; ⚥ ⚲) While located closer to the highway than to the beach, Plantation Hale is popular for its condo amenities (the usual) and online rates. The units have modern layouts featuring a full kitchen, lots of bathroom and closet space, and lanai.

Kapa'a Sands (☎ 822-4901, 800-222-4901; www .kapaasands.com; 380 Papaloa Rd; studios/2-bedroom units from $110/155; ⚲) If you think all condos are aloof and immense, think again. Kapa'a Sands, managed by longtime, on-site staff, features 24 clean, modern units on a primo beachfront locale. While the individually owned units differ in decor, all are 100% nonsmoking (banned even on lanai) and include kitchens, lanai, breeze-catching louvered windows and at least a partial ocean view. The two-bedroom units, which accommodate four people comfortably, are the sweetest deal. Other bonuses are free parking, daily towel service and laundromat.

TOP END
Kaua'i Coast Resort at the Beachboy (☎ 822-3441, 877-977-4355; www.kauaicoastresort.com; 4-484 Kuhio Hwy; r from $180, 1-/2-bedroom units from $225/310; ❄ ❄) If you cannot decide between a 'home away from home' condo and a full-service hotel, this upscale timeshare is your answer. Huge, well-appointed and spotlessly clean, the units are so pleasant you'll wish you *lived* here. All guests enjoy hotel amenities like fitness center, full spa, tennis courts, multiple swimming pools, and a destination restaurant, Hukilau Lanai, on site. Free parking is an added plus. The catch? Of 106 timeshare units, only 10% are available for nonowner rental. Call months in advance.

Lodge at Rosewood B&B (☎ 822-5216; www .rosewoodkauai.com; Kamalu Rd; house $200, plus one-time cleaning fee $200) With gleaming hardwood floors, cathedral ceilings and French windows, the ranch-style Lodge is a classy find. The three bedrooms comfortably sleep six on luxurious pillow-top beds sporting fine linens. The expansive living room space includes a fireplace and comfortable sofas to ward away any travel-related claustrophobia. An enclosed patio lets you enjoy the balmy outdoors without being ravaged by mosquitoes. A true 'home away from home,' the house includes full kitchen, washer/dryer and high-speed DSL hookup.

Eating
Mema (☎ 823-0899; 4-369 Kuhio Hwy; mains $9-18; ❄ 11am-2pm Mon-Fri, 5-9pm nightly) Across the island, you'll find a surprising number of Thai restaurants. Most are owned by different members of the same family, but each is unique – and Mema is among the best. The menu features a list of savory dishes that can be tailored to your meat-philic or meat-phobic preference: you choose either tofu, chicken, pork, beef, fish or shrimp. The stir-

fried eggplant with basil ($9 to $12) and red chili with coconut milk ($9 to $18) are house favorites. Rice includes white, brown or traditional Thai sticky.

Caffé Coco (☎ 822-7990; 4-369 Kuhio Hwy; salads & sandwiches $5-14.50, meals $16-21; ❄ 11am-9pm Tue-Fri, 5-9pm Sat & Sun) Almost hidden behind thick foliage, this open-air café is where the island boho goes for a sit-down meal. It's casually romantic, with hip live music and twinkling strings of lights at night. Chefs have created a winning fusion menu with staples such as the tofu-veggie peanut wrap ($7.50) and the Moroccan-spiced 'ahi (yellowfin tuna) with banana chutney and a curried purple-sweet-potato samosa ($21). Sinful desserts and quality coffees are irresistible finales. Ward off voracious mosquitoes with repellent (remember to cover your ankles!).

Hukilau Lanai (☎ 822-0600; Kaua'i Coast Resort at the Beachboy; dinner $16-27; ❄ 5-9pm Tue-Sun) Ignore the touristy name: Hukilau Lanai is no run-of-the-mill resort restaurant. Here, you'll taste excellent Hawaiian Regional Cuisine in a casually elegant setting. Start with local-style nachos: wonton chips and 'ahi poke (cubed raw yellowfin tuna mixed with shoyu, sesame oil, salt and chili pepper). While it excels in fish prepartion, regular menu items like the feta-and-sweet-potato ravioli and the sugar-cane-skewered shrimp are signature items. If you're an

---

THE AUTHOR'S CHOICE
Kintaro (☎ 822-3341; 4-370 Kuhio Hwy; appetizers $3.50-6, meals $14-20; ❄ 5:30-9:30pm Mon-Sat) From the outside, Kintaro is a plain, boxy building. But inside you find a surprisingly sleek and urban restaurant, always jam-packed with locals and tourists alike. From thick-cut slices of sashimi ($15 to $17) to a shrimp/fish/veg tempura combination ($14), mains shine in quality and quantity. The owner is Korean, but the cuisine is authentic (and excellent) Japanese. A bar near the entrance (with ample seating for waiting patrons) is followed by a mouth-watering sushi counter further inside. A specialty is sizzling, crowd-wowing *teppanyaki*, when chefs show their stuff on steel grills at your table. The only downside is rather abrupt, rushed service.

early-bird diner, the tasting menu pairs six courses with five wines ($40; food only $28) from 5pm to 6pm. It lacks satisfying veg mains, however. Opened by the owners of Gaylord's, Hukilau Lanai is the most oft-mentioned locals' fine-dining pick – and that says a lot.

In a pinch, the following eateries will satisfy folks on a budget and not on a diet:

Eggbert's (☎ 822-3787; Coconut Marketplace, 484 Kuhio Hwy; breakfast mains $5-15, lunch mains $6-10 ; 7:30am-3pm) Hearty breakfast eaters, head to Eggbert's, which serves over 150 types of omelettes.

Lappert's (☎ 822-0744; Coconut Marketplace, 484 Kuhio Hwy; single scoop $3.10) Top off your meal with Kaua'i's premium ice cream.

Whole Enchilada (☎ 822-4993; Kinipopo Shopping Village, 4-356 Kuhio Hwy; meals $5-10; ; 11am-8pm Tue-Sat) Prodigious, fresh and generous Mexican food.

Aloha Pizza (☎ 822-4511; Coconut Marketplace, 484 Kuhio Hwy; pizza $5.50-23; ; 9am-8pm) The aromas will lure you toward delectable calzone and pizza, including a sublime artichoke-garlic version.

Korean Bar-B-Q Restaurant (☎ 823-6744; Kinipopo Shopping Village, 4-356 Kuhio Hwy; plates $7; ; 10am-9pm Wed-Mon, 4:30-9pm Tue) More local than Korean, but generous plate lunches do include kimchi, plus three other veg and two scoops of rice. The grilled meats are nicely done (not too greasy) and locals swear by the macaroni-potato salad.

Fish Hut (☎ 821-0033; Coconut Marketplace, 484 Kuhio Hwy; meals $8; ; 9am-8pm) Specializes in fresh 'ahi and ono (wahoo) served with haole-style coleslaw and fries.

Drinking & Entertainment

Let's face it, even the most populous region on Kaua'i is not a hopping night spot. So if you expect urban polish or bohemian throngs, you'd best head elsewhere.

BARS & NIGHTCLUBS

Tradewinds (☎ 882-1621; Coconut Marketplace; ; 10am-2am) A large 'South Seas' bar, Tradewinds is the Kaua'i version of a neighborhood sports bar, offering daily happy 'hour' from 2pm to 7pm and live bands on weekends (cover charge). There's something for everyone here: darts, karaoke, DJs and dancing, electronic games and nine TVs. Attention football fans: during NFL season, they open at 7am (8am when the mainland switches to daylight saving time).

Kuhio Lounge (☎ 823-6000; Aloha Beach Resort, 3-5920 Kuhio Hwy; admission $5; ; 10pm-2am) Low-key resort bar serving an array of drinks, including the colorful, frothy ones you would not be caught ordering at home.

LUAU & HULA

Smith's Tropical Paradise (☎ 821-6895; www.smiths kauai.com; Wailua Marina; luau adult/child 3-6/child 7-13 $65/19/30; ; 5pm Mon, Wed & Fri) The Smith Family Garden Luau is a Kaua'i institution (since 1985), attracting droves of tourists (many decked out in matching aloha attire) to the sprawling 30-acre gardens. But it's also a lively affair, run by four generations. The 'ohana (family) spirit is palpable, from the moment Kawika Smith (the founder's grandson, who is general manager and also sings and plays the ukulele) initiates the imu (underground cooking pit) ceremony and introduces 'Grandma.' The outdoor setting is another plus, and the show is truly multicultural, featuring Hawaiian, Tahitian, Samoan, Filipino, Chinese, Japanese and New Zealand dances. And of course be prepared to be dragged onstage to join in. To catch the show and skip the food, the price drops (adult/child aged three to 12 $15/7.50).

Courtyard by Marriott Kaua'i at Waipouli Beach (☎ 822-3455, 800-760-8555; www.courtyardmarriott kauai.com; 4-484 Kuhio Hwy; luau adult/child 3-11/child 12-17 $59/26/38; ; 6pm Tue-Sun) This Tahitian-themed Tihati 'Hiva Pasefika' luau is a commercial show with an average buffet dinner, open bar, imu unearthing and Polynesian revue – plus a 'pareo fashion show.' It lacks the down-home charm of family-run affairs, but performers are quite impressive.

Aloha Beach Resort (☎ 823-6000, 800-823-5111; www.abrkauai.com; 3-5920 Kuhio Hwy; luau adult $60-65, child 6-12 $30-35, youth 13-20 $40-45; ; 6pm Tue) The Punua halau (school) of the Kaua'i Beach Resort in Lihue also performs here, so between the two, just choose the closer location. Again, this show is a family affair and, for better or worse, more homey and less glitzy.

Coconut Marketplace (☎ 822-3641; ; 5pm Wed) While the hula shows are light and touristy, they're lively and, hey, you're in Hawaii. Performers might be longtime tutu (grandmothers), supple young men and women or crowd-pleasing keiki (children) hamming it up.

CINEMAS

Coconut Marketplace Cinemas (☎ 821-2324; 4-484 Kuhio Hwy; adult/child/senior $7/4/5.50, shows before 6pm $4) Screens first-run movies in a mall setting.

Shopping

Kaua'i's Hindu Monastery Gift Shop (☎ 822-3012; www.himalayanacademy.com/ssc/hawaii; 107 Kaholalele Rd; ☯ 9am-noon) While not Hawaiian or local, the souvenirs here are unusual – chanting CDs, alarm clocks with the Great Crystal on the face, granite lingams and tiger-eye Ganesha figurines.

Coconut Marketplace (☯ 9am-8pm Mon-Sat, 10am-6pm Sun) Open-air mall with boutiques, surf shops, art galleries and gift shops, including a branch of Crazy Shirts (call ☎ 822-0100). Sporty girls, check out Chicks Who Rip (call ☎ 823-6704, or visit www.chickswhorip.com), a surf shop catering to, well, the name says it all. The Rosie the Riveter logo gear is classic.

Tin Can Mailman (☎ 822-3009; tincan.mailman@ verizon.net; Kinipopo Shopping Village, 4-356 Kuhio Hwy; ☯ 11am-7pm Mon-Fri, noon-5pm Sat), This shop lives up to its description of 'Fine Books and Curiosities.' Amid shelves of rare, new and used books, find delightful Hawaiiana oddities, like vintage LPs, maps, photos and postcards, '50s-era paper dolls and cruise menus. The air-conditioned interior is deliciously chilly, creating a refreshing oasis for bookworms and browsers.

Getting Around

You will need your own transport to reach any sites not on the main stretch of Kuhio Hwy. The **Kaua'i Bus** (☎ 241-6410) offers limited service between Wailua and Lihu'e, and Wailua and Hanalei, Monday to Friday. Main stops are at Coconut Marketplace going north and Wailua Family Restaurant, near Haleilio Rd, going south.

WAIPOULI

Waipouli is the mile-long commercial strip between Coconut Plantation and Kapa'a. The main draw is...shopping centers. And not fancy ones either. Waipouli is where you will find the necessities, including post office, laundromat, business center, Internet access and supermarkets. Note that the distinction between Waipouli and Kapa'a is often confusing. The most simple way to distinguish the two is by shopping center name. Or, as another rule of thumb, Waipouli ends when you notice a gap in the

shops just south of the All Saints Church/ Gym.

In coming years, the already congested town will see even more resort development. On the last two remaining vacant properties in Waipouli – on either side of Courtyard by Marriott Kaua'i at Waipouli Beach – plans are set for almost 550 condo units and 1000 parking stalls.

Information

There are ATMs inside Foodland supermarket in Waipouli Town Center and, just a minute north, inside Safeway in Kaua'i Village. Both are located on the *mauka* (inland) side of Kuhio Hwy.

When driving along Kuhio Hwy, stay in the right lane if you plan to drive past all the shopping centers. Otherwise you'll find yourself in a turn-only lane into a center – and during the rush hour it can take 10 minutes just to flee the parking lot.

ComputerWeb (☎ 821-0077; www.computerweb.us; Kaua'i Village, 4-831 Kuhio Hwy; per 10min $2; ☯ 9am-9pm Mon-Sat) One-stop shop for Internet access, photocopies, faxes, CDs, video games and computer repairs. Interior is bare-bones basic, but staff is helpful and parking is easy.

Longs Drugs (☎ 822-4915; Kaua'i Village; ☯ store 7am-10pm Mon-Sat, 8am-8pm Sun, pharmacy 8am-9pm Mon-Sat, 9am-6pm Sun) Pharmacy and over-the-counter drugs, plus excellent prices on household products, beach supplies, grocery items and souvenirs.

Sights

On clear days you can see the outline of the **Nounou Mountain** (known as the Sleeping Giant) atop Nounou Ridge from a marked viewpoint just north of the Waipouli Complex. According to legend, the amicable giant fell asleep on the hillside after gorging on poi at a luau. When his *menehune* friends needed his help, they tried to rouse him by throwing stones. But the stones bounced from the giant's full belly into his open mouth. The stones lodged in the giant's throat, he died in his sleep and turned into rock. Now he rests, stretched out on the ridge with his head in Wailua and his feet in Kapa'a. At an elevation of almost 1250ft, the giant's forehead is the highest point on the ridge.

Poke around in Kaua'i Village, Waipouli's largest shopping center, and you'll find the **Kaua'i Heritage Center** (☎ 821-2070; admission free;

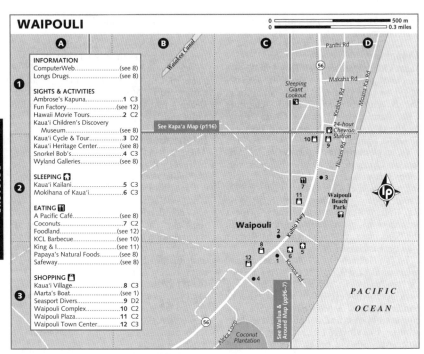

WAIPOULI

INFORMATION
ComputerWeb.......................(see 8)
Longs Drugs.........................(see 8)

SIGHTS & ACTIVITIES
Ambrose's Kapuna....................1 C3
Fun Factory..........................(see 12)
Hawaii Movie Tours...................2 C2
Kaua'i Children's Discovery
    Museum.........................(see 8)
Kaua'i Cycle & Tour..................3 D2
Kaua'i Heritage Center..............(see 8)
Snorkel Bob's.........................4 C3
Wyland Galleries....................(see 8)

SLEEPING
Kaua'i Kailani.........................5 C3
Mokihana of Kaua'i..................6 C3

EATING
A Pacific Café......................(see 8)
Coconuts.............................7 C2
Foodland.............................(see 12)
KCL Barbecue........................(see 10)
King & I.............................(see 11)
Papaya's Natural Foods...........(see 8)
Safeway..............................(see 8)

SHOPPING
Kaua'i Village........................8 C3
Marta's Boat.........................(see 1)
Seasport Divers......................9 D2
Waipouli Complex..................10 C2
Waipouli Plaza.......................11 C2
Waipouli Town Center.............12 C3

9am-5pm Mon-Sat), which displays hand-made wood carvings, feather leis, bamboo nose flutes and other traditional Hawaiian crafts. One-day workshops ($25, reservations required) in hula, lei making and chanting are offered.

On rainy days, head to the nonprofit **Kaua'i Children's Discovery Museum** (☎ 823-8222; www.kcdm.org; Kaua'i Village; adult/child $5/4; 9am-5pm Tue-Sat), an indoor playground for the elementary set. The kid-size replicas of ethnic abodes – Filipino, Japanese and South Indian – along with a 'tree house' are sure to please. The black-light tunnel (which turns ghastly fluorescent anything white) and volcano slide are pure fun. All the modules emphasize learning about science, culture, arts, technology and nature – particularly regarding Hawaii. The museum also offers a day camp (all day $50, per hour $10) for kids in kindergarten to fourth grade, and a well-stocked gift shop with educational toys.

Also in Kaua'i Village is another location of the ubiquitous **Wyland Galleries** (☎ 822-9855; www.wyland.com; Kaua'i Village, 4-831 Kuhio Hwy;

9am-9pm Mon-Sat, 10am-8pm Sun), with over 30 locations, mostly in the US. Wyland (known only by first name, like Madonna and Cher) is famous for his luminous underwater seascapes that by now are either iconic or clichéd. His 'Whaling Wall' murals are indeed breathtaking, however, and since he painted the original in Laguna Beach, his work graces cities including Vancouver, New York, Sydney and Honolulu. He plans to stop at 100 murals worldwide, and at the time of research he had done 91.

Another rainy-day option is **Fun Factory** (Waipouli Town Center; games 50¢-$1; 10am-10pm, to midnight Fri & Sat), with loads of video games, rides and games of skill.

Activities
For hiking trails nearby (with access from Wailua or Kapa'a), see p103.

Kaua'i Cycle & Tour (☎ 821-2115; www.bikehawaii.com/kauaicycle; 4-934 Kuhio Hwy, Waipouli; 18-speed cruiser per day/week $15/75, quality mountain bike with front suspension $20/95, full suspension $35/150; 9am-6pm Mon-Fri, to 4pm Sat) rents bikes maintained by experienced cyclists. Also sells and services bikes.

SNORKELING

The cool thing about **Snorkel Bob's** (☎ 823-9433; www.snorkelbob.com; 4-734 Kuhio Hwy; basic snorkel sets per day/week $2.50/9, good ones $8/32, boogie boards $6.50/26; ⏰ 8am-5pm Mon-Sat), if you're island-hopping: you can rent gear on Kaua'i and return it on the Big Island, O'ahu or Maui.

SURFING

Submit to Kaua'i's surfing Svengali at **Ambrose's Kapuna** (☎ 822-3926; ambrose.curry@verizon .net; 770 Kuhio Hwy; lessons per hr $25), where your mind and body will be coached in the ways of the wave by surf guru Ambrose Curry; lessons 'for the obtuse' are given in waters he has been riding since 1968. Post-lesson you can buy a board shaped by Curry or take home a piece of his art.

Also teaching newbies is the **Wailua Bay Surf Company** (☎ 823-1129, 645-1067; 5111 Nounou Rd; 2hr lesson $45).

Tours

In air-conditioned 'theaters on wheels,' movie buffs can cruise the island with **Hawaii Movie Tours** (☎ 822-1192, 800-628-8432; www .hawaiimovietour.com; 4-885 Kuhio Highway; adult/child under 12 from $111/92; ⏰ office 7:30am-6pm), viewing famous film clips on a video monitor – and the actual filming site right outside the window! The standard land tour is fine, but it's worth paying extra for the 4WD option (adult/child aged five to 11 $123/113), an adventurous eco-tour that takes you off-road to the base of Mt Wai'ale'alea (Jurassic Park territory) and includes lunch at Lydgate Beach Park. Both tours include a look at the private Coco Palms property, where you can pay homage

---

BIG-SCREEN KAUA'I

Hollywood has tapped Kaua'i over 75 times when looking for fantasy film and TV locations. Keep your eyes peeled for these famous settings:

- *South Pacific* (1957): the North Shore's Lumaha'i Beach, with Makana mountain in the background, became an icon.
- *Blue Hawaii* (1961): Elvis remains omnipresent at Wailua's Coco Palms Resort.
- *Donovan's Reef* (1963): the Nawiliwili Harbor area, including the original Kaua'i Inn, were backdrops for Lee Marvin and John Wayne.
- *Gilligan's Island* pilot (1963): Moloa'a Bay was the pilot site for the shipwrecked SS *Minnow*.
- *King Kong* (1976): remote Honopu Valley on the Na Pali Coast was the giant gorilla's island home.
- *Fantasy Island* (1978–84): the waterfall shown during this TV series' opening credits is Kaua'i's own Wailua Falls.
- *Raiders of the Lost Ark* (1981): rugged landscapes near Hule'ia Stream outside Lihu'e and Kalaleo Mountain north of Anahola stood in for South American jungles.
- *The Thorn Birds* (1983): old Hanapepe town became Queenland, Australia, in the Richard Chamberlain TV mini-saga.
- *Honeymoon in Vegas* (1992): Lihu'e sites including the airport, police station and hospital make an appearance along with Nicholas Cage; the manager of Hanalei Inn stars in a bit part as an airline pilot.
- *Jurassic Park* (1993): Hanapepe and Lawa'i Valleys became the valley of the dinosaurs for Steven Spielberg's *Jurassic Park*; all three films in the series were partly filmed on the Garden Isle.

Film buffs can indulge their big-screen fascination with *The Kaua'i Movie Book* by Chris Cook.

You might also see a celebrity in person here, as the following big names own homes on the island: Kareem Abdul-Jabar, Ben Stiller, Pierce Brosnan, Michael Crichton, Bette Midler, Graham Nash and Matt Le Blanc.

to Elvis. Tours provide transport to and from most Eastside and South Shore hotels. While the tour revolves around movie locations, it's actually Kaua'i's best, all-around passenger tour. The company, which began as almost a whim, has expanded to create similar tours in Monterey, Boston and San Francisco.

Sleeping

Accommodations are scarce in Waipouli, but luckily it's sandwiched by Wailua (p106) and Kapa'a (p118), where much better options can be found. **Hawaii Kailani** (☎ 360-676-1434; www.hawaii-kailani.com/index.php; 1201 11th St, Bellingham, Suite 100, WA 98225) manages the following two value Waipouli condos that can be really good or really bad, depending on the unit. Since they're managed from afar, the on-site staff tends to be impersonal. The lobby area is depressingly barren.

Mokihana of Kaua'i (☎ 822-3971; 796 Kuhio Hwy; studio units $72; 🐾) Comprises 80 oceanfront studios that can be excellent bargains, especially in the low season, when rates drop dramatically. Each unit has a kitchen and lanai, plus room to roam. Don't book units ending in 12 or 14, as you'll abut the laundry room. Ground-floor units are wheelchair-accessible.

Kaua'i Kailani (2-bedroom units $72-85) The nearby sister property has 57 units handled by the front desk at Mokihana of Kaua'i. These condos have fully equipped kitchens, two twin beds in one room and a queen bed in the other; rates are good for up to four people, and the same sublet list mentioned above advertises rentals here.

Eating

BUDGET

Papaya's Natural Foods (☎ 823-0190; Kaua'i Village, 4-831 Kuhio Hwy; dishes $5-8, salad per lb $7; 🕑 9am-8pm Mon-Sat, deli to 7pm Mon-Sat) Seeking health foods? Easy. Just follow folks in dreadlocks (especially if blond), lived-in tees or flowing yoga bell-bottoms. Chances are you'll end up at Papaya's, Kaua'i's biggest and best health-food store. Along with bulk items, vitamins and supplements, herbal mosquito repellent (Longs is cheaper), organic produce (very expensive) and bottled water (the Arrowhead jugs are a bargain), you can also chow down on tasty tofu or salad-bar fixings. The convenient courtyard tables attract your typical neighborhood hippie. Papaya's opened a Hanalei store in late 2005.

KCL Barbecue (☎ 823-8168; Waipouli Complex, 4-971 Kuhio Hwy; dishes $4-8; 🕑 10am-10pm) For a meal on the run, this hole-in-the-wall serves perhaps 100 different Chinese, Japanese and Korean dishes. The Korean food is rather greasy, so your best bets are the chicken or pork *katsu* (fried cutlets) or a Chinese standby.

King & I (☎ 822-1642; Waipouli Plaza, 4-901 Kuhio Hwy; mains $7-11; 🕑 4:30-9:30pm) This friendly, family-run restaurant sets the Kaua'ian standard for Thai food with a lengthy menu featuring goodies such as curries popping with kaffir lime and lemongrass, fiery or not, as you like. Vegetarians will find loads of options, like flavorful eggplant and tofu in chili oil or a mound of traditional pad Thai with tofu.

Of the two supermarkets in Waipouli, chain giant **Safeway** (☎ 822-2464; Kaua'i Village, 4-831 Kuhio Hwy; 🕑 24hr) is clearly the tourist choice. Well-stocked, with a deli counter, bakery and fish counter, it caters to mainland-haole tastes. In the same mall is Papaya's Natural Foods for organic produce and Longs Drugs for staples and an impressive, bulk health-food aisle. Another option is local chain supermarket **Foodland** (Waipouli Town Center; 🕑 6am-11pm).

MIDRANGE & TOP END

In case you're wondering, Jean-Marie Josselin's well-renowned A Pacific Café closed abruptly in 2005, after garnering rave reviews since its opening in 1989. At the time of research, it was slated to eventually reopen. Josselin helped put Hawaiian Regional Cuisine on the gourmet radar and he owns a restaurant at Caesar's Palace in Las Vegas.

Coconuts (☎ 823-8777; 4-919 Kuhio Hwy; mains $14-21; 🕑 4-10pm Mon-Sat) With a kitschy facade and the name Coconuts, discriminating diners might bypass this place. Don't make that mistake. Coconuts cranks out consistent, island-influenced food at prices that, while rather steep for locals, won't faze urban mainlanders. Seafood 'cigars' (wrapped rolls) are ubiquitous on Kaua'i but Coconuts' version, with shrimp and *ono* (wahoo), drizzled with teriyaki sauce and accompanied by fresh pineapple-chili chutney, will please those who prefer pungent flavors. Go with an appetite, as portions reflect the local penchant for hearty eating.

Shopping

Waipouli's two main shopping malls are Waipouli Town Center and Kaua'i Village. They cater primarily to basic needs rather than pleasure sprees. But Kaua'i Village in particular is a good, all-purpose stop for supplies, groceries and business services.

Marta's Boat (☎ 822-3926; www.martasboat.com; 770 Kuhio Hwy; ⏲ 10am-6pm Mon-Sat) Whimsical Marta's has soft and sexy threads from the Paris, LA and New York crops. Distinctive lingerie and frocks shine, but jewelry and excruciatingly cute little-girl clothes also enchant. No bargains here, folks.

KAPA'A

pop 9472

It's hard to find a lively, pedestrian-friendly commercial strip within Kaua'i's dozens of rural neighborhoods. You typically find modern malls or 'planned' old-towns. But Kapa'a is a charming authentic community, albeit a tiny one – populated by old timers, nouveau hippies and tourists.

Historically Kapa'a was a plantation town, but the last sugar mill closed in the 1940s, and the last pineapple plant in the early 1960s. But since the 1970s, tourism has mushroomed with new development of condos, hotels, restaurants and shops.

On the inland side of Kuhio Hwy is the island's largest residential population and a public high school that serves the entire North Shore. In Kapa'a's mini 'downtown,' you'll find a New Age vibe, with a marked concentration of organic/vegan/raw cuisine, plus a Hare Krishna devotee who chants and dances along the sidewalk by herself daily. Budget travelers will find value-priced lodging in residents' homes here.

But Kapa'a traffic is a nightmare. During commute hours, cars literally crawl along Kuhio Hwy in both directions. If you're traveling between the north end of Kapa'a to Wailua or beyond, by all means take the Kapa'a By-Pass Rd. Here, you will definitely need a car; walking outside the main commercial strip, even to the closest supermarket, is far from pleasant.

Information

INTERNET ACCESS

Akamai Computer Technologies (☎ 823-0047; www.akamaicomputers.com; 4-1286-A Kuhio Hwy; per 10min $2; ⏲ 9am-4pm Mon-Thu, 9am-noon Fri) This es-tablished outfit offers Internet access and computer repairs (per hour $65). Park in the Ono Family Restaurant lot.

Business Support Services (☎ 822-5504; fax 822-2148; 4-1191 Kuhio Hwy; per hr $10; ⏲ 8am-6pm Mon-Sat, 10am-6pm Sun) No atmosphere but cheap Internet access, plus fax, copies and stamps.

Java Kai (☎ 823-6887; 4-1384 Kuhio Hwy; wi-fi per 15/120min $3/12; ⏲ 6am-5pm) Pleasantly low-key café, but wi-fi only.

LAUNDRY

Kapa'a Laundry Center (☎ 822-3113; Kapa'a Shopping Center, 4-1105 Kuhio Hwy; ⏲ 7:30am-9:30pm, last wash 8pm) Cramped and lacking wheeled carts, but featuring lively piped-in island tunes.

MEDICAL SERVICES

Samuel Mahelona Memorial Hospital (☎ 822-4961; fax 823-4100; 4800 Kawaihau Rd) Primarily a long-term-care facility, this longstanding hospital expanded services to include basic emergency care in late 2005. Serious cases are transferred to Lihu'e's Wilcox Memorial Hospital.

MONEY

First Hawaiian Bank (☎ 822-4966; 4-1366 Kuhio Hwy) 24-hour ATM.

POST

Post office (☎ 800-275-8777; Kapa'a Shopping Center, 4-1101 Kuhio Hwy; ⏲ 8am-4pm Mon-Fri, 9am-2pm Sat)

Sights

KAPA'A BEACH PARK

Low-key and local, this county beach park is a mile-long ribbon of beach beginning at Kapa'a's north end, where there's a ball field, picnic tables and a public pool. At the south end of the beach, near Pono Kai Resort, there's a nice sandy area.

A pretty, shoreline **foot-and-bicycle path** runs the length of the beach park, crossing over a couple of old bridges where families and old-timers drop fishing lines. The path makes an appealing alternative to walking along the highway to and from town.

HAWAIIAN ART MUSEUM

This **museum** (☎ 823-8381; www.huna.org; Dragon Bldg, 4504 Kukui St, Suite 11; ⏲ by appointment) contains the personal collection of Serge Kahili King, the founder of Aloha International and a renowned *huna* (ancient Hawaiian world view and healing process using the

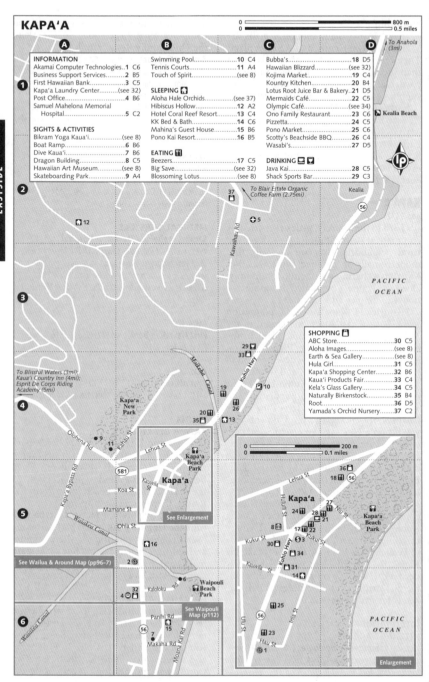

KAPA'A

0 ——————— 800 m
0 ——————— 0.5 miles

INFORMATION
Akamai Computer Technologies..**1** C6
Business Support Services..........**2** B5
First Hawaiian Bank..................**3** C5
Kapa'a Laundry Center.........(see 32)
Post Office..............................**4** B6
Samuel Mahelona Memorial
    Hospital..........................**5** C2

SIGHTS & ACTIVITIES
Bikram Yoga Kaua'i.................(see 8)
Boat Ramp...............................**6** B6
Dive Kaua'i..............................**7** B6
Dragon Building.......................**8** C5
Hawaiian Art Museum.............(see 8)
Skateboarding Park..................**9** A4

Swimming Pool........................**10** C4
Tennis Courts...........................**11** A4
Touch of Spirit........................(see 8)

SLEEPING
Aloha Hale Orchids...............(see 37)
Hibiscus Hollow......................**12** A2
Hotel Coral Reef Resort...........**13** C4
KK Bed & Bath.........................**14** C6
Mahina's Guest House.............**15** B6
Pono Kai Resort.......................**16** B5

EATING
Beezers...................................**17** C5
Big Save.................................(see 32)
Blossoming Lotus....................(see 8)

Bubba's....................................**18** D5
Hawaiian Blizzard...................(see 32)
Kojima Market..........................**19** C4
Kountry Kitchen........................**20** B4
Lotus Root Juice Bar & Bakery..**21** D5
Mermaids Café.........................**22** C5
Olympic Café..........................(see 34)
Ono Family Restaurant.............**23** C6
Pizzetta...................................**24** C5
Pono Market.............................**25** C6
Scotty's Beachside BBQ............**26** C4
Wasabi's..................................**27** D5

DRINKING
Java Kai...................................**28** C5
Shack Sports Bar......................**29** C3

SHOPPING
ABC Store.................................**30** C5
Aloha Images.........................(see 8)
Earth & Sea Gallery................(see 8)
Hula Girl..................................**31** C5
Kapa'a Shopping Center...........**32** B6
Kaua'i Products Fair..................**33** C4
Kela's Glass Gallery.................**34** C6
Naturally Birkenstock...............**35** B4
Root...**36** D5
Yamada's Orchid Nursery........**37** C2

To Anahola
(3mi)

Kealia Beach

To Blair Estate Organic
Coffee Farm (2.75mi)

Kealia

*PACIFIC
OCEAN*

To Blissful Waters (3mi);
Kaua'i Country Inn (4mi);
Esprit De Corps Riding
Academy (5mi)

Kapa'a
New
Park

Olohena Rd

Kapa'a Bypass Rd

Kahau Ldg

Lehua St

Koa St

Kapa'a
Beach
Park

Kauwila St

Kapa'a

Mamane St

Waiakea Canal

Ohia St

See Enlargement

See Wailua & Around Map (pp96–7)

Kaloloku Rd

Waipouli
Beach
Park

See Waipouli
Map (p112)

Waiakea Canal

Panihi Rd

Moana Kai Rd

Makaha Rd

Kawaihau Rd

Moikeha Canal

Kuhio Hwy

0 ——————— 200 m
0 ——————— 0.1 miles

Lehua St

Kapa'a

Hulili St

Niu St

Kapa'a
Beach
Park

Kukui St

Kukui St

Kuhio Hwy

Kauwila St

Niu St

Iila St

Hau St

*PACIFIC
OCEAN*

Enlargement

mind, body and spirit) healer. While the museum (strong on Hawaiiana) can be visited only by appointment, there are free **talk story sessions** at 5pm on Wednesday that focus on Hawaiian culture, as well as hula classes and *huna* healing circles. Visit the website for current offerings.

Activities

Kapa'a is another hotbed for renting sports equipment, especially for **kayaking** the Wailua River (p100) and for arranging scuba dives.

There are free **tennis courts** and a **skateboarding park**, along with a field for baseball, football and soccer in Kapa'a New Park, and a public **swimming pool** (☎ 822-3842; admission free; ⏲ 10am-4:30pm Thu-Mon) at Kapa'a County Beach Park.

DIVING

No, there's no good diving off Kapa'a's coast, but there are good outfits. From here, you must then head to the North Shore or South Shore.

Ocean Quest Watersports (☎ 742-6991, 800-972-3078; www.fathomfive.com) This satellite location of the superlative Fathom Five (p163) outfit in Koloa is geared for the excellent North Shore dive at Tunnels reef.

Seasport Divers (Map p112; ☎ 823-9222, 800-685-5889; www.seasportdivers.com; 4-976 Kuhio Hwy) Rents gear, leads dives, including to Ni'ihau, and offers certification courses. Snorkel gear is available. Its main location is in Po'ipu (p171).

Dive Kaua'i (☎ 822-0452, 800-828-3483; www.dive kauai.com; 1038 Kuhio Hwy; ⏲ 8am-5:30pm Mon-Sat, 9am-3pm Sun) Go here only as Plan B.

FISHING

Setting out from the small boat ramp at the end of Kaloloku Rd, off Kuhio Hwy, is gregarious **Hawaiian Style Fishing** (☎ 635-7335; half-day charter per person $100), which works out of a locally built, owned and operated boat.

CYCLING

A smooth 6-mile coastal pedal starts in Kapa'a, running along Kealia Beach and on to Anahola (p122), before turning into a rough single track for another 9 miles. The jarringly bumpy ride is truly off-road, on gravel and dirt, through overgrown grass and bushes. The pristine shoreline is spectacular, however.

BODYWORK & YOGA

For a mind and body experience, try **Touch of Spirit** (☎ 823-6144; Dragon Bldg, 4504 Kukui St, Suite 8; massage per hr $35-95, body wraps $65-95; ⏲ 10am-5pm Mon-Fri). Hot-rock massage, reflexology, facials, herbal body wraps, waxing, reiki, and tarot and psychic readings ($35) are all offered.

Also in the building is **Bikram Yoga Kaua'i** (☎ 822-5053; www.bikramyogaretreats.com; Dragon Bldg, 4504 Kukui St, Suite 10; drop-in class $15). Ideal for followers of Bikram yoga, especially the classes taught by studio director Judy Louie, a certifed Bikram teacher.

HORSEBACK RIDING

More than just a tour outfit, **Esprit De Corps Riding Academy** (☎ 822-4688; www.kauaihorses.com; Kualapa Pl; ⏲ tours Mon-Fri) offers all levels of training, summer day-camps for all ages, 'pony parties,' and weddings on horseback. The basic tour (three-hour tour including tax $112) teaches stopping, turning and trotting the horse before venturing into the pastureland above Kapa'a. Experienced riders can choose more advanced tours that allow cantering (four-/six-hour tour including tax $148/216). Groups are limited just to five; minimum age is 10. Owner, guide and instructor Dale Rosenfeld is certified by the American Riding Instructors Certification Program and has studied with big names such as Linda Tellington-Jones.

Tours

A good introduction to Kapa'a, the **Kapa'a Town Walking Tour** (☎ 245-3373; khs@hawaiilink.net; adult/child $15/5; ⏲ 10am & 4pm Tue, Thu & Sat) is led by knowledgeable local guides. In about 90 minutes, guides point out landmarks, describe Kapa'a's sugar and pineapple boom days and, best of all, talk story and answer questions. Tours start at Pono Kai Resort (which was once a pineapple cannery), one block south of town. Advance reservations are required.

Blair Estate Organic Coffee Farm (☎ 822-4495, 800-750-5662; www.blairestatecoffee.com, 6200-B Kawaihau Rd; 1hr tour free; ⏲ 9am Mon, Wed & Sat by appointment only) is Kaua'i's only organic coffee farm. Established in 2001, this husband-and-wife operation is a labor of love for founder Leslie Blair Trent (just call him Les), who initiated his coffee career in the early 1990s, roasting coffee on the famed

Kona Coast. Back then he also launched an online coffee business (www.coffeetimes .com) and free publication, *Coffee Times*, which continue to thrive today. The free one-hour tour includes coffee cupping (tasting) of Kona, Kaua'i and other varieties. No unannounced visits, as this is a small working farm.

Festivals & Events

Heiva I Kaua'i Iaorana Tahiti (☎ 245-5010) Dance troupes from as far as Tahiti, Japan and Canada join groups from Hawaii in this Tahitian dance competition in early August at the Kapa'a Ball Park; drumming contests, too.

Coconut Festival (☎ 651-3273; www.kbakauai.org; admission adult/child/teen $5/free/2) Two-day homage in early October to all things coconut! Events include coconut-pie-eating contests, coconut cook-off, coconut-tree-climbing show, cooking demonstrations, coconut-milk bar, music, hula and crafts. Lots of *keiki* (children's) activities, from pony rides to coloring contests to Kaua'i's favorite TV mascot, Russell the Rooster.

Sleeping
BUDGET

KK Bed & Bath (☎ 822-7348, 800-615-6211 ext 32; www.kkbedbath.com; s/d/tr $40/50/60) Smack in the heart of Kapa'a, this studio is perfect for the no-frills traveler. It's spotless and refreshingly minimalist, and the converted storehouse building adds a historic touch. In your 300-sq-ft room, you get a firm bed, spacious bathroom, cable TV, microwave and mini fridge. Multiple windows and ceiling fans keep you cool. Although the location just off Kuhio Hwy can be noisy, businesses close by 9pm. Owner Richard Sugiyama, who lives in the adjacent house, is a local lay historian who turns the studio into 'home.' Three-night minimum.

Aloha Hale Orchids (☎ 822-4148; www.yamada nursery.com; r $50, cottages $80) Tucked away in a working orchid nursery sit two amazing lodging deals. Single travelers can bunk in the compact but cheerful studio, with queen bed, mini refrigerator, TV and sparkling-white tile floor. For more space and privacy, the detached cottage adds separate bedroom, full kitchen, TV, lots of windows, washer and clothesline. Amidst orchid greenhouses in a quiet residential neighborhood, the immaculate rooms are 'just like home.'

Hibiscus Hollow (☎ 823-9004; www.akauaivaca tionrental.com; d/tr/q incl tax $60/65/70) Close your eyes and picture a one-bedroom suite that a surfer buddy might offer you: clean and comfy, if slightly lived-in, with island-style rattan furnishings and colorful mobiles dangling from an open-beam ceiling. If such a mental image makes you smile, you're sure to appreciate the bargain offered by long-time Kaua'i residents Greg and Sue Liddle. The suite includes a handy kitchenette, TV/VCR, phone and lanai.

Mahina's Guest House (☎ 823-9364; www.mahi nas.com; 4433 Panihi Rd; s with shared bathroom $65-95, d with shared bathroom $75-110) In a four-bedroom house near the beach, women travelers can find welcoming, communal lodging with a 'female empowerment' vibe. Rooms are spacious, with hardwood floors, double or queen bed, lots of closet space and sunrise views. Guests share kitchen, bathroom, dining and living room, telephone, stereo and washer/dryer. Ideal for women who want to meet others.

Blissful Waters (☎ 822-5216; www.rosewoodkauai .com; 6393 Waipouli Rd; r $85) Four miles above Kapa'a town, past sleepy pastures, along a

---

THE AUTHOR'S CHOICE

Kaua'i Country Inn (☎ 821-0207; www.kauaicountryinn.com; 6440 Olohena Rd; ste $95-145, 3-bedroom cottages from $225; 🖳) Pastoral setting. Spacious suites. Convenient kitchenettes. Private Beatles museum. Huh? No joke! This classy inn can't be beat in aesthetics, amenities or mod eccentricity. The four suites all have either kitchen or kitchenette, TV/DVD (and over 1500 DVDs available to rent), in-suite Macintosh computers with high-speed Internet access and wi-fi throughout the property. The palatial 1200 sq ft Green Rose suite ($145) is spectacular, with an open-beam, vaulted 18ft ceiling, knotty pine walls, full modern kitchen, funky genuine jukebox stools and expansive 300 sq ft deck. Guests are invited to view an astounding array of Beatles memorabilia, including a 1967 Mini Cooper S car originally owned by Beatles manager Brian Epstein. The British/German hosts are friendly, articulate and technically savvy. No children under 12 in suites; but all ages welcome in the cottage.

bumpy dirt road, what do you find? A classily appointed room in a modern, two-story home. On the ground floor, it includes private entrance, small refrigerator and privileges to use the rest of the elegant house, including kitchen, living room and sleek swimming pool. If you need extra space, inquire about the upstairs room ($70) with two twin beds.

MIDRANGE
Hotel Coral Reef Resort (☎ 822-4481, 800-843-4659; www.hotelcoralreefresort.com; 1516 Kuhio Hwy; r $99-159) While the oceanfront location at the north end of Kapa'a is excellent, the rooms are plain and small. They do include the expected amenities, including phone, cable TV, refrigerator and free parking. Those in the seaside building are better than those in the main building. But the hotel was undergoing renovation during the time of research, and plans included a beachside pool and upscale restaurant. Rates are based on double occupancy, and additional guests cost a steep $25 per person.

Pono Kai Resort (☎ 822-9831, 800-456-0009; www.ponokai.com; 4-1250 Kuhio Hwy; r $79-99, 1-/2-bedroom units from $135/150; 🏊 🎾) While the 240-unit Pono Kai Restort's timeshares are consistent in quality, the 30 to 35 condo vacation rentals are a mixed bag. Thus, it's recommended mainly for the convenient location within walking distance of town. One- and two-bedroom units are quite spacious and include full kitchen, living room with queen sofa bed, cable TV and lanai. There are tennis courts and a decent swath of beach.

Eating
No one goes hungry in Kapa'a, where excellent edibles range from vegan and 'live' (raw) to local-favorite plate lunches and Spam *musubi*. Thus it's perplexing why tourists clamor for a window table and so-so hamburgers from Bubba's. Sure, it's better fast food than McDonald's but isn't the tourist-only queue a tip-off?

BUDGET
Beezers (☎ 822-4411; 4-1380 Kuhio Hwy; items $3-8; 🕙 11am-10pm) If you miss the days of ice-cream parlors (when did they become 'old-fashioned' anyway?), revel in the nostalgia at Beezers. Here you'll find banana splits, malted milkshakes and ice-cream sundaes amid quaint 1960s decor. Sundaes bear names like Peppermint Twist and Mustang Sally, and the entire menu – hot dogs, sloppy joe's and root-beer floats – is a blast from the past. The ice cream is Dreyer's, not super-premium Lappert's, so you're paying for the preparation. A plain ol' single-scoop cone will set you back $3.25.

Bubba's (☎ 823-0069; www.bubbaburger.com; 4-1421 Kuhio Hwy; burgers $3-5; 🕙 10:30am-8pm) You're bound to notice the constant throng of mainland tourists chomping from window seats facing the highway. Sure, Bubba's is a local chain, and their 100% Kaua'i beef burgers are fine. Sure, we appreciate their concession to vegetarians, ginger-teriyaki tempeh burgers. But *puh-leeze* follow the 'When in Rome' maxim and try a local-favorite hangout instead!

Kountry Kitchen (☎ 822-3511; 1485 Kuhio Hwy; meals $4-8; 🕙 6am-2pm) An excellent down-home diner, Kountry Kitchen lets you tailor your meal: Build your own light and crepelike omelette (from $5.25) from a variety of fillings. Choose either one, two or three pancakes ($3 to $5.75), either banana, strawberry or chocolate-chip. Add a luscious tropical fruit salad of papaya, banana, pineapple and orange to your meal for $5.75. The staff make you feel like *'ohana* (family). Breakfast served all day, lunch from 11am.

Ono Family Restaurant (☎ 822-1710; 4-1292 Kuhio Hwy; breakfast mains $7-8.50, burgers & sandwiches $4.50-8.25; 🕙 7am-1:30pm) Kaua'i's old-time diners take seriously their omelettes and pancakes – and you can taste the results at Ono's, a fixture in Kapa'a. Choose from 18 types of omelettes or opt for the incomparable tropical pancakes ($6 to $8) with bananas, macadamia nuts and coconut in batter on top – and 'Aunty Ono's' special coconut syrup, served warm. Ideal for vegetarians craving eggs benedict is the 'eggs veggie,' with two poached eggs, fresh steamed veggies and hollandaise sauce atop an English muffin, plus half a papaya.

Pono Market (☎ 822-4581; 4-1300 Kuhio Hwy; plate lunch $6; 🕙 7am-7pm Mon-Fri, 7am-6pm Sun) Looks can be deceiving. Case in point: Pono Market, a bodega-type hole-in-the-wall. But inspect the deli counter and menu of generous plate lunches and deliciously fresh sushi rolls. Locals head here to nosh on *kalua* pig (pig cooked in an underground pit) with poi or to grab a *musubi* (rice ball) or sushi, packaged and ready for a picnic. Teriyaki chicken, *lomilomi* salmon, *poke* (cubed, marinated raw fish) and abalone or scallop salad ($10.99 per pound) are homemade and worth every penny. (Tip: see p66 for definitions of local eats.)

Lotus Root Juice Bar & Bakery (☎ 823-6658; www.blossominglotus.com; 4-1384 Kuhio Hwy; cookies & scones $2.50-3; ☽ 7am-6pm) For healthful and delicious vegan treats, stop at this bar and bakery run by the Blossoming Lotus folks. You're unlikely to find coconut-lavender cookies, spirulina popcorn or *'awa* (kava) brownies (don't worry, they're legal) anywhere else.

Kojima Market (☎ 822-5221; 4-1543 Kuhio Hwy; ☽ 8am-7pm Mon-Fri, to 6pm Sat, to 1pm Sun) At the north end of town, this market seems small and basic but carries an excellent selection of island-raised meat.

Big Save (☎ 822-4971; Kapa'a Shopping Center; ☽ 7am-11pm) One of Kapa'a's two supermarkets; sells *'ahi* and smoked salmon *poke* for well under $10 per pound.

MIDRANGE

Wasabi's (☎ 822-2700; 4-1388 Kuhio Hwy; sushi rolls $3.50-13, mains $8-18; ☽ 11am-9pm) Can sushi be an expression of creativity? Yes, if you try the house specialties like Lollypop Roll with paper-thin cucumber hugging succulent *hamachi* (yellowtail), *maguro* (tuna) and salmon ($12). With marine-blue walls, well-worn furniture and funky 'under the sea' decor, Wasabi's has just enough grime

for a boho-urban vibe – but not enough to produce the yuck factor. Herbivores can enjoy Tempura Garden Roll wrapped in nori or tofu skin ($9), but clearly this is a place for fish eaters.

Blossoming Lotus (☎ 822-7678; www.blossoming lotus.com; Dragon Bldg, 4504 Kukui St; mains $7-14; ☽ 11am-3pm & 6-9:30pm) The 'vegan world fusion cuisine' served here (sans meat, dairy, eggs or even honey) is both innovative and healthy. But quality is mixed. The lunchtime wraps and sandwiches are fine, showcasing such astounding creations as grilled coconut meat, BBQ tempeh, purple Okinawan-potato salad and live (uncooked) paté du jour. But Pele's Soba Sensation is heavy-handed with the sauce and lacking in vegetables. The overly enormous dinner mains are best shared, family style, for a varied meal. (After all, how much soba noodles can one person consume?) Open only since 2003, Blossoming Lotus already has a gorgeous cookbook, available at the restaurant, at local shops and at www.veganfusion.com.

Scotty's Beachside BBQ (☎ 823-8480; 4-1546 Kuhio Hwy; sandwiches $6-10, mains $11-24; ☽ 11am-9pm Mon-Sat, 10am-8pm Sun) On Kaua'i, barbecued meat is 'marinated in shoyu sauce and grilled.' For the authentic *smoked* stuff, the only option is Scotty's, where they smoke pork, beef and chicken for up to 15 hours. Succulent St Louis–style ribs (half/full rack $16/24) are rubbed with spices and smoked for four hours, then served with your choice of Scotty's secret BBQ sauces, coleslaw, cornbread or garlic bread. Loosen the belt even more with desserts from deep-fried cheesecake to chocolate coma cake.

RAINBOW IN A CUP

On sweltering days, nothing hits the spot like shave ice. This icy island treat might resemble a mainland snow cone but try it and you'll instantly taste the difference. The ice is not crushed but actually shaved by a sharp rotating blade, and the colorful syrups feature the gamut of flavors, from classic strawberry to local-favorite *li hing mui* (crack-seed flavor). Purists can order 'plain' shave ice, but try ice cream or sweet azuki-bean paste underneath for added pleasure.

Shave ice is sold across the island, but it's always best when made by a specialized seller who focuses on the 'art' of shave ice. Eateries that make shave ice on the side usually fail to keep their machine blade sharp, leading to grittier ice. Also beware of overcharging: a small plain should never cost over $2.

For Kaua'i's best shave ice, head to **Hawaiian Blizzard** (☽ noon-5pm Mon-Fri), the white van parked outside Big Save. Owner Aaron Furugen is the low-key guru of shave ice, perfecting the art since the 1980s. He concocts his own syrups – and while some vendors offer 50-plus flavors, Aaron focuses on perhaps a dozen that meet his standards.

THE AUTHOR'S CHOICE

Mermaids Café (☎ 821-2026; 4-1384 Kuhio Hwy; mains $9; ⏱ 11am-9pm) Plate lunches for the hippie-granola set? You bet. And we guarantee you'll be tempted to try everything on the menu, from the classic seared 'ahi and nori wrap to overflowing plates of coconut curry topping veggies, tofu or chicken. The herbs and seasonings are sublimely simple, letting the cornucopia of fresh ingredients speak for itself. Quench your thirst with homemade lemonade or spearmint iced tea, find a seat outside and while away a lazy afternoon. Such scrumptious healthful cuisine will surely convert the worst of junk-food junkies.

Family packs ($54 to $79) serve from four to 10. The only consolation for noncarnivores is a garden burger ($8).

Olympic Café (☎ 822-5825; 4-1354 Kuhio Hwy; breakfast & lunch mains $8-14, dinner mains $12-24; ⏱ 6am-9pm Sun-Thu, to 10pm Fri & Sat) If you need to satisfy eclectic tastebuds and appetites, the menu here can please all. In a sprawling space overlooking the highway, the Olympic Café is a casual, tropical-setting (if LA-inspired) diner. Fill up with the egg and spinach scramble with sun-dried tomatoes and artichoke hearts ($9) or the whopping *kalua* pig burrito ($10.50). Fresh fish is served the way you choose. The bar serves beer and wine and concocts tropical cocktails with names like 'Kaua'i 5-O' and 'The Goofyfoot' for folks so inclined.

Pizzetta (☎ 823-8882; 1387 Kuhio Hwy; pizzas $16-23; ⏱ 11am-10pm) Okay, it does resemble a suburban shopping-mall pizzeria, with the same pseudo-Italian decor and non-Italian diners. But, if you're craving pizza on the Eastside, your only other option is Pizza Hut (which is where the locals go). So, head here for decent combinations, like Milano (fire-roasted veg and feta) or Shrimp Puttanesca (shrimp, capers, Kalamata olives, roma tomatoes and spicy sauce).

Drinking

Java Kai (☎ 823-6887; 4-1384 Kuhio Hwy; coffee drinks $1.50-4.50; ⏱ 6am-5pm) Kaua'i's café culture reflects the attitudes of mainlanders rather than locals, but Java Kai (a mostly local chain) adds a lively touch to any neigh-

borhood. It offers a mind-boggling selection of java drinks, along with coffee beans (Kaua'i-grown $17 per pound, Kona-grown $31 per pound) and fruit smoothies (under $6) in a low-key sidewalk setting. At almost $3, the muffins are pricey, but scrumptious and baked on-site.

Shack Sports Bar (☎ 823-0200; 4-1639 Kuhio Hwy; burgers $6-7, beers $4; ⏱ noon-2am) Twelve beers on tap (yes, Guinness, too), multiple TVs to catch the big game and bar food, including *huge* salads. Merry-makers flock here, especially on $2-pint Thursday.

Shopping

Kapa'a is ideal for rainy-day browsing.

ABC Store (☎ 823-0081; 4-1359 Kuhio Hwy; ⏱ 6am-11pm) This local catchall chain carries everything from snacks to T-shirts to souvenirs to beer. Prices are competitive compared with major stores.

Hula Girl (☎ 822-1950; www.welovehulagirl.com; 4-1340 Kuhio Hwy; ⏱ 9am-6pm Mon-Sat, 10am-5pm Sun) Aloha-shirt aficionados know the real deal from the wannabe, and here you'll find a wide selection of quality, name-brand shirts ($40 to $125). Feel the silky soft Tori Richard line in cotton lawn ($70 to $75) – and note the muted, not garish, prints. Also sells women's dresses, jewelry, island-made ceramics, art prints and other souvenirs.

Kaua'i Products Fair (☎ 246-0988; www.kauaiproductsfair.com; ⏱ 9am-5pm Thu-Sun) Handicrafts (including pottery, jewelry and batik clothing) and produce are sold at this crafts fair on the north side of town.

Naturally Birkenstock (☎ 822-3627; ntrlbirk@mauigateway.com; 4-1467 Kuhio Hwy; ⏱ 10am-5pm Mon-Fri) Wide selection of Birkenstocks and other comfortable shoes, such as Keens and Chacos.

Root (☎ 823-1277; 4-1435 Kuhio Hwy, Suite 103; ⏱ 10am-7pm Mon-Sat, noon-4pm Sun) Owned by a woman in Bozeman, Montana, the Root sells clothing geared toward the youthful female set, with brands like Roxy, Free People and Seven. While rather trendy and overpriced (Kaua'i is not the place to build your wardrobe), the selection includes unique pieces worth a browse.

Yamada's Orchid Nursery (☎ 822-4148; www.yamadanursery.com; 5087-A Kawaihau Rd; ⏱ by appointment) Take home a living, blooming souvenir. Orchids can be carried on-flight or shipped to your home.

Aloha Images (☎ 821-1382; www.alohaimages .com; Dragon Bldg, 4504 Kukui St; ☯ 10am-6:30pm Mon-Sat, to 3pm Sun) Come here to browse through a range of local artists' paintings. Since 1995, Ray Charron, former director of Kapa'a's Wyland Gallery, has displayed and sold paintings by Kaua'i artists. The low-pressure atmosphere is welcoming to art aficionados and novices alike, and pieces range from about $200 to $36,000. To make art afford-able for the average guy or gal, Charron gives discounts for multiple or repeat buyers and interest-free layaway.

Earth & Sea Gallery (☎ 821-2831; Dragon Bldg, 4504 Kukui St; ☯ 9am-9pm) All pocketbooks can find a gift here, from 'beanbag' geckos (filled with Kaua'i sand) to intricately carved wooden frames ($75 to $125) and coconut-shell lamps ($85). The carvings are done in Indo-nesia, so they're not exactly local, but they're based on designs by the shop's owner.

Kela's Glass Gallery (☎ 822-4527, 888-255-3527; www.glass-art.com; 4-1354 Kuhio Hwy; ☯ 10am-7pm Mon-Fri, 10am-6pm Sat, noon-5pm Sun) If glass is your thing, this niche gallery will tempt you, as it showcases quality pieces by over 100 artists from around the world. Only four are Hawaii-based, however.

NORTHEAST COAST

Beyond Kapa'a, the landscape suddenly opens into a vast swath of greens and blues: wild sugarcane, Anahola's rugged Kalalea mountain range, cobalt sea and turquoise sky. No hulking resorts or jammed parking lots or bumper-to-bumper traffic in sight. You are entering a part of Kaua'i well-known only by locals. Just north of Kapa'a, a couple of scenic lookouts present striking views that spur newfound wonder at Kaua'i's beauty – not that you needed reminding.

Kealia Beach

Mainly a locals' surf and boogie board-ing spot, this scenic beach, at the 10-mile marker, is recommended mainly for ex-perts. The powerful waves are mesmerizing but treacherous. A breakwater protects the north end, so swimming and snorkeling are occasionally possible there – but far supe-rior spots exist on the North and South Shores. After rainstorms, the sand may be heavily littered with tree limbs carried down Kealia Stream, which empties at the beach's south side.

Donkey Beach

An easy 10-minute walk down from the highway takes you to golden Donkey Beach. Along the way, a sign warns: 'Nudity is against the law: violators will be pros-ecuted.' Yes, Donkey Beach has long been known as Kaua'i's main nudist beach. But nude sunbathing is illegal on Kaua'i, and police occasionally roll in and bust those in the buff – so shed the trunks at your own risk. The beach is also popular as a gay beach; it certainly draws a mixed crowd.

Summer swells are rideable here, but from October to May dangerous rip cur-rents and a powerful shore break take over. Blustery winds whip ironwood trees away from the shore and, bent so low, they look almost like shrubs (which means lousy shade, so bring sun protection). *Naupaka* and *'ilima,* native ground-creeping flowers, add dashes of color to the sand.

To get to the beach, stop at the paved parking lot at the ocean side of Kuhio Hwy, about halfway between the 11- and 12-mile markers; look for the small 'Public Shore-line Access' sign. From there follow the path down to the beach.

Anahola
pop 1932

You'll miss this small village if you're not looking for it, but find it, scratch below the surface and the Native-Hawaiian town of Anahola will reveal itself as one of Kaua'i's most captivating communities. Two sub-divisions of Hawaiian Homestead lots exist at the southern and northern ends of Ana-hola, which once supported thriving pine-apple and sugar plantations. The few who stay in Anahola will find themselves in rural seclusion among true locals – quite a unique experience on a resort island.

Grouped together at the side of Kuhio Hwy, just south of the 14-mile marker, Ana-hola's modest commercial center includes a **post office** (☯ 8am-4pm Mon-Fri, 9:30-11:30am Sat), renowned burger stand and basic conven-ience store.

SIGHTS & ACTIVITIES
Anahola Beach Park

A county park on Hawaiian Home Lands, Anahola Beach Park sits at the south side of Anahola Bay. The wide bay fringed with lovely sandy beach was an ancient surfing site, and the break is still popular with local surfers. To get here, turn off Kuhio Hwy onto Kukuihale Rd at the 13-mile marker, drive a mile down and then turn onto the dirt beach road. You can also access the north end of the beach from 'Aliomanu Rd; note that there is a 'first' 'Aliomanu Rd at the 14-mile marker and a 'second' one north of the 15-mile marker.

'Aliomanu Beach

Secluded 'Aliomanu Beach is another spot frequently primarily by locals, who pole- and throw-net fish and gather *limu* (seaweed). It's a mile-long stretch of beach; you can get to the prettier north end by turning onto 'Aliomanu Rd (the second), just past the 15-mile marker on Kuhio Hwy. Turn left onto Kalalea View Dr, go 0.5 miles and turn right at the beach access sign. This intimate beach is accessed via a short trail; look for the rope swing to your left.

Massage

TriHealth Ayurveda (☎ 828-2104, 800-455-0770; www.oilbath.com; Kuhio Hwy; treatments $130-275) In a simple bungalow just off the highway, you can sample traditional Ayurvedic therapies, practiced by therapists trained both locally and in Kerala, India. A popular and luxuriously sensual treatment entails a herb-scented hot-oil massage, synchronized by two therapists, followed by a heady steambath lying in a horizontal wooden steamer. Other treatments involve streaming hot oil poured on your forehead or hot oil rhythmically poured over your entire body. TriHealth also sells quality Ayurvedic herb products online. Located between the 20- and 21-mile markers.

SLEEPING

For information about camping in Anahola Beach Park, see p218.

Hale Kiko'o (☎ 822-3922; www.halekikoo.com; 4-4382-B Kuhio Hwy; s $65-80, d $70-85, plus one-time cleaning fee $50) You'll probably struggle to choose between the two lovely studios in this sunny-yellow house just off the highway. Painted in rich colors, the downstairs unit is spacious, with a kitchen overlooking a vibrant lawn and patio. The interior is chic, with stone-tile floors; the indoor-outdoor bathroom qualifies as art, with pebble floor,

---

HAWAIIAN HEALING HANDS

In the late 1970s Angeline Kaihalanaopuna Hopkins Locey moved back to Hawaii after years living in California. Back in her native land, Angeline, who is almost three-quarters Native Hawaiian and grew up on O'ahu, experienced a homecoming, not only geographically but culturally. She embraced Hawaiian healing, studied with *lomilomi kumu* (teacher) Margret Machado on the Big Island, and in the mid-1980s established a homestead in Anahola, where she began to share her gift of therapeutic touch with the community. Over the years, 'Auntie Angeline,' now in her late 70s, became a local icon, and today her son Michael and granddaughter Malia carry on her legacy.

Angeline's Mu'olaulani (☎ 822-3235; www.auntyangelines.com; Kamalomalo'o Pl; signature treatment $130; ☺ 9am-3pm Mon-Fri, by appointment only) is an authentic introduction to Hawaiian healing practices and remains a best-kept secret, frequented mainly by locals. Don't expect plush towels, glossy marble floors or an endless menu of face and nail pamperings. A trip to Angeline's is more like visiting a friend's bungalow, with outdoor shower, wooden-plank deck, massage tables separated by curtains, and simple sarongs to cover up.

The signature treatment includes a steam, vigorous salt scrub and a special four-hands (two-person) *lomilomi* massage (traditional Hawaiian healing massage). The four-hands method prevents you from fixating on a particular tender area (the mind cannot focus on all four hands, so it must disengage and let the body relax and receive the treatment). But if you'd prefer a single massage therapist (or other treatments like hot stones), just request so. During the treatment, therapists might spontaneously break into *oli* (Hawaiian chant), which adds a unique and powerful element. If you chat with Michael or Malia, their reverence for the ancient healing arts is clear, and their desire to share their culture would make any visitor feel welcome.

As an expression of *ho'okipa* (hospitality), the Loceys invite guests to stay and sip a drink on the patio after the treatment. The facilities (including showers and sauna) are unisex, but the staff is glad to provide same-sex facilities upon request.

open shower and crescent-shaped orange wall. The smaller upstairs unit is less creative but brighter, surrounded by windows. Both include cable TV, phone and CD player. Washer/dryer available for $5 per load.

'Ili Noho Kai O Anahola (Hawaiian Style Beachfront B&B; ☎ 821-0179, 639-6317; www.kauai.net/anahola; Aliomanu Rd; r with shared bathroom incl breakfast $75) It's easy to unwind at Sondra and Michael Grace's informal guesthouse fronting Anahola Bay. Four compact but tidy rooms (sharing two bathrooms) surround a central lanai, where guests can talk story, enjoy Michael's spontaneous guitar tunes and fill up on home-cooked breakfasts. Rooms include either king, queen, double or two twin beds. The hosts are Native Hawaiian activists with a dramatic tale (see opposite). An ideal setting if you want to learn about Hawaiian land issues from passionate insiders.

EATING

Duane's Ono Char-Burger (☎ 822-9181; 4-4350 Kuhio Hwy; burgers $5-7; 10am-6pm Mon-Sat, 11am-6pm Sun) Burger mavens know the island's best burgers come from this nondescript drive-up counter. And clearly word has spread. Check out the autographed photos of fans from Chuck Norris to Steve Tyler. Try the 'old fashioned' with cheddar, onions and sprouts, or the 'local girl', smothered in Swiss cheese, pineapple and teriyaki sauce. Crispy thin fries and melt-in-your-mouth onion rings are irresistible complements. Non-meat eaters, you're out of luck. As the menu states, 'This is *not* fish.'

Hole in the Mountain

The *puka* (hole) in Pu'u Konanae is now more like a sliver, since a landslide transformed the once-obvious landmark. Legend says the original hole was created when a giant threw his spear through the mountain, causing the water stored within to gush forth as waterfalls. From slightly north of the 15-mile marker, look back at the mountain, down to the right of the tallest pinnacle, and on sunny days you'll see a smile of light shining through a slit in the rock face.

Ko'olau Road

Ko'olau Rd is a peaceful, scenic loop drive through rich green pastures, dotted with soaring white egrets and bright wild flowers. It makes a nice diversion and is the way to reach untouristed Moloa'a Beach or Larsen's Beach (no facilities at either). Ko'olau Rd connects with Kuhio Hwy 0.5 miles north of the 16-mile marker and again 180yd south of the 20-mile marker.

For a quick bite, the **Moloa'a Sunrise Fruit Stand** (☎ 822-1441; Kuhio Hwy & Ko'olau Rd; juices & smoothies $3-6.25, sandwiches $5.50-7; 7:30am-6pm Mon-Sat, 10am-5pm Sun) is conveniently located, with a healthful menu featuring sandwiches on multigrain bread, taro burgers and brown-rice vegetarian sushi. A luscious 16oz smoothie ($4.50) is a far better deal than the $3 mini gulp of juice. The 'Fruit Stand' moniker is a slight misnomer as the selection of food overshadows its fruit. Located past the 16-mile marker.

MOLOA'A BEACH

With a semicircular bay and gleaming blond sand, this pretty beach is remote enough to escape much traffic. To the north, there's a shallow protected swimming area good for families; to the south, the waters are rougher but there's more sand. When the surf's up, it's still a pleasant spot for beach walking – from one end of the golden crescent to the other. Toward the back of the beach, which is fed by Moloa'a Stream, there's plenty of shade, making for an ideal picnic or daydreaming spot. The pilot for the classic TV series *Gilligan's Island* was filmed here. To get here, follow Ko'olau Rd and turn onto Moloa'a Rd (1.25 miles and 1 mile coming from the south and north respectively). The road ends 0.75 miles down at a few beach houses and a little parking area. The whole bay can have strong currents when the surf is rough.

Get away from it all at the **Jade Lily Pad** (☎ 822-5216; www.rosewoodkauai.com; 2-bedroom house $250), a beach house on stilts aside a tranquil stream. With two bedrooms, two bathrooms, full kitchen, lanai with Jacuzzi and airy cathedral ceilings, it's a spacious retreat for adventurous couples or families. Two kayaks are provided, so you can paddle along the stream to Moloa'a Beach (one block away by foot). The rugged, unpaved road to the house is best traversed by 4WD. Located off Moloa'a Rd.

LARSEN'S BEACH

This long, golden-sand beach, named after L David Larsen (former manager of C Brewer's Kilauea Sugar Company), is good for

WHO OWNS THE LAND?

Land ownership in Hawaii has been a hot-button issue since 1848 when the Great Mahele allowed fee-simple ownership for the first time. Today Kaua'i's real-estate market is booming and the prime (multimillion-dollar) lots almost always end up in outsiders' hands. You'll see bumper stickers reading 'Keep Hawaiian Lands in Hawaiian Hands' and 'Locals Only: We Grew Here, You Flew Here.'

Native Hawaiians are eligible for set-aside lands under the Hawaiian Homes Commission Act, passed by the US Congress in 1920. Kaua'i's own Prince Johah Kuhio Kalaniana'ole, the Territory of Hawai'i's congressional delegate, sponsored the Act, which set aside almost 200,000 acres for Native Hawaiian homesteads. (Of course, this 'generous' gift is only a small fraction of the crown lands taken by the US upon the islands' annexation in 1898 – and the best land was already taken by the sugar industry.)

People of at least 50% Native Hawaiian ancestry became eligible for 99-year leases at $1 per year. Today perhaps 6500 Native Hawaiian families are living on about 30,000 acres of homestead lands. But administration by the Department of Hawaiian Home Lands (DHHL) has proved controversial: much of the land was leased to big businesses or appropriated by federal, state and county governments.

Further, numerous Native Hawaiians have waited for years to receive their parcels. While unverified, estimates show that between 30,000 and 40,000 people have died while on the Hawaiian Home Lands waiting list. In Anahola, sovereignty activists Sondra and Michael Grace (who is Native Hawaiian), along with a handful of others, took action instead of just waiting.

The Graces moved to Anahola Beach Park on July 4, 1986, launching an occupation that would last over a decade. They built simple structures but a cohesive community. But the DHHL would not recognize their quitclaim deed and on July 15, 1991, descended with the National Guard and bulldozers to evict them and destroy the buildings.

Undaunted, they returned, got rearrested and returned again to build a 24-sq-ft Polynesian hut on the beach. The DHHL finally relented, but Hurricane 'Iniki struck in 1992. The hurricane was an ironic blessing because the Graces then qualified for Federal Emergency Management Agency (FEMA) funds due to the quitclaim deed and utility bills. They built a $12,000 cultural center that was again bulldozed in 1995. Finally Michael Grace received his land award and they built the current B&B in 1998. To learn more about the fight for sovereignty, visit www.hawaiiankingdom .org and also check out the documentary video *Anahola*, by Nicholas Rozsa, which the Graces keep on hand at their B&B. It's a compelling indie documentary about the 1991 demolition.

In the 2000s several lawsuits have challenged the constitutionality of programs that benefit Native Hawaiians. In 2002, 18 plaintiffs argued that the DHHL and the Office of Hawaiian Affairs (a state agency) should be abolished because their use of state tax revenues discriminates against non-Hawaiians. The US District Court dismissed the case and the 9th US Circuit Court of Appeals partly affirmed the ruling – ultimately preserving the Hawaiian Homes Commission Act.

Thus, beneath the veneer of 'paradise' lie the age-old struggles for autonomy and ownership by natives for their native land.

solitary strolls and beachcombing. Although shallow, snorkeling can be good when the waters are very calm, which is usually only in the summer. Beware of a vicious current that runs westward along the beach and out through a channel in the reef.

When the tide is low, you might share Larsen's – very much a local beach – with Hawaiian families collecting an edible seaweed called *limu kohu*. The seaweed found here is considered to be some of the finest in all of Hawaii. Otherwise, it will be you, the sand and the waves. Boulder-hop around the point at the western end of the beach to access supremely private sands.

The turnoff to Larsen's Beach is on Ko'olau Rd, a little more than a mile down from the north intersection of Ko'olau Rd and Kuhio Hwy, or just over a mile north of the intersection of Moloa'a and Ko'olau Rds. Turn toward the ocean on the dirt road there (easy to miss if you're coming from the south: look for it just before the cemetery) and take the immediate left. It's 1 mile to the parking area and then a five-minute walk downhill to the beach.

North Shore

Mention Kaua'i, and people immediately fantasize about golden sandy beaches, thundering waterfalls, sheer cliffs overlooking pounding surf, foliage growing wild, suntanned surfers, blue skies and bluer waters.

In reality, the island does not always match such expectations. But the North Shore will not disappoint.

For years the North Shore was truly remote – an off-the-beaten-path adventure for day-trippers or campers. The odd wanderer might perhaps bird watch at Kilauea Point, swim in Hanalei Bay or hike the Kalalau Trail. Today the North Shore is a must-see, and cars zoom nonstop to the end of the road. The 1970s development of Princeville, which is among the priciest second-home markets in the USA, was a major impetus for North Shore tourism, for better or worse.

Still, the vibe here is noticeably laid-back and rural. Residents are a motley mix of original farming families, '70s hippie transplants, surf bums of all ages, part-time-resident homeowners and a new generation of 20-somethings seeking 'the good life.' Folks often recognize one another by name, and the hippie culture still prevails (albeit in a cleaned-up, toned-down form). As in all beach towns, surfing is *the* sport of choice, and catching a few waves *pau hana* (after work) is a way of life.

Unexpected showers are common, but they're gentle, even dreamy. Mountaintops lie shrouded in clouds that drift and lift, revealing plunging waterfalls. In winter it might rain for days on end, but passing summer showers form brilliant rainbows.

The North Shore scenery would seem too pat and idyllic – if you weren't here to witness it.

HIGHLIGHTS

- Catching early-morning waves at **Hanalei Bay** (p143)

- Savoring a frosty at **Banana Joe's Fruit-stand** (p131) in Kilauea

- Trekking the Na Pali Coast's **Kalalau Trail** (p156)

- Identifying native flora at **Limahuli Garden** (p153)

- Learning to windsurf at **'Anini Beach Park** (p133)

- Spotting birds and other wildlife at **Kilauea Point** (p128)

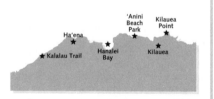

KILAUEA
pop 2092

While still building a critical mass as a town, Kilauea's modest commercial stretch is worth a stop. The main attractions are the picturesque lighthouse and seabird sanctuary at Kilauea Point, but you'll also find a handful of destination eateries – from gourmet pizza and artisan breads to savory fresh fish to the island's best fruit stand. Vacation rentals are springing up in quiet neighborhoods, making Kilauea an up-and-coming sleeping spot for folks who want to experience real-life living on Kaua'i.

The pastoral terrain is peaceful, if less dramatic than the mountainous vistas surrounding Hanalei. But the unhurried, untouristy setting is quite refreshing. Also, it might make a better vacation home base if you're traveling in both directions.

For years the Kilauea Theater & Community Events Center (in the Kong Lung Center) was a popular cultural gathering spot and the only cinema on the North Shore. But in 2005 the center ended its theater function and now rents the property to a Christian church, for steadier income.

Sights & Activities
ROCK QUARRY BEACH

Also known as Kahili Beach, Rock Quarry is a broad sandy beach, with a pretty fringe of ironwood trees. The beach is a river mouth for Kilauea Stream, so the water can be murky. Fairly remote, this beach has rich fishing and, on occasion, surf turf. If the waves are big enough to ride, swimmers should take extreme caution with strong near-shore currents.

Public access is via Wailapa Rd, which begins midway between the 21- and 22-mile markers on Kuhio Hwy (Hwy 56). Follow Wailapa Rd north for less than 0.5 miles beyond Kuhio Hwy and then turn left on the unmarked dirt road that begins at a bright-yellow water valve. The dirt road, which continues for less than 0.5 miles before ending at the beach, is rough. Compact cars can do it, but pick your way slowly over and around the crevices.

NA 'AINA KAI BOTANICAL GARDENS

What started as a retirement landscaping project morphed into this 240-acre extravaganza of **botanical gardens** (☎ 828-0525; www

.naainakai.com; 4101 Wailapa Rd; tours $25-70; ⊙ 9am Tue-Thu), all meticulously groomed. Joyce and Ed Doty, who arrived on Kaua'i from California in 1982, originally planned to keep their property private until their deaths. But in 2000, when she was 75 and he 79, they established a nonprofit entity and donated their $17-million garden to it.

The expansive grounds include 13 gardens, throughout which you'll discover perhaps 70 rather quaint, life-sized, carefully placed bronzes, ranging from an elderly couple sitting on a bench to a lion stalking a jackrabbit. Get lost in the Poinciana maze, a hedge of 2400 mock-orange plants, or play in the Children's Garden, a playground on steroids, with a kid-size railroad train, a log cabin, a covered wagon, a treehouse, a graffiti wall and a $300,000 16ft-tall bronze sculpture-fountain of Jack and the Beanstalk set in a wading pool. Other gardens here include a beach, a bird-watching marsh and a sprawling forest of around 60,000 South and East Asian hardwood trees.

Clearly both a labor of love and of money (Joyce Doty is the former wife of the late Charles M Schulz, the Peanuts comic-strip creator), the gardens are impressive but a tad contrived, especially surrounded by such stark, unadulterated beauty. Bear in mind that the flora found here are modern introductions.

The staff and docents are well-informed, but tours ain't cheap. Request the three-hour 'Formal & Wild Forest Garden' riding tour, if you have mobility issues. To get the best bang for your buck, call about the 'Founder's Tour,' usually held once a week and led by the gentleman farmer whose handiwork you'll be touring.

To reach the gardens, turn right onto Wailapa Rd, between the 21- and 22-mile markers on Kuhio Hwy; the garden is just over 0.75 miles down on your right.

CHRIST MEMORIAL EPISCOPAL CHURCH

After turning onto Kolo Rd, just past the 23-mile marker on Kuhio Hwy, look immediately for the striking Christ Memorial Episcopal Church. Built in 1941 of lava rock, the headstones (also of lava rock) in the churchyard are much older, dating back to when the original Hawaiian Congregational Church stood on this site.

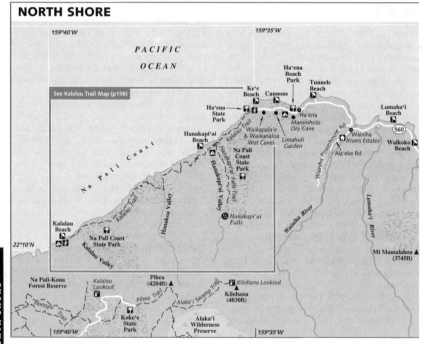

NORTH SHORE

KILAUEA POINT

The **Kilauea Point National Wildlife Refuge**
(☎ 828-0383; www.fws.gov/pacificislands/wnwr/kki
laueanwr.html; adult/child under 16 $3/free; ☼ 10am-
4pm, closed federal holidays) is the northernmost
point of the inhabited Hawaiian Islands.
Topped by **Kilauea Lighthouse**, built in 1913,
it's picture-postcard material. Park staff at
the visitors center are very knowledgeable
and will train the telescope there on nesting
birds. The paved path to the lighthouse is
disabled accessible.

Even if birds bore you, it's worth driving to
the end of Kilauea Rd for the stunning view
of the lighthouse (with the biggest clamshell
lens in the world) and cliffs beyond. Most
of the surrounding refuge is closed to the
public, to protect the wildlife habitat. Binoculars are loaned free at the lighthouse; in
addition to birds, scan for sea turtles, frolicking spinner dolphins in spring and summer,
and humpback whales in winter.

Four species of birds come to Kilauea to
nest, but most leave after their young have
been reared. Red-footed boobies, the most
visible, are abundant on the cliffs to the east
of the point, where they build large stick
nests in the treetops. Boobies nest from
February to September, with their peak egg-
laying occurring in spring.

Wedge-tailed shearwaters arrive by March
and stay until November, nesting in burrows
they dig into Kilauea Point. Other readily
spotted species are the red-tailed and white-
tailed tropic bird, from March to October.
If you're lucky, you'll spot a pair flying in
loops, performing their courtship ritual.

Laysan albatrosses are at Kilauea from
around December to July. Some nest on
Moku'ae'ae Island, straight off the tip of
the point. Other albatross nesting sites lie
on the grassy clearing to the west of Kilauea
Point. Look out beyond this clearing to see
Secret Beach (p132), divided into three
scalloped coves by lava fingers.

Great frigate birds nest on the Northwestern Hawaiian Islands, not Kaua'i, but
these aerial pirates visit Kilauea Point year-
round to steal food from other birds. You
won't see the distinctive red throat balloon
that the male puffs out to attract females,
though, as they're here to feed, not breed.

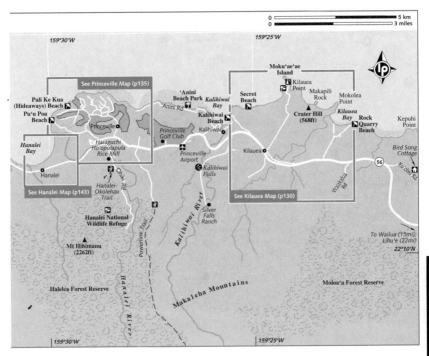

Frigate birds, which have a wingspan of 7ft and a distinctive forked tail, soar with a mesmerizing grace. Golden plovers (the legendary birds believed to have led the ancient Polynesian mariners to these islands) arrive from the Arctic in August and stay through spring.

Some of Kaua'i's estimated 100 nene, the endangered Hawaiian goose that was reintroduced here in 1982, can also be spotted.

GUAVA KAI PLANTATION

Unless you're a guava maniac, this **plantation** (☎ 828-6121; www.guavakai.com; Kuawa Rd; admission free; ☷ 9am-5pm), which cultivates 480 acres of guava trees that produce juice for Ocean Spray and other juice companies, is not a must-see. But the neatly planted orchard is pleasant enough. Juice samples are available at the visitors center, which sells an impressive variety of guava products, jams, hot sauces and syrups. There's a path leading through a garden planted with tropical flowers that makes for a nice short stroll; delve into the orchards to pick as many guava as you like.

Guava is grown commercially mainly in Mexico, as crops here and in Florida suffer from fruit flies. Varieties of guava can be round, ovoid or pear-shaped, 2in to 4in long, soft when ripe, with a moist, subtly sweet taste and a rind that softens to be fully edible. The flesh, which can be white, pink, yellow or red, contains numerous small, edible seeds. Guava Kai's harvest yields of a hybrid whose fruit grows to half a pound (twice the normal size) are close to 4.5 million pounds annually.

To get here, turn inland onto Kuawa Rd from Kuhio Hwy, just north of the 23-mile marker and 0.25 miles south of the Kolo Rd turnoff to Kilauea. The visitors center is about a mile from the highway.

PILATES

The best place for pilates on the island is **Mary Jane's Pilates** (☎ 639-3247; mjpilates@verizon .net; 4433 Kilauea Rd; private sessions per hr $65). At her fully equipped studio, you can tone your body with pilates and gyrotonic sessions, which uses special equipment to exercise the body in fluid, compound movements,

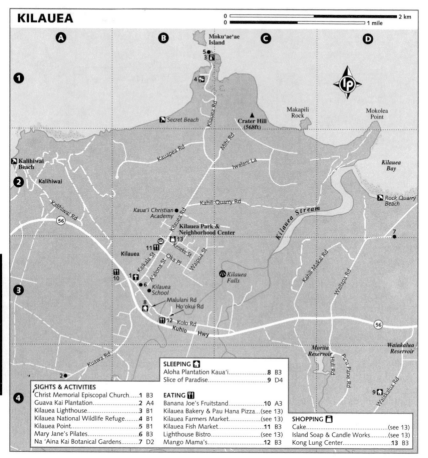

KILAUEA

0 ____ 2 km
0 ____ 1 mile

SLEEPING 🛏
Aloha Plantation Kaua'i......................**8** B3
Slice of Paradise..............................**9** D4

SIGHTS & ACTIVITIES
Christ Memorial Episcopal Church......**1** B3
Guava Kai Plantation.........................**2** A4
Kilauea Lighthouse............................**3** B1
Kilauea National Wildlife Refuge........**4** B1
Kilauea Point....................................**5** B1
Mary Jane's Pilates...........................**6** B3
Na 'Aina Kai Botanical Gardens.........**7** D2

EATING 🍴
Banana Joe's Fruitstand.....................**10** A3
Kilauea Bakery & Pau Hana Pizza...(see 13)
Kilauea Farmers Market..................(see 13)
Kilauea Fish Market...........................**11** B3
Lighthouse Bistro..........................(see 13)
Mango Mama's..................................**12** B3

SHOPPING 🛍
Cake..(see 13)
Island Soap & Candle Works...........(see 13)
Kong Lung Center...............................**13** B3

rather than the linear, isolated method of conventional machines. Mary Jane also offers two-person duet pilates sessions for $40 each.

Sleeping

The number of midrange and especially top-end vacation rentals is burgeoning in Kilauea. Budget travelers should stick to better-value Eastside options. Contact the agencies listed on p137 for listings; of those agencies the best for Kilauea are 'Anini Aloha Properties, Coldwell Banker Bali Hai Realty and North Shore Properties. Rates are typically quoted by the week.

Aloha Plantation Kaua'i (☎ 828-6872, 877-658-6977; www.alohaplantation.com; 4481 Malulani Rd; r $69-99) While modern minimalists might find the decor overwhelming, vintage collectors will be intrigued by this 1920s plantation house filled with antiques, from classic barber chairs to bobble-head hula dolls. The in-house rooms resemble an eccentric aunt's house or a mini museum, rather cluttered and furnished with retro rattan and wrought-iron pieces. The $69 room shares a shower, while the $79 room has a private bathroom. A better deal is the detached studio ($99) with kitchenette. Outdoor cooking patio with modern grill and Jacuzzi available.

Bird Song Cottage (☎ 828-6797, 652-2585; www .kauaibirdsongcottage.com; house per night $135, per week $890, plus one-time cleaning fee $90) Aah... a secluded, airy cottage, surrounded by verdant greenery and within earshot of rhythmically breaking waves. Also known as Manu Mele ('Bird Song' in Hawaiian), this home away from home features a sweeping 12ft ceiling, hardwood furniture, a luxurious tub made of India-imported granite, a full kitchen, a canopy bed and a washer/dryer. On the 6-acre property you can play gardener in the fruit orchard and veggie garden, or laze around in a hammock.

Slice of Paradise (☎ 826-9622; www.rentalsonkauai .com; 4852-A Waiakalua Rd; house per week $1100) In a secluded house southeast of Kilauea town, enjoy the privacy of a cottage surrounded by a 2.5-acre lawn and garden. While only a studio, it feels cozy rather than cramped, with sleek hardwood floors, invitingly fluffy bed and full kitchen, plus a spacious deck and Jacuzzi. The ocean is distant but visible. Contact North Shore Properties.

Eating

Kilauea Bakery & Pau Hana Pizza (☎ 828-2020; Kong Lung Center, Kilauea Rd; pastries $2, pizza $10-30; 🕑 6:30am-9pm, pizza from 10:30am) If you end up eating breakfast, lunch and dinner here, we totally understand. From gooey mac-nut sticky buns to specialty pizzas, this place

---

> **THE AUTHOR'S CHOICE**
>
> Keep your eyes peeled for a banana-yellow shack on the *mauka* (inland) side of Kuhio Hwy near the 24-mile marker. Don't speed, otherwise you might miss the best fruit stand on Kaua'i. **Banana Joe's Fruitstand** (☎ 828-1092; www.bananajoekauai.com; 5-2719 Kuhio Hwy; 🕑 9am-6pm Mon-Sat, to 5pm Sun) sells bursting-fresh produce grown on the adjacent 6-acre lot. You'll find golden starfruit, Sunrise (pink-flesh) and Solo (orange-flesh) papayas, organic greens and all type of citrus, from giant Meyer lemons to rough-skinned, sugar-sweet navel oranges. Also available are Kilauea honey, Hanalei poi, and locally made cheeses and preserves.
>
> Behind the counter you'll see Joe Halasey (the real-life Banana Joe) whipping up his velvety frosties (frozen fruit run through a juicer so that it resembles ice cream) and refreshing smoothies (fruit blended with pineapple juice). This hands-on owner has farmed here since 1986.

has no peer. The Hawaiian sourdough loaf ($4.75) is perfectly tangy and chewy, while the tropical Danish pastries surprise your tastebuds with fillings from *liliko'i* (passion fruit) to guava. On weekends, the sweet treats can sell out just before noon. The pizza, which many tout as Kaua'i's finest, features tasty toppings like smoked *ono* (wahoo), Kilauea goat cheese and fresh sugarloaf pineapple.

Mango Mama's (☎ 828-1020; cnr Kuhio Hwy & Ho'okui Rd; smoothies $4-5.50, sandwiches $5-6.50; 🕑 7am-6pm Mon-Sat) Known as much for its pink, pink, pink decor as for its food, Mango Mama's is a little roadside joint serving smoothies, sandwiches from tempeh burgers to peanut butter and jelly, baked goods and coffee drinks. With nothing-fancy patio table and chairs, the covered dining area is a low-key place to linger.

Kilauea Fish Market (☎ 828-6244; 4270 Kilauea Rd; plates & wraps $8-11; 🕑 11am-8pm Mon-Sat) If there's a traffic jam in Kilauea, it's likely to be here around lunchtime, as people line up for massive plates of seared-*'ahi poke* (cubed, marinated yellowfin tuna) salad ($11) with organic greens or wraps stuffed with sautéed *'ahi* or tofu, brown rice, and lots of veggies ($7 to $10). The *poke* is succulent at an acceptable $12 per pound; while the *'ahi* sashimi block dipped in cajun spices is unique but pricey at $18 per pound. Order at the cramped counter and eat outside at picnic tables under shady trees.

Lighthouse Bistro (☎ 828-0480; Kong Lung Center, 2484 Keneke St; lunch mains $6-12, dinner mains $18-28; 🕑 noon-2pm & 5:30-9pm Mon-Sat, 5:30-9pm Sun) If looks matter (and they do), this rustic, open-air bistro makes a great first impression. Especially at night, it seems to glow with mellow lights and rich woods. And upon closer inspection – of the food – it doesn't disappoint. The menu focuses on local ingredients, such as Kilauea greens and goats cheese. Fresh fish is served grilled, blackened or ginger-crusted (a unique preparation using Japanese pickled ginger). Budget diners can eat their fill at the pasta bar ($14), while vegans can enjoy the Napoleon, a towering stack of polenta, grilled vegetables and greens ($18).

Kilauea Farmers Market (☎ 828-1512; Kong Lung Center, Kilauea Rd; deli items $4-7; 🕑 8am-8pm Sun-Thu, to 8:30pm Fri & Sat) Did someone say *pupu* (appetizer) party on the lanai? No problem, as this upscale bodega has a gourmet beer and wine selection, olives, boutique cheeses, flatbreads and other goodies suited to the yuppie palate. The deli's inventive offerings include a piquant ginger-teriyaki tofu sandwich.

For major grocery shopping, head toward Kapa'a or Princeville, but in Kilauea, you can easily cobble together a meal from the fruit stand, bakery, fish market and longstanding farmers market.

Shopping

Island Soap & Candle Works (☎ 828-1955; www .islandsoap.com; Kong Lung Center, 2474 Keneke St; ☉ 9am-9pm) While not exclusive to Kaua'i or Kilauea, each location makes its own soaps and candles, so you know they're fresh and oh-so-fragrant. The beeswax candles in coconut shells ($8 to $12) make unique gifts. The scents feature tropical fruits and flowers and tend to be subtle rather than cloying.

Cake (☎ 828-6412; Kong Lung Center, 2484 Keneke St; ☉ 10am-6pm) Fun boutique for the young and hip, with sexy, strapless dresses, designer jeans and a rainbow of fitted tees and tanks.

Getting There & Around

Kolo Rd, the main turnoff into Kilauea, is slightly less than 0.5 miles west of the 23-mile marker. Kilauea Rd starts opposite the church, and after 0.5 miles, you'll reach historic Kong Lung Center, with restaurants and shops. Kilauea Rd ends 2 miles later at Kilauea Point.

KALIHIWAI

pop 717

A rural residential area, Kalihiwai, which means 'edge of a steam' in Hawaiian, is known mainly for its beaches. Kalihiwai Rd was a loop road going down past Kalihiwai Beach, connecting with the highway at two points, until the tidal wave of 1957 washed out the Kalihiwai River bridge. The bridge was never rebuilt, and now there are two Kalihiwai Rds, one on each side of the river.

Sights & Activities

KALIHIWAI BEACH

With a wide, deep bay, this sandy stretch of beach (Map p130) is popular for many activities, such as swimming and, when the winter northwest swells roll in, daredevil boogie boarding and surfing along the cliff at the east end of the bay. The Kalihiwai Stream empties into the bay, and kayakers launch here for a scenic paddle up into Kalihiwai Valley, where you can see or hike to Kalihiwai Falls (note: the falls are on land leased by Princeville Ranch Stables and you might be shooed away). The beach has no facilities. For kayak rentals see p144.

To get here, take the first Kalihiwai Rd, 0.5 miles west of Kilauea. On your return to Kuhio Hwy, look to the left as soon as you see the 'Narrow Bridge' sign; you'll spot a picturesque waterfall that's partially hidden in a little valley.

SECRET BEACH

'Secret's Out Beach' might be a better moniker, as this gorgeous, golden-sand beach (Map p130) backed by sea cliffs and jungle-like woods has been 'discovered.' Still, it's a beauty frequented mainly by Kaua'i's alternative community, perhaps because it's accessible only by a steep (and slippery) 10- to 15-minute hike. Its Hawaiian name, Kauapea Beach, appears on some maps.

To get to Secret Beach, turn down Kalihiwai Rd 0.5 miles west of Kilauea and then turn right onto the first dirt road, which is just 0.1 miles from Kuhio Hwy. The road ends at a parking area less than 0.5 miles down. Don't leave anything of value in your car. The well-defined trail begins from the parking lot. After a 2-minute walk it leads downhill through ironwood trees and mixed jungle growth. The descent to the beach is tricky, and if it's just rained, treacherously slippery. The beach is quite idyllic, but if you're up for a stroll or feel the need for more privacy, walk along the beach in the direction of Kilauea Lighthouse.

The beach has open seas, with high winter surf and dangerous currents prevailing from October to May. In summer, water conditions are much calmer, and swimming and snorkeling can be good.

HORSEBACK RIDING

You can satiate your appetite for North Shore landscapes on a scenic horseback ride at **Silver Falls Ranch** (☎ 828-6718; www.silverfalls ranch.com; end of Kamo'okoa Rd; 90min trail ride $80, 2-/3hr ride $100/120). The friendly professionals here lead daily rides, either a shorter jaunt or a combo ride, swim at a natural mountain pool and picnic lunch. The working-ranch grounds are exquisite, with blooming orchids, old-growth trees and water elements enhancing the ride.

'ANINI

Countless 'vacation rental' houses line the road fronting idyllic 'Anini Beach. But this secluded area remains the best-kept secret. The beach park is spacious, with calm water perfect for kids, lazy kayaking, easy snorkeling and the best beginner windsurfing on the island.

There has been talk of connecting Princeville with 'Anini by a direct coastal road, but local resistance has kept the talk just that. For now, 'Anini's dead-end street means little traffic, keeping this area unhurried and quiet. Still, 'Anini is growing, and a number of exclusive homes, including many vacation rentals and Hollywood getaways, have shot up.

To get here, cross Kalihiwai Bridge (look and listen for the thundering waterfall here), turn onto the second Kalihiwai Rd and then bear left onto 'Anini Rd. It's about 1.5 miles from the highway to the beach.

Sights & Activities

'ANINI BEACH PARK

You can't ask for a gentler stretch of beach than 'Anini Beach Park. The water is flat as glass within the lagoon, which is protected by one of the longest and widest fringing reefs in the Hawaiian Islands. At its widest point, the reef extends over 1600ft offshore. The park is unofficially divided into day-use, camping and windsurfing areas. While weekends might draw crowds, weekdays are low key. Facilities include rest rooms, showers, changing rooms, drinking water, picnic pavilions and barbecue grills. There's a mild hippie vibe here, and you might see a bunch of bongo drummers (or, rather, *hear* the lively rhythmic thumping) in a pavilion.

You might be surprised to see polo matches across the street at **Kaua'i Polo Club** (www.kauaipoloclub.org), especially on Sundays. The sport arrived on Kaua'i in 1887 and proved very popular until World War II. Then, after a hiatus, a Canadian named Ken Anderson initiated a polo club in 1979, which moved from the Wilcox Mansion in Hanalei to the Kilohana Mansion in Puhi to the current location in 'Anini in the early 1980s. Famous names who have played here include Memo Gracida and Sylvester Stallone (who once owned a house here).

SWIMMING & SNORKELING

With practically no shore-break and average water depth at 4ft to 5ft, kayaking and lap swimming are practically effortless.

Swimming and snorkeling are good in the day-use area and in front of the camping area; conditions are best when the tide is high. A pretty good spot is opposite the midpoint of Kaua'i Polo Club's fence or at the far end of 'Anini Rd. The snorkeling is shallow, but the long barrier reef means lots of juvenile fish. Be careful over here because the 'Anini Channel cutting across the reef creates dangerous rip currents. The protected lagoon west of the channel provides safer water conditions.

WINDSURFING & KITESURFING

'Anini Beach, with its steady gentle breezes and calm bay, is an excellent place to learn windsurfing and kitesurfing. Lessons are given by the following outfits:

'Anini Beach Windsurfing (☎ 826-9463; 1hr lesson $50, board rental per hr/full day $25/50) An excellent company that teaches all levels. Instructor Foster Ducker also teaches kitesurfing (five-hour lesson $400).

Windsurf Kaua'i (☎ 828-6838; windsurfkauai@aol .com; 3hr lesson $75, board rental per hr/half day/full day $25/50/75; 🕑 9am & 1pm Mon-Fri) Instructor Celeste Harvel specializes in teaching beginners (but she can also give certification courses); also rents boards with gear.

FISHING

Fishing boats out of 'Anini include the following:

'Anini Fishing Charters (☎ 828-1285; www.kauai fishing.com; charter 4hr shared per person $125, private per 6 anglers $675) Captain shares the catch.

North Shore Charters (☎ 828-1379) Similarly priced.

Sleeping

The vacation-rental market is booming, and it's obvious why. Here, you can rent the beach home of your dreams, and play in your own 'private' plot of sand and surf right across the street. Other than the beach park facilities, you'll find no pedestrian traffic, restaurants, shops or other tourist trappings here.

The best way to find an appropriate rental is to search the Internet or contact an agency; see p137 for a list of these. One of the best agencies for rentals here is 'Anini Aloha Properties, which manages houses ranging from about $1100 to $10,500 weekly. Coldwell Banker Bali Hai Realty and North Shore Properties are also recommended. Note that most vacation-rental rates are quoted by the week and require additional cleaning fees and security deposits.

'Anini Beach Hideaway (☎ 828-1051; www.aninibeachhideaway.com; 3635 'Anini Rd; 1-bedroom house per week $875) Sharing an acre of property with a main house, this cottage has lots of fruit trees (guests are invited to pick fruit). Pleasant but no ocean view.

'Anini Beach Hale (☎ 828-6808, 877-262-6688; www.yourbeach.com; 3649 'Anini Rd; 2-bedroom house per day/week $255/1600) On a large 16,000 sq ft lot, this two-bedroom, two-bathroom house with large screened lanai is quiet and private. Both bedrooms have king beds; suitable for two couples. Owners are a longtime Kaua'i couple who live in nearby Kilauea.

Noho Kai (☎ 821-1454, 800-769-3285 ext 00; www.nohokai.com; 3617 'Anini Rd; 3-bedroom house per week $2100) Built in 2000, this modern vacation home with country-white walls is not only spacious at 1750 sq ft but also features sweeping front and back covered lanai (800 sq ft). Very airy, with vaulted ceilings and French doors; two master bedrooms are separated by a large living-room buffer zone. Maximum six people, including kids and babies.

Camping is right on the water, with shaded tent sites. The beach park is relatively spacious, although it crowds up on weekends, when local families arrive. See p218 for county park permit information. No camping is allowed on Tuesdays.

Eating

'Anini Beach Lunch Shak (☎ 635-7425; meals $3.75-7; ☷ 10:30am-3pm Tue-Sat) Seek out this modest lunch truck in the beach parking lot. Nothing beats the fresh fish tacos, flautas and burritos here, especially after a day in the water. Try the pharaoh-style double-wrap taco or the heftier Sara special, and spike it with one of 24 bottled hot sauces or the truck's special cilantro-jalapeño sauce (50¢).

PRINCEVILLE
pop 1698

The grandiose fountain at Princeville's entrance says it all. Welcome to Kaua'i's largest and most exclusive planned community, which emerged after the luxury Princeville Hotel was built in 1985. Before then, the promontory between 'Anini Beach and Hanalei Bay was a swath of pristine ranch land.

Today the 11,000-acre community is both resort and suburb (albeit suburbia for folks with money). The main street is a wide thoroughfare flanked by manicured lawns, two celebrated golf greens and well-marked side streets to 1500 condo units and 600 houses (at last count). The road terminates at the magnificent Princeville Hotel.

In a 2005 *New York Times* study, Princeville ranked ninth among the most-expensive US second-home markets, with a median home price of $715,000 in 2004. The multitude of condos and vacation rentals gives a resort atmosphere, but Princeville is, sadly, not pedestrian oriented. A car is imperative as shopping and dining options are simply too far away or, considering highway traffic, risky. The vibe is more 'bedroom community' than funky surf town, happening beach strip or lively commercial mecca. (Those would be Hanalei, Po'ipu and the Coconut Coast, respectively.)

The influx of outside money into Princeville has modernized the North Shore. Here you'll find the North Shore's only gas station and fire station, plus the main shopping center, located right outside the resort complex, along Kuhio Hwy. A small airport sits south of Princeville, but it serves mainly helicopter tours.

Princeville stands in sharp contrast to its neighboring, rural, free-spirited North Shore communities. But its design tries to tread lightly, with low-rise condos and relatively uncrowded development. Princeville makes a good day trip for swimming at Queen's Bath, relaxing at Hideaways, or just admiring the splendid view outside the Princeville Hotel (join the daily crowd at sunset).

History

Princeville traces its roots to Robert Wyllie, a Scottish doctor who became foreign minister to Kamehameha IV. In the mid-19th

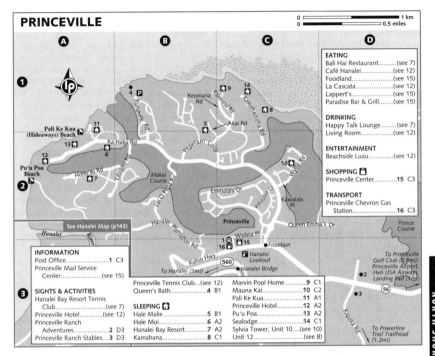

PRINCEVILLE

century Wyllie bought a coffee plantation in Hanalei and began planting sugar. When Queen Emma and Kamehameha IV came to visit in 1860, Wyllie named his plantation and the surrounding lands Princeville in honor of their two-year-old son, Prince Albert, who died only two years later. The plantation later became a cattle ranch.

Orientation
Kuhio Hwy changes from Hwy 56 to Hwy 560 at the 28-mile marker in front of Princeville. The 10-mile stretch from here to Ke'e Beach at the end of the road is perhaps the most scenic drive in all of Hawaii.

Information
Only one shopping center, Princeville Center, serves the entire community, but it only has the basics: supermarket, small medical clinic, banks, library, a restaurant or two, gas station, hardware store, mail facilities and numerous real-estate agencies.

Post office (☎ 800-275-8777; Princeville Center; ☉ 10:30am-3:30pm Mon-Fri, to 12:30pm Sat)

Princeville Mail Service Center (☎ 826-7331; Princeville Center; ☉ 9am-5:30pm Mon-Fri) Just a hole-in-the-wall at the center, but it offers mailing and fax services (including UPS and US Post), Internet access (per 15 minutes $3), dry cleaning, storage, Western Union, photocopying and more. You can send shipments to yourself here but only if you use a private shipping company, not US Post. Address shipments to yourself c/o Princeville Mail Service Center, 5-4280 Kuhio Hwy, Princeville, HI 96722.

Sights
PRINCEVILLE HOTEL
Whether due to the ornate decor, the private promontory location or the stunning view of Hanalei Bay, this hotel is Kaua'i's most luxurious. The grand lobby sweeps you away with floor-to-ceiling windows and 180-degree views of Makana mountain (commonly called 'Bali Hai,' the name popularized by the movie *South Pacific*). All the giant urns, chintz sofas, chandeliers and slabs of gleaming marble inside are no match for the glorious piece of nature outside.

The luxury hotel was erected amid enormous controversy in 1985. Locals, who were ticked at losing one of their favorite sunset spots, nicknamed the bluff-side building 'the Prison.' The original hotel was indeed dark and inward-looking, and it so failed to incorporate its surroundings that the owners closed it down in 1989. Over the next two years the hotel was gutted and virtually rebuilt.

Even if you neither sleep nor dine here, you can partake in the hotel's perfect vantage point for Bali Hai. Just park in the public lot and stroll toward the grassy bank to the right of the main lobby. Every sunset brings a throng of admirers, from enthralled shutterbugs to romantic couples hand in hand – cliché or not, Hanalei sunsets never grow stale!

PALI KE KUA (HIDEAWAYS) & PU'U POA BEACHES

Pali Ke Kua Beach (also called Hideaways Beach) is Princeville's magnificent secluded lozenge of sand. When calm, there's good swimming and snorkeling, and it's perfect for sunset any time. To get here, park in the public lot just after the guardhouse at the Princeville Hotel and take the path between the fences. After several minutes, the trail becomes unbelievably steep, with stairs and ropes to aid your descent. For roomier play, head to Pu'u Poa Beach, between the Princeville Hotel and the mouth of the Hanalei River. High surf, common in winter, can generate dangerous currents at both beaches.

QUEEN'S BATH

This delightful lava-rock pool right on the shoreline provides a natural protected swimming and snorkeling hole. The surf splashes in softly or with a crash, periodically flushing clean the ice-blue pool, which is so salty you float along effortlessly. Look for turtles and monk seals just beyond the pool.

To get here, enter the Princeville Hotel area and drive just under 1.5 miles before turning right onto Punahele Rd. Park in the area at the end of the road and take the trail to the right. It's about a 10-minute walk to the bottom. About halfway down, you'll pass a gushing waterfall, but be careful rinsing off here, as leptospirosis lurks (see p240). When you reach the shore, turn left and walk over the rocks for five minutes.

Activities
HIKING

Due to Princeville's location on a promontory, hiking here generally means scrambling down rocky cliffs to the beach (or hoofing it across the parking lot to your car). The sole major hike is the north end of the **Powerline Trail**, but starting from the south end at Keahua Arboretum (see p105) is recommended. If you do choose to hike from here, the trailhead is on Kapaka Rd, just south of Princeville Ranch Stables.

GOLF

The Robert Trent Jones Jr–designed championship links at the **Princeville Golf Club** (☎ Prince 826-5000, Makai 826-3580; www.princeville .com; 5-3900 Kuhio Hwy; green fees Prince nonguest/guest $175/150, Makai nonguest/guest $125/110, club rental $35) are legendary; the 18-hole par-72 Prince Course, which Jones created in 1990, is Kaua'i's highest-rated course. The 27-hole par-72 Makai Course, c 1971, comprises three aptly named nines – Woods, Lake and Ocean – and it recently enjoyed a $3 million refurbishing. It might interest aficionados to compare the Prince and Makai courses, as they reflect Jones' evolution.

Green fees include cart and day pass to the spa. If you play from noon or later, 'twilight' discounts (Prince $120, Makai $85) save you a bundle, with deeper discounts as the day goes on. Collared shirts are required.

TENNIS

You can hit at either the **Princeville Tennis Club** (☎ 826-1230; www.princeville.com; Princeville Hotel, 5-3900 Kuhio Hwy; court per person per hr $15; ◷ 9am-5pm) or the **Hanalei Bay Resort Tennis Club** (☎ 826-6522; Hanalei Bay Resort; court per person per hr $6; ◷ 9am-9pm).

HORSEBACK RIDING

Saddle up for a horseback ride at **Princeville Ranch Stables** (☎ 826-6777; www.princevilleranch .com; Kuhio Hwy; tours $65-170; ◷ tours Mon-Sat) between the 26- and 27-mile markers, spanning 2500 acres of cattle country, from mountain to ocean. The company is owned by the Carswell family, whose other members own Princeville Ranch Adventures and Kaua'i Backcountry Adventures.

The popular waterfall ride (three-/four-hour tour $110/120) crosses ranch land to

Kalihiwai Falls for a picnic and swim. Or play *paniolo* (cowboy) with a cattle drive ride that lets city slickers help round up a cattle herd and drive them to their next pasture. For a quick jaunt, try the 1½-hour ocean bluff ride. Riders cannot be under eight years old or over 230lb.

MULTIACTIVITY ADVENTURES

Princeville Ranch Adventures (☎ 826-7669, 888-955-7669; www.adventureskauai.com; tours $79-125) offers a 4½-hour tour that combines eight ziplines, a suspension bridge, a swimming hole and lunch. The age and weight minimums are 12 and 80lb, so it allows smaller kids to participate than the other major zipline outfit, Kaua'i Backcountry Adventures.

Another four-hour tour includes a kayak paddle to a waterfall pool plus a picnic lunch – a good, less-crowded substitute for the Wailua River Secret Falls paddle. The shortest and simplest three-hour tour involves a hike to a waterfall–swimming hole and picnic lunch.

Tours

While not the best option on the island, **Heli USA Airways** (☎ 826-6591, 866-936-1234; www.heli usahawaii.com; 30/45/60min tours $109/169/199) flies from Princeville Airport, which is handy if you're on the North Shore. This mega outfit, which also runs O'ahu tours, just seems a tad impersonal. One of its helicopters crashed in the fall of 2005, killing three passengers.

Sleeping

Princeville's condo complexes are either perched on seaside cliffs or sitting peacefully along golf greens. Bear in mind, sea breezes make a huge difference in comfort level (just compare the temperature in inland parking lots versus those along the windy shore).

Most condo complexes do not rely on a single agency, do individual owners either hire an agency or manage their own rentals. If you want to stay at a particular complex, simply do a Google search to find all available units. Note that even within the same complex, units will vary in quality and appearance, as well as in cost.

Get all the details before booking, as there are usually cleaning fees, minimum stays (typically five to seven nights) and

other restrictions. Weekly rates are generally 25% lower than daily rates, giving an incentive to booking seven rather than five nights.

Check www.vrbo.com, an extensive online list of vacation rentals, and contact the following agencies, which have fairly extensive Princeville rentals:

'Anini Aloha Properties (☎ 828-0067, 800-246-5382; www.aninialoha.com; 4270 Kilauea Rd, Suite I-1, Kilauea 96754) Extensive selection of North Shore rentals, including Princeville condos, and an especially good list of dream houses from Anahola to Ha'ena.

Coldwell Banker Bali Hai Realty (☎ 866-400-7368; www.balihai.com; 5-5088 Kuhio Hwy, PO Box 930, Hanalei, HI 96714) Established in 1978, Bali Hai has extensive listings for the North Shore, particularly in Hanalei, 'Anini and Kilauea. Office located in heart of Hanalei. On-staff Japanese translator available.

Kaua'i Vacation Rentals (☎ 245-8841, 800-367-5025; www.kauaivacationrentals.com; 3-3311 Kuhio Hwy, Lihu'e, HI 96766) A longtime all-island agency.

North Shore Properties (☎ 826-9622, 800-488-3336; www.hanaleinorthshoreproperties.com; PO Box 607, Hanalei, HI 96714) Long-standing, female-owned company; specializes in unique North Shore vacation rentals, both condos and getaway houses. Handles properties all the way from Anahola to Ha'ena, including Hanalei, Kilauea and 'Anini.

Oceanfront Realty (☎ 826-6585, 800-222-5541; www.oceanfrontrealty.com; PO Box 223190, Princeville, HI 96722) Handles mainly condos in Princeville.

MIDRANGE

Condos

Condos can be booked through the agencies (see above); unless stated otherwise, prices vary depending on individual owners.

Sealodge (☎ 650-573-0636, 800-585-6101, 866-922-5642; Kamehameha Ave; 1-bedroom unit $120-145, 2-bedroom unit $145-170; 🏊) Slightly weathered, Sealodge is nevertheless a top complex, thanks to its oceanfront setting. Just open the lanai door, feel the breeze and hear the pounding surf – it's a far cry from the still, warm inland air. The units are comfortable, if basic. No in-unit washer/dryer but laundry facilities available on-site. Of 86 total units, 55 are available as vacation rentals; we list the phone numbers of the three agencies who manage about 35 units altogether; also try a Google search and call the agencies listed above.

Kamahana (Kamehameha Rd; 🏊) Most units overlook the sweeping greens of Princeville's

Makai Course, so noise is minimal. Because the complex is not oceanfront, units tend to be hotter (without ocean breezes) and also cheaper.

Unit 12 (☎ 826-9622; www.rentalsonkauai.com; per week $850) This one-bedroom place is among the more economical units at Kamahana. It's compact but smartly decorated, with a slightly sunken living room facing a quiet swath of golf course (and the ocean beyond). With one bedroom plus a sofa pull-out, it sleeps four. Includes washer/dryer. Contact North Shore Properties.

Hale Moi (☎ 826-9394, 800-535-0085; www.marcre sorts.com; Ka Haku Rd; studio cottage $120-220, 1-bedroom cottage $140-250) Rustic-looking wooden buildings on stilts serve as comfy cottages. Guests won't have oceanfront settings or hear crashing waves because the cottages sit on the inland side of the road, but they're more economical.

Mauna Kai (3920 Wyllie Rd; 🏊) This complex, located near the entrance to Princeville, comprises two- or three-story units with lots of windows and a clean, white look. The distance from the ocean means rates are often reasonable.

Sylvia Tower, Unit 10 (☎ 826-9622; www.rent alsonkauai.com; per week $1000) One particularly sweet set-up at Mauna Kai is this three-story condo owned by well-known, California-based professional harpist Sylvia Woods. This two-bedroom, 2.5-bathroom unit lets you spread out: at the top is a sun-filled kitchen; in the middle is the master bedroom with computer and high-speed Ethernet connection, plus washer/dryer. If you want, you can play the Dusty Strings FH-36B harp she leaves there. Ideal for folks who don't mind stairs. Contact North Shore Properties.

Pali Ke Kua (☎ 826-9394, 800-535-0085; www .marcresorts.com; Ka Haku Rd; 1-bedroom unit $150-350, 2-bedroom unit $205-450; 🏊) One of Princeville's upscale properties, Pali Ke Kua shines with subdued style. Many units are managed by Marc Resorts, with an office in the complex. Oceanfront units add between $45 and $80 to the nightly cost. Depending on availability, rates can vary by over 50%. If you can snag an oceanfront one-bedroom unit for $195 instead of the $350 rack rate, it's a steal.

Pu'u Poa (☎ 826-9394, 800-535-0085; www.marc resorts.com; Ka Haku Rd; 2-bedroom unit $275-500; 🏊) Located right next to Princeville Hotel,

Pu'u Poa is another property managed predominantly by Marc Resorts.

Homes

Weekly rates for vacation-rental homes can soar as high as $6500 for mansions. Here are a couple of $1000-per-week homes that offer more privacy than condos.

Marvin Pool Home (☎ 826-9622; www.rental sonkauai.com; 3583 Keoniana Rd; house per week $1000; 🏊) Ideal for families, with three bedrooms and two bathrooms. While the interior design could use a dose of modern chic, the large private swimming pool more than compensates. Secluded and quiet, except for the hypnotic pounding surf just below the property. Contact North Shore Properties.

Hale Malie (☎ 826-9622; www.rentalsonkauai.com; 4911 Akai Rd; house per week $1000) For a couple who wants a sprawling, apartment-size master suite, this is it. While there are three bedrooms and two bathrooms, the entire top floor is the master suite, with Jacuzzi tub in the master bathroom. Windows on virtually all walls let in lots of sunlight; furnishings are standard tropical. Contact North Shore Properties.

TOP END

Hanalei Bay Resort (☎ 826-6522, 800-827-4427; www .hanaleibayresort.com; 5380 Hono'iki Rd; r $185-275, studio unit incl kitchenette $215-240, 1-bedroom unit incl kitchen & breakfast $350-390; 🍽 🏊) While certainly pleasant, the Hanalei Bay Resort suffers slightly in the shadow of the belle-of-the-ball Princeville Resort. The decor is above-average tropical but not luxurious, and staffers lack the easy graciousness of their counterparts at Princeville. But the ocean views are equally stunning and, since you can choose from hotel or condo rooms, it's ideal if you want a kitchen. A small agency called Aloha Condos (☎ 930-1830, 877-782-5642; www .alohacondos.com) manages 10 excellent and competitively priced options here, two with wi-fi.

Princeville Hotel (☎ 826-9644, 800-325-3589; www.princevillehotelhawaii.com; 5520 Ka Haku Rd; r Internet/rack from $302/465, ste Internet/rack from $533/820; 🍽 🏊) Deluxe, over-the-top rooms feature deep-soaking tubs and phenomenal coastal views –plus modern gadgets like liquid-crystal windows between the bedroom and bath that morph from clear to opaque with the flick of a switch. Outside, the magnificent pool resembles endless turquoise glass. It's an exercise in decadence, but the atmosphere is down-to-earth; staffers are not at all snooty (and much more pleasant and friendly than the bored folks at cheap condos). Rates typically run 35% below rack and vary considerably depending on occupancy. The self- and valet-parking rate is $15.

Eating
Beyond the sit-down dining options at the Princeville Hotel and Hanalei Bay Resort, pickings are slim in Princeville. Head to Kilauea or Hanalei for a far superior selection of both grocers and restaurants.

BUDGET
In a pinch, you'll find a basic supermarket, ice-cream shop and burger joint.

Foodland (☎ 826-9880; Princeville Center; ✆ 6am-11pm) Standard supermarket with better selection than Hanalei's Big Save. Cheap bakery and deli with takeaway items for a basic lunch.

Lappert's (☎ 826-7393; single scoop $3.10; Princeville Center; ✆ 10am-9pm) Kaua'i's own ice-creamery, featuring the all-time favorite Kaua'i Pie and other tropical flavors.

Paradise Bar & Grill (☎ 826-1775; sandwiches $7-8.50; Princeville Center; ✆ 11am-11pm) Casual, touristy hangout serving burgers and a panoply of fried creations. Full bar.

MIDRANGE & TOP END
Café Hanalei (☎ 826-2760; Princeville Hotel; breakfast $6-10, lunch $12-20, dinner $21-35, 3-course prix fixe $52; ✆ 6:30am-2:30pm & 5:30-9:30pm) At this breezy terrace restaurant, the food can hardly compete with the staggering Hanalei Bay view. But the cuisine is playful and well-executed, eg an oyster 'martini' appetizer spiked with fiery pepper vodka, rack of lamb marinated in Kaua'i coffee and a 'bento box' filled with *somen* (thin wheat noodles), sushi, grilled tofu and 'ahi poke. Or just drop in for dessert: the signature chocolate baby cake or chocolate tower filled with *liliko'i* mousse are heavenly.

La Cascata (☎ 826-2761; Princeville Hotel; dinner mains $24-36, 3-course prix fixe $52; ✆ 6-10pm) With perhaps the best views of Bali Hai, the food here is pricier and less innovative than at Café Hanalei. The atmosphere is cozier, however, with warm tones and a Mediterranean feel. The menu includes upscale, haute starters, like seared foie gras and 'ahi and roasted beet tartare. Mains are mostly fancy pasta and heavy meats and game. The crispy-skin *onaga* (snapper) with wild mushrooms stands out.

Bali Hai Restaurant (☎ 826-6522; Hanalei Bay Resort; breakfast & lunch $8-15, dinner mains $31-38; ✆ 7-11am, 11:30am-2pm & 5-9pm) Another feast for your eyes awaits at this open-air dining room with a panoramic view of Hanalei Bay. For breakfast, the specialty is fried eggs, Portuguese sausage, poi pancakes and taro hash browns. The dinner menu is heavy on seafood (for good reason), from the 'ahi poke tower ($12) to creamy linguini with lobster, shrimp and scallops ($38); fish preparations change daily. Desserts include a Kahlua-spiked warm chocolate-pudding

---

DINNER ON THE BEACH

If your two biggest fantasies are 'romantic beach' and 'personal gourmet chef,' good news. You can simultaneously make them come true on Kaua'i… for a few hundred bucks.

Princeville Hotel (☎ 826-9644, 800-325-3589; www.princevillehotelhawaii.com; 5520 Ka Haku Rd; dinner per couple $435) can arrange a private dinner for two on the beach (or in a garden). You meet a personal server in the lobby and then proceed to a secluded spot, complete with flickering candlelight and torches (and, of course, a chilled bottle of champagne). The Princeville restaurants prepare the four courses you choose.

If you're not a Princeville Hotel guest, private companies offer similar pampering. **Heavenly Creations** (☎ 877-828-1700; www.heavenlycreations.org; dinner per couple $285), led by chef Steve Star, will serve a gourmet dinner on the beach of your choice. Star, who studied with Jeremiah Tower in San Francisco, might prepare his specialties such as papaya-watercress salad, macadamia-crusted marlin or smoked-'ahi-stuffed mushrooms. But he's also happy to accommodate your preferences (eg Hawaiian Regional Cuisine, low-fat, vegetarian, vegan, French or your own favorite recipes).

cake and a 'low-carb' flourless chocolate torte (yes, *very* healthy!). Cheaper eats are served at the Happy Talk Lounge.

Drinking & Entertainment
BARS & NIGHTCLUBS
Happy Talk Lounge (☎ 826-6522; Hanalei Bay Resort; ☽ 11am-9:45pm) Enjoy the same (or better) views here as at the resort's more buttoned-up Bali Hai Restaurant. There's a tasty bar menu ($7 to $15) from 2pm to 9pm, live jazz from 4pm to 7pm Sunday and Hawaiian music most other nights.

Living Room (☎ 826-9644; Princeville Hotel; ☽ 3-11pm) A spectacular view of Hanalei Bay, thanks to a bodacious location and glass walls, makes this a fine place for a sunset drink and sushi rolls. The lovely live entertainment from 7:30pm to 10:30pm swaddles this lounge in ambience. Catch the Ko'olau Trio (Ken Emerson, Poncho Graham and Kirby Keough) on Sunday nights at 7:30pm.

La Cascata (☎ 826-2761; Princeville Hotel; ☽ 6-10pm) Slack-key tunes by Ken Emerson and Poncho Graham on Monday and Tuesday nights at 7:30.

Landing Pad (☎ 826-9561; Princeville Airport, 5-3541 Kuhio Hwy; admission $3-5; ☽ 9pm-2am Wed-Mon) Odd as it might seem, this airport bar is a decent place to drop in for local reggae or rock bands on Friday or Saturday; karaoke or DJ and dancing on weeknights.

LUAU
Beachside luau (☎ 826-2788; Princeville Hotel; adult/child 6-12/senior 65 and over $69/35/60; ☽ 6pm Mon & Thu) The only luau option on the North Shore is this one, at the Princeville Hotel. The spectacular setting raises this otherwise rather typical dinner – featuring the expected *imu* (underground cooking pit) ceremony and a better-than-average Hawaiian buffet – up a notch. The performances, which feature music and dance from Tahiti, New Zealand, Samoa and Hawaii, aren't as spirited or in-your-face as others, however. Still, any luau near the beach, where you can stroll off for a breather, can't be too bad.

Getting Around
The **Princeville Chevron gas station** (Kuhio Hwy; ☽ 6am-10pm Mon-Sat, to 9pm Sun) is the last stop to buy gas before the end of the road at Ke'e

Beach. Beware: pump prices are always at least 10¢ higher than the cheapest Westside stations.

A car is imperative here. While Princeville is a safe community, with lots of green space, its sprawling layout is not conducive to walking. The vast gulf between condo complexes, restaurants and Princeville Center makes it highly unpleasant to walk – especially with cars zooming past.

HANALEI VALLEY
Round the first curve west of Princeville and – wow! – you enter another realm altogether. It's impossible to describe the North Shore's grandeur without sounding trite, but perfectly curved bays and emerald cliffs do seem magnified in intensity here. Kaua'i is a phenomenon of nature, not of man-made civilization, and the coast from Hanalei to Ha'ena epitomizes its natural wonders. The rustic drive itself, with sharp curves and river crossings, only highlights your journey to a region still relatively remote and untouched. Even before driving through Hanalei, you'll pass a few icons.

Sights & Activities
HANALEI VALLEY LOOKOUT
Just beyond Princeville, on Kuhio Hwy, this lookout (Map p135) provides a spectacular bird's-eye view of the valley floor with its meandering river and spread of patchwork taro fields. It's a beautiful scene, and while many people pull in, jump out, snap photos and move on, take a moment to grasp the valley's serene grace. From the lookout, off to your lower right-hand side you can see the North Shore's first one-lane bridge, which opened in 1912. Visible to the south are the twin peaks of Hihimanu ('beautiful' in Hawaiian).

HANALEI BRIDGE
Seven one-lane bridges, including the Hanalei Bridge (Map p135), mark the drive from the Hanalei River to the end of the road. They might seem quaint and anachronistic, but they serve to protect the North Shore from development, as big cement trucks and heavy construction equipment are beyond the bridges' limits. Even large tour buses cannot venture here. Over the years, developers have introduced numerous proposals to build a two-lane bridge

over the Hanalei River, but North Shore residents have successfully beaten them down. During torrential rains, the road between the taro fields and the river can flood, forcing the Hanalei Bridge to close until the water subsides.

HANALEI VALLEY SCENIC DRIVE

If you like what you saw from the lookout, head into the Hanalei Valley by turning left onto Ohiki Rd immediately after the Hanalei Bridge. This 2-mile scenic drive through the **Hanalei National Wildlife Refuge** (Map pp128-9; http://pacificislands.fws.gov/wnwr /khanaleinwr.html) parallels the Hanalei River, passing taro fields, banana trees, bamboo thickets, *hau* (hibiscus) trees and wild ginger, all encompassing 917 acres of the valley, stretching up both sides of the Hanalei River.

Prior to Western contact, the valley was planted with taro, but in the mid-1800s rice paddies were planted to feed the Chinese laborers who were working in the cane fields. The rice grew so well that by the 1880s it became a major export crop. The demand for rice eventually waned, and while taro once again predominates, what you see is only 5% of that original acreage planted in taro. The wetland taro farms in the refuge produce two-thirds of Hawaii's commercially grown poi taro and also create a habitat for endangered Hawaiian waterbirds.

Established in 1972 the refuge is closed to the public. But even from the roadside, birders can spot some of the 49 types of birds using the habitat, including snow-white egrets and night herons, as well as the valley's endangered native species:

- *alae keʻokeʻo* (Hawaiian coot): slate-gray with white forehead
- *aeʻo* (Hawaiian stilt): slender with black back, white chest and long pink legs
- *ʻalae ʻula* (Hawaiian moorhen): dark-gray with black head and distinctive red-and-yellow bill
- *koloa maoli* (Hawaiian duck): mottled brown with orange legs and feet

You can enter the refuge on the Hoʻopula-pula Haraguchi Rice Mill Tour (p145).

HIKING

For those seeking a punishing hike, torture yourself with the steep **Hanalei-Okolehau Trail**, which ascends 1250ft in under 2 miles, passes through the Hanalei National Wildlife Refuge and offers 360-degree views at the top. It's hard to recommend the hike with a clear conscience because of its merciless grade through so-so scenery. Allow at least three hours for the 4.5-mile round-trip. Note: *okolehau* is a Hawaiian liquor distilled from the ti plant, which you'll see along the path.

To get to the trailhead, follow the Kuhio Hwy until just past the Hanalei Bridge, then take a left onto Ohiki Rd. The signposted trailhead is 0.75 miles down the road across from the dirt parking lot on your left. Cross the footbridge at the start of the trail and enter the confusing network of trails-of-use. Basically, the trail turns right at the first two forks (left turns go to the bird-watching overlooks of the pond inside the

---

RULES OF THE ROAD

Don't play chicken when crossing the one-lane bridges from Hanalei to the end of the road. Follow the local bridge etiquette:

- Stop at the white line. Otherwise you might cause an accident or traffic jam (or receive *da stink eye*).
- If the bridge is empty and you reach it first, go.
- If a car is crossing ahead of you, follow.
- If you see cars approaching from the opposite direction, yield to the entire queue of approaching cars.
- Exception: if you are the sixth or seventh car crossing the bridge, stop and let the opposite side go. It's just common courtesy. And if another person stops and waits to let your side cross, don't forget to give a thank-you wave (or, better yet, the shaka sign!).

refuge). About 10ft before the gate marked 'Unauthorized Entry Prohibited,' turn left up the dirt 4WD road, which later becomes a forest path.

A bit less than 0.75 miles up, you'll see a large concrete powerline tower. The view of Hanalei from here is spectacular, and you could stop here for a more moderate hike. Otherwise, it's just over a mile of impossibly steep scrambling up Kauka'opua Hill to reach a final panoramic viewpoint framed by ti plants. The higher you go, the more exposed the trail becomes. Steep ups and downs might require you to use your hands to brace yourself.

The return trip means no more climbing, but the incessant downhill is killer on the knees. Despite the awesome views, this trail is for diehards only. Remember, the land flanking both sides of the trail is the refuge, so don't stray.

HANALEI
pop 478

While surfers follow the waves wherever they break, Hanalei is the island's only actual surf town. The vibe is palpable, from the daily influx of board-laden trucks to the ubiquitous suntans and board shorts. Here, not only do tourists appear happy and relaxed, but even residents seem permanently on vacation mode – hitting the waves daily after work or school. Many are transplants, who came for the waves or the exotic remoteness (which is fast disappearing) and somehow never left. Hanalei still exudes a casual, slightly hippie vibe, but the flood of new money has added a layer of exclusivity, too.

In the early 1970s Hanalei was still relatively unknown to mass tourism. But today Hanalei is a destination, and traffic is a constant backdrop. Still, as you cross the Hanalei Bridge and pass the lazy Hanalei River drifting past fields of taro, you know you're crossing a threshold. The pace immediately slows, there are no buildings in sight and time feels suspended. Unlike many Kaua'i towns, Hanalei does not reflect the island's sugarcane-plantation history as much as its traditional Hawaiian *kalo* (taro) and fishing roots.

The village took a beating during Hurricane 'Iniki, losing many historic wooden buildings. Fortunately, most reconstruction reflects a period style that matches the town's original rustic character. Lavish vacation homes abound here, making Hanalei ideal for travelers who prefer an escape from the conventional bustling resort atmosphere. Outdoorsy types would also feel at home here, close to the island's most famous surfing and hiking.

Orientation & Information

Nearly anything you might desire can be found in Hanalei Center, on the *mauka* (inland) side of Kuhio Hwy, or Ching Young Village, on the *makai* (seaward) side of the highway. Ching Young Village arose from the old Ching Young Store, the North Shore's main general store since the 19th century, and is now an art gallery called Evolve Love.

Hanalei has no bank (there are none west of Princeville), but there is an ATM in the Ching Young Village's Big Save supermarket.

Bali Hai Photo (☎ 826-9181; Ching Young Village; per hr $9; ⏱ 8am-8pm Mon-Fri, 9am-5pm Sat, 10am-5pm Sun) Internet access.

Java Kai (☎ 826-6717; Hanalei Center; ⏱ 6:30am-6pm) Lively, open-air hangout spot with wi-fi Internet access only.

Post office (☎ 800-275-8777; 5-5226 Kuhio Hwy) In the village center.

Sights
WAI'OLI HUI'IA CHURCH & MISSION HOUSE

Hanalei's first missionaries, the Reverend and Mrs William Alexander, arrived in 1834 in a double-hulled canoe. Their church, hall and mission house remain in the middle of town, set on a huge manicured lawn with a beautiful mountain backdrop.

The pretty green wooden **church** retains an airy Pacific feel, with large, outward-opening windows and high ceilings. The doors remain open during the day, and visitors are welcome. A Bible printed in Hawaiian and dating to 1868 is displayed on top of the old organ. The Wai'oli Church Choir, the island's best, sings hymns in Hawaiian at the 10am Sunday service.

Wai'oli Mission Hall, to the right of the church, was built in 1836. The hall, which originally served as the church, was built of coral lime and plaster with a steeply pitched roof to handle Hanalei's heavy rains.

Behind the church and hall is the **Wai'oli Mission House** (☎ 245-3202; admission by donation;

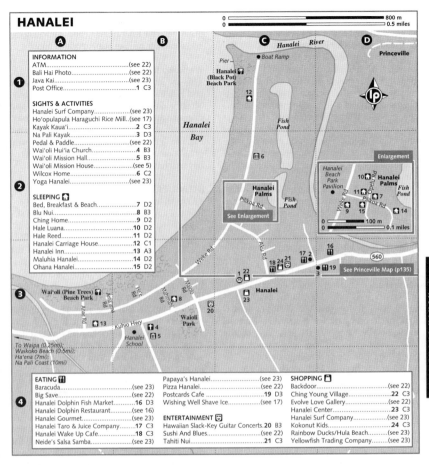

HANALEI

INFORMATION
ATM...(see 22)
Bali Hai Photo................................(see 22)
Java Kai...(see 23)
Post Office...**1** C3

SIGHTS & ACTIVITIES
Hanalei Surf Company.....................(see 23)
Ho'opulapula Haraguchi Rice Mill..(see 17)
Kayak Kaua'i.......................................**2** C3
Na Pali Kayak....................................**3** D3
Pedal & Paddle...............................(see 22)
Wai'oli Hui'ia Church...........................**4** B3
Wai'oli Mission Hall............................**5** B3
Wai'oli Mission House.....................(see 5)
Wilcox Home..**6** C2
Yoga Hanalei..................................(see 23)

SLEEPING
Bed, Breakfast & Beach........................**7** D2
Blu Nui...**8** B3
Ching Home...**9** D2
Hale Luana..**10** D2
Hale Reed..**11** D2
Hanalei Carriage House.......................**12** C1
Hanalei Inn..**13** A3
Maluhia Hanalei.................................**14** D2
Ohana Hanalei....................................**15** D2

EATING
Baracuda..(see 23)
Big Save..(see 22)
Hanalei Dolphin Fish Market............**16** D3
Hanalei Dolphin Restaurant.............(see 16)
Hanalei Gourmet.............................(see 23)
Hanalei Taro & Juice Company........**17** C3
Hanalei Wake Up Cafe......................**18** C3
Neide's Salsa Samba........................(see 23)

Papaya's Hanalei.............................(see 23)
Pizza Hanalei..................................(see 22)
Postcards Cafe...................................**19** D3
Wishing Well Shave Ice...................(see 17)

ENTERTAINMENT
Hawaiian Slack-Key Guitar Concerts.**20** B3
Sushi And Blues...............................(see 22)
Tahiti Nui..**21** C3

SHOPPING
Backdoor...(see 22)
Ching Young Village..........................**22** C3
Evolve Love Gallery.........................(see 22)
Hanalei Center...................................**23** C3
Hanalei Surf Company......................(see 23)
Kokonut Kids....................................**24** C3
Rainbow Ducks/Hula Beach.............(see 23)
Yellowfish Trading Company.........(see 23)

Princeville

Hanalei River

Pier — Boat Ramp

Hanalei (Black Pot) Beach Park

Hanalei Bay

Fish Pond

Hanalei Palms

Hanalei Beach Park Pavilion

See Enlargement

See Princeville Map (p135)

Wai'oli (Pine Trees) Beach Park

Hanalei

Waioli Park

Hanalei School

To Waipa (0.25mi);
Waikoko Beach (0.5mi);
Ha'ena (7mi);
Na Pali Coast (10mi)

NORTH SHORE

9am-3pm Tue, Thu & Sat). The Alexanders spent their first three years living in a grass hut here, but couldn't adjust to living Hawaiian style, so they built this big New England house. It was home to other missionaries over the years, most notably Abner and Luci Wilcox, whose family became the island's most predominant property holders. The main part of the house, built in 1837, has old wavy glass panes, well-preserved period furniture, quality woodwork and notable architecture. They don't build 'em like they used to, do they?

To get to the inconspicuous parking lot, coming from the east turn inland immediately before Hanalei School and then left on the dirt driveway opposite the water hydrant.

HANALEI BAY

Hanalei, which means 'crescent bay,' is a scenic and seemingly endless stretch of sand. The wave action here is changeable: flat in summer and pounding in winter. So it's not the best swimming spot, but surfers arrive in droves from around the island. There are several beaches along the bay: The best are at Hanalei (Black Pot) Beach Park and Wai'oli (Pine Trees) Beach Park, which both have rest rooms, showers, drinking water, picnic tables and grills. Black Pot is the best place for catching the sunset, because you can see Bali Hai from there. Another easy-access public beach is at the **Hanalei Beach Park Pavilion** (also with facilities) on Weke Rd near Aku Rd.

On the opposite side of the road, midway between the beach pavilion and Hanalei Beach Park, check out the rustic brown mansion with the wraparound porch, sitting sedately in a sprawling lawn. This is the private **Wilcox Home**, which traces its roots to early Hanalei missionaries Abner and Luci Wilcox. The remains of a narrow-gauge railway track, once used to haul Hanalei rice, lead to the long pier jutting into the bay.

You can learn the names of Hawaiian fish simply by memorizing the road names along the beach, as each is named after a different fish.

Hanalei (Black Pot) Beach Park

Often dubbed simply 'Hanalei Pier,' due to its unmistakable landmark, this stretch of sand shaded by ironwood trees at Hanalei Beach Park is popular mainly with surfers. The sandy-bottom beach slopes gently, making it very safe for beginners. Lessons are typically taught here, just west of the pier, where you find surf schools lining up big ol' softboards and rashguards daily. In summer, swimming and snorkeling are decent, as are camping and kayaking. As always, take extreme caution during periods of high surf as dangerous shore breaks and rip currents are common.

At the eastern end of the park, the mouth of the Hanalei River opens into the beach, and you'll find a small boat ramp where kayakers launch for trips up the river. This spot is called **Black Pot**, after a big black wok owned by Henry Tai Hook, who used to cook community meals here in the late 1800s or early 1900s.

Wai'oli (Pine Trees) Beach Park

Pine Trees boasts perhaps the bay's highest winter surf; it's the site of various surfing contests, including the **Pine Trees Longboard Classic**, held in late April, which showcases local talent from up-and-coming kids to aging legends. Pro surfers Bruce and Andy Iron cut their teeth here and each February they sponsor the Pine Trees Classic, an event for kids to compete, meet their idols and win prizes. Swimming is hazardous here except during the calmest summer surf. A section, known locally as **Toilet Bowls**, on Ama'ama Rd has rest rooms and showers. Gaze on million-dollar views here.

Waikoko Beach

This beach (no facilities), protected by a reef on the western bend of Hanalei Bay, offers a sandy bottom and shallower and calmer waters than the middle of the bay. Pull off the highway around the 4-mile marker. Winter surfing is sometimes good off Makahoa Point, the western point of the bay; surfers call this break **Waikokos**.

Activities

KAYAKING

For the independent kayaker, the Hanalei River is ideal. The 6-mile round-trip journey through the Hanalei National Wildlife Refuge is way less congested than the Wailua River, and occasionally the riverbed is luxuriantly canopied by overhanging trees. Your paddling distance depends on the water level in the river.

The Hanalei River is perfect for novice paddlers to practice solo, or for children. You can launch your kayak right at the dock, and it's impossible to get lost. A self-guided paddle is nice and flexible: you can paddle all day or for just an hour,

For kayak rentals try **Pedal & Paddle** (☎ 826-9069; www.pedalnpaddle.com; Ching Young Village; single kayaks per day/week $15/60, double kayaks $35/140; 🕑 9am-6pm), which offers all equipment, and gear to secure it to your car. Check out the clear-bottomed kayaks (per day $45) for use at Hanalei or 'Anini. Rent snorkel sets (per day/week $5/20), boogie boards (per day/week $5/20), beach chairs and umbrellas, tents (per day/week $12/35), sleeping bags (per day/week $3/10) and backpacks (per day/week $5/20). Another option for rental is Kayak Kaua'i.

If you want to get hardcore, consider the 17-mile Na Pali Coast trip. This strenuous, all-day paddle is only possible from May to September, due to rough seas. Even in the summer calm you should take motion-sickness preventives the day before (the biggest obstacles are seasickness and the mental challenge).

The put-in is at Ha'ena and the take-out at Polihale, where a van picks you up to return to Hanalei, meaning you circumnavigate Kaua'i in a day. When conditions are right, you'll enter several caves, including (if you're lucky) the **Double Door Cave**, with a freshwater cascade pouring through the cave roof.

For the Na Pali Coast trip:

Kayak Kaua'i (☎ 826-9844, 800-437-3507; www .kayakkauai.com; Kuhio Hwy; single kayaks per day/week $28/112, double kayaks $52/208; ☼ 8am-5pm, to 8pm in summer) Hawaii's biggest outfitter. For the Hanalei River paddle, you put in right outside the shop. Tours include a Na Pali Coast thriller ($185) from May to September, Blue Lagoon kayak and snorkel ($60), or open-ocean paddle on the South Shore (winter; $115). It also rents snorkel gear (per day/week $8/20) if you want to get a closer look at all those sea turtles. This outfit also offers camping gear, including the basics plus stoves (per day/week $6/24) and foam sleeping pads (per day/week $4/16). They also store gear and cars (per day/week $5/10).

Na Pali Kayak (☎ 826-6900, 866-977-6900; www .napalikayak.com; Kuhio Hwy; tours $175) The Na Pali Coast trip is the only tour these folks lead and their guides have over a decade of experience paddling these waters.

Outfitters Kaua'i (☎ 742-9667, 888-742-9887; www .outfitterskauai.com; Po'ipu Plaza, 2827-A Po'ipu Rd; Na Pali Coast tour $185; ☼ reservations taken 8am-9pm) Located in Po'ipu, but offers tours islandwide.

SNORKELING

While most snorkeling cruises depart from Port Allen on the Westside, three are based in Hanalei. No doubt, starting from the North Shore is preferable, as you'll see the lushest parts of Na Pali that the Westside cruises simply have no time to reach. These catamarans depart from Hanalei:

Na Pali Catamaran (☎ 826-6853, 866-255-6853; www.napalicatamaran.com) Offers four-hour tours (adult/child $135/110), morning and afternoon, in summer months, generally May to September. On calm days the 34ft cat (16 passengers maximum) enters sea caves. During winter, three-hour sightseeing tours (no snorkeling) are scheduled when weather permits. No shade.

Captain Sundown (☎ 826-5585; www.captainsundown.com) Long, six-hour tour (adult/child 7-12 $148/125) is comfortable on a 40ft sailing cat, but the crew cannot go as far toward the coast (or into sea caves) as does Na Pali Catamaran. A three-hour sightseeing tour (adult/child 7-12 $120/99) omits the snorkeling. Both are offered only during summer. Lunch is a roast beef pastrami sandwich, with no substitutions.

SURFING & WINDSURFING

Hanalei Bay swells are generally best in winter, but Hawaiian ocean weather is fickle, so you never know.

Hanalei Surf Company (☎ 826-9000; www.hanaleisurf.com; Hanalei Center, 5-5161 Kuhio Hwy; 2½hr lesson $65-150, surfboards per day/week $15/65, boogie boards per day/week $5/20; ☼ 8am-9pm) An established outfit; fins are a couple of dollars more. Call the shop to set up surfing lessons. It also has economical snorkel sets. Surf instructors here (Russell Lewis and Ian Vernon) have an excellent reputation and are especially suited for advanced surfers.

Hawaiian School of Surfing (☎ 652-1116; 1½hr lesson $65; ☼ lessons 8am, 10am and noon) You cannot miss the red rashguards and line-up of boards near Hanalei Pier. Stop by (or call in advance) for a lesson by legendary pro big-wave surfer Titus Kinimaka or, more likely, one of his guys. No more than three students per instructor.

Hawaiian Surfing Adventures (☎ 482-0749; www .hawaiiansurfingadventures.com; 2hr lesson group/private $55/75, surfboards per day/week $30/100; ☼ 8am-2pm) Longtime Kaua'i surfer Mitchell Alapa and his team give group (up to four but often fewer) or private (single or couple) lessons in Hanalei Bay. Long and thorough lesson with half-hour on land and one hour in the water – then you can keep the board to practice for another hour. Look for the yellow rashguards.

Kayak Kaua'i (☎ 826-9844; www.kayakkauai.com; Kuhio Hwy; 1hr lesson $50, surfboards per day $20, boogie boards per day $6; ☼ lessons 10am & 2pm) If you rent gear for four days, you get three more days free.

Windsurf Kaua'i (☎ 828-6838; windsurfkauai@aol .com; 2hr lesson $60) Lessons at Hanalei Bay and also 'Anini Beach Park .

YOGA

One of Kaua'i's first yoga studios, **Yoga Hanalei** (☎ 826-9642; www.yogahanalei.com; Hanalei Center, 2nd fl, 5-5161E Kuhio Hwy, upstairs; per class $15) is directed by Bhavani Maki, an outstanding teacher who has studied for many years with Pattabhi Jois. Classes are geared mainly toward different levels of Ashtanga and Bikram, but include other methods and the restorative 'Relax Deeply' class.

Tours

Ho'opulapula Haraguchi Rice Mill Tour (☎ 651-3399; www.haraguchiricemill.org; Kuhio Hwy; 3hr tour incl lunch per person $65) The Haraguchi family, who also own the Hanalei Taro & Juice Company, offers tours (10am Thursday, by appointment only) of their historic rice mill and wetland taro farm located on inaccessible Hanalei National Wildlife Refuge land. The tour is both ecotour and cultural lesson: you'll see endangered and rare native birds and learn about the ancient staple taro, and

---

HOMAGE TO TARO

To locals, describing poi as 'wallpaper paste' is not only absurd, it's an insult. Taro is a sacred food, considered the root of all life. The taro stem is called *oha*, from which *ohana* (family) is derived. In old Hawaii, only men could tend the taro fields because women menstruate and were considered unclean. Traditional Hawaiian households always show respect for taro: when the poi bowl sits on the table, one is expected to refrain from arguing or speaking in anger.

In the 1970s a cultural resurgence pushed taro cultivation into the mass commercial market, but production has ebbed and flowed over the years. Until recently, taro farms struggled in part because younger generations showed less interest in farming, and fungus disease and snail infestation devastated crops.

Lately taro has made a comeback. Terry Shintani, a University of Hawai'i (UH) MD, has developed a 'Hawaii Diet' that emphasizes taro over rice (half the calories!), and celebrity chefs are featuring taro at their upscale restaurants. At supermarkets you can find many brands of poi on sale, along with taro chips and baked goods.

In the early 2000s UH conducted genetic modification research on Hawaiian varieties of taro, which spurred strong outcry from Hawaiians. In May 2005, the university agreed not to tamper with taro without consulting Hawaiians about their cultural concerns.

On Kaua'i, you can taste unique taro specialties at the Hanalei Taro & Juice Company kiosk and the best taro chips from Taro Ko Chip Factory (p191) in Hanapepe. To see an excellent example of taro fields, stroll through Limahuli Garden in Ha'ena. Even McDonald's offers taro pie, with flaky crust, creamy filling and Hanalei taro, during special promotions – a big hit among locals.

Hawaii's immigrant history. A family member (who's the fifth generation to farm taro on Kaua'i) leads the educational, personal tours, which are limited to 14 people. The $65 is steep, but the nonprofit historic rice mill survives by donations and grants – and the tour does include outstanding food: fruit-poi smoothie, deli sandwich and special taro creations from the Hanalei Taro & Juice Company. Tours start at the Rice Mill kiosk next to the Hanalei Taro & Juice Company.

Sleeping

See the list of vacation-rental agencies on p137. Coldwell Banker Bali Hai Realty has a long list for Hanalei.

BUDGET

Except for camping, $80-and-under lodging is rare in Hanalei. The following two options come close, however. Also see the Ching Home studio review.

Ohana Hanalei (☎ 826-4116; www.hanalei-kauai .com; r incl tax per day/week $95/615) A large studio half a block from sandy beach...for under $100? Yes, if you're seeking simple lodging mainly for sleeping. The downstairs room is slightly cavernous and furnishings are not posh, but it's clean and comfy, with kitchenette, private entrance, phone, cable

TV and convenient parking. The hosts are easygoing, longtime residents who give guests lots of privacy. Rates drop if you stay a week.

Hanalei Inn (☎ 826-9333; www.hanaleiinn.com; 5-5468 Kuhio Hwy; r $99) If you're the nothing-fancy type, the four studios with kitchens at Hanalei Inn should suffice. The compact rooms sport hardwood floors, stone-tile bathrooms, small dining table and wi-fi. If you stay for a week, no taxes are charged. One studio ($89) lacks a kitchen and TV, but does include a fridge, a microwave and a coffeemaker. The amiable on-site manager, Bill Gaus, has lots of experience in the hotel industry (formerly with Hyatt) and he's an excellent local source. Also ask about the Pine Trees Beach House, run by the same owners, which has three units ($109 to $189) that sleep between one and four.

Camping at Hanalei (Black Pot) Beach Park is permitted on Friday, Saturday and holidays only, with a county permit (see p218).

MIDRANGE & TOP END

The following options are all located in the same neighborhood, Hanalei Palms, a block or less from the beach. Note the lack of utility poles here: the lines are underground.

Ching Home (☎ 826-9622, 800-488-3336; 5119 Weke Rd; 2-bedroom ste per week $850, 1-bedroom ste per week $750, studio per week $550) Welcome, surfers! For dudes and chicks who don't mind the 'public' location directly across Hanalei Pavilion, this is your ideal surfer pad. Downstairs, the A-frame two-bedroom suite includes a full kitchen and cozy loft space, while the studio is a basic bed and kitchenette deal. Upstairs you'll find the best of the bunch: a one-bedroom suite, light and airy, with high ceiling and full kitchen. Each can be rented individually. Outside, the yard is merely a struggling lawn. The pavilion lot across the street is packed all day, and cars zoom past on their way to the pier, but all's quiet at night. Contact North Shore Properties.

Bed, Breakfast & Beach (☎ 826-6111; www .bestofhawaii.com/hanalei; r incl breakfast $90-145) In a three-story house, three guest rooms will suit folks seeking a traditional B&B experience. Rooms are decorated in country-cute florals and white wicker, with hardwood floors, calico wallpaper and shared living room. On the 2nd floor, the two smaller rooms enjoy nice views from a wraparound lanai. The 3rd-floor room, spacious at 700 sq ft, features spectacular views of Hanalei Bay and Bali Hai mountain. While refrigerator space is provided, none of the rooms include a kitchen.

Hale Luana (☎ 826-6931; Opelu Rd; ste $150, plus one-time cleaning fee $85) Utterly charming, this enormous loft suite might be your trip highlight. A private entrance leads to this one-bedroom suite, painted in classic white, with a soaring cathedral ceiling. The romantic, open-air spiral staircase overlooks a spacious kitchen and dining room. In the loft bedroom you can laze in bed, gazing at the ocean through a window. Complimentary washer/dryer available. Contact Coldwell Banker Bali Hai Realty.

Hale Reed (☎ 415-459-1858; www.hanalei-vacation.com; 4441 Pilikoa St; 2-/3-bedroom apt per week from $1000/$1300, partly refundable security deposit $300-500) This superb three-story home is impeccable down to details like all-matching silverware, luxury linens, and both wi-fi and DSL Ethernet connections. The three-bedroom apartment (which sleeps 10) is the entire main house, with sweeping ceilings, well-stocked kitchen and tasteful furnishings. A stairway leads to a fantastic 3rd-floor 'secret' room, streaming with sunlight and panoramic views. On the ground floor, the two-bedroom apartment (which sleeps four) is simpler but no less comfortable, with windows all around and full kitchen. There's free use of washer/dryer. The security deposit is refunded minus the cleaning fee ($80 to $125 for downstairs, $150 to $300 for upstairs).

Maluhia Hanalei (☎ 415-382-8918, 415-310 1919; www.hanaleivacationrental.com; 3-bedroom ste per day/ week $235/1600, 2-bedroom ste per day/week $150/1050, partly refundable security deposit $500) At the end of a quiet cul-de-sac, a large group (up to 10) can settle comfortably in a lovely, island-style house. Downstairs, the two-bedroom unit features a compact kitchen with classy tile floor and modern tropical furnishings including a gorgeous armoire. Upstairs, the three-bedroom 'suite' is really the main part of the house, with three bathrooms, enormous kitchen and plantation-style living room with wicker rockers. The property is bordered by a nature preserve and thus wonderfully peaceful. Rates jump during summer months and winter holidays. The cleaning fee (deducted from the deposit) ranges from $80 to $250 (for the whole house).

Blu Nui (☎ 826-9622, 800-488-3336; 4435 Mahimahi Rd; 2-bedroom house per week $1500) On a side street near Hanalei Bay, Blu Nui is not the greatest bargain for two bedrooms without a view, but it buys you the privacy of your own house. With hardwood floor and high ceiling, the airy, island-style bungalow includes a comfy living room (with sofa bed), well-equipped kitchen, covered garage and backyard patio. The two standard-size bedrooms share a bathroom. Contact North Shore Properties.

Hanalei Carriage House (☎ 826 6946; www.hana leibaycarriagehouse.com; 2-bedroom house per week $1750, plus one-time cleaning fee $125 & security deposit $400) Revel in the luxury of a dreamy private house just steps from the beach, near Hanalei Pier. While the main house blocks any ocean view, this oasis is surrounded by a stunningly green lawn, lily pond and tropical garden bursting with color from over 100 orchids, hanging in trees. The two-bedroom, one-bathroom house is airy, with sun-filled windows all around, and it offers all the expected amenities, including full kitchen, satellite TV and washer/dryer.

NORTH SHORE

Eating & Drinking
BUDGET
Wishing Well Shave Ice (Kuhio Hwy; shave ice from $2; noon-5pm Tue-Sun) Can't miss the colorful van parked near the Hanalei Taro & Juice Company kiosk! While the claim to be the oldest shave-ice vendor on Kaua'i may or may not be true, it does serve a fine product. Try the *li hing mui* (Chinese crack seed) flavor, which is better than most.

Hanalei Taro & Juice Company (826-1059; 5-5070-B Kuhio Hwy; smoothies $3-4.50, sandwiches $6.50; 10:30am-5pm Mon-Sat) In a mobile kiosk permanently parked in a grassy lot near the town's eastern boundary, this family-run fixture specializes in unique, Hanalei-grown taro products. Specialties include 'Kalo Koolers' (fruit smoothies with a taro base), taro hummus (per 8oz $4) and addictive taro-coconut *mochi* (a Japanese sticky-rice dessert; per piece 50¢). Fill up on sandwiches piled with freshly cut deli meats or taro hummus and veggies. Also check out its reasonably priced selection of local produce.

Java Kai (826-6717; Hanalei Center; 6:30am-6pm) Take your coffee and tempting pastries on the lanai at casual Java Kai. Hot dishes include a Belgian waffle with fruit, macs and whipped cream ($8) and a papaya fruit bowl with yogurt ($7.50).

Hanalei Wake Up Café (826-5551; cnr Kuhio Hwy & Aku Rd; breakfast $5-7; 6-11:30am) The best place for major early birds to find a wholesome, hot breakfast.

Or grab something to go:

Big Save (826-6652; Ching Young Village; 7am-9pm) Bland and basic, barely more than a convenience store, this is the only supermarket west of Princeville – with the prices to show for it.

TAHITI NUI'S GLORY DAYS

Nowadays glitzy luau shows are the norm across the islands. But for 40 years, lucky Kaua'i visitors would stumble upon the casual, family-run Tahiti Nui luau in Hanalei.

In 1964 a Tahitian woman, Louise Hauata, and her husband Bruce Marston, founded the still-iconic **Tahiti Nui** (826-6277; Tahiti Nui Bldg, Kuhio Hwy; dinner mains $14.50; 2pm-2am), a classic South Seas–style restaurant and bar. It was *the* North Shore gathering place, where folks could jam on guitars and ukulele, eat, drink and just talk story. As its reputation grew, the Nui drew people as famous as Jacqueline Kennedy, who arrived unexpectedly, preceded only minutes earlier by secret service agents.

When Bruce died in 1975, Louise continued the luau tradition with even more vigor. She was known to greet strangers with great aloha and to break into renditions of Tahitian songs in English, French or Tahitian.

Within the community, Louise often opened her heart (and the doors of Tahiti Nui) for fundraisers and events. When the Hanalei River overflowed, leaving people stranded on the North Shore, she would let them spend the night at the Nui and provide not only blankets and pillows but also a home-cooked breakfast the next day.

Louise died in 2003, and Tahiti Nui is now run by her son, Christian Marston, her nephew, William Marston, and the president and CEO John Austin. Today, there's no luau, as the Tahiti Nui building now rents out the space formerly used for the luau, but the management plans to revive the luau at a different venue. (Note to Hawaiian music fans: Austin is married to celebrated singer Amy Hanaiali'i Gilliom.)

The Tahiti Nui remains a lively, loud hang-out spot – and gets louder and rowdier as the night advances. Nothing fancy, it's a well-worn favorite, with woven mats and paddle fans on the ceiling, intimate wraparound wooden bar and large, street-facing front lanai. The restaurant serves dinner classics like kiawe-wood-smoked *huli huli* (rotisserie) chicken and a Hawaiian plate with *laulau* (a bundle made of pork or chicken and salted butterfish, wrapped in taro and ti), poi and *lomilomi* salmon.

The bar offers generous happy hours (4pm to 6pm Monday to Saturday, all day Sunday), mouth-watering *pupu* (appetizers; $8 to $11), nightly live music – and with a live-and-let-live attitude, you smokers can light up with impunity. Tuesday evenings feature an especially talented and well-known musician, Keli'i Keali'i, who was formerly half of the duo Hapa, from 6pm to 9pm.

Hanalei Dolphin Fish Market (☎ 826-6113; 5-5016 Kuhio Hwy; ☷ 10am-7pm) 'Ahi sushi rolls ($8), 'ahi poke (per lb $14) and clam chowder (per pint $5) make yummy picnic fixings. Fresh fish (per lb $10 to $17) is a relative bargain.

Papaya's Hanalei (☎ 826-0089; Hanalei Center, 5-5161 Kuhio Hwy; ☷ 9am-8pm) Opened in late 2005, the second Papaya is a fresh-scrubbed, slightly smaller sibling to the original Kapa'a store, Papaya's Natural Foods. Find tasty deli meals and the usual array of healthy cereals, meat substitutes and soy yogurts. Organic produce is dismayingly expensive.

MIDRANGE & TOP END

Polynesia Café (☎ 826-1999; Ching Young Village; mains $7-16; ☷ 8am-9pm) The locals' kudos and constant queue at this patio café proves the truth of its slogan: 'Gourmet food on paper plates.' Here, the plate lunch rises to another level. Try the 'ahi crusted in mac-nut or pecan pesto ($15 to $16) or the tofu glazed with orange-ginger sauce ($11), both with rice and veggies. Or sample the Hawaiian variety plate ($7), which includes kalua pork (pork cooked in a traditional underground pit) and cabbage over rice, plus lomilomi salmon (minced, salted salmon, diced tomatoes and green onion). In the dessert showcase, massive pieces of cake and brownies will no doubt prove to be irresistible.

Pizza Hanalei (☎ 826-9494; Ching Young Village; pizza from $12; ☷ 11am-9pm) The pizzas are made with care and it shows. Choose from whole wheat or white crust with a small but decent topping selection, including pleasantly pungent basil pesto. Carnivores dig the meaty Lizzy Special with pepperoni, Canadian bacon and sausage, while herbivores savor the aptly named Veggie Special, chock-full of mushrooms, bell peppers, black olives, zucchini and fresh tomato. If you want just a slice, the only options are cheese ($3) or pepperoni ($3.45).

Hanalei Gourmet (☎ 826-2524; www.hanaleigourmet.com; Hanalei Center; sandwiches $7-10, dinner mains $14-26; ☷ 8am-9:30pm, to 10:30pm summer) You cannot go wrong at this lively café/bar/deli that indeed succeeds at 'em all. From sampler of lox-style local smoked fish to crunchy mac-nut fried chicken, the food is tasty and unpretentious. Most preparations are healthy but you can also find beer-battered fish and chips (served island-style with Asian coleslaw and soy-wasabi

sauce!). Its forte, however, is the meal-size deli sandwiches, made with fresh, house-baked bread.

Neide's Salsa Samba (☎ 826-1851; Hanalei Center; dishes $9-17; ☷ 11am-2:30pm, 5-9pm) Unique flavors and a quiet veranda are the main attractions at this little owner-run restaurant serving Mexican and Brazilian fare. In addition to the usual Mexican dishes, like huevos rancheros and burritos, you can gorge on traditional Brazilian offerings, such as panqueca (a veggie or chicken crepe stuffed with pumpkin). Neide also makes a fantastic passion-fruit margarita.

Baracuda (☎ 826-7081; Hanalei Center; small plates $5-12; ☷ 11:30am-2:30pm & 6-9:30pm Tue-Sat) Sleek and sophisticated, this restaurant and bar seems incongruously yuppie-urban for a casual surf town. Indeed, the chef-owner, Jim Moffat, hails from San Francisco, where he'd established two successful restaurants, and it seems many of the staff are imported, too. Moffat knows his way around a kitchen, however, and the menu features unimpeachable California cuisine, such as Medjool date-and-celery salad ($7), smoked trout with avocado ($9) and grilled tiger prawns ($9), plus an extensive wine list.

Postcards Café (☎ 826-1191; www.postcardscafe.com; 5-5075 Kuhio Hwy; mains $18-27; ☷ 6-9pm) Outside, Postcards looks like a plain, old wooden building. Inside, the rustic dining room simultaneously feels special and homey. The creative, healthy, gourmet cuisine is well worth the price. Start off with polenta-crusted taro fritters and the signature seafood rockets (shrimp, fish and coconut, fried in lumpia). The menu is ideal for vegetarians, with delicious savory selections like sautéed tofu with vegetables and cashews in tamari-ginger sauce. While fish and seafood are mainstays, no meat is served here.

Hanalei Dolphin Restaurant (☎ 826-6113; www.hanaleidolphin.com; 5-5016 Kuhio Hwy; mains $20-32; ☷ 11am-9:30pm) One of the Hanalei originals, this riverside restaurant still draws 'em in with its specialty fresh fish, plus ginger chicken, veggie casseroles and loads of shrimp dishes. Quality is decent but with a revolving door of chefs, it can be unpredictable. Buying fresh fish from the Hanalei Dolphin Fish Market to cook yourself might be preferable, if you're good in the kitchen.

Entertainment

Sushi & Blues (☎ 826-9701; www.sushiandblues.com; Ching Young Village; ☷ 6pm-2am) The sushi will please all; the cigarette smoke, probably not. Live blues and jazz nightly.

Hawaiian Slack-Key Guitar Concerts (☎ 826-1469; www.hawaiianslackkeyguitar.com; Hanalei Community Center; adult/child & senior $10/8; ☷ 4pm Fri & 3pm Sun) Slack-key guitar and ukulele concerts by longtime musicians Doug and Sandy McMaster year-round, in a refreshingly informal atmosphere.

Shopping

Kokonut Kids (☎ 826-0353; 5-5290 Kuhio Hwy; ☷ 10am-6:30pm Mon-Sat, 10:30am-5pm Sun) A smorgasbord of unique, top-quality, locally made children's clothing and toys. The colorful screen-printed tees and handmade sun hats are irresistible. And where else can you find a tropical-print Barbie camping tent and sleeping bag?

Rainbow Ducks/Hula Beach (☎ 826-4741; Hanalei Center; ☷ 10am-8pm) Stylish, Bohemian-chic clothing for the whole family. Funky bags and accessories, with a Southeast Asian touch.

Hanalei Surf Company (☎ 826-9000; www.hanaleisurf.com; Hanalei Center, 5-5161 Kuhio Hwy; ☷ 8am-9pm) The archetypal surf shop, with lots of gear, board shorts, bikinis and nonchalant staffers.

Backdoor (☎ 826-1900; Ching Young Village; 5-5190 Kuhio Hwy; ☷ 9am-9pm) The Hanalei Surf Company's sister company is similar in youthful vibe, but carries skateboards and a wider selection of alternative street clothes by brands including Luci Love, Volcom, Paul Frank and Billabong.

Evolve Love Gallery (☎ 826-6441; Ching Young Village; ☷ 10am-6pm) Fine selection of art by local artists.

Yellowfish Trading Company (☎ 826-1227; Hanalei Center; ☷ 10am-8pm Mon-Sat, to 7pm Sun) Nostalgia rules at this Hawaii memorabilia shop. You'll find a wide selection, from kitschy reproductions to genuine collectibles.

Getting Around

Pedal & Paddle (☎ 826-9069; www.pedalnpaddle.com; Ching Young Village; ☷ 9am-6pm) rents cruisers (per day/week $10/30) and mountain bikes ($20/80); alternatively, you could try **Kayak Kaua'i** (☎ 826-9844; www.kayakkauai.com; Kuhio Hwy; ☷ 8am-5pm), also with cruisers ($15/60) and mountain bikes ($20/80).

Remember, if driving west, the last chance to fill your tank was back in Princeville.

AROUND HANALEI

Lumaha'i Beach

You cannot find a beach more gorgeous than this mile-long stretch, where Mitzi Gaynor promised to wash that man right out of her hair in the 1958 musical *South Pacific*. The broad, white-sand beach, with jungle growth looming on one side and tempestuous open sea on the other, is perfect for strolling. Look around the lava outcrops for deep-green sand made of the mineral olivine.

But don't plan to swim here. There is no reef barrier and waves are almost always too powerful, with perilous shore breaks – do not underestimate the risks here. It's particularly treacherous in winter, though strong currents prevail year-round.

There are two ways onto Lumaha'i Beach. The first and more scenic is a three-minute walk that begins at the parking area 0.75 miles past the 4-mile marker. The trail slopes to the left at the end of the retaining wall (take the other steep trail from the 'no beach access sign' to reach a shoreline rock shelf perfect for a private picnic). Seek shelter from the wind at the lava point at the eastern end here. These rocks are popular for sunbathing and being photographed, but size it up carefully, as people have been washed away by high surf and rogue waves.

The other way to access Lumaha'i is along the road at sea level at the western end of the beach, just before crossing the Lumaha'i River Bridge. The beach at this end is lined with ironwood trees. Across the way is pastoral Lumaha'i Valley, all grazing horses and rainbows.

If you prefer to admire from the road, there are two **lookouts** with views down onto Lumaha'i. The first pull-out is at the 5-mile marker; the second pops up around the bend and offers a better angle. Beware of speeding traffic on the narrow, winding highway.

Wainiha

Ancient house sites, heiau (ancient Hawaiian religious sites) and old taro patches reach deep into Wainiha Valley, a narrow valley with steep green walls. This valley is said to have been the last hideout of the

---

HOUSES ON STILTS

Along the North Shore, especially in coastal Wainiha and Ha'ena, otherwise-normal houses sit way above the ground – to guard against tsunami flooding. After the last tsunami struck in 1957, the county has required all new homes in flood- and tsunami-prone zones to be built on 'pilings' (poles or concrete posts) about 10ft to 16ft high. But existing homes may stay on ground level, even if they're remodeled (as long as the old footprint is kept). So far no big wave has tested the protective measure.

---

menehune, the ancient little people. In fact, as late as the 1850s, 65 people in the valley were officially listed as *menehune* on the government census!

SLEEPING & EATING

Hale Ho'omaha B&B (☎ 826-7083, 800-851-0291; www.aloha.net/~hoomaha; 7083 Alamihi Rd; r incl breakfast $150-175; 🖥) Ride an elevator up this *tall* house on stilts, to enter a spectacular home, built in 2005 especially to accommodate a B&B. Guests enjoy the run of the house, including the sleekly modern kitchen and airy living room (gleaming hardwood everywhere) showcasing a fine collection of Hawaiian hula implements and lei. Bedrooms are richly appointed and the dual massage showerheads (tub is large enough for two) aren't found anywhere else. The iconic Pineapple Room features a unique 7ft-diameter round bed. Hot breakfasts, washer/dryer, wi-fi and computer – the friendly hosts sure take care of you.

River Estates (☎ 826-5118, 800-399-8444; www.riverestate.com; house $175) You'll feel like the king of the castle in this secluded house on stilts, surrounded by lush foliage, fruit orchard, and the Wainiha River running through the backyard. The spacious house includes two bedrooms, two bathrooms, gourmet kitchen with modern appliances galore, lanai with views, washer/dryer, TV/VCR, and all the other comforts of home. Furnishings are upscale, and privacy is guaranteed – making the house especially popular with couples and honeymooners. Five-night minimum, with exceptions.

Red Hot Mama's (☎ 826-7266; 5-6607 Kuhio Hwy; meals $6-8.50; 🕙 11am-5pm) The last eatery before the end of the road, this little counter serves up generous burritos, tacos ($3.25 each) and fresh Caesar or tuna salads. Note the collection of hot sauces displayed outside (with the warning not to disturb any!).

SHOPPING

Wainiha General Store (☎ 826-6251; 5-6600 Kuhio Hwy; 🕙 10:30am-dusk) Just the basics, but it's the last place to grab groceries or beer before the end of the road. Friendly staff, who rightfully yell at folks who speed around here.

End of the Rainbow (☎ 826-9980; endoftherainbow@hawaii.rr.com; 5-6607 Kuhio Hwy; 🕙 10:30am-dusk) Handmade jewelry, island-style clothing and sarongs, art prints and photography – all featuring mainly Kaua'i artists. The collection of genuine *puka*-shell necklaces ($75 to $200) is a far cry from cheapo fakes. Friendly proprietor makes browsers feel welcome.

HA'ENA

Ha'ena is a rural community with singular houses on stilts, a YMCA camp, the only large hotel beyond Princeville, mysterious caves and still-pristine sandy beaches. Visitors who want to disconnect from the stress of modern, fast-paced life will find an oasis here.

In the 1870s a group of Native Hawaiians from Na Pali and Ha'ena called the Ha'ena Hui (group) bought this area, a traditional *ahupua'a* (land division from mountains to sea). They lived as a close community on the land, until it was partitioned starting in 1955. The *hui* disbanded in 1967, and since then newcomers have bought large parcels, including the oceanfront lots where beach mansions sit today.

Two tsunamis struck Ha'ena in the 20th century: both the first in 1946 and the second in 1957 devastated homes along the beach. Thus any new house built today must be elevated (see left).

To learn more about Ha'ena's history, see the outstanding website www.pacificworlds.com/haena.

Sights & Activities
TUNNELS BEACH

Tunnels is a big horseshoe-shaped reef with great diving and snorkeling when the water is calm (which is generally limited to summer months). There's a current as you head into deeper water. When conditions are right, you can start snorkeling near the east point and let the current carry you westward. It's more adventurous (and less crowded) than Ke'e Beach and features interesting coral formations.

Approaching the parking area midway between the 8- and 9-mile markers, you'll notice trucks with board racks and surfboard lawn art. No surprise since the reef drops to 60ft out in the bay, forming a deep trough that generates a tubular winter surf break (hence the name Tunnels). Be aware that dangerous rip currents prevail from October to May, making it suitable for experts only.

It was here on October 21, 2003 that competitive surfer Bethany Hamilton, then 13, lost her left arm in a shark attack. Undaunted, Bethany resumed her surfing career, wrote a book, made a media splash and continues to dominate at national competitions. See www.bethanyhamilton.com for her remarkable story.

You can walk from Tunnels to Ha'ena Beach Park.

HA'ENA BEACH PARK
Ha'ena Beach is yet another beautiful curve of white sand, but beware of astoundingly strong rip currents and shore breaks from October to May. To the right, you can see the horseshoe shape of Tunnels outlined by breaking waves. To the far left is **Cannons**, a particularly good wall dive, with crevices and

lava tubes sheltering all sorts of marine life. You'll wonder how sea turtles can be endangered, with so many coasting in these waters; playful dolphins visit early in the morning. Lifeguard (and snack truck) on duty here.

MANINIHOLO DRY CAVE
Directly across Ha'ena Beach Park, Maniniholo Dry Cave is deep and broad and high enough to explore. Drippy and creepy, a constant seep of water from the cave walls keeps the interior damp and humid.

The cave is named after the head fisherman of the *menehune*, the legendary race of small people who built ponds and other structures at night. Maniniholo had caught a huge haul of fish just when his people were preparing to leave Kaua'i. They piled half the fish on the beach and the other half at the base of the cliff abutting the current cave. An *akua* (ghost) stole the fish near the cliff and hid within the mountain. The *menehune* began to dig from both the top and the bottom of the cliff to pursue the *akua*, whom they caught and immediately killed (can ghosts die another death?). The hole dug to catch it is today's Maniniholo Dry Cave.

YOGA & MASSAGE
Offering a wide range of massages, face and body treatments, waxing, manicures and yoga classes is the **Hanalei Day Spa** (☎ 826-6621; www.hanaleidayspa.com; massage per 30/60/90min $60/85/125; ☼ 10am-6pm). Diverse offerings include Zen shiatsu healing, Ayurvedic

---

INVASION OF THE HIPPIES

No place was remote enough to escape the '60s hippie invasion – not even out-of-the-way Ha'ena. In the late 1960s Howard Taylor (Elizabeth's brother) acquired a large parcel of the current Ha'ena State Park. He had wanted to build a house there, but the state was condemning the land and wouldn't grant him a permit, yet required tax payment. In retaliation he lent the land to the 'flower-power people,' already squatting on Kaua'i parks since 1968.

Living in shacks, treehouses and tarp shelters, a hippie community dubbed **Taylor Camp** soon formed. They used a communal shower and open-air toilet, established a Church of the Brotherhood of the Paradise Children, sunbathed nude and relied on junker cars to get around. Some survived on welfare, while others grew *pakalolo* (marijuana) or held conventional jobs elsewhere on the island. At one point, the group numbered over 100, to the chagrin of locals suspicious of the oddball, pot-smoking, unwashed haole flocking to the remote North Shore.

In 1977 the state finally condemned the property for park use, spurred by neighbors' complaints about the lack of modern toilets and garbage disposal. Some say the sanitation problem killed off mullet and other fish formerly plentiful in Ha'ena's waters.

Go to www.pacificworlds.com/haena/memories/memory5.cfm for an intriguing account of Taylor Camp.

NAME THAT PLANT

Kaua'i is a green garden wonderland, but much of the foliage commonly seen around the island was not around in ancient Hawaii. To differentiate between plants that are native, Polynesian introduced (between 200AD and 1300AD) and modern introductions (since Captain Cook's arrival in 1778), head to **Limahuli Garden** (☎ 826-1053; www.ntbg.org; self-guided/guided tour $10/15; ☺ 9:30am-4pm Tue-Fri & Sun).

Here, you'll find well-marked examples of Hawaiian ethnobotanical and medicinal plants and endangered native species, along with commonly seen modern introductions. The layout creates a pleasant 0.75-mile loop trail for self-guided guests. Benches here and there allow stops for rest or contemplation. Upon entering the garden you see an impressive taro 'amphitheater,' with small and large plants growing within ancient stone terraces. You might be surprised to discover that stereotypical 'Hawaiian' fruits and flowers, such as the mango, guava and plumeria, weren't around in ancient Hawaii. With either tour, guests receive an outstanding booklet packed with interesting plant descriptions, Hawaiian history and legends (by itself it's worth the admission fee!).

Beyond Limahuli Garden's 17-acre visitor-accessible area is the vast 985-acre Limahuli Preserve: lush, virgin forest that is slowly recovering from Hurricane 'Iniki's devastation. Juliet Rice Wichman had acquired the entire property in 1967, with the goal to preserve Limahuli Valley as a 'living classroom' on ancient Hawaii. In 1976 she gifted the garden to the National Tropical Botanical Garden (NTBG), a nonprofit organization that protects rare native plants (see p167). In 1994 her grandson Charles 'Chipper' Wichman, director of the NTBG, generously gave the adjoining 985 acres to the NTBG.

To get here, turn inland just before the stream that marks the boundary of Ha'ena State Park.

consultations and meditation lessons. For delicious decadence, try a massage with chocolate or mint massage oil.

Sleeping

Ha'ena Beach Park has campsites, covered picnic tables, rest rooms and showers. Many hikers from the Kalalau Trail camp here, using it as a base before starting the trail. The trailhead at the end of the road is slightly over a mile away, but this might be a safer parking place if your car will be unattended for a few days. See p218 for county camping permit information.

Ha'ena is a hotspot for vacation rentals, so if your fantasy is the perfect beach house, go for it. A Google search is most effective, but you can also call the agencies listed on p137.

One famous house is owned by the entertainer Charo, famous for her flamenco-guitar music and of course her signature 'cuchi-cuchi!' line. In the 1980s she moved to the Hawaiian Islands, performed on O'ahu and owned a restaurant on the North Shore of Kaua'i. She's back in California now but still owns property here, including her vacation rental dubbed Charo's Bali Hai Villa.

Wedding parties often rent multisuite houses for lodging the group but while the setting might seem ideal for the ceremony and reception, agents do charge a higher rate and deposit, plus an additional insurance policy. Guest numbers are limited (eg 75 guests maximum at Charo's).

Charo's Bali Hai Villa (☎ 826-9622, 828-0067; 5-7553 Kuhio Hwy; per week $7700) This white-stucco, Spanish-style villa includes seven bedrooms all facing the ocean and Bali Hai mountain, six bathrooms, ample living space and a detached patio – all on lush grounds right on the beach.

Hanalei Colony Resort (☎ 826-6235, 800-628-3004; www.hcr.com; Hwy 560; 1-/2-bedroom unit from $210/250; ☒ ☐ ☒) Its slogan: 'Unspoiled. Unplugged. Unforgettable.' In other words, forget the TV, stereo and phone – and soak up pure, natural Kaua'i. This longstanding condo complex located on Tunnels Beach just before the 8-mile marker has a secluded feel: it's the only resort west of Princeville. The units are comfortable, with full kitchen and lanai, but quality is mixed: you might find bent screen doors, peeling paint or worn furnishings. But while it's not the most luxurious, the remote location is peaceful and the staff is friendly, with a reputation for service. Two computers with high-speed Internet access (and wi-fi or Ethernet connections) are available free to guests. For weekly stays, the seventh night is free.

Kaua'i YMCA-Camp Naue (☎ individuals 826-6419, groups 246-9090; fax 246-4411; off Hwy 560; campsite & dm per person $12) Booked solid by groups from June to August, these bare-bones bunkhouses and campsite are ideal for backpackers. The five bunkhouses each hold 15 guests on average and have screened windows, cement floors and multiple bunks. No linen is provided. The camp is geared to groups but accepts individual travelers if there's room. Separate men's and women's showers are available; the kitchen is reserved for large groups. Check vacancy before arrival. The camp, located before the 8-mile marker, is a 10-minute walk from Tunnels Beach.

Eating & Drinking

Sustenance is at a bare minimum here, so stock up in Hanalei.

Na Pali Art Gallery & Coffee House (☎ 826-1844; Hanalei Colony Resort; snacks $2-3; ☽ 7am-5pm) Brews up excellent coffee drinks, all hot or iced as you like.

HA'ENA STATE PARK

Commonly called 'end of the road,' the 230-acre Ha'ena State Park is a fitting finale to the picturesque North Shore drive. Ke'e Beach is postcard pretty, with clear, calm waters framed by the distinctive 1280ft cliff commonly known as Bali Hai, its name in the movie *South Pacific*. Hawaiians prefer to use its Hawaiian name, 'Makana', which aptly means 'gift.'

Sights & Activities
WET CAVES

Two wet caves are within the boundaries of Ha'ena State Park. The first, **Waikapala'e Wet Cave**, is just a few minutes' walk uphill from the main road along a rutted dirt drive opposite the visitor parking overflow area. The second, **Waikanaloa Wet Cave**, is right on the south side of the main road. Both caves are deep, dark and dripping, with pools of very cold water.

According to legend, the caves were created when the goddess Pele first arrived in the Hawaiian Islands after leaving her South Pacific homeland, seeking refuge from a jeal-

ous sister (my, epic jealousy was certainly rampant among the immortals). She dug into the mountains looking for a place on Kaua'i's North Shore to call home. After striking water, she rejected the caves as a dwelling and moved to the Big Island of Hawai'i, where she still resides in Kilauea Volcano.

KE'E BEACH

Snorkeling is good at Ke'e Beach, which has a variety of tropical fish. A reef protects the right side of the cove and, except on high surf days, it's usually calm. The left side is open and can have a powerful current, particularly in winter. When it's exceptionally calm – almost never – snorkelers can cross the reef to the open ocean where there's great visibility, big fish, interesting coral and the occasional sea turtle. It makes the inside of the bay look like kid stuff, but breaking surf and strong currents create conditions that simply are not worth the risk. For the majority of people, it's wise to stay within the reef. When the tide's extremely low, however, you can walk far out on the reef without getting your feet wet and peer into tide pools.

There are several ways to behold the Na Pali Coast from here. One way is to walk the first 30 minutes of the Kalalau Trail (p156). Another is to take the short walk out around the point at the left side of the beach, toward the heiau. Or, simply walk down the beach to the right for a few minutes and look back as the cliffs unfold, one after the other.

Showers, drinking water, rest rooms and a pay phone are tucked back in the woods behind the parking lot.

KAULU PAOA HEIAU

The remains of Kaulu Paoa Heiau stand just five minutes from Ke'e Beach. Here, beneath the cliff face, large stones create a long flat grassy platform where a thatched-roof *halau* (a longhouse used as a hula school) once ran the entire length of the terrace. Here, dances to Laka, the goddess of hula, were performed. In ancient Hawai'i this was Kaua'i's most sacred hula school, where the legendary Kaua'i chief Lohi'au (see opposite) and his friend Paoa trained, and students aspiring to learn hula came from all of the Hawaiian Islands.

Present-day hula *halau* (troupes) still leave fern wreaths, rocks wrapped in ti leaves, lei

PASSIONATE GODDESSES

Legend says that the volcano goddess Pele was napping one day under a *hala* tree on the Big Island when her spirit was awakened by the sound of distant drums. Her spirit rode the wind toward the sound, searching each island until she finally arrived at Ke'e Beach. Here, above the heiau (ancient Hawaiian religious site), she found Lohi'au, a 16th-century chief, beating a hula drum, surrounded by graceful hula dancers.

Pele took the form of an enchanting woman and captured Lohi'au's heart. They became lovers and moved into his house. In time Pele had to go home to the Big Island, leaving lovesick Lohi'au behind. Later, she sent her sister Hi'iaka to fetch him within 40 days (all the other sisters refused the task, fearing Pele's monumental jealousy), forbidding Hi'iaka even to hug Lohi'au. In return, Pele vowed to watch over Hi'iaka's friend Hopoe, a human woman who lived in an ohia-lehua grove.

After Pele left, Lohi'au, heartbroken and distraught, had become deathly ill. When Hi'iaka arrived he was dead and she had to undergo a perilous journey to find his wandering spirit, then perform a series of rituals to revive him. When 40 days passed, Pele, in a fit of rage, brought lava and destruction to the Big Island, killing Hopoe. On her return with Lohi'au, Hi'iaka saw the ruins and knew Pele had not kept her promise so she embraced Lohi'au and placed a lei around his neck.

Pele then circled Lohi'au in a ring of lava fire, which incited Hi'iaka to attack Kilauea Volcano and prepare to let loose the seas. Pele realized her faithlessness (in the face of her sister's faithfulness) and she relented, telling Hi'iaka where to find Lohi'au's spirit. Lohi'au (revived yet again) and Hi'iaka then returned to Kaua'i, where they lived until Lohi'au died a mortal death.

You can see Lohi'au's House Site near Ke'e Beach, just a minute's walk above the parking lot – but you must ramp up your imagination into overdrive. At the Kalalau Trail sign, go left along the barely discernible dirt path to a vine-covered rock wall. This overgrown level terrace, which runs back 54ft to the bluff, is the historical home of Lohi'au.

and other offerings to Laka in crevices in the cliff face. Under no circumstances should these be disturbed. This site is sacred to Hawaiians and should be treated with respect. Night hula dances are still performed here on special occasions.

To make the five-minute walk through almond trees to the remains of the heiau, take the path on the western side of the beach. Follow the stone wall as it curves uphill, and you'll reach the heiau almost immediately. The overgrown section at the foot of the hill is one of the more intact parts of the heiau, but keep walking up the terraces toward the cliff face. Surf pounding below, vertical cliffs above – quite a memorable place to worship the gods.

NA PALI COAST STATE PARK

On virtually every visitor's must-see, must-do list is Na Pali, which in Hawaiian means simply 'the cliffs.' Nowhere else in Hawaii will you see such grand, sharply fluted cliffs (though the highest are on Moloka'i).

Na Pali Coast State Park encompasses the rugged, corrugated 22-mile stretch be-tween the end of the road at Ke'e Beach in the north and the road's opposite end at Polihale State Park in the west.

History

Kalalau, Honopu, Awa'awapuhi, Nu'alolo and Mioli'i are the five major valleys on the Na Pali Coast. Since the first waves of Tahitian settlers, these deep river valleys contained sizable settlements. When winter seas prevented canoes from landing on the northern shore, trails down precipitous ridges and rope ladders provided access.

In the mid-19th century missionaries established a school in Kalalau, the largest valley, and registered the valley population at about 200. Influenced by Western ways, people gradually began moving to towns, and by century's end the valleys were largely abandoned.

The Na Pali valleys, with limited accessibility, fresh water and abundant fertility, have long been a natural refuge for people wanting to escape one scene or another, like modern-day 'Kalalau outlaws,' who drop out back here.

Sights & Activities

For a close-up view of the Na Pali Coast, hiking the 11-mile Kalalau coastal trail into Hanakapi'ai, Hanakoa and Kalalau Valleys is a backpacking adventure rated among the world's most beautiful. From the opposite side, in Koke'e State Park, a couple of strenuous hikes reach clifftops with gorgeous views into Awa'awapuhi and Nu'alolo Valleys for a different perspective.

You can also access the Na Pali Coast by sea on a 17-mile kayak adventure (p144). An attractive way to combine kayaking, hiking and camping on the coast: paddle to the Kalalau campground with one of the outfits (you supply the permit) for around $125 per person. Find local guys to carry in your gear for around $80. There's no specific tour like this, so you'd need to ask around in Hanalei – and find guys you trust.

Expect to 'escape into nature' along the Na Pali Coast? Yes and no. Certainly you will be smack atop one of Hawaii's natural wonders, miles from any roads and towns. But realize that you'll also be surrounded by fellow admirers (especially on the first leg of the Kalalau Trail), and you'll hear helicopters droning and loudspeaker announcements from cruise ships all day. The Na Pali Coast is Kaua'i's marquee show, and you will certainly not be alone out there.

KALALAU TRAIL

Kalalau is Hawaii's premier trail. Here, it's common to meet hikers who have trekked in Nepal or climbed to Machu Picchu. The Na Pali Coast is similarly spectacular, a place of singular beauty.

The Kalalau Trail is basically the same ancient route used by the Hawaiians who once lived in these remote north-coast valleys. The trail runs along high sea cliffs, and winds up and down across lush valleys before it finally ends below the steep fluted *pali* of Kalalau.

The state parks office in Lihu'e can provide a Kalalau Trail brochure with a map. Basic information is posted at the Ke'e Beach trailhead, but the small print is hard to read.

The hike itself can be divided into three parts:

Ke'e Beach–Hanakapi'ai Valley (2 miles)
Hanakapi'ai Valley–Hanakoa Valley (4 miles)
Hanakoa Valley–Kalalau Valley (5 miles)

The first 2 miles of the trail to Hanakapi'ai Valley are insanely popular: 500,000 people hike it annually, and it shows in the eroded trail edges, muddy passages with ankle-deep puddles and, especially in summer, boisterous children. No permit is required for the hike to Hanakapi'ai Valley.

Hardy hikers in good shape can walk the 11-mile trail straight through in about

---

LETHAL BEAUTY

The Kalalau Trail leads you through rugged wilderness and hikers should be well prepared. The entire trail is rough and rocky and, especially during the rainy winter season, it can be impassable. Try to hike the Kalalau Trail after a dry spell, otherwise it can be treacherously slippery. The muddiness is mostly an inconvenience until the smooth stones become coated and slick. Find a walking stick at the trailhead (or bring your own) – they make a big difference!

The farther you go, the more you'll traverse steep cliffs on an unnervingly narrow path, occasionally just a little more than a foot in width. Hardy hikers accustomed to high-country trails don't consider it unduly hazardous, however.

Accidents happen. Most casualties along the Kalalau Trail are the result of people fording swollen streams, walking after dark on cliff-edge trails or swimming in treacherous surf. Keep in mind that the cliffs are composed of loose and crumbly rocks; don't try to climb them and don't camp directly beneath them, as goats commonly dislodge stones that can tumble down on top of you. Still, for someone who's fit, cautious and aware, the hike will be unforgettable.

There's no shortage of water sources along the trail, but all drinking water must be boiled or treated. Campers should bring only what is necessary (travel light!) because an unwieldy backpack will markedly compromise your footing on this terrain. You don't want extra weight shifting on stream crossings or along cliff edges.

Pack out what you pack in. Garbage and jettisoned weight from departing campers is a serious problem at Kalalau, and it cannot be overstated: take your detritus with you.

Last, mosquitoes are voracious so be sure to wear repellent.

seven hours. Until the Hanakoa Valley campground reopens, however, it's not possible to (legally) break the trip beyond Hanakapi'ai. In winter there are generally only a few people at any one time hiking all the way in to Kalalau Valley, but foot traffic is thick in summer. Weekends are busiest.

Even if you're not planning to camp, a permit is officially required to continue on the Kalalau Trail beyond Hanakapi'ai. Free day-use hiking permits are available from the **Division of State Parks** (Map p78; ☎ 274-3444; www.hawaii.gov/dlnr/dsp; Department of Land & Natural Resources, Division of State Parks, 3060 Eiwa St, Rm 306, Lihue, HI 96766; ☒ 8am-3:30pm Mon-Fri), which also issues the required camping permits for the Hanakapi'ai (one night maximum) and Kalalau (five nights maximum) Valleys. For more information on permits see p217).

Ke'e Beach to Hanakapi'ai Valley

The 2-mile trail from Ke'e Beach to Hanakapi'ai Valley is a delightfully scenic hike. Morning is the best time to head west on the first leg of the trail, while afternoon is ideal when returning east, as the sun thus strikes your back and provides good light for photography.

Just 0.25 mile up the trail, you catch a fine view of Ke'e Beach and the surrounding reef. The trail weaves through *hala* (screw pine), *kukui* (candlenut) and *'ohi'a* trees and then back out to clearings with fine coastal views. There are purple orchids, wildflowers and a couple of mini waterfalls en route. At the 0.5-mile mark, you come to a finger of cliff with your first view of the Na Pali Coast on one side and Ke'e Beach

on the other. Even if you weren't planning on a hike, it's well worth coming this far.

The trail ascends steadily for another 0.5 miles, then starts to dip under soft-needled ironwoods and through stream gulches. The smooth rocks on the trail are often coated in mud and thus precariously slippery. At about the 1.5-mile point, you'll see a black-and-yellow striped tsunami pole marker, which indicates the lowest point of safety in case of a tsunami.

You will soon reach Hanakapi'ai Valley, where you must ford the stream to continue. Hanakapi'ai Beach is sandy in the summer, but a beach of only boulders during winter, when storms sweep out the sand. It's sometimes not accessible across a flooded river. The western side of the beach has a small cave with dripping water and a miniature fern grotto.

The ocean is dangerous here, with unpredictable rip currents year-round. It's particularly treacherous during winter high-surf conditions, but summer trades also bring very powerful currents. Hanakapi'ai Beach is the deadliest beach on the island, causing one drowning per year on average since the 1970s.

The campsite closest to the oceanfront cliffs is overused and under-maintained; don't add to the trash left here. Another slightly better campsite is located a little way up the trail to Hanakapi'ai Falls (see p159).

If you're just doing a day hike and want to walk further, it makes more sense to head up the valley to Hanakapi'ai Falls than it does to continue another couple of miles on the coastal trail.

NORTH SHORE

SWEAT-FREE NA PALI COAST

Be honest: you're a weekend walker more than vigorous trekker. Don't be deterred if you cannot hike or kayak the Kalalau Trail. You have a handful of gentle options. And, yes, we believe you'll train hard for your next trip here.

- Walk a few minutes west on **Ke'e Beach** (p154) to glimpse the cliffs, scurrying over rocks for a better view. Highly recommended in early-morning light.
- Drive up to the **Kalalau Lookout** and the **Pu'u o Kila Lookout** in Koke'e State Park (p207).
- Take a **helicopter tour** (p62).
- Take a **catamaran** or **raft tour** from Hanalei (p145), Waimea (p194) or Port Allen (p185).
- Treat yourself to spectacular scenery underwater, too, and go snorkeling (p145). Leave from Hanalei (only in summer) for the shortest transit time.
- Buy the **screen saver**. Take Na Pali home with you.

Hanakapi'ai Valley to Hanakoa Valley

After 10 minutes, up from Hanakapi'ai Valley on the way to Hanakoa Valley, there's a nice view of Hanakapi'ai Beach. From there the trail goes into bush, and the next coastal view is not for another mile. This is the least scenic part of the trail.

Craggy cliffs begin to tower overhead following some well-cut, but hot and exposed switchbacks that climb 800ft in elevation. The trail traverses rocks where rivulets of water tumble over the cliff into a pool. The trail keeps climbing past the 3-mile marker; this final section of the switchbacks over rocks and mud can be brutal, and the grade is steep. Soon the trail reaches its highest point at **Space Rock**, a prominent boulder overlooking the coast (a popular rest stop).

Winding from waterfall gulch to ridge and back again, the trail then passes through several mini valleys within the greater Ho'olulu Valley, finally reaching Waiahuakua Valley. These are 'hanging valleys,' which end abruptly at sea cliffs rather than gradually sloping into a beach. When streams reach the coast, they simply pour off the cliffs as waterfalls. Old Hawaiian stone terraces announce the trail's entrance into Hanakoa Valley, passing a helipad and hunting shack.

The valley is pretty, and in **Hanakoa Stream** you'll find pools large enough for swimming. About 0.5 mile up the valley there's a **waterfall**, but it's a tough climb on a very overgrown path.

Hanakoa Valley to Kalalau Valley

By far the most difficult part of the trail, the last 5 miles are also without question the most beautiful. Make sure you have at least three hours of daylight left. There are very narrow and steep stretches, so pack your gear securely and watch your footing. Don't go off-trail trying to chart a new course; this is no time for experimentation and hikers have gotten fatally lost here.

About a mile out of Hanakoa Valley, ascending past coffee shrubs and ti plants, you'll reach the coast again and begin to get fantastic views of Na Pali's jagged edges. The red-dirt switchbacks show incredible erosion due to salty seaspray, sparse rainfall and feral goats that consume the vegetation.

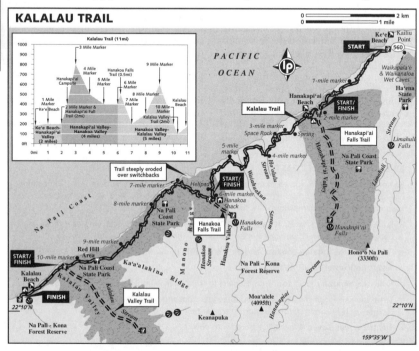

DETOUR: HANAKAPI'AI FALLS

The 2-mile hike from Hanakapi'ai Beach to Hanakapi'ai Falls – a Kalalau Trail side trip – tacks an extra 2½-hour round-trip on to the Ke'e Beach to Hanakapi'ai Valley walk. Due to tricky rock crossings, this trek is tougher than the walk from Ke'e Beach to Hanakapi'ai Beach. During heavy rain, flash floods are likely in the narrow valley, so do this hike only in fair weather.

The trail itself is periodically washed out by floodwaters, and sections occasionally get redrawn, but path direction basically ascends gradually up the side of Hanakapi'ai Stream. The trail is not well-maintained, however; in places you may have to scramble over and around tree trunks and branches. If you find the trail occasionally disappears into the surrounding forest, look for little tiny tags of colored plastic ribbon tied to branches here and there. Be prepared to lose your way and find it again.

Trails line both sides of the stream, but the main route heads up the stream's western side. Big old mango trees along the way might have fruit for the picking. Ten minutes' walk from the trailhead, you'll find thickets of green bamboo interspersed with eucalyptus. Also along the trail is the site of an old coffee mill, though all that remains is a little of the chimney.

The first of three major stream crossings is about one mile (25 minutes' walk) up, at a sign that warns: 'Hazardous. Keep away from stream during heavy rainfall. Stream floods suddenly.' Be particularly careful of your footing on the rocky upper part of the trail. Some of the rocks are covered with a barely visible film of slick algae – worse than walking on ice.

Hanakapi'ai Falls is spectacular, falling 100ft into a wide pool gentle enough for swimming. Directly under the falls, the cascading water forces you back from the rock face – a warning from nature, as falling rocks are common. The setting is idyllic, though not very sunny near the falls because of the incredible steepness.

The coast is much drier here, and the trail winds in and out of gulches, some dry and some with fast-flowing streams that must be crossed, past sissal grasses, lantana and guava trees. The vegetation is sparse here, so you can clearly see the sheer drop to the sea (just beyond your feet). You'll continue making steep descents and ascents until you reach a final climb just before the 10-mile marker on an eroded slope called **Red Hill**, for obvious reasons. You'll have to find a way to slide down the red-dirt rubble because the original route has crumbled away. Cross Kalalau Stream and start down the final mile of track into Kalalau Valley.

The large valley has a beach, small waterfall and heiau site, plus ruins of ancient houses and a few caves. If you make it all the way here, you'll find a communal scene, with drum circles and new friends sharing campfire stories.

An easy 2-mile trail leads back into the valley to a pool in Kalalau Stream where there's a natural water slide. Valley terraces where Hawaiians cultivated taro until 1920 are now largely overgrown with bitter Java plum, and edible guava and passion fruit. Feral goats scurry up and down the crumbly cliffs and drink from the stream.

During the 1960s and '70s people wanting to get away from it all tried to settle in Kalalau, but forestry rangers eventually routed them out. Rangers still swoop in by helicopter every six months or so to check camping permits; those caught without permits are forced to hike out immediately.

Getting There & Away

The parking lot at Ke'e Beach trailhead is quite large but fills quickly during the jammed summer months. Cars are generally safe during the day due to high foot traffic. But if you're camping, break-ins of cars left overnight are common. Some advise leaving cars empty and unlocked to prevent smashed windows. Consider parking at the campground at Ha'ena Beach Park. Whatever you do, don't leave valuables in a locked car.

You could also store everything in Hanalei or Wainiha and take a taxi to the trailhead. Kayak Kaua'i stores gear and cars.

North Shore Cab (☎ 826-4118) charges a hefty $20 for the roughly 6-mile ride from Hanalei to Ke'e Beach. En route to Ha'ena from Hanalei, Wainiha General Store stores bags for $3 a day.

South Shore

Of all Kaua'i's resort meccas, the sun-drenched South Shore is the tourist favorite. It's no wonder, as Po'ipu boasts sunny skies and friendly surf all year round. If it's gloomy on the North Shore, head south for an uplifting UV dose.

For those seeking a convivial, rather than secluded, atmosphere, Po'ipu boasts enough of a critical mass for that resort vibe. Beaches are bustling but not jammed, and, despite the mega condos and hotels clustered near the coast, there's easy beach access for all. The off-highway location is a boon, and parking is generally trouble-free.

Just inland are the former plantation towns Koloa and Kalaheo, both excellent antidotes to the resort scene. Koloa's restored historic 'old town' is the South Shore's lively commercial center, while Kalaheo, one-stop town (literally) and gateway to the Westside, presents a handful of worthy dining options.

Accommodations are plentiful here, and most visitors flock to the coast to stroll on primo beaches and admire picture-perfect Pacific sunsets (with nary a building obstructing the view). But for a change of scenery, consider staying in Kalaheo's unpretentious neighborhoods or around Koloa, with lush jungle growth and vistas encompassing the Lawa'i Valley.

While Po'ipu dwellers can walk to the beach, a car is necessary to reach all other destinations. The distances separating Po'ipu sleeping and eating spots preclude walking – and the nearest town for groceries is over 2 miles away.

SOUTH SHORE

HIGHLIGHTS

- Walking the southeastern coast to **Maha'ulepu Beach** (p172)
- Admiring the lush greenery of the **National Tropical Botanical Garden** (p167)
- Surfing and swimming along **Po'ipu Beach Park** (p170)
- Tasting *poke* (marinated raw fish) and seared *'ahi* (yellowfin tuna) at **Koloa Fish Market** (p165)
- Playing an $8 round at **Kukuiolono Golf Course** (p182) in Kalaheo
- Exploring the underwater world by **scuba diving** (p171)

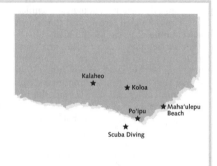

SOUTH SHORE

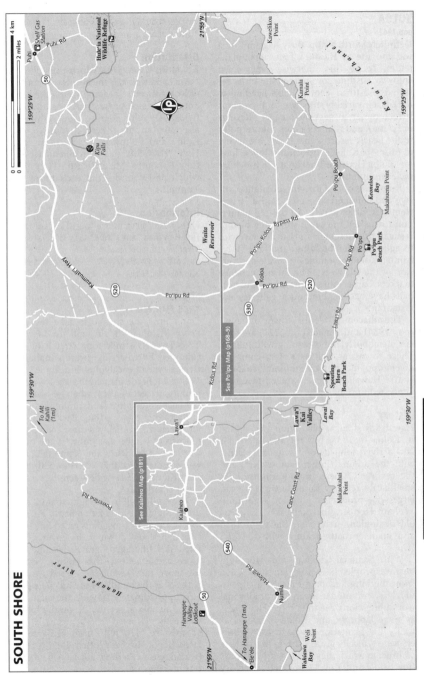

SOUTH SHORE

KOLOA
pop 1942

Definitely worth a stop, the village of Koloa was the site of Hawaii's first sugar plantation. Today, this otherwise-sleepy town enjoys a bustling commercial life in its restored 'old-town' center. Folks heading to the coast invariably stop here for provisions (which by far surpass the meager offerings in Po'ipu), and it offers a nice counterpart to the beach-resort scene. Locals are trying to promote Koloa's historical essence; look for 'Koloa Heritage Trail' maps in brochure racks around here.

Koloa was once a thriving plantation village and commercial center until it largely went bust after WWII. All the old plantation towns tell the same story: the history is sugar, the present is tourism. Today, with its aging wooden buildings and false storefronts, Koloa resembles a clean-cut version of the Old West. The former produce markets, barbershops, bathhouses and beer halls have become boutiques, galleries and restaurants.

The adjacent residential towns of Lawa'i (pop 1984) and Omao (pop 1221) are low-key, neighborly and blooming with foliage. These towns, as well as Koloa, comprise diverse populations of Filipino, Japanese, Native Hawaii, white and mixed-race residents, with no majority.

History

Hawaii's first sugar plantation was started in Koloa in 1835, but the raw materials had arrived long before; sugarcane came with the original Polynesian settlers, and the earliest Chinese immigrants brought small-scale refinery know-how. However, large-scale production did not begin until William Hooper, an enterprising 24-year-old Bostonian, arrived on Kaua'i in 1835 and made inroads dealing with the *ali'i* (chiefs).

With financial backing from Honolulu businesspeople, he leased land in Koloa from the king and paid the *ali'i* a stipend to release commoners from their traditional work obligations. He then hired Hawaiians as wage laborers, and Koloa became Hawaii's first plantation town. In 1888 workers were typically given a three- to five-year contract in which they had to work 10 hours (for field hands) or 12 hours (for factory

workers) a day, six days a week. The wage? Nine dollars a month.

Orientation

Koloa Rd (Hwy 530), which runs between Lawa'i and Koloa, is the best way in and out of Koloa if you're heading west – the pleasant rural drive passes pastures and cane fields. If you're coming from Lihu'e, an alternate (and more scenic) route to reach Koloa and Po'ipu is to take Kaumuali'i Hwy (Hwy 50) and turn *makai* (toward the sea) onto Maluhia Rd (Hwy 520), which passes under the enchanting Tree Tunnel.

Information

Only basic services are found in Koloa:

First Hawaiian Bank (☎ 742-1642; 3506 Waikomo Rd) At the east end of town.

Post office (☎ 800-275-8777; 5485 Koloa Rd) Serves both Koloa and Po'ipu.

Sights
TREE TUNNEL

Don't miss the chance to take the drive down Maluhia Rd, through the fairy-tale Tree Tunnel, a mile-long stretch of road canopied by towering swamp mahogany trees, a type of eucalyptus. Pineapple baron Walter McBryde planted the trees as a community project in 1911, when he had leftover eucalyptus after landscaping his estate at Kukuiolono (see p180). Back then, with 900 trees, the tunnel was more than double its current length; alas, most of the tunnel was lopped off when the Kaumuali'i Hwy was rerouted. Maluhia Rd (Hwy 520) intersects Kaumuali'i Hwy between the six- and 7-mile markers.

The cinder hill to the right about 2 miles down Maluhia Rd is **Pu'u o Hewa**. From its top, the ancient Hawaiians raced *he'e holua* (wooden sleds) down paths covered with oiled *pili* (thatched) grass. To add even more excitement to this popular spectator sport, the Hawaiians crossed two sled paths near the middle of the hill. The paths were approximately 5ft wide; the eagle-eyed might be able to see the 'X' on the hillside where they crossed. Hewa means 'wrong' or 'mistake.' The hill's original name was lost when a surveyor jotted 'Pu'u o Hewa' (which means 'wrong hill') on a map he was making.

OLD KOLOA HISTORIC BUILDINGS
Until recently the building that houses **Crazy Shirts** (☎ 742-7161; 🕑 10am-9pm Mon-Sat, to 6pm Sun) was the Yamamoto General Store. Check out the huge monkey-pod tree planted alongside in 1925 by Howard Yamamoto. Before the theater across the street burned down, moviegoers would line up at Yamamoto's for crack seed (Chinese preserved fruit) and soft drinks. A couple of wooden sculptures by the late Maui artist Reems Mitchell sit on the sidewalk in front of the store. In the courtyard behind, you'll find the site of the former town hotel, along with a little **historical display** that includes a Japanese bath and some period photos.

At the east side of town is the **Koloa Jodo Mission** (☎ 742-6735; 2480 Waikomo Rd; 🕑 services 6pm Mon-Fri, 9:30am Sun), which follows Pure Land Buddhism, a non-meditating form, popular in Japan since the 12th century. The Buddhist temple on the left is the original, which dates back to 1910, while next to it is a newer and larger temple where services are now held. During services, the smell of incense and the sound of beating drums fill the air. Obon (Japanese Festival of the Dead) dances (see p223) are held here each June.

St Raphael's Catholic Church, Kaua'i's oldest Catholic church, is the burial site of some of Hawaii's first Portuguese immigrants. The original church, built in 1854, was made of lava rock and coral mortar with walls 3ft thick – a type of construction that can be seen in the ruins of the adjacent rectory. When the church was enlarged in 1936, it was plastered over, and it now has a more typical whitewashed appearance. To get here from Koloa Rd, turn onto Weliweli Rd, then right onto Hapa Rd and proceed half a mile to the church.

SUGAR EXHIBITS
Any sugarologists in the crowd? The **field** on Koloa Rd, opposite Sueoka Store, is for you. In a tiny, clumped garden, you'll find a dozen varieties of sugarcane all twisted together and labeled with faded interpretive markers. The stone smokestack in another corner of the field is a relic from one of Koloa's early mills, and dates back to 1841.

In the center of the field, the principal ethnic groups that worked the plantations are immortalized in a **sculpture**. The Hawaiian wears a *malo* (loincloth) and has a poi dog by his side. The Chinese, Korean, Japanese, Portuguese, Filipino and Puerto Rican groups are likewise in indigenous field dress. You may notice that the plaque on the wall curiously makes reference to a haole (Caucasian) overseer – present-day islanders found the depiction of this Caucasian plantation boss seated on a high horse so unacceptable that he was actually omitted from the sculpture at the 11th hour.

Activities
Koloa is mostly a commercial (and community) base from where you go elsewhere to explore the outdoors. A number of watersports outfits are based here. Free municipal **tennis courts** are found in Knudsen Park.

DIVING
While Koloa is not even on the coast, the island's best dive outfit, **Fathom Five Divers** (☎ 742-6991, 800-972-3078; www.fathomfive.com; 3450 Po'ipu Rd; shore dives $65-95, boat dives $100-140), is located here. Run by a husband-and-wife team, Jeannette and George Thompson, this outfit can't be beat for knowledgeable, personal and flexible service. They offer the whole range, from Ni'ihau boat dives to night dives to certification courses. Groups max out at just six divers (no kidding!) and they avoid mixing skill levels. Unlike the typical outfit, they let divers choose sites instead of running the same tour over and over, allowing for diverse multiday dives. And if you bring your own equipment, they'll store and clean it for you. Private charters (including overnighters) are possible, too. The Thompsons and their kids are a diving family, and their love of the sport and the island is contagious. Their shore-diving sister company is Ocean Quest Watersports (p117) but all bookings are handled here. Call well in advance.

See p59 for more on diving.

SNORKELING
For snorkel gear rental and sales, a standby is **Snorkel Bob's** (☎ 742-2206; www.snorkelbob.com; 3236 Po'ipu Rd; rental mask, snorkel & fins per week $9-32; 🕑 8am-5pm), which also rents boogie boards (per day/week $6.50/26).

SOUTH SHORE

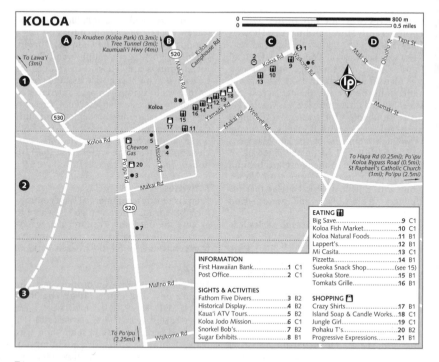

KOLOA

Tours

ATV

Kaua'i ATV Tours (☎ 742-2734, 877-707-7088; www
.kauaiatv.com; 5330 Koloa Rd) takes groups from
six to 12 over 22,000 acres of pastureland
mauka (inland) of Koloa and Lihu'e, a vast
area that's middling in scenery until you
reach the lusher upcountry. Don't expect a
wild and woolly ride; it's a controlled tour
and not one can let loose. The four-hour waterfall tour costs $145 per person (⌚ 7am,
8am, noon & 1pm) and is more rewarding
since you splash at two private waterfalls
(you also get splattered with mud). The
automatic Yamaha Bruins meet California
emission-control standards. Private tours,
including transportation to a wedding site
by ATV, can be arranged.

Festivals & Events

Koloa Plantation Days Celebration (☎ 822-0734;
www.koloaplantationdays.com), the South Shore's
biggest annual celebration, spans nine days
of lively family fun in late July. Events (in
Koloa and Po'ipu) include a parade, block
party, craft fairs, luau dinner and show,

golf tournaments, guided walks and more.
Many events are free.

Sleeping

The following inns are located near Koloa,
which makes a convenient, central home
base. From here, the Po'ipu beaches are
a quick drive away, but you can unwind
in the cooler, greener uplands amid local
residences. You will also be closer to the
highway and more eating options.

Boulay Inn (☎ 742-1120, 635-5539; http://home
.hawaii.rr.com/boulayinn; apt per day/week/month
$75/450/1400) A private one-bedroom apart-
ment with wraparound lanai (porch), full
kitchen and washer/dryer for $75? You're
not dreaming. In quiet Omao, a residential
neighborhood between Koloa and Po'ipu,
this breezy apartment (which can sleep
four) is perfect for those seeking homey
comfort rather than an ocean view. Sliding
glass doors fill the place with sunlight, while
overhead fans cool it down. Guests have an
easy-access, off-street parking space. The
second-floor unit sits atop the owners' ga-
rage, so there are no shared walls. Don't

hesitate – this is among Kaua'i's best deals. Please call for address details.

Hale Kua (Map p181; ☎ 332-8570, 800-440-4353; www.halekua.com; 4896-E Kua Rd; 1-bedroom apt $105, 1-bedroom cottages $115, 3-bedroom apt $125-175) Escape into a jungle world of misty rain, giant trees and…modern apartments with every creature comfort you could desire. Hale Kua is an alternative for anyone seeking a comfortable retreat away from tourist throngs. The spacious units resemble upscale townhouses, and each unit includes, lanai, washer/dryer and full kitchen. The location is way up a narrow road, so it's best for folks who return home and stay put for the night. The 1300-sq-ft three-bedroom apartment upstairs is ample space for a family. Big discounts for weeklong-plus stays.

Marjorie's Kaua'i Inn (Map p181; ☎ 332-8838, 800-717-8838; www.marjorieskauaiinn.com; r $130-160; 🖭) Classy to the nth degree, this inn overlooking the verdant hills of Lawa'i Valley is a refreshing alternative to the standard beach-house setting. Each room features an expansive private lanai, glossy hardwood floors, luxury linens and kitchenettes. The priciest room includes a private hot tub (state of the art, with 25 massage jets). All guests can use the inviting 50ft lap pool, plus a poolside barbecue grill. Ownership transferred in 2005, but the quality has held steady to date.

Eating

The following eateries are strung along Koloa Rd near its intersection with Maluhia Rd.

Sueoka Snack Shop (☎ 742-1112; 5392 Koloa Rd; snacks $1.50-4.50, plate lunch $4; ⏱ 9am-3pm, from 9:30am Sun) If you're off the diet wagon and game to try the heart-clogging local fast-food favorites, you can find them all for under $5 each at this take-out window adjacent to the Sueoka Store: Portuguese bean soup, chili and rice, *loco moco* (fried egg, hamburger patty, rice and gravy), plate lunches, sandwiches, burgers and saimin (local-style noodle soup). No seating.

Lappert's (☎ 742-1272; Koloa Rd; ice cream single scoop $3.50; ⏱ 6am-10pm) You can find Kaua'i's famous premium ice cream at four locations on the island. This one was where the late founder Walter Lappert often hung out. Kaua'i Pie flavor (coffee ice cream with chocolate fudge, mac nuts and coconut flakes) is a bestseller, while luscious sorbets in guava and mango let you stick to the ol' diet.

Koloa Fish Market (☎ 742-6199; 5482 Koloa Rd; lunch $4-7; ⏱ 10am-6pm Mon-Fri, to 5pm Sat) Locals are constantly lined up to buy *bento* (Japanese meal) boxes, sushi, plate lunches and fresh fish. The *poke* (cubed marinated raw fish) comes in mouth-watering varieties (per pound $9 to $9.50), and the seared-'*ahi* (yellowfin tuna) slices (per pound $13) are gourmet quality. For dessert, try the sweet hunk of *haupia* (coconut dessert). Fresh sashimi-quality fish is a steal.

Pizzetta (☎ 742-8881; 5408 Koloa Rd; pizza $16-23, mains $12-18; ⏱ 11am-9:30pm) It looks like any suburban pizzeria, decorated in no-brainer green, red and white. And it lacks the local cachet of Brick Oven Pizza in nearby Kalaheo. But pickings are slim in Koloa, and the thin-crust gourmet pizza, in combos like fire-roasted vegetables with feta cheese, are tasty, as are the tarragon-chicken *panini* (sandwiches) during lunch or eggplant lasagna during dinner. There's a children's menu, happy hour (from 3pm to 5:30pm) and pizza by the slice ($3 to $4, until 6pm). Free delivery service (from 5pm) on orders over $20.

Mi Casita (☎ 742-2323; 5470 Koloa Rd; appetizers $6-9.50, meals $6-19; ⏱ 5-9pm Mon-Sat) The colorful mural and lively, piped-in music add just the right atmosphere for the filling Mexican fare served at this cozy family-run restaurant. Standouts include the seafood lover's fajitas, with sautéed *ono* (wahoo) and tiger shrimp, fresh fish tacos and, if you're not counting your fat calories, *chile rellanos* (chiles stuffed with cheese, egg-batter-fried and topped with more cheese). They tend to be inconsistent in keeping opening hours so call ahead.

Tomkats Grille (☎ 742-8887; 5404 Koloa Rd; breakfast $5-9, lunch $8-13, dinner $15-20; ⏱ 7am-10pm) The predominant customers are tourists, and the menu reflects it. The *pupu* (appetizer) selections swim in oil and meat, from pork wontons to beer-battered shrimp to pork ribs. Lunch means burgers and grilled sandwiches; forgo the overpriced plate lunches. Dinner continues the steak and burger theme, with a seafood menu including the fresh catch, fish-and-chips and non-local crab legs. The happy hour (from 3pm to 6pm), with $2 beers and $4 margaritas, mimics the scene at sportbars in Anytown, USA.

Check out the following for groceries:

Big Save (cnr Waikomo Rd & Koloa Rd; 6am-11pm) One of the better Big Save branches, with deli.

Koloa Natural Foods (☎ 742-8910; 5356 Koloa Rd; 10am-8pm Tue-Sat, to 4pm Sun & Mon) Limited selection of bulk and packaged items, fresh produce, natural toiletries and supplements. Rather pricey (eg Tom's of Maine toothpaste, 6oz, $6) but the only game in town for spirulina and whole-wheat, no-trans-fat cookies.

Sueoka Store (☎ 742-1611; 5392 Koloa Rd; 7am-9pm) A small market with good selection of local produce and take-out sushi and other Japanese dishes. Try the boiled peanuts, sold by weight in pre-packaged bags. Mainland imports like boxed cereal are expensive.

Shopping

Progressive Expressions (☎ 742-6041; www.progressiveexpressions.com; 5420 Koloa Rd; 9am-9pm) Established in 1972, 'Progressive's' is the South Shore's first surf shop. Original owners Marty and Joe Kuala sold the shop to the Hanalei Surf Company in 2005 but Joe still designs and crafts boards sold here.

Pohaku T's (☎ 742-7500; www.pohaku.com; 3430 Po'ipu Rd; 10am-8pm Mon-Sat, to 6pm Sun) At Pohaku T's, a smorgasbord of quality tees and tanks showcase original Kaua'i-theme designs. Also available are handmade aloha shirts by well-known local seamstress Jacqueline Vienna, who also invented 'Kaua'i chicks,' cute little beanbags or Christmas ornaments that commemorate the island's post-'Iniki recovery (they make great souvenirs). All items sold here are made by Kaua'i residents.

Island Soap & Candle Works (☎ 742-1945, 888-528-7627; www.kauaisoap.com; 5428 Koloa Rd; 9am-10pm) Follow your nose toward the soothing fragrances of plumeria, pineapple and dozens more. Established in 1984 to recreate the art of soap- and candle-making, the company is now a mini chain. They also carry locally made items, including the unique 'recycled crayons' – old crayons are melted by color and molded into island shapes, including a brown tiki and glorious orange-and-yellow sun ($8.50).

Jungle Girl (☎ 742-9649; 5424 Koloa Rd; 9am-9pm) Trendy fashions for females of all ages, from flowing, earthy skirts to bikinis. Around Halloween, look for the candy-colored fairy tutus for girly girls who'll beg to wear them day and night.

Crazy Shirts (☎ 742-7161; 5356 Koloa Rd; 10am-9pm Mon-Sat, to 6pm Sun) Across the Hawaiian Islands, Crazy Shirts is ubiquitous, selling top-quality, clean-cut T-shirts with original, island-inspired designs. Grungy bohos, this is probably not for you.

PO'IPU

pop 1075

Po'ipu, which ironically means 'completely overcast' in Hawaiian, is a major tourist destination about 3 miles south of Koloa down Po'ipu Rd. Here you'll find a string of condos, timeshares and two major hotels, all sharing a stretch of sand and surf. No Po'ipu 'town' as such exists – so don't bother looking for it. Families tend to prefer Po'ipu for its kid-friendly waters and safe environment. Folks staying elsewhere should spend a day here to check out the beaches, especially out-of-the-way Maha'ulepu Beach (p172). The unpredictable Spouting Horn blowhole is a major attraction.

Orientation

Po'ipu is a town in name only, so reaching sights beyond the beach means driving. (Even the beach might require a drive if your lodging place is not near swimmable waters.) The main entry road is Po'ipu Rd (Hwy 520), which first splits into Ho'onani Rd if you veer right, and then into Lawa'i Rd (toward Spouting Horn Beach Park) if you again veer right. If you stay left, you will remain on Po'ipu Rd, from which you can access most condos and hotels.

If you want to skip Koloa en route to Po'ipu, take Maluhia Rd (Hwy 520) then veer left onto Ala Kino'iki Rd (Po'ipu-Koloa Bypass Rd). You'll end up at the intersection of Po'ipu Rd and Pe'e Rd (at Po'ipu Kai Resort).

Information

Services are limited in Po'ipu, but for Internet access, one convenient, if overpriced, option is the business center at the **Grand Hyatt Kaua'i Resort & Spa** (☎ 742-1234, 800-554-9288; www.kauai.hyatt.com; 1571 Po'ipu Rd; per 15min $7.50) which has a handful of computers.

Sights

PRINCE KUHIO PARK

In a quiet field of green, a **monument** commemorates Prince Jonah Kuhio Kalaniana'ole, born nearby in 1871. He was the Territory of

Hawaii's first delegate to the US Congress and he spearheaded the Hawaiian Homes Commission Act, which set aside 200,000 acres of land for indigenous Hawaiians, many of whom are still waiting for it. You'll also find **Ho'ai Heiau**, the remains of a fishpond and an ancient Hawaiian house platform. The park is about 0.5 miles down Lawa'i Rd, across from Ho'ai Bay.

BABY BEACH

This protected swimming beach is just deep enough for little kiddies. It's located off Ho'ona Rd, east of Prince Kuhio Park. Look for the beach access post that marks the pathway between the road and the beach. Big kids can find deeper water with fewer rocks just a short stroll west of this narrow beach.

LAWA'I (BEACH HOUSE) BEACH

While small and rather rocky, this beach (nicknamed 'Beach House Beach' for the adjacent restaurant) opposite Lawa'i Beach Resort can be rich snorkel turf, especially during winter. Entry is rough with just a roadside strip of sand and scads of rocks, but when the water is calm, it's quite clear and there's an abundance of tropical fish, including orange-shouldered tangs, rainbow parrotfish, raccoon butterfly fish and white-spotted puffer fish. When the surf's up in summer, the snorkelers share the beach with surfers. Across from the beach are rest rooms, a shower and public parking.

SPOUTING HORN BEACH PARK

As long as you maintain a 'no expectations' attitude, this famous, if fickle, **geyser** is worth a visit. A stream of water might shoot 25ft into the air accompanied by a whooshing basso. Or a ho-hum spurt of water might taunt a swarm of bored tourists. How much water surges through Spouting Horn all depends on the waves, tides and overall force of the sea rushing through the hole in the basalt rock reef. Nevertheless, it's a mandatory stop on the tour-bus circuit.

Coming during high tide gives you more chance of seeing impressive aquatic displays here, which can reach 30ft when the surf is truly up. You can avoid the tour-bus crowd by arriving in the late afternoon, which is also the best time to see rainbows dancing in the spray. To get here, turn right off Po'ipu Rd onto Lawa'i Rd, just past Po'ipu Plaza, and continue for 1.75 miles.

NATIONAL TROPICAL BOTANICAL GARDEN

With a mission of propagating tropical and endangered plant species and researching ethnobotanical and medicinal plants, **National Tropical Botanical Garden** (NTBG; ☎ 742-2623; www.ntbg.org; 4425 Lawa'i Rd; admission free; ☒ 8:30am-5pm) is worth a look, even if plants aren't your thing. The 10 acres surrounding the visitors center are lush with multi-hued hibiscus blossoms, sprays of orchids, ti plants, topiaries and palms.

The NTBG manages much of Lawa'i Kai, the coastal valley west of Spouting Horn Beach Park, including the 80-acre **Allerton**

LONGING LOVERS

Across Kaua'i, the native *naupaka* plant thrives both near the sea and in the mountains. More wide than tall, it has thick, pulpy, bright-green leaves and small, white flowers with light-purple streaks. Eight types exist and, intriguingly, they feature 'half' flowers: the beach *naupaka* has petals only on the lower half, while the mountain *naupaka* is just the opposite, with petals only on the upper half.

A variety of myths explain this mystery. Some say that the passionate volcano goddess Pele noticed two lovers, very much in love. She desired the young man and approached him as a beautiful stranger, but no matter how she enticed him, he remained faithful. Angered, Pele chased him into the mountains, throwing molten lava at him. Her sisters (always saving the day) rescued the man from sure death by transforming him into the mountain *naupaka*. Then when Pele pursued the young woman toward the sea, Pele's sisters changed her into the beach *naupaka*.

Other tales tell of a Princess Naupaka who is forced to abandon her true love, a fisherman, because he is a commoner. Upon their final parting, she gives him half of a flower from her lei. She returns to the mountains and he returns to the sea.

In any case, the unique half-flower always emphasizes the universal mourning of lost love.

PO'IPU

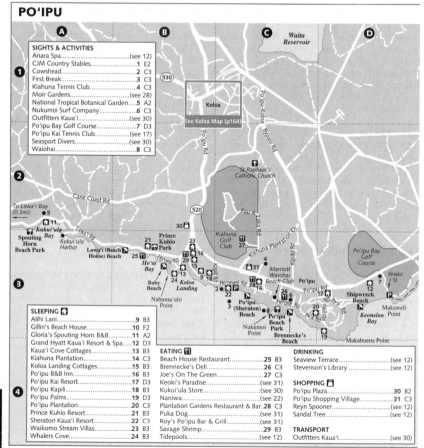

SIGHTS & ACTIVITIES
Anara Spa...................................(see 12)
CJM Country Stables......................1 E2
Cowshead....................................2 C3
First Break...................................3 C3
Kiahuna Tennis Club......................4 C3
Moir Gardens............................(see 28)
National Tropical Botanical Garden....5 A2
Nukumoi Surf Company..................6 C3
Outfitters Kaua'i.........................(see 30)
Po'ipu Bay Golf Course...................7 D3
Po'ipu Kai Tennis Club.................(see 17)
Seasport Divers..........................(see 30)
Waiohai.......................................8 C3

SLEEPING
Alihi Lani.....................................9 B3
Gillin's Beach House.....................10 F2
Gloria's Spouting Horn B&B...........11 A2
Grand Hyatt Kaua'i Resort & Spa....12 D3
Kaua'i Cove Cottages...................13 B3
Kiahuna Plantation.......................14 C3
Koloa Landing Cottages................15 B3
Po'ipu B&B Inn............................16 B3
Po'ipu Kai Resort.........................17 D3
Po'ipu Kapili...............................18 B3
Po'ipu Palms...............................19 D3
Po'ipu Plantation.........................20 C3
Prince Kuhio Resort......................21 B3
Sheraton Kaua'i Resort.................22 C3
Waikomo Stream Villas.................23 B3
Whalers Cove..............................24 B3

EATING
Beach House Restaurant................25 B3
Brennecke's Deli..........................26 C3
Joe's On The Green.......................27 C3
Keoki's Paradise........................(see 31)
Kukui'ula Store...........................(see 30)
Naniwa.....................................(see 22)
Plantation Gardens Restaurant & Bar..28 C3
Puka Dog...................................(see 31)
Roy's Po'ipu Bar & Grill...............(see 31)
Savage Shrimp............................29 B3
Tidepools................................(see 12)

DRINKING
Seaview Terrace........................(see 12)
Stevenson's Library.....................(see 12)

SHOPPING
Po'ipu Plaza...............................30 B2
Po'ipu Shopping Village................31 C3
Reyn Spooner...........................(see 12)
Sandal Tree..............................(see 12)

TRANSPORT
Outfitters Kaua'i.......................(see 30)

Garden, a work of landscape art originated in the 1870s by Queen Emma, the wife of Kamehameha IV, who built a summer cottage that still stands. In 1885 Scottish immigrant Alexander McBryde, the namesake for McBryde Sugar, bought the vast property from Queen Emma's estate. Then, in 1937, Chicago industrialist Robert Allerton bought the lower 67 acres of Lawa'i Kai and, with his adopted son John Gregg Allerton, he significantly expanded the diverse gardens. Upon Robert Allerton's death in 1964, he left $1 million to establish a tropical botanical garden on upper valley lands, and the NTBG assumed management in 1971.

Visits to Allerton Garden are only by **guided tour** (2½hr tour $30; ⊙ 9am, 10am, 1pm &

2pm Mon-Sat). Knowledgeable guides pepper the tour with interesting tidbits and enhance visitors' appreciation of the garden (they're definitely worth the fee), and Japanese-speaking guides are available. Iconic sights include the giant Moreton Bay fig trees (with roots that dwarf humans), the meditative 'undulating' fountain, Queen Emma's cottage, the Allertons' own home – and an eye-popping variety of tropical plants. Guides might point out where Laura Dern hightailed it from a predatory dinosaur in *Jurassic Park*. Reservations are required; meet at the visitors center.

The NTBG's **McBryde Garden**, in the upper part of the valley, can be visited on a self-guided tour ($15). No reservations are re-

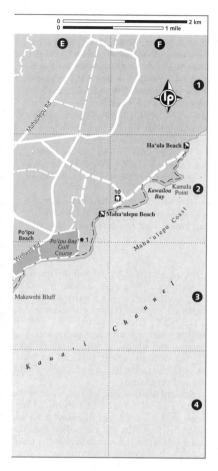

quired, you just hop on a **tram** (☉ every 30 min, 9:30am-2:30pm Mon-Sat, returning on the hour 10am-4pm) from the visitors center to the valley.

KOLOA LANDING

Koloa Landing, at the mouth of Waikomo Stream, was once Kaua'i's largest port. Sugar grown on Koloa Plantation was shipped from here, and whalers called at Koloa Landing to resupply provisions. Back then, perhaps 40 to 50 ships annually anchored off the landing. In the 1850s farmers used the landing to ship Kaua'i-grown oranges and sweet potatoes to California gold miners, and it was the third busiest whaling port among the Hawaiian Islands, surpassed only by Honolulu and Lahaina,

Maui. The landing lost its importance after the road system was built, and it was abandoned in the 1920s. Today there's nothing to see other than a small county boat ramp.

Beneath the water is another story; Koloa Landing is popular for **snorkeling**, and the best **shore-diving** spot on the South Shore. Introductory and certification scuba lessons are often held here. Its protected waters reach depths of about 30ft, and it's generally calm all year, although *kona* (leeward) winds can sometimes create rough water conditions. It has some underwater tunnels, and a good variety of coral and fish. Sea turtles are commonly seen, and monk seals make occasional appearances as well. For the best sights, swim out to the right after entering the water.

MOIR GARDENS

Contrary to popular belief, cacti and succulents are temperamental rather than hardy creatures, prone to over- and underwatering. Thus, it's remarkable that **Moir Gardens** (☎ 742-6411; Kiahuna Plantation Resort, 2253 Po'ipu Rd; admission free; ☉ sunrise-sunset), a modest oasis amid parking lots and condos, has survived since the 1930s.

The gardens, now part of the Kiahuna Plantation resort, were originally the estate of Hector Moir, manager of Koloa Sugar Plantation, and Alexandra 'Sandie' Knudsen Moir: they were a gift from her father. They named their estate Pa'u a Laka, 'skirt of Laka,' the Hawaiian goddess of hula, and it was the site of many gala social gatherings back then.

The Moirs were once avid gardeners who switched from tropical flowering plants to drought-tolerant ones before it became trendy. In 1948 the Brooklyn Botanical Garden ranked Moir Gardens one of the 10 best cactus-and-succulent gardens in the world, in the same league as the Huntington Gardens and the Royal Gardens of Monaco.

Today the mature cactus and succulent garden remains preserved in its entirety, with the resort built around its perimeter. It's a low-key, approachable collection, interspersed with winding paths, lily pond and colorful shocks of orchids. The old lava-stone plantation house, which fronts the gardens, is also here. The plantation

SOUTH SHORE

LOOK BUT DON'T TOUCH

You're almost guaranteed to spot **monk seals** along the Po'ipu coast, half-ton piles of dark blubber. Thus it might be hard to believe they're among the most endangered species on Kaua'i – and one of Hawaii's only two endemic mammals, found nowhere else in the world (the other is a species of bat). The once-thriving monk seal population across the Hawaiian Islands is today estimated at about 1300 and declining by 4% annually. Most live on the remote Northwestern Hawaiian Islands but at least 50 live in the state of Hawaii, and at least half on Kaua'i.

Monk seals live for 25 to 30 years and molt annually – females are typically larger than males. The breeding season runs from December to mid August, and pups are born from March to June. In fall 2005, when a pup was born on Po'ipu, government officials and volunteers tried to shield the mother and baby from beachgoers, surrounding them with fencing and signs and taking turns at keeping vigil. After weeks of feeding her pup and teaching it to swim, she left and the pup was transferred to a protected location. Despite such successes, monk seals, like too many endemic species, remain at grave risk.

If you see a monk seal, remember that you are in its natural habitat. Never approach the animal – keep a distance of 100ft. By all means do not provoke it to move or 'do something.'

For more information see the website of the **Kaua'i Monk Seal Watch Program** (www.kauai monkseal.com).

---

manor is now Plantation Gardens Restaurant & Bar.

It's more of a sideshow than a showstopper, but check it out if you're staying nearby or dining at the restaurant – or if you're a fan of desert flora.

PO'IPU (SHERATON) BEACH

The long ribbon of golden sand running from the Sheraton Kaua'i Resort east to Po'ipu Beach Park is known simply as Po'ipu or Sheraton Beach. It's actually three attractive crescent beaches separated by narrow rocky points. Depending on location and wave action, the waters are good for swimming, bodysurfing, board surfing, windsurfing or snorkeling.

Cowshead, the rocky outcropping at the west end of the beach near the Sheraton, offers Po'ipu Beach's best boogie boarding breaks. Top surfing spots include **First Break**, offshore in front of the Sheraton; inshore along the beach are slower, milder waves more suitable for beginners. **Waiohai**, at the east end of the beach in front of the sprawling new Marriott Waiohai Beach Club timeshare, also sees swells.

PO'IPU BEACH PARK

If you're seeking a safe, lively, family-friendly beach, this is it. You won't find monster waves or idyllic solitude here, but parents with young children enjoy the convenience of Po'ipu Beach Park. Located at the end of Ho'owili Rd (off Po'ipu Rd), it features a lifeguard station and shallow, gentle waters. The narrow beach is crowded, especially during weekends, but it's a family-friendly scene; kids without siblings can quickly find playmates and parents end up recognizing familiar faces among their ilk. Older kids can try snorkeling here, as the fish are relatively plentiful and very tame.

Nukumoi Point extends into the water at the western side of the park. Also known as Tortugas, it is indeed home to many green sea turtles. At low tide, you can walk out on the point and explore tide pools that shelter small fish. The best **snorkeling** is at the west side of the point, where there are swarms of curious fish. It's also a good, shallow **diving** spot for beginners through to advanced divers.

Beach facilities include rest rooms, showers and picnic tables, plus a convenient playground for kids. Beach toys can be rented across the street at Nukumoi Surf Company.

BRENNECKE'S BEACH

With a good shore break, this beach is awesome for **bodysurfing** and **boogie boarding**. However, it breaks really close to shore, making it dangerous for novices. While it's best when surf is highest, generally in summer, there's respectable action in winter, too. Beware of strong rips that are present with high surf. The beach is only a small pocket of sand and the waters can get crowded. For safety reasons, fins are not allowed and surfboards are prohibited.

Brennecke's is named for Dr Marvin Brennecke, who once owned a home on the sea wall against the beach. The beach suffered severe damage during both Hurricanes 'Iwa and 'Iniki, exposing rock boulders along the shorebreak.

SHIPWRECK BEACH
At Keoneloa Bay, this half-mile-long sandy beach fronts the Grand Hyatt Kaua'i Resort & Spa. The surf can be challenging, but ideal for **bodysurfing** and **boogie boarding**. A couple of near-shore surf breaks attract local board surfers as well. Water conditions are suited for the experienced only, as the pounding shore-break and high surf make for dangerous swimming. Toward the left of the bay, daredevils leap off **Makawehi Point**, the gigantic rock cliff.

The name comes from, yes, a shipwrecked wooden boat that washed ashore and remained for years. In 1982, Hurricane 'Iwa swept the boat back to sea.

Activities
DIVING
Dive boats and catamaran cruises usually depart from Kukui'ula Bay, where there's a small-boat harbor about 0.5 miles east of Spouting Horn.

Seasport Divers (☎ 742-9303, 800-685-5889; www .seasportdivers.com; Po'ipu Plaza, 2827 Po'ipu Rd; 2-tank dive $110-140; ☒ check-in 7:30am & 12:45pm) leads a range of dives from shore or boat, including a three-tank dive to the 'forbidden' island of Ni'ihau ($260), offered only in summer. Snorkelers can hop on dive boats, too ($65). All dives are guided by instructor-level divemasters, and any group with noncertified divers includes an additional instructor (for the novices). Its 48ft boat can hold 36 people but they limit groups to 18, and the typical count is eight to 12. You can also rent snorkeling or scuba gear.

There's also Fathom Five Divers in Koloa (p163).

KAYAKING
Outfitters Kaua'i (☎ 742-9667, 888-742-9887; www .outfitterskauai.com; Po'ipu Plaza, 2827-A Po'ipu Rd; ☒ reservations taken 8am-9pm) rents double kayaks (per day $80). Here in Po'ipu, you can go sea kayaking near Spouting Horn; the eight-hour paddle make a good training prelude to the grueling Na Pali challenge.

SURFING
Po'ipu is a popular spot for lessons because it's got killer breaks and year-round sun. If you sign up for lessons, check how big your class will be. Four is maximum density. Lessons listed below are for groups, unless otherwise noted.

Margo Oberg's Surfing School (☎ 332-6100, 888-742-6924; 2hr lesson $48) offers highly regarded classes designed by this World Cup surfing champion.

Also try **Kaua'i Surf School** (☎ 742-8019; www .kauaisurfschool.com; 2hr lesson $60). Classes meet at the Nukumoi Surf Company.

Instructors are CPR-, lifeguard- and first aid-certified at the **Garden Island Surf School** (☎ 652-4841; www.gardenislandsurfschool.com; 2hr lesson $60; ☒ lessons 8am, 10am, noon & 2pm) The lesson includes one hour with instructor and one hour free surfing. Instructors know how to encourage kids to let loose and have fun. They tout a 97% success rate (wonder what 'success' means here), but groups can max out at six.

At **Aloha Surf Lessons** (☎ 639-8614; 2hr lesson group/private $60/125; ☒ lessons 9am, 11am, 1pm & 3pm), pro surfer Chava Greenlee and his staff teach groups of six max, with 15 minutes on land, 45 minutes in water with instructor and one hour on your own.

Nukumoi Surf Company (☎ 742-8019; www .nukumoi.com; 2100 Ho'one Rd; ☒ 7:45am-6:30pm Mon-Sat, 10:45am-6pm Sun), a well-stocked surf shop, rents gear and books lessons with the Kaua'i Surf School. Rental costs: softtop boards per hour/day/week $5/20/60, hard boards $7.50/30/80, boogie boards per day/week $5/15, snorkel gear $5/15. There is also a wide selection of surf shorts, swimsuits and sportswear, sold by teenage gals who might or might not surf themselves. The shop is right across Po'ipu Beach Park.

Seasport Divers (☎ 742-9303, 800-685-5889; www .seasportdivers.com; Po'ipu Plaza, 2827 Po'ipu Rd) rents surfboards (per day/week $20/100) and boogie boards (per day/week from $4/15).

Progressive Expressions (☎ 742-6041; www.pro gressiveexpressions.com; 5420 Koloa Rd; ☒ 9am-9pm), a surf shop in Koloa, rents boards for comparable prices.

DETOUR: MAHA'ULEPU BEACH

Locals consider this pristine swath of **beach** (7:30am-6pm, to 7pm summer) to be Kaua'i's last undeveloped coast. Just a couple of miles beyond Shipwreck Beach, it's not far, but it's unpaved access road is bumpy and most tourists ignore it. The rugged surroundings are unforgettable: limestone (ancient lithified sand) cliffs, pounding surf and either blazing sun or winds that shower you with sea spray and threaten to whisk away your hat. An outstanding primer to appreciating the Maha'ulepu coast's fascinating geology is *Kaua'i's Geologic History: A Simplified Guide* by Chuck Blay and Robert Siemers. Another good resource is **Malama Maha'ulepu** (www .malama-mahaulepu.org).

Maha'ulepu waters are choppy and better suited for experienced surfers, boogie boarders, kitesurfers and windsurfers than once-a-year tourists. But hiking and exploring here is enticing all year round. Before Westerners arrived, this coast was heavily settled, and important historic sites lie buried beneath cane fields and shifting sands. Local believers claim to see ghost marchers approaching from the sea at night. AOL founder Steve Case, who owns the property, has not yet announced plans to develop the area, which abuts the Po'ipu Bay Golf Course. Come before bulldozers clear the way for more resorts.

Access hours are strictly enforced; if you miss the 6pm or 7pm closing time, you car is stuck for the night. The old cane-haul access road is rough – sans 4WD, drive slowly. To get here, drive past the Grand Hyatt Kaua'i, proceed for 1.5 miles and turn right where it dead-ends at a gate. Continue past the gatehouse until you reach the beach parking area. Two short trails to the beach begin at the parking area.

For a closer look at the fascinating windswept coast, you can hike an easy 2 miles from Shipwreck Beach to get here. From Po'ipu Rd, turn *makai* (toward the sea) on Ainako and park in the Grand Hyatt lot at the end. Start at the ironwood trees at the east end of the beach and just stay along the coast. You will walk over craggy cliffs and pass spectacular limesand formations (unfortunately carved with local graffiti here and there). You'll also see tide pools in rocky coves and perhaps a beached monk seal, oblivious to the waves crashing around it. The pristine greens of Po'ipu Bay Golf Course seem incongruous compared with the stark, windswept coast, especially when you see the protected remains of a heiau (ancient Hawaiian religious site).

The Maha'ulepu coast comprises a string of beaches – **Maha'ulepu Beach**, **Kawailoa Bay** and **Ha'ula Beach** – from west to east. Near Maha'ulepu Beach (nicknamed Gillin's – you'll see why) is the sole house on the entire coast, the **Gillin Beach House** (742-7561; www.gillinbeachhouse.com; per week $2675-2900, winter holiday rate $3300), which you can rent. The three-bedroom, two-bathroom house sees more passersby nowadays. It's a unique, if pricey, escape. The original Gillin house (destroyed in 1992 by Hurricane 'Iniki) was built in 1946 by Elbert Gillin, a civil engineer with the Koloa Sugar Plantation. The current house sits on the same property.

From there, keep walking east to reach Kawailoa Bay, surrounded by sand dunes to the west and protected by jutting sea cliffs to the east. Here you might see Hawaiians net-fishing in the waters along the shore, plus windsurfers and kitesurfers skimming across the surf. Ironwood trees backing the beach make a pleasant spot for a picnic. Continue on to reach Ha'ula Beach, a stunning curved bay with pounding white-crested waves.

The coastline is exposed and you'll likely encounter either blazing sunshine or turbulent seawinds. Bring a hat that cannot blow away (stiff visors seem to stay put), sunscreen, sunglasses and ample water.

HORSEBACK RIDING

If you want a break from hoofin' it yourself, you can hop on a horse at **CJM Country Stables** (742-6096; www.cjmstables.com; tours Mon-Sat). The rides are the slow, nose-to-tail, follow-the-leader variety, so they're safe but might bore experienced riders. Choose from a short two-hour basic ride ($90), a three-hour breakfast ride to a secret beach ($105) or a 3½-hour ride with a swim and picnic ($115), all in the secluded Maha'ulepu Beach area. The stables are conveniently located in Po'ipu, along the main dirt road 1.5 miles east of the Grand Hyatt Kaua'i. The maximum weight is 250lb.

GOLF & TENNIS

You're almost guaranted a good day of golf in Po'ipu – at least regarding the weather (no guarantees for a good *game*). The economical **Kiahuna Golf Club** (☎ 742-9595; www.kiahunagolf .com; 2545 Kiahuna Plantation Dr; green fees before/after 11am $90/50, club rental from $20) is a relatively forgiving 18-hole, par-70 Robert Trent Jones Jr course. Established in 1983, this compact, inland course uses smaller targets and awkward stances to pose challenges. Prices include cart and drop even lower after 2:30pm weekdays.

The South Shore's jewel is the **Po'ipu Bay Golf Course** (☎ 742-8711, 800-858-6300; www.kauai -hyatt.com/golf; 2250 Ainako St; green fees nonguest/guest $185/125, club rental $40). This 18-hole, par-72 course adjacent to the Grand Hyatt covers 210 seaside acres alongside the cliffs above Maha'ulepu Beach. Tee times after noon are discounted and after 3pm they drop to $65. Carts are included in the fee.

For tennis, your best bet is the pleasant **Kiahuna Tennis Club** (☎ 742-9533; kiahuna tennisclb@aol.com; 2290 Po'ipu Rd; court rental per person per hr $10; ☼ 8am-6pm), with tennis courts and a pool (cool waterslide!). The **Po'ipu Kai Tennis Club** (☎ 742-8706; 1775 Po'ipu Rd; per day guest/non-guest $10/20) has two synthetic courts and six hard courts, plus round robins, clinics and private lessons.

BODYWORK & FITNESS CENTER

Anara Spa (☎ 742-1234, 800-554-9288; www.anaraspa .com; Grand Hyatt Kaua'i, 1571 Po'ipu Rd; massage per hr $75-250, treatments $65-75) offers all manner of massages, herbal wraps, body scrubs and polishing in a lush, indulgent setting.

The spa also includes plush weight and fitness rooms, a 25yd pool and classes.

Tours

Sunset cruises, however clichéd, draw 'em in year-round. **Capt Andy's Sailing Adventures** (☎ 335-6833, 800-535-0830; www.napali.com; Lawa'i Rd; adult/child 2-12 $69/50) departs from Kukui'ula Harbor between 4pm and 5pm for a two-hour cruise. Eat and drink all you want but, lest you get too excited, the menu is…buffalo wings (ie chicken), vegetable crudités (ie carrot sticks), spinach dip, pretzels and pineapple.

Also check the myriad cruise options departing from Port Allen Marina Center (p185), farther west along the coast. If you're keen to sail Kaua'i's waters, try a snorkel tour, which lets you sail, snorkel and see whales in winter.

Festivals & Events

New Year's Eve Fireworks (☎ 742-7444; www .poipubeach.org) Free fireworks on the beach at Po'ipu Beach Park on December 31.

Prince Kuhio Celebration of the Arts (☎ 240-6369; admission free except luau) Day-long celebration, in late March, to honor Prince Johah Kuhio Kalaniana'ole, who was born in 1872 on the site of Prince Kuhio Park (p166). Events include commemorative ceremonies, educational sessions on Hawaiian culture and music, and an evening luau.

Kaua'i Products Council Craft Fair (☎ 823-8714) When on Kaua'i, buy Kaua'i-made. At this all-day fair in mid-August, you'll find quality products made primarily on Kaua'i, secondarily within Hawaii. The fair, typically located across from Po'ipu Beach Park, also features music and hula.

beb Festival Rodeo (☎ 639-6695; www.kauairodeo .org, www.alohafestivals.org) Held at CJM Stables in mid-September, this rodeo features roping competitions sure to impress city slickers. This event is part of the statewide Aloha Festivals.

Kaua'i Mokihana Festival Hula Competition (☎ 822-2166; www.mokihana.kauai.net; Grand Hyatt Po'ipu Resort & Spa; admission $5-10) Three days of serious hula performances in late September, both *kahiko* (ancient) and *'auana* (modern).

Hawaiiana Festival (☎ 742-1234; www.alohafesti vals.com; Grand Hyatt Kaua'i Resort & Spa; admission free except luau; ☼ 8am-noon) Part of the Aloha Festival, this mid-October three-day event features Hawaiian crafts, demonstrations, educational displays, hula and a luau.

PGA Grand Slam of Golf (www.pga.com/grandslam) Since 1994, the Po'ipu Bay Golf Course has hosted this exclusive, two-day PGA event among the year's four elite players. Late November.

Sleeping

Before navigating through Po'ipu's condo morass, get your bearings at the **Po'ipu Beach Resort Association** (☎ 742-7444; www.poipubeach .org; PO Box 730, Po'ipu, HI 96756) website. The association can also mail a brochure listing many Po'ipu accommodations. For a general idea of what's available, check **Vacation Rentals By Owner** (www.vrbo.com), a lengthy online list of condos and private homes.

Note that some condo complexes are managed primarily by one agency, which makes arrangements simple. At other complexes, multiple agencies or individual owners handle units. People try to avoid agencies, leery of extra fees, but often they are the best way to widen your options without spending days doing Google searches.

Bear in mind that condo units are individually owned, so even within the same complex, units can vary considerably in quality and interior design.

The following vacation rental companies are good starting points:

Gloria's Vacation Rentals (☎ 742-2850, 800-684-5133; www.gloriasvacationrentals.com; PO Box 1258, Koloa, HI 96756) Excellent selection of homes, cottages and condos in all price ranges; an easy-to-navigate website with thumbnail pics and rates shown at a glance.

Grantham Resorts (☎ 742-2000, 800-325-5701; www.grantham-resorts.com; 3176 Po'ipu Rd, Ste 1, Koloa, HI 96756) Well-established agency for homes and condos; main agency for Waikomo Stream Villas and Nihi Kai Villas.

Kaua'i Vacation Rentals (☎ 245-8841, 800-367-5025; www.kauaivacationrentals.com; 3-3311 Kuhio Hwy, Lihu'e, HI 96766) A longtime all-island agency.

Po'ipu Connection Realty (☎ 800-742-2260; www.poipuconnection.com; PO Box 1022, Koloa, HI 96756) Founded in 1994, this husband-and-wife team gives personalized service; limited selection of properties, but includes gems in small, oceanfront complexes.

Suite Paradise (☎ 742-7400, 800-367-8020; www.suite-paradise.com; 1941 Po'ipu Rd, Po'ipu-Koloa, HI 96756; ☺ reception hours 8am-9pm) Manages about 200 units for Po'ipu Kai Resort, the largest complex in Po'ipu (and a mixed bag). Also handles about 20 units each at other complexes such as Kiahuna Plantation. Book by Internet and get 10% off; but it you want a specific unit, you must call.

MIDRANGE

Prince Kuhio Resort (5061 Lawa'i Rd; studio/1-bedroom units from about $75/135; ☒ ☒) A 90-unit economy complex across Lawa'i (Beach House) Beach, Prince Kuhio is basic and showing its age, but it's a fantastic value. The grounds are pleasantly landscaped with tall trees and a decent-size pool. Adjacent on the east boundary is Prince Kuhio Park, which provides a quiet buffer zone. Units vary markedly in quality and you might book a gem or a dud. To contact the Prince Kuhio, call the agencies listed above. Po'ipu Connection Realty manages 16 units, including a particularly cute studio, Unit 331 (per night $75 to $95, per week $550), with king bed, distant ocean view, stylish tile floor, new linens and funky-cool decorations.

Po'ipu B&B Inn (☎ 742-1146, 800-808-2330; www.poipu-inn.com; 2720 Ho'onani Rd; r incl breakfast $95-155) This 1933 plantation home, country cute with lots of white wicker and carousel horses, would appeal mainly to diehard B&B fans. Slightly worn and homey, each room has a king bed, kitchenette and tiled bath (two have soaking whirlpool units). The B&B keeps the main entrance unlocked all day, so if walk-ins or curiosity seekers irk you, choose a more secure place. The owners also run Kaua'i Inn in Lihu'e and rent condos in Po'ipu.

Waikomo Stream Villas (☎ 742-7220, 800-325-5701; www.grantham-resorts.com; 2721 Po'ipu Rd; low season 1-/2-bedroom units $119/149, high season $149/179; ☒) Among the large condos at Po'ipu, Waikomo Stream Villas gives the most for your money – it feels upscale despite surprisingly midrange rates. The pretty landscaping, complete with peaceful stream, provides an oasis from the asphalt heat (and consolation for the non-beachfront location). The 60 units are modern, clean and spacious (averaging 1100 to 1500 sq ft), with soaring vaulted ceilings, lanai, well-equipped kitchen and washer/dryer. Upgrade to a two-bedroom for a split-level layout with lots of light. Four-night minimum stay.

Koloa Landing Cottages (☎ 742-1470, 800-779-8773; www.koloa-landing.com; 2704B Ho'onani Rd; studio cottages $105, 1-/2-bedroom cottages from $130/160) Charming and cheerful, in crayon colors, these five cottages across from Koloa Landing can't help but make you smile. Hidden amid lush landscaping, they seem rustic but come with all the modern amenities, including wi-fi and full kitchen, with playful touches like vividly painted walls, shoji doors or thatched-roof dining nook. All two-bedroom cottages include two bathrooms. Additional cleaning fees apply. Also available is a large two-bedroom, one-bath house in Koloa ($150).

Po'ipu Plantation Resort (☎ 742-6757, 800-634-0263; www.poipubeach.com; 1792 Pe'e Rd; B&B r incl breakfast $120-190, 1-/2-bedroom units from $115/165; ☒) If you want to avoid a large-resort atmosphere, this nine-unit condo is ideal. It's a quick walk from the beach (hence the reasonable rates) and the units feature spacious rooms, high ceilings, hardwood floors, bedding for four, fully equipped kitchens and lanai. The B&B rooms are rather steep, especially the smaller rooms in the 1930s house; if you can afford it, upgrade to the Ali'i Suite, with ocean view, whirlpool tub and, believe it or not, fireplace (for atmosphere rather than necessity).

Kaua'i Cove Cottages (☎ 651-0279, 800-631-9313; www.kauaicove.com; 2672 Pu'uholo Rd; studio units $125-145) From the outside, the units look boxy and plain. But inside – wow! Bamboo canopy beds, open-beam ceilings, reams of sheer mosquito netting, and lots of windows create a romantic tropical retreat. The patios are small, but the kitchens are fully loaded and the cool hardwood floors refresh beached-out feet. Parking stalls are right outside the door, meaning no lugging suitcases or beach gear. Ask about the good-value, private Palm Room (from $95) and Garden Suite (from $145) located in a subdivision near the Grand Hyatt.

Po'ipu Kai Resort (☎ 742-7400, 800-367-8020; www.suite-paradise.com; 1941 Po'ipu Rd; low-season 1-/2-bedroom units from $147/168, high-season from $178/205; 🛋) The largest condo complex in Po'ipu, its varied buildings range in style, quality and location. The Kahala complex, for example, is across-the-board average: unsurprising tropical theme, worn furnishings and a hike to the beach. But the Manualoha townhouse-style buildings are newer, with master bedroom upstairs and kitchen, living room and second bedroom downstairs – and close to the beach. Po'ipu Sands, while a trek to the beach, is spacious and well-maintained. All units include washer/dryer except the Mill studios (kitchenette only, $112), an acceptable value for one or two. Rates quoted apply for two-to-four nights, but the longer you stay, the more they drop. Book by Internet for a 10% discount (but you cannot request a particular unit).

Po'ipu Palms (☎ 800-742-2260; www.poipuconnection.com; 1697 Pe'e Rd; per day/week from $165-225; 🛋) Location, location, location. Po'ipu Palms might resemble a modest two-story complex, but its primo perch overlooking the ocean catapults it to Class A status. The 12 two-bedroom, two-bathroom oceanfront units are 900 sq ft and all decently appointed, but they definitely vary in chic appeal. Request Unit 304, stylishly decked with matching burnished hardwood furniture, luxury linens and immaculate carpeting. All units included washer/dryer and, of course, the soothing soundtrack of endless

waves. Contact agent is Po'ipu Connection Realty.

TOP END

Alihi Lani (☎ 800-742-2260; www.poipuconnection.com; 2564 Ho'onani Rd; per day $195-325; 🚫 🛋) For a contemporary boutique condo (with only six units) overlooking the ocean, Alihi Lani's two-bedroom, two-bathroom units should more than satisfy. At 1150 sq ft, they're spacious, with huge, full kitchens, washer/dryer and wide doors begging to be flung open toward the lanai and glorious ocean beyond. The basic tropical decor includes white walls and blond wood cabinetry, but units vary in furnishings. The complex sits on the *mauka* (inland) side of the road, so while oceanfront, they're not literally on the beach. But with no buildings opposite, nothing mars the view. The contact agent is Po'ipu Connection Realty.

Sheraton Kaua'i Resort (☎ 742-1661, 800-782-9488; www.sheraton-kauai.com; 2440 Ho'onani Rd; r Internet/rack from $205/325; 🚫 🛋) On the pro side, the Sheraton radiates a welcoming atmosphere, with open-air lobby and the best beachfront location in Po'ipu. On the con side, the hotel is sprawled like an amoeba, even divided into two by Ho'onani Rd, meaning rooms might entail a hike to the beach (and to the parking lot). Until you reach the pricey Deluxe Garden category ($475), you'll be in the so-so wing across the road. Rooms are decent, with the expected business-class amenities, and there's valet parking ($8) – but if you want 'luxury,' dis ain't da one. Still, you can't beat its proximity to Po'ipu Beach.

Po'ipu Kapili (☎ 742-6449, 800-443-7714; www.poipukapili.com; 2221 Kapili Rd; 1-/2-bedroom units from $220/290; 🛋) Epitomizing functional luxury, this condo complex shines. While not beachfront, it's close to Po'ipu Beach and the best rooms do enjoy lovely ocean views. The 60 units are extremely roomy and clearly a step above, with lots of hardwood, big plush beds, two bathrooms, digital cable and Internet access. The complex has tennis courts, barbecue area, and an extensive book and video library. Only two-bedroom units include washer/dryer. Five-day minimum stay.

Kiahuna Plantation (☎ 742-6411, 800-688-7444; www.outrigger.com; 2253 Po'ipu Rd; 1-/2-bedroom units from $225/365; 🛋) Amid luxuriant trees and giant Monstera leaves, Kiahuna Plantation feels like a garden retreat. The airy units are spread between Po'ipu Rd and a swimmable bit of Po'ipu Beach. Each has a fully equipped kitchen, living room and large lanai; the one-bedroom unit sleeps four adults, the two-bedroom units, six adults. Third-floor units are best; try for one overlooking Moir Garden. The only thing missing is an in-unit washer/dryer, however there is a laundromat available on-site. Online discounts available.

Grand Hyatt Kaua'i Resort & Spa (☎ 742-1234, 800-554-9288; www.kauai.hyatt.com; 1571 Po'ipu Rd; r Internet $340-520, rack $455-685; 🔌 🖳) Po'ipu's most exclusive hotel is a class act – and in 2005 it got promoted from Hyatt Regency to Grand Hyatt status. When you enter the airy lobby, adorned with striking antiques and orchids, the view suddenly pans wide toward the Pacific panorama – the architecture manages to complement the natural magnificence outside. Inside, the room decor is typically tropical, but obviously a class above. The Hyatt is also home to the classy Anara Spa (p173), the world-famous Po'ipu Bay Golf Course (p173) and a swimming-pool extravaganza featuring a 150ft waterslide. The only downside is its distance from swimmable waters (eg 1 mile to Brennecke's Beach).

Whalers Cove (☎ 742-7571, 800-225-2683; www .whalers-cove.com; 2640 Pu'uholo Rd; 1-/2-bedroom units from $349/479; 🔌 🖳) Discriminating travelers who want luxury without a smidgen of tourist fuss, welcome. Whalers Cove, the most luxurious condo in Po'ipu, exudes understated confidence. Units are spacious, elegant and utterly immaculate, with markedly upmarket furniture, gleaming marble-tile floors and carpeting that positively pampers your toes. Premier Resorts manages most vacation rentals, and their on-site staff overflow with aloha spirit. The location off the main drag adds to the peace. Daily maid service. Rates drop by 30% when occupancy is low.

Gloria's Spouting Horn B&B (☎ 742-6995; www .gloriasbedandbreakfast.com; 4464 Lawa'i Rd; r incl breakfast $350; 🖳) Featured in many glossy books

---

TIME OUT FOR MOMMY AND DADDY

If you need a break from the kids (or they need one from you!), the major resorts offer professionally supervised 'day camps.'

In Po'ipu the Keiki Aloha Club at the Sheraton Kaua'i Resort also accepts three- to 12-year-olds for full-day (guest/nonguest with lunch $45/70) and half-day (guest with/without lunch $30/25, nonguest with/without lunch $40/35) sessions. Here, the program seems more creative and geared toward teaching kids about the island. Kids might learn hula and ukulele, go bamboo-pole fishing, play games, hear stories, fly kites, build sand castles or just swim in the resort pool. Full-day campers receive a T-shirt and cap. Kiahuna Plantation offers a similar program.

Nearby, Camp Hyatt Kaua'i at the Grand Hyatt Kaua'i Resort & Spa takes toilet-trained kids from three to 12 for full-day (with lunch $70), half-day (with/without lunch $55/45) or evening sessions (per hour $10). During the day, kids learn hula and make Hawaiian crafts like lei and shell bracelets. In the evening, they might also play computer games. Guests only.

The Kaua'i Marriott Resort in Lihu'e invites kids from five to 12 to its Kalapaki Kids Club for full-day (with lunch $45), half-day (morning $25, afternoon $35) or evening sessions (6pm to 10pm Wed) to come and play beach and pool games, go on treasure hunts and obstacle races, do face painting and other island-oriented activities. Full-day campers receive a 'Kalapaki Kids' T-shirt. The maximum is only six kids, and Marriott guests get first priority.

The Princeville Hotel offers a full-day ($65) Keiki Aloha Program for kids from five to 12. Activities include making ti-leaf crafts, lei and sand art. Kids also learn about Hawaii's history, folklore and music. For kids under five years old, babysitting is available (per child per hour $15; discounts for multiple children from same family) with a maximum of three kids per sitter.

Another option is to hire a babysitter: **Babysitters of Kaua'i** (☎ 632-2252; www.babysittersofkauai .com; per hr $15, 3-hr minimum) offers sitters who are insured, licensed, TB tested, background checked and CPR and first-aid certified.

Also an option on the Eastside is the summer day camp at Kaua'i Children's Discovery Museum (p112), an indoor playground that combines fun and education.

and magazines, Gloria's is indeed picturesque: spectacular ocean perch; exquisite furnishings; hearty breakfasts; private seaside pool; complimentary liquor selection; and charming hosts. So, is it worth the cost? If you need tons of space, a full kitchen or hotel service, no. But for the quintessential B&B experience, Gloria's is justly famous. The three guestrooms are similar, each with private oceanfront lanai, canopy bed, Japanese-style *furo* bathtub (deep, for soaking), kitchenette and no shared walls. Three-day minimum stay; rate drops to $325 nightly for weeklong stays; no credit cards.

Eating

As in any resort town, Po'ipu's eating options are limited mainly to touristy fast food and extravagant steak and seafood.

BUDGET

Brennecke's Deli (☎ 742-1582; 2100 Ho'one Rd; sandwiches $4-6; ☼ 8am-9pm) Don't be put off by the convenience-store vibe here because the deli serves thick sandwiches, tailored to your tastes. Choose from seven types of bread, including a savory onion-and-dill roll, and a laundry list of cheese, protein (including taro burgers or honey ham) and veggies. Forgo the exorbitantly priced shave ice ($3.50 for a small cup that should never run over $2). Think twice before dining at the upstairs restaurant, which by all accounts has slipped in quality over the years.

Joe's on the Green (☎ 742-9696; Kiahuna Plantation Dr; breakfast $5-8, lunch $7-10; ☼ 7am-5:30pm Fri-Tue, to 8:30pm Wed & Thu) Join the locals at this open-air eatery at Kiahuna Golf Club for the early-bird special ($5, served until 9am, Monday to Saturday) or arrive at your leisure for mouth-watering Hawaiian sweet-bread French toast or stick-to-your-ribs biscuits and gravy. For a casual clubhouse setting, the food is quite gourmet, from shrimp cakes with chipotle aioli to 'ahi tempura rolls to smoked pork ribs falling off the bone. Live Hawaiian music accompanies dinner on Wednesday and Thursday.

Puka Dog (☎ 742-6044; Po'ipu Shopping Village; hot dogs $6; ☼ 11am-6pm Mon-Sat) Hot dogs go gourmet at this leafy, bamboo shack tucked away at the mall. Choose from Polish sausage or veggie dog and slather with your choice of tropical or traditional relish. Wash it down with freshly squeezed lemonade.

Savage Shrimp (☎ 635-0267; cnr Po'ipu & Ho'onani Rds; meals $10; ☼ 11am-2pm) Driving south on Poi'pu Rd, veer right, and you'll see a white van parked in the middle of nowhere on a grassy roadside clearing. Here, garlic lovers will find heaven in huge plates of garlic shrimp with a Brazilian twist (coconut milk, cilantro and tomatoes). A couple of patio tables offer a bit of shade from the blazing sun.

Kukui'ula Store (☎ 742-1601; Po'ipu Plaza, 2827 Po'ipu Rd; ☼ 8am-6:30pm) If you need groceries, head to this small but well-stocked supermarket.

MIDRANGE & TOP END

Keoki's Paradise (☎ 742-7535; Po'ipu Shopping Village; café menu $5-11, dinner $17-25; ☼ 11am-11pm, bar 11pm-midnight) Either you like the tropical onslaught of tiki torches and faux waterfalls or you don't. Regardless, the food served here is good considering the mall setting. For the fresh catch, you can choose from five preparations (the 'naturally grilled' option lets fresh island fish shine), and other mains feature shellfish and steak. The under-$10 lunches, such as fish tacos or veg-cashew stir-fry, are great value.

Roy's Po'ipu Bar & Grill (☎ 742-5000; www .roysrestaurant.com; Po'ipu Shopping Village; appetizers $7-12, mains $19-25; ☼ 5:30-9:30pm) Yes, Roy's remains a darling of foodies and in-flight magazines as *the* place for Hawaii Regional Cuisine. Yes, the food is delicious, with signature dishes like shrimp and asparagus crepes with chèvre, pesto-steamed whitefish with cilantro-ginger-peanut oil and grilled shrimp with smoked tomato *beurre blanc* (classic French butter sauce). On the con side, be prepared for long waits and loud crowds (this is no place for an intimate conversation). One surprise: it's family-friendly, with high chairs, kids' menu and accommodating staff.

Plantation Gardens Restaurant & Bar (☎ 742-2121; www.pgrestaurant.com; Kiahuna Plantation, 2253 Po'ipu Rd; appetizers $8-15, mains $19-26; ☼ pupu 4pm, dinner 5:30-9pm) The open-air, plantation-house dining room is ideal for folks who want fine food without a scene. The mercifully concise menu features locally grown ingredients and unique preparations, such as the steamer basket of fish and shoyu-glazed vegetables or the jumbo scallops stir-fried with Koloa asparagus and soba noodles. You could cobble together a tasty meal of *pupu*. The veranda overlooking Moir Gardens holds the best seats in the house.

Tidepools (☎ 742-6260; Grand Hyatt Kaua'i Resort & Spa, 1571 Po'ipu Rd; mains $23-30; ☼ 6-10pm) All top oceanfront restaurants start to look alike after a while. But Tidepools manages to stand out with its open-air thatched huts, cascading waterfalls and a tranquil carp pond. Choose from crab cakes with passion-fruit salsa, 'ahi sashimi and steamed mussels to start, followed by the signature macadamia nut-crusted mahi-mahi in a ginger-butter sauce. A special *keiki* (children's) menu is also available. Tidepools is less loud and bustling than other destination restaurants in Po'ipu, thus it's popular for 'romantic' occasions.

Beach House Restaurant (☎ 742-1424; www.the -beach-house.com; 5022 Lawa'i Rd; dinner mains $25-40; ☼ 6-10pm) A South Shore icon, the Beach House surpasses its peers in oceanfront location, sunset views and all-around cachet. Start with their signature 'ahi taster, which include 'ahi poke sushi, 'ahi tostadas and 'ahi hash spring roll. Never boring, their creations range from crab-topped fish with seared scallops and *edamame* (lightly boiled green soybeans) risotto to a Kahlua taro cheesecake. The *keiki* menu, clearly not just an afterthought, serves mains that include an ice-cream sundae – plus virgin tropical drinks, sweet and colorful. A special-occasion favorite, the Beach House is always packed; reservations are recommended.

Naniwa (☎ 742-1661; Sheraton Kaua'i Resort, 2440 Ho'onani Rd; dinner mains $25-45; ☼ 6-9:30pm Tue-Sat) The Sheraton's three fine-dining restaurants are clustered side by side opposite the lobby, as if forcing a choice among them. Go with your mood, but the cozy Naniwa will certainly satisfy any sushi cravings (the nearest Japanese alternative is in Lihu'e). The food is impeccably presented and the raw fish flawlessly fresh. But prices can seem exorbitant, with two-piece nigiri priced at $11 and maki rolls between $12 and $16, but the combinations are creative, eg 'Tuna Luvva' ('ahi roll laced with extra tuna) and the curiously named 'Sixty-Nine Roll' (California crab roll topped with freshwater eel).

Drinking & Entertainment

For nighttime entertainment in Po'ipu, the Grand Hyatt's gloss is hard to top.

BARS

Stevenson's Library (☎ 742-1234, 800-554-9288; Grand Hyatt Kaua'i Resort & Spa; 1571 Po'ipu Rd; ☼ 6-11:45pm) Take an exclusive gentleman's-club library. Plop it on a tropical beach. Might seem incongruous but, hey, why not. Enjoy an impressive selection of ports and cognacs, fine cigars, live jazz, pool and chess. Browse walls lined with literary classics or sidle up to the gleaming 27ft koa-wood bar.

Seaview Terrace (☎ 742-1234, 800-554-9288; Grand Hyatt Kaua'i Resort & Spa; 1571 Po'ipu Rd; ☼ 4-11pm) Catch the sunset from indoors here, as the aptly named bar boasts a perfect view. Entertainment includes a nightly torch-lighting ceremony at sunset and either Hawaiian music or *keiki* hula shows. Times vary throughout the year, depending on day length. All free (albeit with the cost of your cocktails).

LUAU & HULA

Grand Hyatt Kaua'i Resort & Spa (☎ 240-6456; www.hyatt.com/gallery/kauailuau/index.html; 1571 Po'ipu Rd; adult/junior 13-20/child 6-12 $75/65/37.50; ☼ 5:15pm Sun, Tue & Thu) The Drums of Paradise Luau is a well-oiled production befitting the Grand Hyatt setting. For an all-you-can-eat buffet, the food is good, including steamed fish on baby bok choy, teriyaki steak, grilled chicken with fresh pineapple and *kalua* pork (pork baked in an underground pit). The show is more glossy than homey and of course includes the Samoan fire dance. All ages can catch only the show for $45.

Sheraton Kaua'i Resort (☎ 742-1661, 800-782-9488; www.sheraton-kauai.com; 2440 Ho'onani Rd; adult/child $68/34; ☼ 6pm Mon & Fri) Advertised as Kaua'i's only 'oceanfront' luau, the Sheraton's 'Surf to Sunset Luau' is the standard all-you-can-eat buffet and bar, followed by a Polynesian revue.

Polynesian dance show (☎ 742-2831; ☼ 5pm Tue & Thu) This free show is performed at Po'ipu Shopping Village.

Shopping

Po'ipu Shopping Village (Po'ipu Rd) A resort-y mall plopped on Po'ipu Rd; offers a bank, jewelry and clothing shops, art galleries

LOVE, KAUA'IAN STYLE

Tropical islands, with their promise of sultry air and glowing sunsets, have symbolized romance since time immemorial. Thus couples from around the world throw clichés to the wind and keep returning to Kaua'i...to get hitched. Most choose a lavish resort, secluded beach, blooming garden Eden or the ever-popular Fern Grotto. But lots of eccentric settings exist, too. It's not unprecedented to marry while midair in a helicopter, underwater wearing scuba gear or trotting along atop horses – you get the idea.

To help with planning, major resorts offer convenient packages, with ready-to-go wedding gazebos or tents on-site and experienced wedding coordinators on staff. Fully prepared to run wedding extravaganzas are the Princeville Hotel, Grand Hyatt Kaua'i Resort & Spa in Po'ipu, Kaua'i Marriott Resort in Lihu'e, Sheraton Kaua'i Resort in Po'ipu and Hanalei Bay Resort in Princeville. Study carefully any wedding package deals, as you might not want the included amenities, which range from the standard bottle of bubbly to massages and meals.

For intimate weddings, a private vacation-rental villa would provide much more intimacy and perhaps ritzier surroundings. Inquire with rental agencies about special rules and fees for such events. Or you can go island-style kitschy and plan a Blue Hawaii wedding on the grounds of the Coco Palms Resort (p97) or the Fern Grotto (p105).

The wedding 'industry' is well-established across the Hawaiian Islands, and you can find local wedding consultants to do all the groundwork for you. Choosing a consultant is very subjective, but the established ones are listed in the **Kaua'i Visitors Bureau Travel Planner** (www .kauaidiscovery.com). On the North Shore, longtime resident Kirby Guyer of Hale Ho'omaha B&B in Wainihi is a wedding coordinator, and her company, **Different Drummer Weddings** (☎ 828-1341, 800-851-0291; www.differentdrummerweddingskauai.com), specializes in genuine Hawaiian-style ceremonies in picturesque outdoor settings (her handmade lei are exquisite).

If you are a control freak or would prefer a simple, hands-on approach, planning your own wedding is quite feasible, especially using the Internet. One good starting point is the website of the **Kaua'i Wedding Professionals Association** (www.kauaiwedpro.com). Also check out the local newspaper, **The Garden Island** (www.kauaiworld.com), for classified advertisements regarding marriage services. One good source could steer you to the top locations, caterers, musicians and photographers.

Bear in mind the state's marriage requirements:

- Minimum age is 16. If under 18, parental consent is required.
- Valid photo identification is required (driver's license or passport).
- A completed application form is required prior to the marriage license appointment. You can either download the form at www.hawaii.gov/health or request the form by phone (☎ Honolulu 808-586-4544, 🕑 8am-4pm Monday to Friday) or by mail (State of Hawaii Marriage License Office, PO Box 3378, Honolulu, HI 96801).
- You must meet with a marriage license agent, who must witness your signing of the form.
- You must contact the marriage license agent for an appointment prior to arrival. Some agents do not book appointments over two weeks before the event. Both parties must be present. For a list of agents, call ☎ 241-3498; you can leave messages, which are promptly returned, on this pre-recorded information line.
- The current licensing fee is $60 (cash only), payable to the agent at the appointment. The agent might charge an additional $5 fee.
- The marriage license is issued immediately and remains valid for 30 days only in Hawaii (which means you must conquer any cold feet within a month or else pay $60 again for another license).

Obviously the appeal of Hawaii as a marriage setting is the islands' natural beauty. But locals, if they likewise choose to marry outside Hawaii, go to...Las Vegas, an utterly man-made city.

SOUTH SHORE

(the type with multiple locations) and a handful of restaurants.

Additional boutiques are found at the Grand Hyatt Kaua'i Resort & Spa, where **Reyn Spooner** (☎ 742-7279; ☼ 9am-9pm) sells classy aloha wear for the whole family (it's the brand of choice for local businessmen). **Sandal Tree** (☎ 742-2009; ☼ 9am-9pm) is your best bet for name-brand footwear.

Getting Around

For car and motorcycle rentals, see p236. **Outfitters Kaua'i** (☎ 742-9667, 888-742-9887; www .outfitterskauai.com; Po'ipu Plaza, 2827-A Po'ipu Rd; ☼ reservations 8am-9pm) rents cruiser (per day $20), mountain (per day $30) and full-suspension (per day $45) bikes. It also rents kid bikes (per day $20) and baby seats (per day $5). Bike rentals include helmet and lock.

KALAHEO

pop 3913

A quintessential local town where the tallest structure is still the Iglesia Ni Cristo steeple, Kalaheo is home to a down-to-earth, traditionally Portuguese-now mixed community. The wooden houses sport plantation-days tin roofs, local boys roar by in monster trucks and residents rarely tend to venture beyond Lihu'e.

Kalaheo is definitely off the tourist track, but, tucked away, you'll find peaceful accommodations that let you become part of the neighborhood. If you plan to hike at Waimea Canyon and Koke'e State Parks but also want easy access to Po'ipu beaches, Kalaheo's central location is ideal.

The town's post office and handful of restaurants are clustered around the intersection of Kaumuali'i Hwy and Papalina Rd.

Sights

KUKUIOLONO PARK

Perfect for jogging or strolling, this **park** (☼ 6:30am-6:30pm) is a residential oasis of green. You'll see only locals here, walking dogs in the evening or playing a quick round of golf. From the south end of the green, the setting is enhanced by a panoramic vista of the South Shore, including verdant Lawa'i Valley, the resorts in Po'ipu and the endless Pacific beyond.

Kukuiolono means 'light of Lono,' referring to the torches that Hawaiians once placed on this hill to help guide canoes safely to the shore. In 1860 King Kamehameha III leased the land to Duncan McBryde, whose son, Walter, the pineapple baron, eventually purchased the 178-acre estate. He built the public golf course here in 1929, and later he deeded the entire site to an irrevocable trust, for use as a public park upon his death. Walter McBryde is now buried near the 8th hole of the golf course, which features a modest Japanese garden.

NONENDANGERED SPECIES

The first wildlife you'll see on Kaua'i will probably be a chicken. They're everywhere, from mountainous Koke'e State Park to crowded resort parking lots – and they're here to stay.

From the old plantation days, Kaua'i has always had a wild-chicken population living in sugarcane fields. Back then, fields were burned before harvest, to eliminate the sugarcane leaves so only the stalks would remain, thus allowing more efficient reaping. The fires would kill some birds and drive others away, while also destroying nests. Thus the population was held in check. When the sugar industry left, chickens inevitably proliferated.

Further, when Hurricane 'Iwa and Hurricane 'Iniki struck in 1982 and 1992 respectively, they obliterated the cages of Kaua'i's fighting cocks, releasing them into the wild, and adding to the wild population. Finally, unlike the other Hawaiian Islands, Kaua'i has no mongoose population to prey on birds, which benefits endangered avian species – and the chickens.

When other islands see their wild-chicken numbers burgeoning, they typically take measures to stop it. But on Kaua'i the attitude is not to fight them but to live with them. Some consider the chickens a sign of post-hurricane recovery. Today you will find souvenirs, T-shirts and logos featuring chickens.

With the rampant population of chickens literally in its backyard, one would understandably be leery of avian flu hitting Kaua'i. But the state takes seriously its role as a front line against the virus, as the islands are the gateway to Asia.

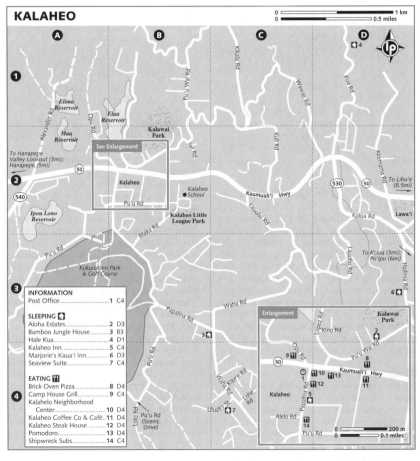

KALAHEO

INFORMATION
Post Office..........................1 C4

SLEEPING
Aloha Estates.....................2 D3
Bamboo Jungle House........3 B3
Hale Kua...........................4 D1
Kalaheo Inn.......................5 C4
Marjorie's Kaua'i Inn..........6 D3
Seaview Suite....................7 C4

EATING
Brick Oven Pizza................8 D4
Camp House Grill...............9 C4
Kalahelo Neighborhood
  Center............................10 D4
Kalaheo Coffee Co & Café..11 D4
Kalaheo Steak House..........12 D4
Pomodoro........................13 D4
Shipwreck Subs.................14 C4

To get here, turn left onto Papalina Rd from Kaumuali'i Hwy (heading west). The sole stoplight at Papalina Rd marks the town center. Drive *makai* (seaward) on Papalina Rd for about 0.75 miles until you reach the park on your right. You may enter under an old stone archway and park in the free lot. But the gates are locked when the golf course closes at 6:30pm. So if you arrive near dusk, park along the road just outside the gate (since you, but not your car, can exit around the gate).

PU'U ROAD SCENIC DRIVE
Pu'u Rd is a scenic side-loop passing small ranches, grand mango trees and fine coastal views. It's a winding country road, only one lane with some blind curves, but nothing tricky if you go slow and honk on the hairpins. And it's so quiet, you might not even encounter another car.

After leaving Kukuiolono Park, turn right onto Pu'u Rd to start the drive. It's just over 3 miles back to Kaumuali'i Hwy this way. About halfway along, you'll look down on Port Allen's oil tanks and the town of Numila, with its old sugar mill.

Down the slope on the west side of the road are coffee trees, part of a total of 4000 acres that have been planted between Koloa and 'Ele'ele. The coffee, on McBryde Sugar Company property, is one of the company's grander schemes for diversifying crops on land formerly planted solely with sugarcane.

HANAPEPE VALLEY LOOKOUT

The scenic lookout that pops up shortly after the 14-mile marker offers a view deep into Hanapepe Valley. The red-clay walls of the cliffs are topped by a layer of green cane, like frosting on a cake. This sight is but a teaser of the dramatic vistas awaiting at Waimea Canyon.

While old king sugar might still dominate the scene surrounding Hanapepe Valley, glance toward the opposite side of the road and you'll see the island's newest major commercial crop: coffee.

Activities

You will find some free **tennis courts** in Kalawai Park.

Kukuiolono Golf Course (☎ 332-9151; Kukuiolono Park; green fees adult/child $8/3, pull carts $6; ☺ 6:30am-6:30pm) is an unassuming, nine-hole, par-36 golf course with grand hilltop views and earthy appeal (bags of chicken feed for the fowl on the fairway and super-friendly locals are just the start). Grab a bucket of balls for $2 and hit the driving range, with its gorgeous sea and coffee plantation views. No tee times: first come, first served. If hunger strikes, go for the cheap vittles at the snack bar (from 8am to 3:30pm).

Sleeping

Kalaheo is more of a bedroom community than a tourist spot, so you'll find just one commercial inn plus rooms and cottages among private homes. Note that a bunch of oft-cited 'classic' cottages have sorely declined in quality.

Aloha Estates (☎ 332-7812; www.kalaheo-plantation.com; 4579 Pu'u Wai Rd; r $45-75) This rambling 1926 plantation house might be rough around the edges, but for budget travelers, it fulfills the basics: cheap, safe and decently clean. With so many rooms, noise might be a problem. If you can afford it, choose an upstairs room, as they're brighter, and overlook the garden; most have private bathrooms and kitchenettes. The basement rooms are rather cavernous. Weekly and monthly discounts up the value for longer stays.

Seaview Suite (☎ 332-9744; www.seakauai.com; 3913 Uluali'i Street; r/ste $65/75) Seaview Suite is a sweet deal indeed. Located on a quiet street just south of the Kukuiolono Golf Course, the ground-floor main suite is simple rather than fancy, but spacious, tidy and comfort-able. It includes full kitchen, separate living and dining areas and bedding for four. Single travelers can bunk in the Ti Room, a cozy studio with kitchenette (including full-size refrigerator). Both include TV and other electronics, plus pretty Japanese shoji doors. The friendly, easygoing hosts live upstairs and rent the Boathouse, another top-value studio, in Kekaha.

Kalaheo Inn (☎ 332-6023, 888-332-6023; www.kalaheoinn.com; 4444 Papalina Rd; studio/1-/2-bedrooms $80/90/120) Like the surrounding town, Kalaheo Inn is unpretentious, dependable and quietly pleasant. The 14 spic-and-span units come in a range of sizes. Longtime manager Herb Brun, born and raised in Kalaheo, is personable and brimming with local sincerity. Most rooms have fully equipped kitchens (otherwise they have kitchenettes) and all have TV, VCR and comfortably firm beds. The biggest three-bedroom units ($160) are extremely homey and are economical for groups. On-site laundromat available; discounts for weeklong stays.

Bamboo Jungle House (☎ 332-5515, 888-332-5115; www.bamboojunglehouse.com; 3829 Waha Rd; r/ste incl breakfast from $120/140; ☒) Behind an inscrutable stone wall sits a secret oasis: a charming plantation-style home with a long lap pool, flanked by a lava-rock waterfall and wild foliage. The three units overlooking the tropical scene are immaculate, with fresh white walls and stylish touches, from fluffy canopy beds to sparkling French doors. All rooms have wi-fi and share an airy kitchen, while the suite comes with its own kitchenette. A truly distinctive property, it's geared toward couples and no kids are allowed.

Eating

Kalaheo Coffee Co & Café (☎ 332-5858; www.kalaheo.com; 2-2560 Kaumuali'i Hwy; breakfast $4-7, lunch $5-8; ☺ 6am-2:30pm) Feel free to linger over coffee at this spacious, open-air patio café, a favorite neighborhood hangout famous for a melt-in-your-mouth pastry called a 'cinnamon knuckle' ($2.75). Breakfast is more imaginative than most: try the tasty bagel Benny, with piles of ham, turkey or grilled vegetables, a poached egg and hollandaise sauce or salsa. Lunches range from a grilled tofu-and-eggplant wrap to a heaping tuna salad on a cornucopia of veggies. Finally, healthy cuisine with zero pretentiousness.

Shipwreck Subs (☎ 651-9132, 635-6562; 4414 Papalina Rd; 6-/13-inch sub $4.50/9.50; ☼ 11am-6pm) Sandwiches that rival those at NYC's finest delis are the specialties here. Choose from any cold cut you can imagine, plus five types of cheese and loads of veggies. Great to pick up en route to Koke'e State Park trailheads. Big Island Tropical Dreams ice cream (scoop $3) is also here.

Brick Oven Pizza (☎ 332-8561; Kaumuali'i Hwy; 10-/12-/15-inch pizza from $10/14/20; ☼ 11am-10pm Tue-Sun) Your patience will be tested here, as you circle the parking lot and wait for a table. But that's the price for tasting the creations of this classic pizzeria, established in 1977. Real brick-oven pies with either white or whole-wheat crust come with surprises, such as a truly vegetarian version piled with premium veggies and stock-free sauce (about $15 to $30). Locals tend to regard Brick Oven as too expensive 'just for pizza' and the majority of diners are tourists.

Camp House Grill (☎ 332-9755; Kaumuali'i Hwy; breakfast $5-6, dinner $10-12; ☼ 6:30am-9:30pm) Established in 1987, this old-time diner joint serves lots of burgers ($4.25 to $6.25) and pies (per slice $3.50, whole $10 to $15), in-cluding pineapple or coconut cream. Mains are the standards: catch of the day, *huli huli* (rotisserie) chicken and barbecued ribs. But don't expect fancy or spotless, 'cause this place is neither.

Pomodoro (☎ 332-5945; Rainbow Plaza, Kaumuali'i Hwy; dinner mains $10-20; ☼ 6-9pm) No restaurant in Kalaheo has a view – so the food must stand on its own. The casual, neighborly Pomodoro, run by a longtime Kaua'i couple, has no problem. The hearty, traditional Italian food is a surprise, as few Italian restaurants exist on Kaua'i. The minestrone soup is hearty (with veggies still nice and crisp) and the pastas are homemade. Service is prompt and friendly, and the owners often remember customers from year to year.

Kalaheo Steak House (☎ 332-9780; 4444 Papalina Rd; dinner $20-33; ☼ 6-10pm) An island fixture, Kalaheo Steak House is masculinely cozy and dimly lit, with faux-leather-upholstered booths, empty adjoining bar and a working-class clubby feel. Dig into 'real food,' like steak, from a 12oz sirloin to an insanely huge 24oz prime rib. All dinners come with a green salad and bread.

Westside

Can a 555-sq-mile island have a frontier? If the island is Kaua'i, certainly. And that last, vast territory is the Westside. The farther west you drive, the more palpably the landscape changes. Dusty vermillion hills and green fields of cane and coffee form an earthy palette under sweeping azure skies. There is a sense of rugged freedom here that calls to mind Tom Petty's iconic lyrics: 'Into the great wide open, Under them skies of blue.'

Toward the sea, the sandy shoreline and straight southern horizon seem to stretch forever. While striking, the landscape is rough around the edges – and might seem stark compared with the sublime, fertile beauty of the North Shore. The Westside is a place for down-to-earth explorers.

The star attraction in the west is Waimea Canyon, a massive chasm revealing layers of ancient lava flows. Steep hikes in and around the canyon illustrate Kaua'i's unique geology and ecology – and challenge even the most surefooted trekkers.

Quiet villages are throwbacks to the Old West and old plantation era – and they might seem deserted to a mainlander's eye. 'God's Country,' they call the Westside, for its multitude of Christian churches, simple wooden structures that match the surroundings.

Nowadays, as little on Kaua'i remains a secret, locals and tourists alike appreciate the Westside – especially the expansive wilderness of Koke'e State Park, the island's most untouched, still-local region.

HIGHLIGHTS

- Flying high in an open-door **chopper** (p190)
- Traversing the otherworldly **Alaka'i Swamp** (p211)
- Visiting **Hanapepe** (p188), a mix of Old West and artists colony
- Strolling an endless stretch of **Kekaha** (p197) sand at sunset
- Exploring the miraculous **Waimea Canyon** (p199)
- **Sailing** (opposite) to the Na Pali Coast

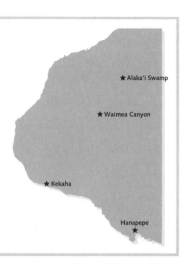

★ Alaka'i Swamp

★ Waimea Canyon

★ Kekaha

Hanapepe
★

'ELE'ELE

pop 2040

'Ele'ele is just a tiny residential cluster, but it draws folks from surrounding towns for its shopping center, at the 16-mile marker. Don't expect more than a supermarket, bank, **post office** (8am-4pm Mon-Fri, 9-11am Sat), laundromat and a couple of restaurants.

Locals come to **Toi's Thai Kitchen** (335-3111; 'Ele'ele Shopping Center, 4469 Waialo Rd; mains $12-18; take-out 11am-2pm Tue-Sat, restaurant 5:30-9pm Tue-Sat) for decent Thai cuisine in a family-style setting. You can choose the preparation for mains – from an invigorating ginger stir-fry to fragrant basil and bamboo – and your choice of tofu, meat, poultry, fish or seafood, or veg only.

Grinds Café (335-6027; www.grindscafe.net; 'Ele'ele Shopping Center, 4469 Waialo Rd; breakfast $4-7, lunch $4.50-9; 5:30am-6pm) has a mixed bag for an American menu, with decent if conventional sandwiches and pastries, but lackadaisical (or simply laidback?) service.

An alternate route between Kalaheo and 'Ele'ele is Halewili Rd (Hwy 540), which intersects Kaumuali'i Hwy just after Kalaheo and connects back again at 'Ele'ele. This route passes acres of neatly planted coffee trees then swings by **Numila**, a former cane town with tin-roof wooden houses surrounding a defunct sugar mill. At the southwest edge of Numila is the **Kaua'i Coffee Company** (335-0813, 800-545-8605; www .kauaicoffee.com; Halewili Rd; 9am-5pm), the state's largest coffee operation. The little **museum** (admission free) with simple displays is just a mechanism to get you to buy the product, which you can sample for free at the café on the premises.

PORT ALLEN

In the late 1800s Port Allen was a major port on Kaua'i, known as 'Ele'ele Landing. In 1909 it was named in honor of Samuel Cresson Allen, a well-known Honolulu businessman who funded early harbor improvements. Today the port, located immediately south of 'Ele'ele on Hanapepe Bay, is one of Kaua'i's busiest recreational boat harbors.

Don't expect a picturesque dock: Port Allen is the unloading point for fuel serving the adjacent electric plant, and it provides a dock for vessels working with the Pacific Missile Range Facility (p198).

Information

The Port Allen Marina Center just up from the harbor has most of the tour offices.

West Side Copy Center (335-9990; Port Allen Marina Center, 4353 Waialo Rd; per hr $6; 8am-6pm Mon-Fri, 8am-noon Sat) has Internet access.

Sights

Dig your toes into drifts of colorful bits of glass at **Glass Beach**, just east of Port Allen. The smooth glass 'pebbles' wash in from a long-abandoned dumpsite nearby, worn and weathered after decades of wave action. Sometimes the glass is plentiful, other times most is washed out to sea. There is terrific exploring east along the rocky coast pocked with tide pools and strewn with odd flotsam. On the path above the beach, do not miss the Japanese cemetery with a view.

To get to the little cove, take Aka'ula St, the last left before entering the Port Allen commercial harbor, go past the fuel storage tanks and then curve to the right down a rutted dirt road that leads 100yd to the beach.

Activities

DIVING

Mana Divers (335-0881; www.manadivers.com; Bay 3, Port Allen Boat Harbor, 4310 Waialo Rd) offers boat dives, night dives and certification courses, but Fathom Five Divers (p163) in Koloa is superior.

You can also jump aboard a snorkeling cruise and pay as little as $25 extra to dive. The problem is snorkeling and diving don't mix, and divers won't see the best sites. But if your group includes both divers and nondivers, it's a convenient way to spend the day together – and you can't beat the price.

SNORKELING & WHALE WATCHING

Port Allen is the launching point for the majority of Kaua'i's catamaran and raft tours, but also consider the tours departing from Hanalei Bay (p145), during summer months only, and Kikialoha Small Boat Harbor (p194) in Kekaha, both of which start closer to the North Shore.

Most snorkeling tours head to the Na Pali Coast, and the main decision is whether to go by catamaran or by raft. Remember, not all tours are offered year-round, so inquire

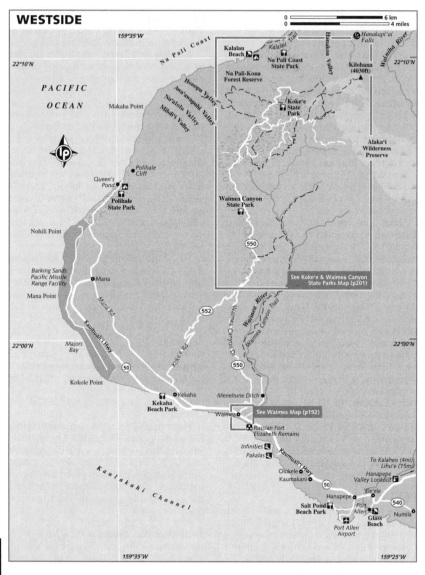

first. If you book online, you often pay less and receive token gifts such as a free T-shirt. Discounters often advertise snorkel cruises and they can save you money; but if you want a particular outfitter, book directly.

Many of the catamarans that run snorkeling cruises also offer spectator sailing tours, typically along the Po'ipu coast at sunset.

Catamarans

The best two are Holoholo Charters and Catamaran Kahanu.

A major player in the cruise business, **Holoholo Charters** (☎ 335-0815, 800-848-6130; www

.holoholocharters.com; Port Allen Marina Center, Waialo Rd; ☯ 6am-8pm) sails two catamarans: On the 65ft power 'cat,' you can take a seven-hour Ni'ihau and Na Pali snorkel tour (adult/child aged six to 12 $169/119) or a 3½-hour sunset-watching cruise (adult/child $89/70). Or you can choose the 48ft sailing catamaran for a five-hour morning snorkel tour (adult/child aged six to 12 $119/85) or a two-hour dinner cruise ($75) for adults only (for 'romance,' they say). The menu includes teriyaki chicken or sautéed beef slices and the usual giveaway of mai tais and champagne. The big boat is cushy, with lots of shade, easy water access, shower hose, decent snorkel gear and professional staff.

The longtime Hawaiian-owned **Catamaran Kahanu** (☎ 645-6176, 888-213-7711; www.catamaran kahanu.com; Port Allen Marina Center, Waialo Rd) offers either five-hour snorkeling tours (adult/child aged four to 11 $115/75) or four-hour sightseeing tours (adult/child aged four to 11 $85/65) with no snorkeling or lunch. This outfit feels local and less commercial, and on tour you can watch a demonstration on weaving ti leaves and *hau* (pandanas) and coconut fibers into fishing lines, nets, etc. Whale-watching tours also offered.

The power catamaran tours run by **Capt Andy's Sailing Adventures** (☎ 335-6833, 800-535-0830; www.napali.com; Port Allen Marina Center, Waialo Rd) go to Na Pali for a five-hour snorkeling tour (adult/child aged two to 12 $139/99) including both breakfast and lunch, or an afternoon dinner cruise (adult/child aged two to 12 $105/80). Groups tend to be large. A two-hour Po'ipu sunset cruise (adult/child aged two to 12 $69/50) for sightseeing and imbibing is also offered.

Blue Dolphin Charters (☎ 335-5553, 877-511-1311; www.kauaiboats.com; Port Allen Marina Center, Waialo Rd) offers snorkeling and diving tours, including a seven-hour Ni'ihau jaunt (Internet/regular $175/196) and the standard five-hour Na Pali deal (Internet/regular $126/147). Scuba divers pay $35 more. Two sunset cruises bring yet more options to get wasted (tours Internet/regular from $73/94). Prices include tax.

Kaua'i Sea Tours (☎ 826-7254, 800-733-7997; www.kauaiseatours.com; Aka'ula St, Port Allen) offers Na

---

THAR SHE BLOWS!

You might assume the Hawaiian Islands lack seasons, but it's only the *signs* that are different. Winter is announced not by snow and ice, but by the arrival of 2000 to 5000 whales. The shallow, warm waters surrounding the major Hawaiian Islands constitute a key habitat for the endangered humpback whale, and nearly two-thirds of the entire North Pacific population migrates 3000 miles from Alaska, typically arriving by November and December.

Here they breed, calve and nurse their young. Humpback whales are not the largest whale species, but they are the most watched – due to their distinctive physical features, dramatic movements and proximity to shore.

Humpback whales average 45ft in body length and weigh approximately 40 to 45 tons. Calves are typically 14ft at birth and weigh as much as 2 tons. Of all whale species, humpbacks have the longest pectoral flipper, about one third of body length. The undersides of their tail flukes are as distinctive as our fingerprints.

In breeding waters, males compete for access to receptive females, slamming each other with their powerful tail flukes and emitting mysterious (to humans) sounds. The females and the young are showy, too, slapping the surface of the water with their pectoral fins and tails and launching themselves into the air (jumping behavior called 'breaching').

The 11½-month gestation period means that females impregnated in a given winter will return to the same waters to give birth the next winter. Then, after feeding all summer in the Gulf of Alaska, a newly weaned calf may follow its mother back to the breeding grounds the following winter. Humpbacks reach young adulthood at four to six years.

The **Hawaiian Islands Humpback Whale National Marine Sanctuary** (☎ 246-2860; www.hawaii humpbackwhale.noaa.gov; 4370 Kukui Grove Street, Suite 206, Lihu'e, HI 96766) offers excellent opportunities to learn more about whales. The sanctuary tries to protect the Hawaiian habitat from too much encroachment by commercial snorkeling, diving and whale-watching cruises. Check the website for upcoming events.

WISE WORDS

A T-shirt is a T-shirt is a T-shirt is a T-shirt? Minds might differ, but on Kaua'i it's caveat emptor regarding the iconic 'Kimo's Hawaiian Rules' t-shirts and paraphernalia. The authentic producer of those words is **Nite Owl T-Shirts** (☎ 335-6110, 888-430-9907; www.niteowlt-shirts.com; Waiaolo Rd; ⏰ 9am-5pm Fri-Tue, 7am-4pm Wed & Thu), a screenprinting company established in 1985. Don't be fooled by copycats who have swiped their famous words. You can find reasonably priced shirts in assorted styles, including femme tanks and extra-extra-extra-large sizes, at the Port Allen headquarters.

Kimo's Hawaiian Rules are as follows:

▥ Never judge a day by the weather.

▥ The best things in life aren't things.

▥ Tell the truth – there's less to remember.

▥ Speak softly and wear a loud shirt.

▥ Goals are deceptive – the unaimed arrow never misses.

▥ He who dies with the most toys – still dies.

▥ Age is relative – when you're over the hill you pick up speed.

▥ There are two ways to be rich – make more or desire less.

▥ Beauty is internal – looks mean nothing.

▥ No rain – no rainbows.

Pali tours by catamaran (adult/child from $133/101) or by rigid hull raft (adult/child from $126/94). Cheaper whale-watching tours also offered, but the snorkeling tours let you do both. Scuba-diving option for $25 more. Prices include tax.

Rafts

For zippier excitement, tour Na Pali in Zodiac rafts instead. Capt Andy's sister outfit, **Captain Zodiac Raft Adventures** (☎ 335-6833, 800-535-0830; www.napali.com; Port Allen Marina Center, Waialo Rd), offers a six-hour tour (adult/child aged five to 12 $159/109) that allows you to snorkel, see amazing sea caves and land on a remote beach. But you can enjoy almost all the same sights with a five-hour tour (adult/child aged five to 12 $129/89). Remember, no shade and no rest rooms.

FISHING

Deep-sea fishing charters also leave from Port Allen. Try **Sport Fishing Kaua'i** (☎ 742-7013; 4hr shared charter per person $95).

Eating

Kaua'i Coffee Café (☎ 335-5333; Port Allen Marina Center, 4353 Waialo Rd; sandwiches $4-6; ⏰ 6:30am-2pm) Has coffee, smoothies, wraps and *panini* sandwiches.

Kauai Chocolate Company (☎ 335-0448; www.kauaichocolate.com; 4341 Waialo Road; ⏰ 11am-5pm Mon-Sat, noon-5pm Sun) Chocoholics, get your fix here. Signature treats include the 'Krabs' (with caramel, pretzels and macs), luscious fudge, 'Piko Paint' (edible body goo) and lots of sugar-free options. For massive decadence, buy 'Da Brick' ($18.50), a 16oz hunk of macadamia toffee, caramel, chocolate and more.

HANAPEPE

pop 2153

Stroll through Hanapepe and you'll swear you're in the Wild West. Behind the simple wooden facades must lurk a western saloon and barbershop, and the 2nd-floor balconies overlook dusty roads where surely horses will soon trot by. No, sorry, fooled you.

Welcome to Hanapepe, a former commercial center that is now undergoing revitalization and considered a 'destination' town. The town is recognized as Kaua'i's artists colony, with almost a dozen galleries and a lively 'art night' each Friday. Hollywood, too, adores quaint Hanapepe, which provided the backdrop for the TV miniseries *The Thorn Birds* (filmed here to portray the long-gone Australian outback), the Filipino Olongapo City in the movie *Flight of the Intruder* and the hometown of Disney's lively animated feature *Lilo & Stitch*.

Unfortunately Hurricane 'Iniki obliterated about half of Hanapepe's irreplaceable buildings in 1992, but the town's traditional essence remains. Even now, it is one of the best-preserved historic towns in the state, with over 43 sites that meet State or National Historic Register criteria.

History

In the early 1800s, Hanapepe (meaning 'crushed bay'), which refers to a town, a valley and a river, was a thriving taro-farming Native Hawaiian community with a population larger than Waimea's. But by the 1840s, Hanapepe's Hawaiians suffered from a host of introduced diseases and only a small village remained by 1870. Chinese rice growers began planting here in the 1860s, while Japanese immigrants arrived in the early 1900s. Many were entrepreneurial immigrants trying to escape the yoke of plantation life. Some were retired laborers, while others chose to start small businesses or to grow taro or rice. Labor-union organizers, barred from living at plantation camps, also ended up living here.

From 1910 to 1930, Hanapepe was a bustling commercial center, a popular stop for military R&R and active shipping and trading at Port Allen. There were two movie theaters, two roller-skating rinks and many restaurants and shops. But in the late 1930s, Lihu'e became the island's business and political seat, with Nawiliwili Harbor as the main port and, later, Lihu'e Airport as the island's main airfield instead of Burns Field. Further exacerbating Hanapepe's decline was the 1938 rerouting of Kaua'i's belt road to bypass the town center, which shifted new development along the Kaumuali'i Hwy.

Orientation

The heart of Hanapepe is off Kaumuali'i Hwy so veer *mauka* (inland) onto Hanapepe Rd, which is impossible to miss with the 'Kaua'i's Biggest Little Town' sign splashed along the highway. Free parking is available in a small lot just around the first bend.

Information

American Savings Bank (☎ 335-3118; 4548 Kona Rd)
Bank of Hawaii (☎ 335-5021; 3764 Hanapepe Rd) On the western end of Hanapepe Rd.
Post office (☎ 335-5433, 800-275-8777; 3817 Kona Rd; 🕑 8:30am-12:30pm & 1-4pm Mon-Fri, 9:30-11:30am Sat)
Talk Story Bookstore & Café (☎ 335-6469; www .talkstorybookstore.com; 3567 Hanapepe Rd; per 15min $2.50) Airy setting, friendly proprietors and cheap high-speed Internet access on two computers.

Sights & Activities

First, get a 'Walking Tour Map' for $2 (but free with a coupon from the freebie guide *This Week Kaua'i*) at stores including **Banana Patch** (☎ 335-5944; 800-914-5944; www .bananapatchstudio.com; 3865 Hanapepe Rd; 🕑 10am-4:30pm). With lively drawings and text, it describes the historic buildings still standing in town. Along the way, be sure to take a stroll (or skip for full effect) over the **Swinging Bridge**, which crosses the Hanapepe River; the path begins opposite the Koa Wood Gallery. Its funky old predecessor fell victim to 'Iniki, but in a community-wide effort this new bridge was erected in 1996.

SALT POND BEACH PARK

Salt Pond Beach Park is one of Kaua'i's best family beaches – and even better because it remains untouristy. Beyond the long stretch of sand, the water in the cove reaches up to 10ft deep and works well for swimming laps (four times across equals 0.5 miles). Both ends of the cove are shallow and good for kids. You might see folks windsurfing here, too. Amenities include covered picnic tables, barbecue grills, showers and camp-sites, and there's a lifeguard.

The park is named for its famous salt ponds toward the east, where Hawaiians have traditionally made rock salt from sea-water. The salt is made by letting seawater into shallow basins, about 2 sq yd and 6in deep, letting it evaporate for several months and scraping off the dried crystals. Often, this *alae* salt has a reddish tint from adding a bit of the iron-rich earth you see everywhere. Indigenous Hawaiians still make salt here, the only known remaining such site in the state.

To get here, turn left just past the 17-mile marker, onto Lele Rd, then right onto Lokokai Rd; the beach is about a mile from the highway.

WESTSIDE

HANAPEPE GALLERY CRAWL

A sleepy village by day, Hanapepe boasts one of the best weekly nighttime events on the island: **Hanapepe Art Night** (🕑 6-9pm Fri). Along the main street, Hanapepe Rd, shops and galleries stay open late, accompanied by live music and other performances. The majority of the 15 or so galleries are owner-run, making Hanapepe a true artists colony. Notables include the following:

Arius Hopman Gallery (☎ 335-0227; www.hopmanart.com; 3840-C Hanapepe Rd; 🕑 10:30am-3:30pm Mon-Thu, to 9pm Fri) A Kaua'i resident since the early 1990s, the well-traveled Hopman is an engineer-turned-watercolorist; his representational renderings of Kaua'i are easy on the eye.

Art of Marbling (☎ 482-1472; 3890 Hanapepe Rd; 🕑 10am-5pm Sat-Thu, to 9pm Fri) Becky J Wold creates exquisite marbled silks, which make unique wall art or clothing. The smallest 40in square is an affordable $40 piece of art. Within the space is another gallery featuring Robert Bader's wood sculpture, including translucent Norfolk pine bowls. Prices range from $100 to several grand.

Banana Patch (☎ 335-5944; 800-914-5944; www.bananapatchstudio.com; 3865 Hanapepe Rd; square tiles 4/6in $17/28; 🕑 10am-4:30pm Sat-Thu, to 9pm Fri) Everywhere on Kaua'i you'll see colorfully painted tiles hanging at front doors, with messages like 'Mahalo for removing your shoes.' These ubiquitous tiles come from Joanna Carolan's cheerful studio, where you can see her staff meticulously adorning plain white tiles. Other handpainted ceramics include platters and bowls. It's pop rather than fine art – perfect for the casual home. The shop also carries handmade jewelry, including certified Ni'ihau shell necklaces (see p214).

Kauai Fine Arts (☎ 335-3778; www.brunias.com; 3751 Hanapepe Rd; 🕑 9:30am-4:30pm Mon-Thu & Sat, to 9pm Fri) A wide-ranging collection of antique maps and prints, plus Ni'ihau shell jewelry and other exquisite handiwork.

Koa Wood Gallery (☎ 335-5483; 3848 Hanapepe Rd; 🕑 11am-6pm Mon-Thu & Sat, to 9pm Fri) Indulge in classic Hawaiian woodworking, which manifests in gorgeous koa (Hawaiian timber) rocking chairs (around $2000 each) or more affordable items like cribbage boards and bowls.

Talk Story Bookstore & Café (☎ 335-6469; www.talkstorybookstore.com; 3567 Hanapepe Rd; 🕑 11am-5:30pm Wed, Thu & Sat, to 11pm Fri, noon-5pm Sun) Here you can combine your passion for art, books and food.

Timespace Contemporary Art (☎ 335-0094; www.timespaceintl.com; 4545 Kona Rd; 🕑 noon-5pm Mon-Sat) For uber-modern photography and paintings, this gallery is a must. Don't miss the unique works by gallery owner Antonio Arellanes, whose mixed-media pieces juxtapose motifs from philosophy to physics.

FLYING

For a real adrenaline high, take an ultralight lesson with **Birds in Paradise** (☎ 822-5309; www.birdsinparadise.com; Burns Field, Puolo Rd; 30-min/1hr lesson $96/165). You can also do a round-the-island lesson on one of these powered hang gliders for $300. Take the road for Salt Pond Beach Park to reach the airport.

Tours

For anyone with fantasies of riding *MASH* copters with Hawkeye, **Inter-Island Helicopter** (☎ 335-5009, 800-656-5009; http://hawaiian.net/~interisland/; 1-3410 Kaumuali'i Hwy; flights regular/waterfall $185/250) is the only way to go. Their copters fly without doors, meaning you feel the wind on your face (and perhaps a spray of mist) and enjoy wide-open views. An outstanding, if costly, tour lands at an otherwise inaccessible waterfall, where passengers can splash in a pool and eat a deli lunch. Tours depart from Burns Field on Lokokai Rd, en route to

Salt Pond Beach Park. The company office is on Kaumuali'i Hwy, next to Lappert's.

For a truly off-the-beaten-track trip, fly to Ni'ihau with Ni'ihau Helicopters (p215).

Eating

Hanapepe is more a daytripper spot than a home base, but Salt Pond Beach Park offers convenient camping (see p218 for permit information). Eating options are few but unique and worth a special stop. Sympathy to fans of Green Garden restaurant, which closed in 2005 after 57 years (and three generations) of serving local-style meals and their famous *liliko'i* (passion fruit) chiffon pie. You can still see the retro building and can't-miss-it green awning from the highway.

Kaua'i Pupu Factory (☎ 335-0084; 1-3566 Kaumuali'i Hwy; 🕑 9am-5:30pm Mon-Fri, to 3pm Sat) Locals never eat boring ol' sandwiches for a picnic, they pack the good stuff: succulent raw-fish *pupu* (appetizers), deep-fried *ika* (squid) and purple-sweet-potato tempura. At this take-out counter, you can load up on island favorites sold prepackaged, from dried, smoked fish (under $5) to *laulau* (bundles of meat and fish and edible taro leaves wrapped in a ti leaf, $5 for two) and *'ahi poke* (cubed, raw yellowfin tuna with spices, per lb $9). It's also ideal for a first-time taste of Hawaiian food: *laulau* or *kalua*-pork (traditional method of cooking in an underground pit) lunch plate with two scoops of rice, *lomilomi* salmon (salmon and fresh tomatoes) and *poke* (cubed, marinated raw fish, $6).

Talk Story Bookstore & Café (☎ 335-6469; www.talkstorybookstore.com; 3567 Hanapepe Rd; mains $6.50-8.50; ⏰ 11am-5:30pm Wed, Thu & Sat, to 11pm Fri, noon-5pm Sun) Hang out at this welcoming gathering place run by a youthful couple, mainland transplants who fit like gloves into sleepy Hanapepe. The bookstore resembles a bright sunroom library (complete with cats), and the outdoor café features a changing menu, with everything from heaping tuna sandwiches to decadent *liliko'i* cheesecake – all homemade, of course. Adjoining the bookstore is an art gallery featuring local artists. There are occasional events and music; call for the schedule.

Omoide Bakery & Wong's Chinese Restaurant (☎ 335-5066, 335-5291; 1-3543 Kaumuali'i Hwy; mains $7.50-9.75; ⏰ 9:30am-9pm Tue-Sat) With Green Garden gone, Omoide has become the Westside's purveyor of *liliko'i* chiffon pie (per slice/whole $2/9.25). Established in 1956, it's another well-worn, slightly sketchy eatery that oddly combines a pie bakery and Chinese restaurant. The Hong Kong and Cantonese menu features the usual laundry list of chicken, beef, pork and seafood dishes, but it's especially known for its Hong Kong roast duck (half/whole $10.25/17.50) and convenient take-out. Located between the 16- and 17-mile markers on the *makai* (seaward) side of the highway.

Hanapepe Café (☎ 335-5011; 3830 Hanapepe Rd; lunch $6-10, dinner $18-24; ⏰ 11am-3pm Mon-Thu, 11am-2pm & 6pm-9pm Fri) Behind an unassuming facade, you'll find one of the island's finest gourmet vegetarian restaurants. The food is simple but inspired, from the smoked-mozzarella frittata to Swiss-chard-filled ravioli in walnut sauce. The Friday dinner

menu changes every two weeks and includes seafood – and with nightfall comes white tablecloths and live music by notable slack-key artist Cindy Combs. The classic apple pie à la mode is worth the splurge.

Assuage a snack attack with shave ice and crack seed at **Hawaiian Hut Delights** (☎ 335-3781; Hanapepe Rd; shave ice from $2; ⏰ noon-5pm Mon-Fri) or irresistible taro chips from **Taro Ko Chips Factory** (☎ 335-5586; 3940 Hanapepe Rd; per small bag $2.50; ⏰ 8am-5pm), a dilapidated kitchen 'factory' where elderly Mrs Nagamine still fries the sliced taro (and potato and purple sweet potato) in massive black woks at dawn. In Hanapepe you'll find the Kaua'i headquarters and factory of **Lappert's** (☎ 335-6121; www.lapperts.com; 1-3555 Kaumuali'i Hwy; ⏰ 10am-6pm), which sells Hawaii's most famous premium ice cream.

OLOKELE & KAUMAKANI

Olokele exists only for the Olokele Sugar Company, the last remaining sugar producer on Kaua'i, and Kaumakani exists only as the headquarters of **Gay & Robinson** (☎ 335-2824; www.gandrtours-kauai.com; 2 Kaumakani Av), owners of this plantation and the island of Ni'ihau (see p214).

Sugar once ruled Kaua'i's economy, but when Lihue Plantation closed in 2000 due to unprofitability, Gay & Robinson became the sole diehard. In the entire state, only one other sugar company remains: Hawaii Commercial & Sugar on Maui.

The road to Gay & Robinson headquarters and the sugar mill, which comes up immediately after the 19-mile marker, is shaded by lovely tall trees and lined with classic, century-old lampposts. Taking this short drive offers a glimpse into plantation life. Everything is covered with a layer of red dust from the surrounding fields. Quite a few indigenous Ni'ihauans live in this area, many of them working for the Robinsons.

At the end of the road is a simple **visitors center** (admission free; ⏰ 8am-4pm Mon-Fri, 11am-3pm Sat), which is more gift shop than anything. More interesting are the two-hour **mill tours** (⏰ 8:45am & 12:45pm Mon-Fri), especially when the mill is actually munching the cane and cranking out the sugar, which isn't always the case. To further explore the vast ranchland, Gay & Robinson also offers ATV tours ($99 to $145; reservations required).

WESTSIDE

Unlike other ATV tours, this one focuses on the landscape and history, not thrill riding, and reaches an elevation of 1500ft.

WAIMEA

pop 1787

Waimea (literally 'reddish water'), the capital of Kaua'i until the mid-1800s, is a site rich in history. Polynesians populated this river valley upon arriving and it was subsequently the site of an ancient Hawaiian settlement. It was here that Captain Cook of the British Navy first came ashore the Hawaiian Islands, and where Kaumuali'i welcomed the first missionaries in 1820. In 1884 Waimea Sugar moved in, and Waimea bloomed into a plantation town. The old sugar mill, now abandoned, sits along the highway on the west side of town.

Located along the highway, Waimea is still the Westside's largest town. But it offers just the basics, so don't expect a lively commercial strip or lots of lodging. While nightlife is nonexistent, Waimea boasts the only movie theater on the Westside and South Shore. It makes a convenient base for exploring Waimea Canyon and Koke'e State Parks. To get there, you can drive up either Waimea Canyon Dr (Hwy 550) or Koke'e Rd (Hwy 552).

Note that Waimea also refers to a district, a river, a valley and a town on Kaua'i – and there is a Waimea Valley on O'ahu and another Waimea town on the Big Island.

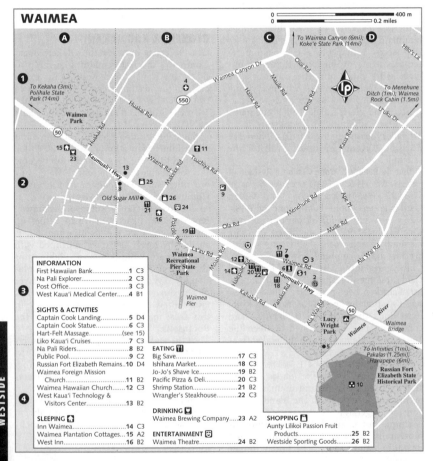

WAIMEA

INFORMATION	
First Hawaiian Bank................1	C3
Na Pali Explorer...................2	C3
Post Office..........................3	C3
West Kaua'i Medical Center......4	B1

SIGHTS & ACTIVITIES	
Captain Cook Landing...............5	D4
Captain Cook Statue................6	C3
Hart-Felt Massage..............(see 15)	
Liko Kaua'i Cruises.................7	C3
Na Pali Riders......................8	B2
Public Pool.........................9	C2
Russian Fort Elizabeth Remains..10	D4
Waimea Foreign Mission	
Church..........................11	B2
Waimea Hawaiian Church......12	C3
West Kaua'i Technology &	
Visitors Center................13	B2

SLEEPING	
Inn Waimea........................14	C3
Waimea Plantation Cottages...15	A2
West Inn..........................16	B2

EATING	
Big Save...........................17	C3
Ishihara Market....................18	C3
Jo-Jo's Shave Ice..................19	B2
Pacific Pizza & Deli...............20	C3
Shrimp Station....................21	B2
Wrangler's Steakhouse..........22	C3

DRINKING	
Waimea Brewing Company.....23	A2

ENTERTAINMENT	
Waimea Theatre...................24	B2

SHOPPING	
Aunty Lilikoi Passion Fruit	
Products.........................25	B2
Westside Sporting Goods........26	B2

Information

First Hawaiian Bank (☎ 338-1611; 4525 Panako Rd)
On Waimea's central square.

Na Pali Explorer (☎ 338-9999, 877-335-9909; www
.napali-explorer.com; Kaumuali'i Hwy; Internet per min
26¢, per hr $6.25; ☺ 7am-5pm) A one-stop shop for
Internet access, simple souvenirs, light snacks and snorkel-
cruise bookings.

Post office (☎ 800-275-8777; 9911 Waimea Rd)

West Kaua'i Medical Center (☎ 338-9431; Waimea
Canyon Dr) Emergency-room services 24 hours.

Sights

WEST KAUA'I TECHNOLOGY & VISITORS CENTER

This state-funded **center** (☎ 338-1332; 9565
Kaumuali'i Hwy; admission free; ☺ 9:30am-5pm Mon-
Fri, 9am-noon Sat) has some interesting photo
and artifact displays on local history from
a technology perspective, and a great assortment of books for sale. Volunteers from
the center lead 90-minute **walking tours** (donations accepted; ☺ 9:30am Mon), reservations preferred, of historic Waimea. On Fridays, free
workshops (donations accepted; ☺ 9:30am Fri) on lei
making are given; reservations preferred.

HISTORIC TOWN CENTER

Downtown Waimea's classic style comes
from wooden buildings with historic facades, such as the neoclassical **First Hawaiian Bank** (1929) and the Art Deco **Waimea
Theatre** (1938).

The **statue** of Captain Cook in the center
of town is a replica of the original statue
by Sir John Tweed that stands in Whitby,
England. The great navigator, clutching his
charts and decked out in his finest captain-
ing threads, now watches over traffic on
Kaumuali'i Hwy.

Waimea Foreign Mission Church (cnr Huakai &
Makeke Rds) was originally a thatched struc-
ture built in 1826 by the Reverend Samuel
Whitney, the first missionary to Waimea.
The present church was built of sandstone
blocks and coral mortar in 1858 by an-
other missionary, the Reverend George
Rowell.

In 1865 Reverend Rowell had a spat with
some folks in the congregation and went off
to build the **Waimea Hawaiian Church** (Kaumuali'i
Hwy; ☺ service 8:30am Sun), a wooden frame
church that was downed in the 1992 hurricane, but has been rebuilt. Sunday services
include hymns sung in Hawaiian.

RUSSIAN FORT ELIZABETH

The remains of this fort (1816–64) stand
above the east bank of the Waimea River.
Like other historical ruins on Kaua'i, it looks
like a boring, abandoned stone wall. Read
the back story (above) for a bit of context.

You can take a short walk through this
curious period of Kaua'i's history. The
most intact part of the fort is the exterior
lava-rock wall, which is 8ft to 10ft high in
places and largely overgrown with scrub.
The *makai* side was designed like the points
of a star, but it takes close observation to
appreciate the effect.

The fort has a good view of the western
bank of the Waimea River, where Captain
Cook landed. Bear right down the dirt
road that continues past the parking lot
and you'll find a vantage point above the
river mouth with a view of Waimea Pier
and Ni'ihau.

LUCY WRIGHT PARK

The Captain Cook landing site is noted
with a plaque on a nondescript rock on the
western side of the Waimea River at Lucy
Wright Park. Notice how it's named after
a prominent Waimea resident and not the
captain himself? It's located on Ala Wai Rd,
as soon as you cross the Waimea Bridge.
This county park also has a ball field, picnic tables, rest rooms and showers. Camping is permitted on a flat grassy area, but
it is a roadside site without much appeal;
see p218 for information about camping
permits.

WAIMEA PIER

Until Port Allen was built, Waimea served
as the region's main pier. It was a major
port of call for whalers and traders during the mid-19th century, and plantations
started exporting sugar from Waimea later
on in the century. Picturesque Waimea
Pier, off Pokole Rd, is now used for pole
fishing, crabbing and picnicking.

MENEHUNE DITCH

Constructed prior to Western contact, this
stone and earthen aqueduct is an engin-
eering masterpiece, with rocks carefully
squared, smoothed and joined to create a
watertight seal. According to legend, Ola,
a king, ordered Pi, a kahuna (priest), to
create a dam and ditch to water his lands

RUSSIANS ON KAUA'I?

Around the time the British arrived in the Hawaiian Islands in the late 1700s, the Russians were actively hunting seals and otters in the Pacific Northwest. The Russian-American Company held a monopoly on the extremely valuable fur trade. Russian ships took nine months to travel from St Petersburg to their North American headquarters in Sitka, Alaska – and the company sought a closer source of supplies.

In 1815 they sent Georg Anton Scheffer, who was fluent in English, to retrieve the skins from a shipwreck off the Waimea coast. When Scheffer arrived, he cured King Kamehameha the Great and his favorite wife, Ka'ahumanu, of an illness, thus garnering the king's gratitude – and a promised Hawaii outpost for the Russians. Soon, however, Kamehameha's British and American advisors warned him that the Russians were a threat, and Scheffer fled O'ahu to Kaua'i, barely saving his life.

On Kaua'i, he ingratiated himself with Chief Kaumuali'i, again by a medical cure. Kaumuali'i saw Scheffer as a means to escape Kamehameha's dominance and promised to help the Russians. Thus he offered the Russians half of O'ahu, plus all the sandalwood on O'ahu and Kaua'i. The wily and opportunistic Scheffer promised to provide a ship and military assistance for Kaumuali'i to invade O'ahu.

In September 1816 Hawaiian laborers under Scheffer's direction began to build Fort Elizabeth, named after the consort of the Czar of Russia. Accounts differ about who gave Scheffer the boot: some say Kamehameha forced Kaumuali'i (who was also suspicious of Scheffer by then) to oust the Russian. Others say the Americans grew wary of the Russian presence and started a rumor that the US was at war with Russia. Either way, in May 1817, Scheffer was forced to leave Kaua'i.

Fort Elizabeth was nevertheless completed and Hawaiian troops used it until they dismantled it in 1864.

---

west of the Waimea River. Pi contracted with the *menehune* (little people) living on the canyon rim to build the ditch for payment of one *'opae* (shrimp) per *menehune*. As always, they finished the project in one night, received their payment and returned to their mountain home, humming so loudly that their voices were heard as far as O'ahu; see also opposite.

When Captain Vancouver visited Waimea at the close of the 18th century, he walked up the river valley atop the wall of this ditch, estimating the walls to be around 24ft high. These days most of the ancient waterway lies buried beneath the road, except for one section about 2ft high. Even today, the ditch continues to divert water from the Waimea River along, and through, the cliff to irrigate the taro patches below.

To get here, turn at the police station onto Menehune Rd and go almost 1.5 miles up the Waimea River. The ditch is along the left side of the road after a tiny parking area.

On the drive up to the ditch, notice the scattered holes in the cliffs to the left. These are **Hawaiian burial caves**. One group of seven caves behind the Waimea Shingon Mission was explored by Wendell Bennett of the Bishop Museum in the 1920s. At that time, each of the caves held a number of skeletal remains, some in canoe-shaped coffins and others in hollowed-out logs.

Activities
SNORKELING
Two outfitters doing Na Pali Coast boat tours are based in Waimea and depart from Kikiaola Small Boat Harbor in Kekaha, instead of Port Allen in Hanapepe. This gives snorkelers the most time in Na Pali waters instead of just cruising there.

Catamarans
Run by Liko Ho'okano, a Native Hawaiian born and raised on Kaua'i, **Liko Kaua'i Cruises** (☎ 338-0333, 888-732-5456; www.liko-kauai.com; 9875 Waimea Rd) sails a 49ft power catamaran to the Na Pali Coast for a four-hour cruise (adult/child aged four to 12 $120/80). Max group size is 34, and tours go as far as Ke'e Beach. This is a friendly, homegrown outfit. Office located east of Big Save.

Rafts

The super-friendly **Na Pali Explorer** (☎ 338-9999, 877-335-9909; www.napali-explorer.com; 3.5/5hr tour $79/125; Kaumuali'i Hwy) has 26ft and 48ft rafts doing snorkel and scenic trips, plus whale watching along South Shore in winter (which are not recommended since you'll see whales on snorkel tours anyway). Its rafts are rigid-hull inflatables (hard bottom with inflatable sides), which give a smoother ride than standard Zodiacs. Group size ranges from 16 to 35 passengers. The larger raft includes a rest room and canopy for shade. It also rents snorkel gear, boogie boards and other beach toys.

If you want a wild raft adventure, **Na Pali Riders** (☎ 742-6331; www.napaliriders.com; Kaumuali'i Hwy; 4hr tour adult/child 5-12 $99/89) fits the bill – but the rigid-hull inflatables are markedly more comfortable. The four-hour tour explores the entire Na Pali Coast, enters sea caves, encounters dolphins and other marine life, and bounces you up and down with each wave. If waters are choppy, you'll feel it.

SURFING

Just before the entrance to Russian Fort Elizabeth, immediately after the 21-mile marker, you'll notice cars parked on the side of the highway. This is the access point to a popular surf break called **Pakalas**. Park here and take the short dirt path to the beach. East of the stone jetty, you'll find good-sized swells and a stretch of gorgeous golden beach backed by swaying palms. Another break nearby is called **Infinities** for its long ride. Both are suitable for experienced surfers only.

MASSAGE & YOGA

Hart-Felt Massage (☎ 338-2240; www.hartfeltmassage.com; Waimea Plantation Cottages, Unit 40, 9400 Kaumuali'i Hwy; massage $46-155, spa & skin treatments $55-130; ☯ 9am-6pm Mon-Sat, by appointment Sun) offers an array of massages, spa and skin treatments, including a novel oil-raindrop therapy, kava-ginger muscle wrap and a nonsurgical 'facelift' using microcurrent electricity and traditional Chinese medicine. Standard services like waxing and pore extraction are also available.

An oceanfront **yoga class** (☎ 338-2240; $13) is offered at Waimea Plantation Cottages. The mixed-level class is geared toward beginners and clearly a tourist 'thang'.

SWIMMING

For lap swimming, there's a **public pool** (☎ 338-1271; 9707 Tsuchiya Rd) at Waimea High School; call for schedule.

Festivals & Events

Waimea Town Celebration (☎ 338-1332; www.wkbpa.org; admission free) Free fun on the Westside includes rodeo, canoe race, food, crafts, ice-cream-eating contest and lei and hula competitions. Held in mid-February.

Waimea Lighted Christmas Parade (☎ 338-9957) Watch lighted floats be led by fire engines through Waimea town. Parade starts at dusk, a week before Christmas.

Sleeping

For a rural place, Waimea lodging is steep. Thus Waimea Rock Cabin is a real gem (beg pardon). Also check the Kekaha vacation-rental listings (p198).

Waimea Rock Cabin (☎ 822-7944, 338-9015; www.a1vacations.com/kauaiwaimearockcabin/1/; Menehune Rd; cabins $40, plus one-time cleaning fee $50) Amid vistas

---

BUSY BUILDERS

According to legend, the *menehune* (little people) were Kaua'i's earliest settlers, who were displaced by subsequent Polynesian migration. *Menehune* were short and stocky in stature, eccentric in character and known for building some amazing stone structures, always within a single night. On Kaua'i, celebrated *menehune* projects still standing today include the Menehune Ditch, Alekoko (Menehune) Fishpond (p80) along the Hule'ia Stream and Maniniholo Dry Cave (p152).

It is believed that the *menehune* population numbered in the hundreds of thousands. And, believe it or not, in the 1850s census, 65 people were counted as *menehune* in Wainiha (but they were of normal size).

Today, locals still believe the *menehune* are lurking, especially when things go bump late at night.

of red dirt and rocky hills, this cabin is a real escape from touristy people, places and prettiness (in the conventional sense). Instead, find peace and quiet in the starker beauty of western Kaua'i. This studio cabin, surrounded by citrus trees and local neighbors, is clean and surprisingly airy, with a high ceiling and an exposed corrugated-metal roof that adds to the rustic atmosphere. The king bed, kitchenette, satellite TV and phone make for a cozy stay. During winter, the cabin is usually booked solid.

Inn Waimea (☎ 338-0031; www.innwaimea.com; 4469 Halepule Rd; r 1 night $135-145, 2 or more nights $110-120; 🖥) Close to the heart of Waimea, this lovely old missionary home with four guest rooms combines historic character with modern comforts. Rooms include the expected amenities plus high-speed Internet connections. The shared living room and lanai (porch) create a communal atmosphere. The cheapest room is wheelchair accessible, while the largest room has a king bed and a Jacuzzi. Weekly discounts are available. For more privacy, try one of their three nearby cottages (one-bedroom cottage $100, two-bedroom cottage $125 to $150).

West Inn (☎ 338-1107, 866-937-8466; www.the westinn.com; 9686 Kaumuali'i Hwy; r $139; 🐾) You can't miss this little motel-style inn, located right on the main drag, across from Waimea Theatre. Renovated in 2004, the rooms would fit the Best Western motel category: clean and comfy, with either king or double beds, phone, cable TV, wi-fi, lanai and kitchenette with bar sink, fridge, microwave and coffeemaker. The price is steep for motel quality, but competition is scarce around here.

Waimea Plantation Cottages (☎ 338-1625, 800-992-7866; www.waimea-plantation.com; 9400 Kaumuali'i Hwy; r from $140, 1-/2-/3-bedroom cottages from $195/240/280; 🐾) The notion of staying in a genuine early-1900s plantation cottage is compelling. From the outside, the simple wooden buildings with tin-roof porches differ little from today's local homes on adjacent side streets. The trouble is the variation in quality from cottage to cottage; if possible, look before you book. Each unit includes cable TV, stereo and full kitchen; wi-fi is available in the lobby and conference room. The less appealing hotel rooms are hardly worth the cost. For large groups,

inquire about the oceanfront four- and five-bedroom houses ($405 to $620). The 27-acre property abuts a decent, if murky, beach. Despite such caveats, the cottages are wildly popular and usually book up solid.

Eating & Drinking
BUDGET
Jo-Jo's Shave Ice (9740 Kaumuali'i Hwy; shave ice $2-4; 🕙 10am-6pm) While still a worthwhile stop with dozens and dozens of syrup flavors, the quality has declined since new owners took over. The shave ice is not bad, just inconsistent, sometimes with skimpy syrup or gritty ice (from dull blades). Still, the colorful sign above the rickety screen door is a beacon and, heck, a small cup is just two bucks. Try unusual flavors like lychee, tamarind and rum.

Shrimp Station (☎ 338-1242; 9652 Kaumuali'i Hwy; dishes $4.75-12; 🕙 11am-5pm) Follow your nose to this little side-of-the-road lunch window serving fresh, aromatic shrimp plates. Varieties include coconut and sweet chili. Each comes with a half-pound of the critters and, of course, two scoops of rice.

Ishihara Market (9946 Kaumuali'i Hwy; 🕙 6am-8:30pm Mon-Fri, 7am-8:30pm Sat & Sun) The town's best grocer is an indie with an extensive deli selling take-out sushi, green salads and a mouth-watering selection of 'ahi poke.

Big Save (🕙 7am-9pm) Waimea branch; this is another option across the street from Ishihara Market.

MIDRANGE & TOP END
Pacific Pizza & Deli (☎ 338-1020; 9850 Kaumuali'i Hwy; pizza $9-22; 🕙 11am-9pm Mon-Sat) Traditional or wacky, it's all here, from Mexican (ground beef and refried beans) to Filipino (Langanisa sausage and grilled eggplant) to lomilomi salmon. The calzones, offered in each pizza-combo flavor, are ideal for single diners. Crust thickness might be inconsistent: the pizza throwers are young local girls who say it depends on 'how tired our arms feel.'

Waimea Brewing Company (☎ 338-9733; www .waimea-plantation.com/brew; Waimea Plantation Cottages, 9400 Kaumuali'i Hwy; appetizers $7-13, dishes $9-30; 🕙 11am-10pm Sun-Thu, to 2am Fri & Sat) Located adjacent to Waimea Plantation Cottages, this microbrewery is slightly suburban-mall-ish compared with its setting amid swaying coconut trees. But the open-air plantation

WESTSIDE

building is pleasant and the island-inspired pub food is tasty; forgo the heavy mains for a variety of *pupu* (appetizers). Two creative uses of '*ahi poke*: a seared *poke* wrap and a sushi roll filled with *poke* and flash-fried. As for the US's westernmost microbrewery's beer, the eight house selections, including its flagship Wai'ale'ale Ale, a light golden brew, are a refreshing alternative to the supermarket stuff.

Wrangler's Steakhouse (☎ 338-1218; dinner mains $17-25; 🕑 11am-9pm Mon-Fri, 4-9pm Sat) If you can ignore the commercial name, this cozy, ranch-style restaurant will more than satisfy a hearty appetite. Meat eaters should try the signature 'sizzling' New York–cut steak, juicy and prepared to your liking, while indecisive types can choose a main of Japanese shrimp and veg tempura, teriyaki beef and sashimi. While the menu offers an '*ahi* penne pasta option, vegetarians will go hungry here.

Entertainment

Waimea Theatre (☎ 338-0282; 9691 Kaumuali'i Hwy; 🕑 7:30pm Wed-Sun) Variety of movies, including new releases, indies and classics, shown here. This is also a venue for the Hawaii International Film Festival (see its website at www.hiff.org).

Shopping

Shopoholics will save a bundle here because Waimea is not exactly a retail extravaganza. A handful of gift stores in the Wrangler's Steakhouse building are worth a browse.

Aunty Lilikoi Passion Fruit Products (☎ 338-1296; 866-545-4564; www.auntylilikoi.com; 9633 Kaumuali'i Hwy; condiments per 10oz $4.50; 🕑 10am-5pm) This homegrown company run by Tony and Lori Cardenas concocts the gamut of delectable passion fruit jellies and other condiments. The *liliko'i*-wasabi mustard beat over 300 rivals to win the 2005 Grand Champion Medal in the Napa Valley Mustard Competition. This is a genuine mom-and-pop affair, and if you stop by the factory, you might see Lori cooking up 100 cases of dressing (she is the sole cook). The *liliko'i* is the same variety you see growing wild on Kaua'i (with yellow skin and seedy orange pulp), but she uses a pure fruit puree imported from Ecuador because locally grown fruit isn't available in such quantity or quality yet. The prod-

ucts are available at retailers islandwide but prices can vary, so buy at this store or online.

Westside Sporting Goods (☎ 338-1411; 9681 Kaumuali'i Hwy; 🕑 9:30am-5:30pm Mon-Fri, to 4:30pm Sat) Head here for outdoor gear, including camping and hiking supplies such as fleece sleeping bags ($15), camp-stove fuel, *tabi* (reef-walking sandals) and first-aid kits.

KEKAHA
pop 3175

Locals like to claim that Kekaha is the westernmost town in the US, but Adak, Alaska, holds that distinction. Still, Kekaha is the westernmost in the state of Hawaii – and proud of it! Check out 'The Unofficial Guide to Kekaha Town' (http://home .hawaii.rr.com/webguides/kekaha.html) for a hilarious introduction to the town.

The coastal highway seems to stretch forever here, along a glorious carpet of golden sand as far as the eye can see. Kekaha Beach Park is perfect for vigorous beach walking or sunset strolling – or you can drive all the way to Polihale State Park (with a 4WD and a dose of patience). The road is flanked by fields of corn and sunflowers, picturesque but purposeful for seed production, too. Cattle and cattle egrets feed in vast pastures.

Rural by choice, Kekaha is rarely visited, even by locals. For years land was cheap – who wanted to live way out here? But since the early 2000s, real estate values have jumped as more prospective landowners flock to Kekaha, one of Kaua'i's last affordable areas.

Heavy-duty hikers who are planning for multiple forays on Waimea Canyon and Koke'e trails will find Kekaha a convenient home base, as would anyone seeking solitude. For others, it might be too out of the way. Since waters on the Westside are generally too rough for swimming, places like Po'ipu would better suit families with children.

Orientation

Kaumuali'i Hwy borders the coast, while Kekaha Rd, the main drag, lies parallel a few blocks inland. Along Kekaha Rd there's a post office and a couple of stores. Welcome to downtown Kekaha, folks! The village's most dominant feature is its old sugar mill, visible from just about everywhere, including the beach.

On its eastern end, Kekaha Rd and Kaumuali'i Hwy meet near the Kikiaola Small Boat Harbor, a state harbor with a launch ramp. Some snorkeling cruises launch here (see p185).

Sights & Activities

Kekaha is primarily a residential town, so its only real draw is the luxuriously long, empty, sandy beach. It's a place to get away from it all.

Free **tennis courts** are available at the junction of Koke'e Rd and Kaumuali'i Hwy.

KEKAHA BEACH PARK

Just west of Kekaha town, this vast beach is ideal for solitary walking. Without any shade, however, the sun is brutal and you can fry your skin (and your bare feet, if you forget to wear *rubbah slippah* – rubber flip-flops – on the scorching sand). Before you jump in, watch the tide carefully. This is unprotected open ocean, and when the surf is high currents are extremely dangerous; under the right conditions, it can be good for surfing, boogie boarding and even swimming. Perhaps the best time to visit is sunset – and you're guaranteed to find a private viewing spot.

Ni'ihau and its offshore islet, Lehua, are visible from the beach. An inconspicuous shower can be found just inland from the highway between Alae and Amakihi Rds; rest rooms and picnic tables are nearby.

Sleeping & Eating

Two good websites for finding places to lay your head in Kekaha are the **Kekaha Info Page** (www.aloha.net/~inazoo/index.htm.htm) and **Kekaha Oceanside** (www.kekahaoceansidekauai.com).

Mindy's (☎ 337-9275; mindys@hgea.org; 8842 Kekaha Rd; s/d $75/85) This sunny 2nd-story apartment is a charmer, with private deck and peaceful mountain views combined with full kitchen, TV, sofa bed for additional guests (per person $5), and ceiling fans throughout. Complimentary fruit and coffee are provided. Reserve well in advance.

Boathouse (☎ 332-9744; www.seakauai.com; 4518-A Nene St; r $85) Within walking distance of an uncrowded sandy beach, the Boathouse is a clean, spacious, ground-floor studio with wraparound covered lanai – great for out-door dining and relaxing. It's perfect for either one or two, with kitchenette, king bed and TV. Free use of washer/dryer. The friendly owners also rent the Seaview Suite in Kalaheo.

Obsessions (☎ 337-2224; Waimea Canyon Plaza, cnr Koke'e Rd & Kekaha Rd; breakfast & lunch $4-7; ⏰ 8:30am-6pm Mon-Fri, 6:30am-3pm Sat & Sun) Luckily (because it's the only game in town) this little place grills a mean *panini*. From the bread for the French toast to the homegrown salads, everything is homemade here. Even the coffee comes from the owner's 5-acre coffee patch. The menu includes five different flavors of fluffy pancakes and a selection of omelettes, sandwiches and salads.

Also in the Waimea Canyon Plaza is Menehune Food Mart, basically a 7-11-type corner store that sells wrapped sandwiches and simple hot items, and Aloha Ice Cream, selling Lappert's ice cream.

BARKING SANDS

Between Kekaha Beach Park and Polihale State Park, the beach stretches for roughly 15 miles. But there is only limited public access near the US Navy base at **Barking Sands Pacific Missile Range Facility** (PMRF; ☎ general information 335-4229, beach access 335-4111). The Navy closed access after the September 11 terrorist attacks, and locals, from environmental activists to local surfers, were livid. Not only did the closure violate the open coastal-access policy, it barred surfers from some favorite Westside winter swells. Following public outcry, the Navy reopened a piece of the coast, but only to Kaua'i residents without felony convictions or to those with connections to the military.

Barking Sands earned its nickname because on days both sunny and windy (with the planets lined up just right) the moving sands make sounds akin to those of barking dogs. (Please send us a recording if you hear them.) The missile-range facility at Barking Sands provides the aboveground link to a sophisticated sonar network that tracks more than 1000 sq miles of the Pacific. Established during WWII, it's been developed into the world's largest underwater listening device. The supersensitive equipment even picks up the songs of humpback whales – the base has gathered the most comprehensive collection of humpback whale soundtracks ever recorded.

The Navy presence on Kaua'i is, as one would expect, controversial. The Navy is Kaua'i's largest employer and it occupies and prohibits access to indigenous Hawaiian territory. New US military initiatives suggest that the naval presence on Kaua'i is likely to be expanded, a move sure to generate protest. Indeed, at the time of writing the Navy was negotiating an easement and lease for 6300 additional acres adjacent to the existing facility.

POLIHALE STATE PARK

If you want remote, come to the immense **white-sand beach** at Polihale. It might attract beachgoers when rain is pouring everywhere else, but it's way out there, past 3.5 miles of rutted dirt road. Mainly you'll see locals here, especially those who enjoy hot-rodding in big trucks. Veterans of Polihale know to drop their tire pressure to at most 20lb for the best traction in the sand. A 4WD is recommended but unless the road is muddy, standard cars can make it.

Polihale is almost overwhelming in its magnitude of sand, sea and sky. Dunes are dozens of feet tall (don't try dune-buggying over them). During the day, brilliant aqua waves pound the shore, and at sunset the horizon is awash in a fiery show. Expert surfers and boogie boarders shred at Polihale (and get punished doing it), but strong rip currents mean the waters are too treacherous for swimming. Bring sun protection, as not a single tree shades the beach.

Polihale State Park is about 5 miles from the Barking Sands military base. Turn left 0.75 miles north of the base entrance at the (subtle) sign for the park onto a wide dirt road that passes through abandoned sugarcane fields.

After almost 3.5 miles, at a large monkeypod tree in the middle of the road, a turnoff leads to the only safe swimming spot in the area. To get there, turn left at the tree, go 0.25 miles, then follow the road north, up the hill toward the base of the dunes. Walk north along the beach and you'll come to **Queen's Pond**, where a large semicircular reef almost reaches the shore, creating a protected pool. When the seas are calm, the reef blocks the ocean currents. But when surf breaks over the reef and into the pool, a dangerous rip runs toward an opening at the reef's southern end.

To get to the state park facilities, go back to monkeypod tree, turn right and continue another mile. A turnoff on the left leads to a camping area with rest rooms, outdoor showers, drinking water and a picnic pavilion. Other camping areas are located in the dunes just above the beach amid thorny kiawe trees (see p217 for camping permit information). Due to its remoteness, Polihale attracts a motley crowd of adventurers, Hawaiians and hippies. The mood is festive and renegade; if you're looking for contemplative solitude, this probably isn't the place.

At the very end of the beach is **Polihale Cliff**, marking the western end of the Na Pali Coast. Combined with the untamed ocean and expansive beach, it's a magnificent sight. Look for the terraced heiau (ancient Hawaiian religious site) toward the cliffs. It was originally on the beach, but over the years ever-shifting sands have added a 300ft buffer toward the sea. Bushwhacking to the heiau through wasp nests and tangled brush isn't worth it.

WAIMEA CANYON STATE PARK

Of all Kaua'i's unique wonders, none can touch Waimea Canyon for utter grandeur. While one expects to find tropical beaches and gardens here, few expect a gargantuan chasm of ancient lava rock, 13 miles long and 2500ft deep to the river bed (and 3700ft above sea level). Flowing through the canyon is the Waimea River, Kaua'i's longest, which is fed by three eastern tributaries that bring reddish-brown waters from the mountaintop bog, Alaka'i Swamp – hence spurring the name Waimea, *wai* (freshwater), *mea* (red or reddish). You might notice higher figures for the canyon's depth, but those do not account for the elevation of the streambed at the canyon bottom.

It's understandable why Waimea Canyon is dubbed the 'Grand Canyon of the Pacific,' but geologically there is no comparison. Arizona's mega wonder is much larger (277 miles long, 10 miles wide on average and up to 5700ft deep) and much older (250 million to 570 million years old, compared to Waimea Canyon's four to five million years).

From afar, the view of the canyon tends to be hazy. The optimum viewing conditions are sunny days following heavy rain, when the lava layers turn deeper red and waterfalls cascade throughout the canyon. Don't miss the **Waimea Canyon Lookout**, which is clearly signposted north of the 10-mile marker, offering sweeping views from a perch of 3400ft. The prominent canyon running in an easterly direction off Waimea Canyon is Koai'e Canyon, to which you can hike.

Waimea Canyon was formed when Kaua'i's original shield volcano, Wai'ale'ale, slumped along an ancient fault line, creating a sharp east-facing line of cliffs. Then another shield volcano, Lihu'e, developed the island's east side, producing new lava flows that ponded against the cliffs. Thus the western canyon walls are taller, thinner and more eroded – a contrast most theatrically apparent while hiking along the canyon floor. The black and red horizontal striations along the canyon walls represent successive volcanic eruptions; the red color indicates that water seeped through the rocks, creating rust from the iron inside.

Orientation

The southern boundary of Waimea Canyon State Park is about 6 miles up the road from Waimea. You can reach the park by two roads: Waimea Canyon Dr (Hwy 550) starts in Waimea just beyond the 23-mile marker, while Koke'e Rd (Hwy 552) starts in Kekaha off Mana Rd. They merge between the 6-mile and 7-mile markers.

State officials generally prefer visitors to use Waimea Canyon Dr, which is 19 miles long and passes the canyon lookouts with terrific views into Kalalau Valley on the Na Pali Coast. Koke'e Rd is shorter by 3 miles and also offers scenic views, but not of the canyon.

On Waimea Canyon Dr, awesome views start about a mile up from Waimea and get better as the road climbs. The lookout point at 1.75 miles up encompasses the Waimea River and the taro patches irrigated by the Menehune Ditch. About 2.5 miles up, you can see Kekaha Beach with Ni'ihau in the background.

Dangers & Annoyances

It's a bad idea to explore Waimea Canyon on rainy days. The red-dirt trails quickly become slick and river fords can swell to impassable levels. Winter is generally rainier than summer, but Kaua'i weather is capricious and you can hike during any dry spell year-round. Hiking poles or a sturdy walking stick will ease the steep descent into the canyon.

Always note the time of sunset and plan to return well before it's dark. Note that daylight will fade inside the canyon long before sunset.

While packing light is recommended, take enough water for your entire trip, especially the return journey, which will be relentlessly uphill. Any available fresh water along the trails must be treated before drinking.

Waimea Canyon trails are remote, and cell phones do not work here. If possible, hike with a companion or at least tell someone your expected return time.

Sights

Along Waimea Canyon Dr, you can see naturally growing examples of native trees, including kiawe (mesquite) and wiliwili. The valuable hardwood koa proliferates at the hunter's check station along the way. Look for the trees with narrow, crescent-shaped leaves. (Note: the area is popular for deer hunting, which is obvious by the photo collage of proud hunters with their fallen quarry at the station.)

SCENIC LOOKOUTS

The most scenic of the lookout points along this stretch of Waimea Canyon Rd is **Waimea Canyon Lookout**, signposted 585yd north of the 10-mile marker, at an elevation of 3400ft. The prominent canyon running in an easterly direction off Waimea is Koai'e Canyon, which is accessible to backcountry hikers. Conventional tour buses go no farther than this lookout.

As you continue up the road, the 800ft **Waipo'o Falls** can be seen from a couple of small unmarked lookouts before the 12-mile marker and then from a lookout opposite the picnic area shortly before the 13-mile marker. The picnic area includes barbecue pits, rest rooms, drinking water, a pay phone and Camp Hale Koa, a Seventh Day Adventist camp.

Pu'u Hinahina Lookout (3640ft) offers two lookouts near the parking lot at a marked turnoff between the 13- and 14-mile mark-

KOKE'E & WAIMEA CANYON STATE PARKS

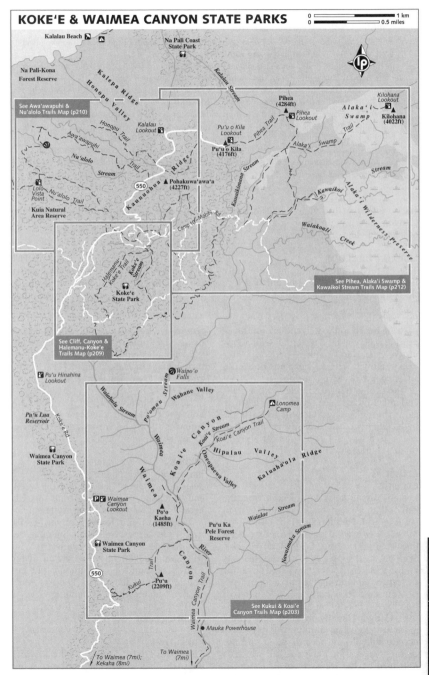

0 ——————— 1 km
0 ——————— 0.5 miles

Kalalau Beach

Na Pali Coast State Park

Na Pali-Kona Forest Reserve

Kalepa Ridge

Honopu Valley

Kalalau Stream

Pihea (4284ft)

Pihea Lookout

Kilohana Lookout

Alaka'i Swamp

Kilohana (4022ft)

See Awa'awapuhi & Nu'alolo Trails Map (p210)

Honopu Trail

Kalalau Lookout

Pu'u o Kila Lookout

Pihea Trail

Awa'awapuhi Trail

Pu'u o Kila (4176ft)

Alaka'i Swamp Trail

Nu'alolo Stream

Nu'alolo Trail

Kaunuohua Ridge

Pohakuwa'awa'a (422ft)

Kawaikoi Stream

Alaka'i Wilderness Preserve

Lolo Vista Point

Kuia Natural Area Reserve

550

Camp 10-Mohihi Rd

Kawaikoi Creek

Waiakoali

Stream

Halemanu-Koke'e Trail

Koke'e Stream

See Pihea, Alaka'i Swamp & Kawaikoi Stream Trails Map (p212)

Koke'e State Park

See Cliff, Canyon & Halemanu-Koke'e Trails Map (p209)

Pu'u Hinahina Lookout

Waipo'o Falls

Pu'u Lua Reservoir

Koke'e Rd

Waialhulu Stream

Po'omau Stream

Wahane Valley

Lonomea Camp

Koai'e Canyon

Koai'e Stream

Koai'e Canyon Trail

Waimea Canyon State Park

Waimea

Koaie Canyon

Hipalau Valley

Kaluaha'ula Ridge

Oneopaewa Valley

Waimea Canyon Lookout

Po'o Kaeha (1485ft)

Pu'u Ka Pele Forest Reserve

Waialae Stream

Nawaimaka Stream

Waimea Canyon State Park

Canyon

River

550

Kukui Trail

Pu'u (2209ft)

Waimea Canyon Trail

See Kukui & Koai'e Canyon Trails Map (p203)

Mauka Powerhouse

To Waimea (7mi); Kekaha (8mi)

To Waimea (7mi)

WESTSIDE

THE MARK TWAIN MYTH

It's common knowledge that Mark Twain coined the 'Grand Canyon of the Pacific' moniker, isn't it? Well, while Twain indeed had a way with words, these aren't his.

In their excellent book, *Kaua'i's Geologic History: A Simplified Guide*, Chuck Blay and Robert Siemers debunk this myth. Twain did spend time on the Hawaiian Islands in 1866, writing his oft-quoted letters compiled in *Mark Twain's Letters from Hawaii*. But he apparently never visited the island of Kaua'i nor saw Waimea Canyon, as his writings mention neither.

Further, extensive research by the Bishop Museum in Honolulu discovered that renowned geologist John Wesley Powell began exploring the Colorado River wonder in 1867, ultimately publishing his findings in 1875 – and he never once referred to a 'Grand Canyon.' Only in 1908 did US President Theodore Roosevelt establish the 'Grand Canyon' as a national monument. So, unless Mark Twain also invented the name of the Grand Canyon itself (before it was even on the map), he could not have made the comparison back in 1866. Twain died in 1910.

---

ers. One has a fine view down Waimea Canyon clear out to the coast, while the other has a view of Ni'ihau.

ILIAU NATURE LOOP

The marked trailhead for the 10-minute Iliau Nature Loop comes up shortly before the 9-mile marker. This is also the trailhead for the longer Kukui Trail. At the start of the trail there's a bench with a view; go past the bench to the left, and after a three-minute walk you'll be rewarded with a top-notch vista into Waimea Canyon. After heavy rainfall, waterfalls explode down the sheer rock walls across the gorge.

The trail is named for the *iliau*, a plant endemic to Kaua'i's Westside, which grows along the trail and produces stalks up to 10ft high. Like its cousin the silversword, *iliau* grows to a ripe old age. Then for a grand finale it bursts into blossom and dies.

Activities

CYCLING

Let loose for 13 miles, all downhill, from the rim of Waimea Canyon (elevation 3500ft) to sea level with **Outfitters Kaua'i** (☎ 742-9667, 888-742-9887; www.outfitterskauai.com; Po'ipu Plaza, 2827-A Po'ipu Rd, Po'ipu; tour adult/child 12-14 $90/70; ☺ check-in 6am & 2:30pm). It supplies the cruisers, helmets and snacks. Remember, you'll be a target for the setting sun during the afternoon ride.

Mountain bikers can also find miles of bumpy, 4WD hunting-area roads off Waimea Canyon Dr. Even when the yellow gates are closed on nonhunting days, bikers are still allowed to go around and use them – except for Papa'alai Rd, which is managed by the Department of Hawaiian

Home Lands and open for hunting, but not recreational use.

FISHING

You can fish for rainbow trout at the **Pu'u Lua Reservoir** (☎ 274-3344; www.hawaii.gov/dlnr /dar; 7-day tourist license adult/child $10/4) from the first Saturday in August for 16 days, then on weekends and holidays till the end of September. The laundry list of rules (from requiring a freshwater game fishing license to net-size limits) is daunting. For locals, it's a popular family activity. To get here, turn *makai* on Ha'ele'ele Rd (4WD only) and the reservoir quickly appears on your right.

In case you're wondering how the rainbow trout got here: the State Division of Aquatic Resources introduced the species to five streams on Kaua'i in 1920.

HIKING

For serious hikers, there are trails that lead deep into Waimea Canyon. During weekends and holidays, all of these trails are fairly heavily used by pig and deer hunters.

The Kukui and Koai'e Canyon Trails, two of the steepest on Kaua'i, are often described together since they connect at Wili-wili Camp, 2000ft into the canyon. If the entire trek sounds too strenuous, hike just one mile down the Kukui Trail, as you'll reach a bench with an astounding view.

The hiking mileage given for each trail following is for one way only.

Kukui Trail

The Kukui Trail (2.5 miles) trailhead, which is also the Iliau Nature Loop entrance, is just before the 9-mile marker. It officially starts just beyond it at a hunter checking station on the right. It passes a picnic table before starting its switchback descent through forest, entering archery Hunting Unit K. At first the way is not overly steep. Because much of it is so exposed, the trail tends to dry out quickly here, even after rain.

From the picnic table onward, keep a sharp eye out for the switchback turns during the descent. When in doubt about where the trail actually is, stick with the more level forks and ignore the steeply rutted bits going down the deepest gashes in the canyon wall. If the going starts to feel too precipitous, it probably is; backtracking to the last switchback junction may be

the best option. There are also tempting places to perch on canyon outcroppings, but unstable, crumbly soil makes it dangerous to do so.

Around the 0.5-mile marker are some washed-away sections of trail that may well require some light, quick steps to safely cross the scree. Past the eroded traverse the switchbacks resume as the descent steepens and the trail enters Hunting Unit B. Only short-cut the switchbacks if they look much safer than the main route. Views of the river canyon open up from the bench around the 1-mile mark.

Continue sharply switchbacking, the trail still in the vicinity of *iliau* and an unnamed tree-topped *pu'u* (a hill, marked '2209' on

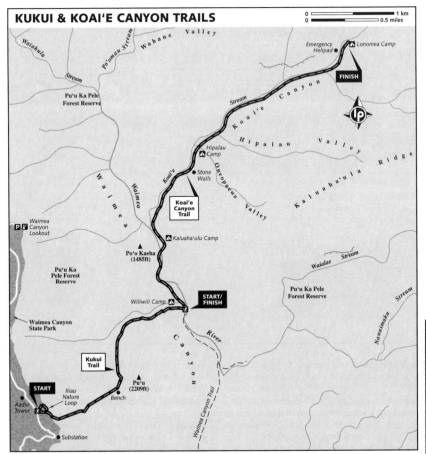

KUKUI & KOAI'E CANYON TRAILS

WESTSIDE KAUA'I TRAIL ELEVATION CHARTS

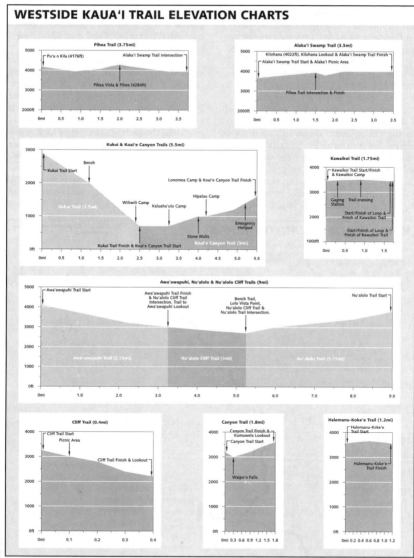

topographic maps) with a big gash in its side prominent. Do not veer toward hill 2209. Instead keep it on the right and where the trail abruptly stops its descent for a moment, look for a small sign directing hikers to turn left. Then with hill 2209 at your back, hike down through deeply rutted and colorful dirt, curving right to start slowly

picking out a path down over a severely eroded soil slope, meanwhile losing at least 500ft in elevation. At the 1.5-mile mark, the trail is still descending as if it's heading for the opposite canyon wall, and a distinctive butte, Po'o Kaeha, is visible down below. Do not veer right into the forest before reaching the bottom of the steep slope, where there's a broken pole sticking up and a rock covered with graffiti.

About an hour from the start, the trail enters thick forest and tree roots form natural steps going downhill. It requires minor boulder-hopping in parts. The first of the forested switchbacks are the steepest, gradually easing as the path travels downhill and becomes overgrown and scratchy in parts. Kukui nuts crunch and swivel underfoot. After pushing through a section of sisal grasses, the path shortly rises and falls once again over boulders. As the sounds of rushing river water become clearly audible, the picnic shelter and toilet of Wiliwili Camp come into view. From here, you're only a few steps away from the river itself, plus a signposted junction for both the Koai'e Canyon and Waimea Canyon Trails.

Overnight camping is allowed at Wiliwili Camp, although it's mostly used by hunters and might be filled with trash. The camp has an open-air picnic shelter and pit toilet, but there are no other facilities.

Koai'e Canyon Trail

A few steps from Wiliwili Camp, the Kukui Trail leads to the Koai'e Canyon Trail (3 miles), a wide dirt road running north across a small streambed, then uphill on switchbacks before turning left and heading along the canyon wall, with beautiful views of the river below. At an indistinct junction, stay on the right-hand lower path, which is filled with small rocks that roll underfoot. Growing in the canyon's shade are giant fanlike ferns, and beautiful red cliffs can be seen stretching out in front. Ignore any false spur trails that divert right down to the river. Soon there's a little plank across a stream (test it before trusting it).

The trail narrows to only foot width as it edges along a slippery, mossy rock face above the river. After only a minute or so, the rocks dry out and the going gets easier. When the trail rejoins the old dirt road, it quickly descends back to the river, then crosses over it. The ford is not especially wide, and sometimes it's possible to boulder-hop across it. On the other bank, which is lined by elegant umbrella grass, turn left (north) and walk along an extremely rutted road to Kaluaha'ulu Camp, marked by another picnic table shelter and pit toilet.

All three backcountry camps on the Koai'e Canyon Trail are part of the forest reserve system. Although the camps have open-air picnic shelters and toilets, there are no other facilities, and all freshwater needs to be treated before drinking. Staying overnight is not an inviting option, however, considering the amount of trash other campers leave behind.

Beyond the camp, the trail continues as a single track. Po'o Keaha, a striking-looking butte also seen from the Kukui Trail, rises up directly on the left. Inundated with leaf litter, the trail widens out but grows fainter. Be sure to stay on the east bank of the river and do not cross it, even when trails-of-use seem to suggest doing so. A Na Ala Hele trailhead sign signals the start of the Koai'e Canyon Trail. Initially it's overgrown and some minor bushwhacking may be required. Spongy, loose soil on the sides of the path can conceal steep drop-offs, so watch your step.

Follow the gently rolling trail underneath the east canyon wall, as kukui nuts bounce around underfoot. At about 2 miles from Wiliwili Camp, the trail meets a couple of stone walls. Sisal grasses and guava line the rest of the way to Hipalau Camp, reached after about an hour of hiking. Making noises as you hike will most likely scare away any wild pigs that may be wandering around, snuffling in the trash. Beyond Hipalau Camp the trail becomes indistinct, but generally keep heading north. Look for an orange-pointed stake at the point where the path becomes visible again, scrambling up over large boulders. Do not veer off toward the river, but continue ascending at approximately the same point midway between the canyon walls and the river.

Becoming ever more steep, the trail has now entered Koai'e Canyon, judging by the red-rock walls rising to the left. Although made up of crumbly soil in parts, the trail is not unnerving by any means. In many places it appears to become lost in forest clearings, often hidden by leaf litter and covered in mud. Just head straight across any such clearing and pick up the trail heading upslope on the other side by keeping to the midlevel below the ridge, but not too close to the river. Many of these clearings have interesting old Hawaiian stone walls.

About a half-hour's hike from Hipalau Camp, grand views of the canyon reward the perseverance of hikers. A stake on the right is labeled '2¼', which is the approximate distance from the official Na Ala Hele trail sign north of Kaluaha'ulu Camp. Entering a deep forest corridor, the path drags through spider webs, hops across a little stream and passes a circular stone enclosure near the 2.5-mile marker stake. In just another 0.5 miles the trail empties out at Lonomea Camp. However, the most rewarding views come just before the end of the trail by the emergency helipad, a grassy area that's perfect for picnicking (no camping) or simply gazing at the river and a small waterfall. When ready, retrace your steps back to the Na Ala Hele trailhead sign, then the first river crossing and Wiliwili Camp.

Waimea Canyon Trail

A third trail in this area is the 8-mile Waimea Canyon Trail, which runs south from Wiliwili Camp to the town of Waimea, ending on Menehune Rd. But it's not recommended. Much of the trail is along a 4WD road that leads to a hydroelectric power station, and it's not particularly scenic. Further, there are numerous river crossings that are frequently impassable.

Sleeping

All four camps on the canyon trails are part of the forest reserve system. Although they have simple open-air shelters, there are no facilities, and the stream water needs to be treated before drinking. See p217 for camping permit information.

KOKE'E STATE PARK

Sprawling Koke'e State Park is the starting point for almost 50 miles of outstanding hiking trails. Here, you'll see terrain unlike that found anywhere else on the island, including the largest concentration of extant native bird species in Hawaii. Remote Alaka'i Swamp in particular is a unique view of Kaua'i's native ecosystem; not only is the swamp inhospitable to exotic species, but due to its high elevation, it is one of the few places across Hawaii where mosquitoes, which transmit avian diseases, do not flourish.

Ancient Hawaiians never established a permanent village in these chilly highlands

---

INVASION OF THE ALIEN SPECIES

Strolling through Koke'e State Park and its surrounding forest-reserve land, you're bound the admire the verdant foliage. Unfortunately, few of them are native – and some of these aliens are threatening to overwhelm the ecosystem. You are sure to see the following noxious weeds on Kaua'i:

- Kalihi ginger: in the 19th century, Chinese immigrants introduced this hardy species with long broad leaves and fragrant 6in to 18in spikes of yellow blossoms as an ornamental. Native to the Himalayas, its creeping growth patterns can overtake forest undercover.
- Waiawi (strawberry guava): introduced to Hawaii in the early 1800s from tropical America, this prolific pest, obvious by its small red fruit, forms dense thickets in pastures and forests and provides a food source for fruit flies, which cause untold damage to Hawaii's agriculture.
- Fayatree: introduced by the Portuguese immigrants around 1900 as an ornamental and for making wine, this small tree forms dense stands in forest and pastures. This nitrogen-fixing plant rapidly colonizes nitrogen-poor volcanic soils, thus shading out native vegetation.

The Department of Land and Natural Resources, Division of Forestry & Wildlife is actively fighting to preserve native species by destroying the weeds, finding rare seeds, planting them in nurseries, reintroducing them to their natural habitat and informing and instructing the public about the problem.

You can help the fight against interloping weeds as a volunteer or intern with the Koke'e Resource Conservation Program (p228) – and simply by cleaning your shoes before entering pristine park land.

For more on invasive species, see www.state.hi.us/dlnr/dofaw/hortweeds.

and came mainly to collect feathers from forest birds and to cut koa trees for canoes. But an extraordinarily steep ancient Hawaiian trail once ran down the cliffs from Koke'e (pronounced ko-*keh*-eh) to Kalalau Valley on the Na Pali Coast. But today the park's only paved road terminates at the Kalalau Lookout, a coastal overlook among the most breathtaking across the Hawaiian islands. Many of the state park's trails also enjoy excellent vantage points into Kalalau Valley and even more isolated valleys along the Na Pali Coast. Note that some trails are maintained by the Division of State Parks and some by the Division of Forestry & Wildlife; contact the right division regarding permits and general information.

Visitors often assume that Waimea Canyon and Koke'e State Parks are completely separate, but they are actually contiguous. Large tour buses go only as far as the Waimea Canyon lookout point, so Koke'e State Park, and especially the hiking trails on forest-reserve land, is relatively uncrowded. Interestingly, you will see few locals here; they might come to hunt, fish, gather plants for hula performances or pick plums in season, but rarely do they come for the hiking and sightseeing that attract the rest of the world.

Orientation & Information

This park's boundary starts beyond the Pu'u Hinahina Lookout. After the 15-mile marker, you'll pass park cabins, Koke'e Lodge, a museum and a campground one after the other. (By the way, Koke'e Lodge is not an overnight lodge but a restaurant and concessionaire station for the nearby cabins.)

The helpful people at the Koke'e Museum sell inexpensive trail maps and provide basic information on trail conditions; you can also call them for real-time **mountain weather reports** (☎ 335-9975).

If you're staying in the cabins or camping, be sure to bring ample provisions, as the nearest stores (and gas) are in Waimea, 15 miles away.

Dangers & Annoyances

All of the suggestions listed for Waimea Canyon State Park (p200) apply. Further, the higher elevation produces a cooler and wetter climate, so bring rain gear and a

fleece or wool sweater. Consider bringing a dry change of clothing and shoes to leave in your car. Then, after a muddy hike, you can stuff your wet items in a plastic bag to avoid permanently staining everything with Kaua'i's famous red dirt. Another threat are ground hornets, which sometimes attack humans. They are disturbed by vibrations of footsteps. If they swarm, you must run and guard your hair, where they gravitate during an attack.

Sights
KOKE'E NATURAL HISTORY MUSEUM

A good place to learn about Kaua'i's ecology is this **museum** (☎ 335-9975; www.kokee .org; donation $1; 🕙 10am-4pm), which features displays of local flora, fauna, climate and geology, along with detailed topographical maps of the area, and a glass case of poi pounders, stone adze heads and other historic artifacts. Some good-quality handicrafts, and an extensive selection of books heavy on Hawaiiana, flora, fauna, culture and history, are for sale.

Ask at the museum for the brochure to the short **nature trail** out back. The brochure, which can be borrowed free or purchased for $1.50, offers interpretive information corresponding to the trail's numbered plants and trees, many of them native Hawaiian species.

The chickens that congregate in the museum's parking lot are not the common garden variety but *moa* (red junglefowl). Early Polynesian settlers brought *moa* to Hawaii, and they were once common on all the main islands. Now the *moa* remain solely on Kaua'i, the only island that's free of the mongoose, an introduced mammal that preys on the eggs of ground-nesting birds.

KALALAU LOOKOUTS

The Kalalau Valley lookouts, two spectacular coastal viewpoints at the northern end of the road beyond the lodge and museum, are not to be missed. The views are among the most breathtaking in all Hawaii – when not obscured by mist.

The first, **Kalalau Lookout**, is at the 18-mile marker. From a height of 4000ft, you can look deep into the green depths of the valley and straight out to sea. When the weather is cooperative, late-afternoon rainbows sweep so deeply into Kalalau Valley that the bottom part of the bows curve back inward. Bright-red 'apapane birds feed from the flowers of the ohia lehua trees near the lookout railings.

Kalalau Valley was once the site of a large settlement and was joined to Koke'e by a very steep trail that ran down the cliffs. Today the only way into the valley is along the coastal Kalalau Trail (p156) from Ha'ena on the North Shore or by kayak (p144). One legend says that rain has sculpted the cliffs into the shapes of the proud chiefs who are buried in the mountains; the cone-shaped pinnacles along the valley walls do look rather like a row of sentinels standing to attention.

The paved road continues another mile to **Pu'u o Kila Lookout**, where it dead-ends at a parking lot. At the time of research, this last stretch of road was closed to vehicular traffic – so you must walk a mile to the lookout. This is actually the last leg of the aborted Koke'e–Ha'ena Hwy, which would have linked Koke'e with the North Shore, thus creating a circle-island road. One look at the cliffs at road's end, and you'll understand why the scheme was scrapped. The Pihea Trail that climbs the ridge straight ahead runs along what was to be the road.

From this lookout, you can enjoy another grand view into Kalalau Valley and a glance inland toward the Alaka'i Wilderness Preserve. A sign here points to Mt Wai'ale'ale, the wettest spot on earth.

Activities
HIKING
Almost 50 miles of hiking trails offer varied terrain for all fitness levels. Generally the toughest trails are those with the steepest changes in elevation. Be aware that pig, deer and goat hunters use some of these trails, so you might want to bust out your garish orange jacket. The camping sites here are strewn with the detritus of ignorant, lazy or disrespectful users (in this case that includes hunters). Please take your trash with you.

The starting point for several scenic hikes, Halemanu Rd is just north of the 14-mile marker on Waimea Canyon Dr. Whether or not the road is passable in a non-4WD vehicle usually depends on re-

cent rainfall. The wet, clay roads here make for a skid fest, providing no traction when wet, so even if you can drive in, if it starts raining, you might not be able to get out. Thus, if you're without a 4WD, park on the west shoulder of Waimea Canyon Dr, opposite Halemanu Rd, and walk the 0.8 miles down.

During summer weekends, trained volunteers lead **Wonder Walks** (from June to September, nominal donation), which are guided hikes on various trails at Waimea Canyon and Koke'e State Parks. Contact the **museum** (☎ 335-9975; www.kokee.org) for schedules and reservations.

Cliff & Canyon Trails
The first of the hikes off Halemanu Rd is the **Cliff Trail** (0.1 miles), a short, simple walk that ends at an overlook peering into Waimea Canyon. From there, you can continue on the **Canyon Trail** (1.8 miles), a steep, but not terribly strenuous 1.75 miles one way that follows the canyon rim, passes Waipo'o Falls and ends at **Kumuwela Lookout**, with views down the canyon to the ocean beyond.

Starting from the highway, walk down Halemanu Rd for just over 0.5 miles, passing under some koa trees, until reaching a well-signed junction. Veer to the right and continue to the next fork in the road, keeping Halemanu Stream on the left and ignoring a hunting trail-of-use on the right. Leave the road by turning right onto the footpath that's signposted for both the Cliff and Canyon Trails.

At the next trail junction, the Cliff Trail takes off to the right and wanders for less than 0.25 miles uphill to the **Cliff Viewpoint**; at the far end of the green-painted guardrails are the very best, and windiest, views of the canyon. There's a good chance of spotting feral goats scrambling along the canyon walls.

When you're ready, backtrack to the previous junction and turn right onto the Canyon Trail, which now descends though more koa and blackberry plants and through a gully beside an old irrigation ditch, which was once used to supply sugarcane fields in the canyon far below. It's easy to miss the obscure junction with the Black Pipe Trail, past which the Canyon Trail keeps descending past 'iliahi (Ha-

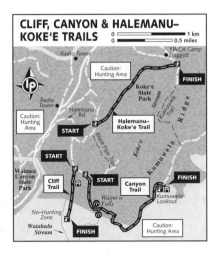

waiian sandalwood) to the edge of Waimea Canyon.

The trail then runs parallel to the canyon rim over some very eroded, bare sections of rock and red soil. Strong winds seem to threaten to blow the wildlife right over the canyon walls, so be sure to anchor every step you take carefully. Views are tremendous from this point, but don't venture too close to the walls, as the soil is not entirely stable.

Just shy of the one-hour point, the Canyon Trail veers away from the rim into another gulch en route to the 800ft **Waipo'o Falls**. A sign may still be standing, identifying 'Falls No 1', also called 'Ginger Pool' for obvious reasons. Further along is 'Falls No 2' and it may be tricky to cross, as Koke'e Stream plummets over the canyon walls here. If the water levels and speed look menacing, turn around here.

Otherwise, after hopping boulders across the stream, the trail clambers onto Kumuwela Ridge and has a reunion with the canyon rim for more breathtaking views. The trail ends at **Kumuwela Lookout**, where there's a picnic table from which to take it all in before turning around and backtracking to Halemanu Rd.

Those who can't stand backtracking the entire way can detour onto the Black Pipe Trail from the start of the Canyon Trail for a gentle rolling 0.5-mile walk through *iliau* plants and other native vegetation. This trail eventually empties out onto Halemanu Rd. After turning left, it's less than a mile's walk back up the dirt road to the highway.

Halemanu-Koke'e Trail

Another trail off Halemanu Rd, which starts farther down the road than the Cliff and Canyon Trails is Halemanu-Koke'e Trail (1.25 miles). An easy recreational nature trail, it passes through a native forest of koa and ohia trees that provide a habitat for native birds, including the 'i'iwi, 'apapane, 'amakihi and 'elepaio. One of the common plants found on this trail is banana *poka*, a member of the passion-fruit family and a serious invasive pest. It has pretty pink flowers, but it drapes the forest with its vines and chokes out less-aggressive native plants. The trail ends near YWCA Camp Sloggett, about 0.5 miles from Koke'e Lodge.

Awa'awapuhi & Nu'alolo Trails

The Awa'awapuhi Trail (3.25 miles) and the Nu'alolo Trail (3.75 miles) each traverses the edges of sheer 2000ft cliffs, allowing you a bird's-eye view into valleys otherwise accessible only by boat. These trails connect via the **Nu'alolo Cliffs Trail** (2 miles), also very scenic, but which, as numerous warning signs point out, contains nervewrackingly narrow and washed-out stretches, right along precipices thousands of feet below. Not recommended for acrophobics! The Nu'alolo Cliffs Trail connects the Nu'alolo Trail near the 3.25-mile mark and to the Awa'awapuhi Trail just a little short of the 3-mile mark.

If you're undecided as to which trail to take, Awa'awapuhi Trail is recommended because the Nu'alolo Trail is steeper and, especially when muddy, ascending it can be rather treacherous. Also, if you are a solo hiker, you'll encounter more traffic on this trail – which is preferable for safety. The views of Nu'alolo Valley clear to the Pacific Ocean are outstanding on both of these trails.

If you're up for a hardcore day hike of all three trails, do the Nu'alolo Trail first to avoid its merciless ascent, especially near the top. Also, if you start on the Nu'alolo Trail, your car will be parked 2 miles downhill (rather than uphill) at the Nu'alolo Trail trailhead.

WESTSIDE

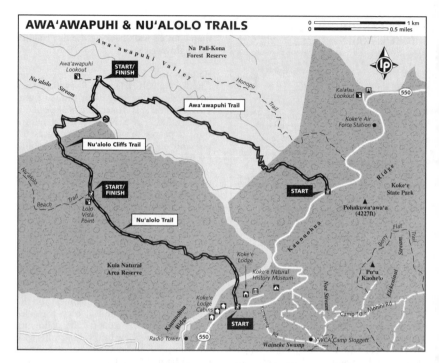

Prolific wild goats are readily spotted along the cliff walls. Capable of breeding at five months of age, the goats have no natural predators in Hawaii, and their unchecked numbers have caused a fair amount of ecological damage.

The trailhead for the Awa'awapuhi Trail begins at a parking area that lies just after the 17-mile marker. The trail starts atop Kaunuohua Ridge, descending in an ohia forest. About 0.5 miles down, the forest becomes drier, and koa mixes in with the ohia. The path widens out, becoming very muddy in spots, and gains partial ocean views around the 1.5-mile marker. If weather conditions at the trailhead were foggy or rainy, there's a chance of walking out from underneath the clouds and escaping the weather soon. Some viewpoints look *makai* into lush valleys over Honopu Ridge, with the sharply eroded *pali* (cliff) dropping away below the trail.

Before the 2-mile marker, the trail dries out and curves around the ridge past rocks and low-lying shrubs, including *a'ali'i* with sticky foliage and *pukiawe* berries. Shade cover is intermittent here, revealing on the left steep *pali* covered with red dirt and segments of the narrow Nu'alolo Cliffs Trail snaking out among them. Shortly after the 2.5-mile marker you'll find a jaw-dropping **viewpoint** right at the level of the clouds, with hardly anything to distinguish between the blue of the sky and the ocean on sunny days. Choppers can often be heard overhead.

From there the trail turns left and cuts back into the forest, becoming overgrown in some parts. Be careful of steep drop-offs as the trail runs right along the side of a ridge. At the next trail junction, a little short of the 3-mile mark, the Nu'alolo Cliffs Trail comes in on the left. Although the painted arrows may be misleading, turn right here to reach the vista point, **Awa'awapuhi Lookout**, in just another 0.25 miles. The views into Awa'awapuhi Valley straight ahead, and Nu'alolo Valley off to the left, are indescribable. State officials warn thrill-seekers not to venture past the guardrails as the high winds and unstable soil are extremely perilous. If you slip, the drop is 2000ft. When ready, walk back to the trail junction and return the way you came.

To complete the entire three-trail trek, start on the Nu'alolo Trail between the cabins and Koke'e Lodge, off Waimea Canyon Dr. The trail begins in cool upland forest (where you'll see banana *poka* and redwoods), and descends 1500ft, ending after a badly eroded stretch with a fine view from **Lolo Vista Point**, a lookout on the valley rim. There's a USGS survey marker at the lookout, at an elevation of 2234ft. After turning onto the Nu'alolo Cliffs Trail, hikers contour above the valley for less than 2 miles, passing the waterfall, to the place where the trail meets the Awa'awapuhi Trail at a junction just uphill from the lookout.

Pihea Trail to Alaka'i Swamp Trail

The Alaka'i Swamp Trail (3.5 miles) and the Pihea Trail (3.75 miles) are often hiked in conjunction because they cross paths – thus allowing you to traverse parts of both. Most hikers start on the Pihea Trail because the trailhead is accessible by the paved road to **Pu'u o Kila Lookout** (p207); at the time of research, the road was closed to vehicular traffic after the Kalalau Lookout, so hikers must walk an extra mile to the trailhead. The alternate Alaka'i Swamp Trail starting point is discussed later. The trails are well-maintained, with mile markers and signs.

The Pihea Trail trailhead is just beyond the lookout. The first mile of the trail runs along the ridge, offering fine views into Kalalau Valley, before coming to the small fork for **Pihea Vista**, a viewpoint that requires a steep scramble to reach. The Pihea Trail then turns inland through wetland forest and, at about 1.75 miles, arrives at aptly named **Alaka'i Crossing**. At this fairy-tale crossroads deep in the misty forest, four boardwalks intersect and lead to opposite directions.

Taking a hard left, the trail continues for 2 miles through rain forest and exposed bogs filled with ferns, perfectly blossoming ohia and old telephone poles before reaching **Kilohana Lookout**, perched on the rim of Wainiha Pali.

While most of the swamp trail has been spanned with boardwalks, it can still be extremely wet and slippery; in places you can expect to slog through mud and even rock-hop across a stream before reaching the lookout, which is the turn-around point for this trip. The stretch between Alaka'i Crossing and Kilohana Lookout includes hundreds of steps, which can be hell on your knees.

THE OTHERWORLDLY ALAKA'I SWAMP

The swamp is a unique ecosystem, where you'll see dwarf trees and mossy undergrowth amid a series of misty bogs. Here and there toppled trees show a massive network of roots, spreading horizontally as the hard-packed soil prevents them from penetrating more than a foot or so deep. The flora is subdued rather than flashy and includes many natives, from *ohia lehua* (tree with orange-red flowers) to *mokihana* (vinelike tree with green berries) to *maile* (vine with aromatic leaves and bark).

In the swamp there are 10 times more native birds than introduced birds. (Elsewhere in Hawaii, introduced birds outnumber natives many times over.) Many of these species are endangered, some having fewer than 100 birds remaining. The Kaua'i *'o'o*, the last of four species of Hawaiian honeyeaters, was thought to be extinct until a nest with two chicks was discovered in Alaka'i Swamp in 1971. However, the call of the *'o'o* – that of a single male – was last heard in 1987.

You'll notice that the trail is virtually completely spanned with wood planks. It was not created to be 'nice' but rather because the trail was previously so muddy that hikers would often go off-trail to find stable footing. This created multiple trails in place of just one, thus hikers trampled more ground and caused more environmental harm. The Department of Land & Natural Resources, Forestry & Wildlife Division, started laying planks around 1989 to preserve the swamp. It was a time-consuming (and crazy, according to some) process that got delayed when Hurricane 'Iniki hit in 1992. Today the project continues, with a plan to cover more of the Pihea Trail.

Alaka'i Swamp Trail to Pihea Trail

If your vehicle has 4WD, you can start at the Alaka'i Swamp trailhead, located on Camp 10-Mohihi Rd, which is up past the Koke'e Museum on the right. If you drive an ordinary car on this rutted dirt road, you're asking for trouble, especially in wet weather.

Starting on the Alaka'i Swamp Trail means you can avoid the most strenuous, muddy parts of the Pihea Trail, substituting a gentle stroll on a grassy ridge and then over boardwalks through the swamp to Alaka'i Crossing.

From here continue straight (heading east) to Kilohana Lookout. On the return from the lookout, you can either retrace your steps or detour at Alaka'i Crossing onto either the Pihea Trail by turning left and hiking to Kawaikoi Camp. From here you must walk back up Mohihi Road to retrieve your vehicle at the Alaka'i Swamp trailhead. This combination of trails lets you experience the swamp and the unusual boardwalk trail and then hike on a dirt path that borders and crosses Kawaikoi Stream.

Kawaikoi Stream Trail

A scenic mountain stream trail, the Kawaikoi Stream Trail (1.7 miles) begins between the Sugi Grove and Kawaikoi campgrounds, off Camp 10-Mohihi Rd. It starts out following the southern side of Kawaikoi Stream, then heads away from the stream and makes a loop, coming down the northern side of the stream before reconnecting with the southern side. If the stream is running high, don't make the crossing.

Kawaikoi Stream is popular for rainbow-trout fishing, which is allowed during an annual open season in August and September. Fishing licenses (p61) are required.

Courses

Koke'e Natural History Museum (☎ 335-9975; www .kokee.org) offers basket-weaving workshops ($15) using plants such as banana *poka* and black wattle. Call the museum to register.

Festivals & Events

Hula *halau* (troops) from all over Hawaii participate in the **Annual Eo e Emalani I Alaka'i** (☎ 335-9975; www.aloha.net/~kokee; admission free;

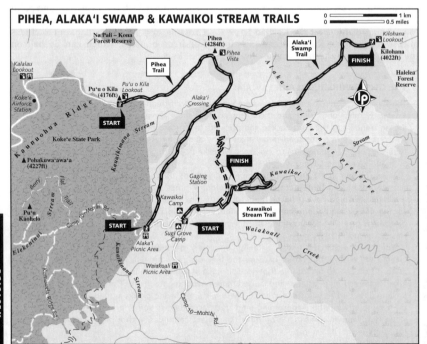

PIHEA, ALAKA'I SWAMP & KAWAIKOI STREAM TRAILS

CAMPING IN KOKE'E STATE PARK

Koke'e campgrounds are at an elevation of almost 4000ft, so nights are chilly. Take a sleeping bag and warm clothing. See p217 for details on all camping options below.

The most accessible camping area is the Koke'e State Park Campground, which is north of the meadow, just a few minutes' walk from Koke'e Lodge. The campsites sit in an uncrowded grassy area beside the woods, along with picnic tables, drinking water, rest rooms and showers. The permit costs $5 from the Division of State Parks.

Further off the main track, Kawaikoi and Sugi Grove campgrounds are about 4 miles east of Koke'e Lodge, off the 4WD Camp 10-Mohihi Rd in the forest reserve adjacent to the state park. Each campground has pit toilets, picnic shelters and fire pits. But there's no water source, so you'll need to bring your own or treat the stream water. These forest-reserve campgrounds have a three-night maximum stay and require camping permits (free) in advance from the Division of Forestry and Wildlife.

The Kawaikoi campground sits on a well-maintained 3.5-acre grassy field, and it is recommended if you are camping in a large group (ie 10 or more). The Sugi Grove site is picturesque, under Sugi trees (commonly called a pine but actually a cedar), a fragrant softwood native to Japan. This site is shaded, making it ideal during hot summer months, and it is closer to Kawaikoi stream.

10am), an outdoor dance festival at the Koke'e Natural History Museum in early October, which re-enacts the historic 1871 journey of Queen Emma, accompanied by a group of 100, to see the spectacular views from Koke'e toward the Kalalau Valley and beyond. The festival includes a royal procession, hula, music and crafts.

Sleeping

Koke'e Lodge (☎ 335-6061; PO Box 819, Waimea, HI 96796; cabins $35-45) The 12 cabins in Koke'e State Park are managed by the lodge, which is actually a restaurant. The bargain oldest cabins are studios with just one large room. Newer are the two-bedroom cedar cabins. Each cabin, old and new, has one double and four twin beds, and a kitchen with a refrigerator and oven, as well as linens, blankets, shower and wood stove. Of the newer cedar cabins, No 2 Lehua is particularly comfortable and includes a wheelchair ramp. State park rules limit stays to five days. The cabins are often booked up well in advance, but cancellations do occur, and you can occasionally snag a cabin at the last moment.

YWCA Camp Sloggett (☎ 245-5959; www.camping kauai.com; campsites per person $10, bunk beds $20, 1-bedroom cabins $65) Right in Koke'e State Park, the Y has a one-bedroom cottage, a bunkhouse that holds 40 and a cement-slab platform for tent camping. Guests must provide their own linens for the bunkhouse, but there are bathrooms with hot showers and a kitchenette. Tent campers can use a barbecue pit for cooking and showers and toilets in the bunkhouse. No reservations are needed for the bunkhouse and tent sites, but the cabin (which sleeps two) has a two-night minimum stay and requires a reservation. It also has a lodge that sleeps 10, which could work for groups or families. Camp Sloggett is about 0.5 miles east of the park museum down a rutted dirt road passable by standard cars, except when muddy.

Eating

Koke'e Lodge (☎ 335-6061; snacks $3-7; 9am-3:30pm) This is the only place to eat north of Waimea. It serves smoked-salmon quiche, granola and other breakfast fare all day long, plus hearty soups (try the Portuguese bean soup), sandwiches and interesting salads, like the Moroccan sampler with couscous, hummus and Mediterranean veggies. The attached gift shop (open 9am to 4pm), sells candy bars, potato chips and a few canned goods.

WESTSIDE

NI'IHAU

Long closed to outsiders, the island of Ni'ihau has spurned change much more than any other place in Hawaii. Due to its unusual inaccessibility, no other island so captivates the imagination as this social experiment dating back to the 1860s.

History

Captain Cook anchored off Ni'ihau on January 29, 1778, two weeks after 'discovering' Hawaii. Cook noted in his log that the island was lightly populated and largely barren – a description still true today. His visit was short, but it had a lasting impact. It was on little Ni'ihau that Cook introduced two things that would quickly change the face of Hawaii. He left two goats, the first of the grazing animals that would devastate the islands' native flora and fauna. And his men introduced syphilis, the first of several Western diseases that would strike the Hawaiian people.

In 1864 Elizabeth Sinclair, a Scottish widow who was moving from New Zealand to Vancouver when she got sidetracked in Hawaii, bought Ni'ihau from King Kamehameha V for $10,000 in gold. He originally tried to sell her the 'swampland' of Waikiki, but she passed it up for the 'desert island.' Interestingly, no two places in Hawaii today could be further apart, either culturally or in land value. Mrs Sinclair brought the first sheep to Ni'ihau from New Zealand and started the ranching operation that her great-grandsons continue today.

Lifestyle & Culture

Today Ni'ihau is a Native Hawaiian preserve and the only island where the primary language is still Hawaiian. It has no paved roads, no airport and no islandwide electricity. The entire island, right down to the church, belongs to the Ni'ihau Ranch, which is privately owned by the non-Hawaiian Robinson family. The Robinsons are highly protective of Ni'ihau's isolation and its people. They provide shelter, food staples and medical care, plus higher education for residents, in a privatized sort of socialism.

Most of Ni'ihau's 250 residents live in Pu'uwai (meaning 'heart' in Hawaiian), a settlement on the dry western coast. Each house in the village is surrounded by a stone wall to keep grazing animals out of the gardens. It's a simple life; water is collected in catchments, and the toilets are in outhouses.

Ni'ihauans speak their own melodic Hawaiian dialect. Business is conducted in Hawaiian, as are Sunday church services. The two Robinson brothers who manage the ranch speak Hawaiian fluently. Ni'ihau has a two-room schoolhouse where three teachers hold classes from kindergarten through 12th grade for the island's 50 students. Although courses are taught solely in Hawaiian up to the fourth grade, students learn English as a second language.

Environment

Ni'ihau is the smallest of the inhabited Hawaiian Islands, with a total land area of 70 sq miles and 45 miles of coast. The island is semiarid, lying in the lee of Kaua'i. Ni'ihau's 860-acre Halalii Lake is the largest in Hawaii, though even during the rainy winter season, it's only a few feet deep. In summer, it sometimes dries up to a mud pond.

Of the approximately 50 Hawaiian monk seals that reside in the populated Hawaiian Islands, more than 30 live on Ni'ihau. About half of all Hawaii's endangered 'alae ke'oke'o (coots) breed on Ni'ihau. Introduced creatures also proliferate: the island has an estimated 6000 feral pigs, as well as wild sheep, goats and turkeys. Many of these animals are now hunted on guided expeditions run by Gay & Robinson tours.

Ni'ihau shells – lustrous, colorful and delicate sea jewels strung into exquisite and coveted lei costing anywhere from $125 to $25,000 – are unique to this small island; in late 2004, protective legislation was before the governor so that only items made of 100% Ni'ihau shells and crafted entirely in Hawaii could carry the Ni'ihau label.

Economy & Politics

The island economy has long depended on sheep and cattle ranching, which has always been a marginal operation on windswept Ni'ihau. Major droughts in recent decades have taken a toll on the herds, and consequently the place has been through some hard times. Ni'ihau rainfall averages a scant 12in annually.

Ranch activities, which once provided most of the work on Ni'ihau, are no longer commercially viable. Consequently, the Robinsons have been looking toward the federal government as a potential source of income and employment. For several years Ni'ihau has leased sites to the government that are used for the placement of unmanned radars linked to missile-tracking facilities on Kaua'i.

In addition, since 1999, military special operations forces have staged periodic training maneuvers on Ni'ihau, using the uninhabited southern end of the island. The operations are small-scale, typically with teams of a dozen soldiers practicing a mock rescue operation or the like. There are ongoing negotiations to increase the military presence on Ni'ihau as part of the testing program for new US weapons technology. The hope is that the military, as a secretive tenant, won't interfere with the rest of Ni'ihau's affairs.

Ni'ihau is 17 miles from Kaua'i and is connected by a weekly supply boat that travels between the two islands. The boat docks in Kaua'i at Kaumakani, headquarters of Ni'ihau Ranch and the Robinson family. Kaumakani is also home to a settlement of Ni'ihauans who prefer to live on Kaua'i, though many of them still work for the Robinsons. Politically, Ni'ihau falls under the jurisdiction of Kaua'i county.

Snapshot: Ni'ihau Today

Ni'ihau is by no means a living-history museum of Hawaiians stuck in time. Although it's got a foot in the past, it takes what it wants from the present. The supply boat brings soda pop as well as poi (fermented taro), and the island has more dirt bikes than outrigger canoes. Ni'ihau residents are free to go to Kaua'i to shop, down a few beers (Ni'ihau itself is dry) or just hang out. But they cannot bring friends from other islands back home with them. Those Ni'ihauans who marry people from other islands, as well as those whom the Robinsons come to see as undesirable, are rarely allowed to return.

Still, for the most part, Ni'ihauans accept that that's the way things are. Some of those who leave are critical, but those who stay don't appear to be looking for any changes. To outsiders, Ni'ihau is an enigma. Some romanticize it as a pristine preserve of Hawaiian culture, while others see it as a throwback to feudalism. The Robinsons view Ni'ihau as a private sanctuary and themselves as its protectors. It's that kind of paternalism that often rubs outside Native Hawaiian groups the wrong way, though for the most part Ni'ihauans don't seem to share those sentiments, and they resist outside interference.

Visiting Ni'ihau

Although outsiders are not allowed to visit Ni'ihau, the Robinsons have 'opened up' the island – at least to a degree – via expensive helicopter flights and hunting excursions. Either of the following trips can be arranged through **Gay & Robinson** (☎ 335-2824; www.gandrtours-kauai.com; 2 Kaumakani, Kauai):

Ni'ihau Helicopters (per person $325) Has no set schedule; tours should be arranged well in advance. Half-day tours take off from Burns Field on Kaua'i. The helicopter – an Agusta 109A, not one of the big-window type of choppers used on other aerial tours – makes a stop at a beach (location depends on weather), where lunch is provided and the snorkeling is revelatory. The pilot flies over much of Ni'ihau but avoids the population center of Pu'uwai village.

Ni'ihau Safaris (per hunter/observer $1810/400) Provides everything you'll need (rifle, license, transportation, guide and preparation and shipping of trophies) to hunt Polynesian boar and feral sheep mostly, but also wild eland, Barbary sheep and wild oryx. Organizers promote this as 'useful harvesting of game' and obey norms of free-chase hunting.

You can also scuba dive the waters around Ni'ihau (but cannot set foot on the island) with several dive operators on Kaua'i; a typical three-tank dive costs around $280. See p59 for more information.

Directory

CONTENTS

ACCOMMODATIONS

Kaua'i accommodations run the gamut, but condos are most prevalent. Our reviews indicate rates for single occupancy (s), double (d), triple (tr) or simply the room (r), when there's no difference in the rate for one or two people. A double room in our budget category costs up to $80; midrange doubles cost $80 to $200; top-end rooms exceed $200. Reviews are listed by price, from lowest to highest within each category.

Unless otherwise noted, breakfast is *not* included, bathrooms are private and all lodging is open year-round; our rates don't include taxes of 11.41%. Smoking is generally prohibited indoors. A reservation guarantees your room, but most reservations require a deposit, after which, if you change your mind, the establishment will refund your money only if your room can be rebooked within a certain period. Note the cancellation policies and other restrictions before making a deposit.

Rates often vary by occupancy and/or by season (high season generally runs from mid-December to mid-April). Rates might jump even more around Christmas and the New Year. Other holidays and special occasions also command premium prices, and the best accommodations are booked well in advance. Off-season, rates are cheaper, except at family-friendly places during summer vacation. Occasionally rates fluctuate depending on weekday or weekend stays. Never pay rack rates at hotels and condos without first checking online for ongoing Internet deals.

Timeshares are not covered in this book, as only owners can use or transfer their vacation period. The timeshare market is burgeoning and you're likely to encounter offers to hear a no-obligation pitch in exchange for discounts and other bonuses. Owning a timeshare means basically that you own an annual vacation period (typically a week or two) at a particular complex. Your vacation period might be floating (variable dates each year) or fixed (same dates each year). You can use your vacation period yourself, rent it through the management company, gift it to someone or exchange it for a week elsewhere.

For an explanation of the icons used in this book, see Quick Reference on the inside front cover.

B&Bs, Inns & Vacation Homes

Residential accommodations include traditional B&Bs (room and breakfast); inns (larger rooms or suites in owner-occupied homes) and vacation homes (ranging from cute cottages to posh mansions). The number of residential accommodations is burgeoning, and in places like Wailua Homesteads,

Hanalei and 'Anini, many homes are now geared toward vacationers.

True to their name, B&Bs offer continental or full breakfasts, or provide food for guests to prepare on their own. If you're traveling with kids, note that some B&Bs do not accept children as guests. Most discourage unannounced drop-ins; for security reasons, a few are not mapped in our book. The cheapest 'in-law' rooms cost around $40, but the average price for B&B and inn rooms start closer to $100, and swanky vacation rentals start at $150. Many require a minimum stay of two or three nights and charge extra for additional guests; weekly discounts often apply. Vacation homes are typically owned by nonoccupant mainlanders, managed by condo agencies (see p173 and p137 for listings) and rent by the week.

A great website for vacation rentals across the islands is **Vacation Rentals By Owner** (www.vrbo.com), which lists hundreds of homes sans any middle man.

Camping & Cabins

Kaua'i offers camping at all levels of 'roughin' it.' Some campgrounds, such as 'Anini Beach Park (p133), are within view of houses; others, such as the campsite in Kalalau Valley (p156), are miles from civilization. For camping supplies and rentals, the best rental sources are Pedal & Paddle and Kayak Kaua'i, both in Hanalei (p144). You can also buy gear from Pedal & Paddle

or from big-box retailers like Kmart and Wal-Mart in Lihu'e.

STATE PARKS

State park campsites can be found at Na Pali Coast State Park (Hanakapi'ai and Kalalau Valleys; p156), Koke'e State Park (p213) and Polihale State Park (p199), while backcountry camping is managed by the Division of Forestry & Wildlife around Waimea Canyon State Park (p206) and Koke'e State Park (p213).

For state park camping, permits are required: Na Pali Coast State Park costs $10 per campsite per night and Koke'e and Polihale cost $5 per campsite per night. Camping is limited to five consecutive nights within a 30-day period (ie you only have five total nights on the entire Kalalau Trail in the Na Pali Coast Park). The Hanakoa Valley campsite along the Kalalau Trail remains closed. You cannot camp for more than two consecutive nights in Hanakapi'ai Valley. Additionally, there are cabins at Koke'e State Park, providing easy access to trailheads.

You can obtain permits in person or by mail from the **Division of State Parks** (Map p78; ☎ 274-3444; www.hawaii.gov/dlnr/dsp; Department of Land & Natural Resources, Division of State Parks, 3060 Eiwa St, Room 306, Lihu'e, HI 96766; ⏰ 8am-3:30pm Mon-Fri) and at state park offices on other islands. Up to five may be listed on each permit, but a picture ID for each person must be shown. You can download the permit application

---

PRACTICALITIES

- Electrical voltage is 110/120V, 60 cycles, as elsewhere in the US.

- Major hotels offer laundry services or coin-operated laundry facilities; condos and vacation-rental homes typically include private washers and dryers. Laundromats are available in most towns and can be found in local *Yellow Pages*.

- Kaua'i's daily newspaper, **The Garden Island** (www.kauaiworld.com), is available islandwide. The website www.islandbreath.org is an online indie publication. Also see the Honolulu dailies: **Honolulu Star-Bulletin** (www.starbulletin.com) and the **Honolulu Advertiser** (www.honoluluadvertiser.com).

- Kaua'i broadcasts from about 11 FM stations and two AM stations; some Honolulu stations are also audible on Kaua'i. All major US TV networks are represented, as well as cable channels featuring locally produced shows and Japanese-language programs.

- Video systems use the NTSC standard, which is not compatible with the PAL system.

- Distances are measured in feet, yards and miles; weights in ounces, pounds and tons; liquid volumes in cups, pints, quarts and gallons.

or send a letter to the office specifying the park(s) at which you want to stay and the dates you wish to stay at each park. Your application must include a photocopy of each camper's ID, with the ID number and birth date. You can apply for a permit as early as a year in advance, and many people do, particularly for Na Pali Coast campsites in summer. So apply for your permits as soon as is practical, and if your plans change once you get the permit, be sure to cancel, as you'll be tying up an empty site and preventing someone else from camping.

For remote backcountry camping in Waimea Canyon, there is no charge. The **Division of Forestry & Wildlife** (Map p78; ☎ 274-3433; www .hawaiitrails.org; Department of Land & Natural Resources, Division of Forestry & Wildlife, 3060 Eiwa St, Rm 306, Lihu'e, HI 96766; ☺ 8am-4pm Mon-Fri) issues free, backcountry camping permits for four sites in Waimea Canyon, two sites (Sugi Grove and Kawaikoi) in the Koke'e State Park area, and the Waialae site near the Alaka'i Wilderness Preserve. This last option, with its high concentration of endangered and native bird populations, is prime turf for birders. Camping is limited to four nights in the canyon, three nights in the Koke'e area and two nights in the Alaka'i Wilderness Preserve within a 30-day period. You can reserve a permit a maximum of 30 days in advance by phone, but you'll still need to collect the permit in person, with proper ID.

COUNTY PARKS
The county maintains seven campgrounds on Kaua'i. Moving clockwise around the island, these are: Ha'ena Beach Park (p152), Hanalei (Black Pot) Beach Park (p144), 'Anini Beach Park (p133), Anahola Beach Park (p122), Hanama'ulu Beach Park (p84), Salt Pond Beach Park (p189) and Lucy Wright Park (p193). The best are the coastal parks at Ha'ena and 'Anini, which is particularly secluded and idyllic. The parks at Anahola and Hanama'ulu tend to attract a rougher, shadier crowd and are not recommended for solo or female campers.

Camping permits cost $3 per night per adult camper (children under 18 free) and can be applied for six consecutive nights, for a total of 60 nights in a calendar year.

Each campground is closed one day a week for cleaning and for preventing permanent squatting. Ha'ena Beach Park and

Lucy Wright Park are closed Monday; 'Anini Beach Park and Salt Pond Beach Park are closed Tuesday; Hanama'ulu Beach Park is closed Wednesday; and Anahola Beach Park is closed Thursday. Hanalei (Black Pot) Beach Park is open only on weekends and holidays. All county campgrounds have showers and toilets, and most have covered picnic pavilions and barbecue grills.

Like most things on Kaua'i, enforcement of permit compliance is laid-back. If you just set up camp and pay the rangers when they come around, it will cost $5 per person. Of course, if you're caught without a permit, they *can* ask you to move. Permits are issued in person or by mail (at least one month in advance) at the **Division of Parks & Recreation** (Map p78; ☎ 241-4463; www.kauai.gov; Lihu'e Civic Center, Division of Parks & Recreation, 4444 Rice St, Suite 150, Lihu'e, HI 96766). Permits are issued between 8:15am and 4pm Monday to Friday.

Following are two handy satellite offices that also issue permits:
Kalaheo Neighborhood Center (☎ 332-9770; 4480 Papalina Rd, Kalaheo; ☺ 8:30am-12:30pm Mon-Fri)
Kapa'a Neighborhood Center (☎ 822-1931; 4491 Kou St, Kapa'a; ☺ 8:30am-12:30pm Mon-Fri)

Condos
More spacious than similarly priced hotel rooms, condos are individually owned apartments furnished with kitchen and, often, washer and dryer. They range in quality from upscale to basic, and they're generally economical, especially if you're traveling with a group. Most units have a three- to seven-day minimum stay. The weekly rate is often six times the daily rate and the monthly is three times the weekly. Inquire about cleaning fees, which might be tacked onto your bill.

The problem with condos is their variability, even within the same complex. Unless you request the exact unit you rented the last time, you might find quite different conditions on a subsequent stay. We try not to list condos with huge variation in unit quality, and we include a few reviews of specific units that you can request.

Most condos are rented through agencies, which are listed in the Po'ipu (p173) and Princeville (p137) sections because of the prevalence of condos there. You could surf the Internet and book directly instead of reserving through agencies – and perhaps save a few bucks. But rental agencies can be helpful in emergencies such as plumbing disasters in the middle of the night. Agencies vary greatly, however, in the extent of on-site services they provide; some run the condo like a hotel while others leave you on your own at night.

A jam-packed, if rather overwhelming, resource is **Vacation Rentals By Owner** (www.vrbo.com), which lists scads of condos (and private homes) and lets you bypass agencies.

Hostels

Kaua'i is woefully lacking in the hostel category. A couple exist in Kapa'a but due to consistent user complaints about safety, drugs and cleanliness, they are not included in this book.

Hotels & Resorts

If a vacation is not a vacation without full hotel service, you'll have to choose from the comparatively small number of hotels on Kaua'i. You'll find top-end hotels in Po'ipu and Princeville, midrange options along the Coconut Coast and a handful of motel-level places islandwide. Hotels and resorts almost always undercut their published 'rack rates' (which are the highest rates they charge) to remain as close to capacity as possible. Always book online, where discounts are offered most frequently. Within a particular hotel, the main factor determining room rates is the view and floor. An ocean view can cost 50% to 100% more than a parking-lot view (euphemistically called a 'garden' or 'mountain' view). Resorts are mega hotels that pamper guests with every imaginable amenity, including restaurants, spa, beach, gym and activities, on sprawling, landscaped grounds; they are more prevalent on O'ahu, Maui and the Big Island.

ACTIVITIES

Kaua'i is not a man-made masterpiece but a wonder of nature. Here, a range of outdoor activities are suited for elite athletes and vacation dabblers alike. Most companies offer lessons for beginners, so don't be shy about paddling a kayak or scuba diving for the first time. River kayaking is a virtual industry here, and surfing, the quintessential Hawaiian pastime, is a star attraction.

If you're not into water sports, try whale watching in winter or a sunset catamaran cruise. On dry land, hiking can mean strenuous backpacking to remote valleys and mountaintops, or it can mean walking across paved trails or along scenic coastline. Kaua'i has only nine golf courses, but they include the top-ranked course in the state, plus scenery found nowhere else. In rolling pastureland on the North Shore to seaside cliffs on the South Shore, horseback riding and mountain biking are spectacular.

For further details, see p54 and the destination chapters' Activities sections.

BUSINESS HOURS

While specific hours are given in most individual reviews, the following opening hours are a good rule of thumb:

Banks Open 8:30am to 4pm weekdays; some banks open to 6pm Friday and 9am to noon Saturday.

Bars and clubs Open to midnight daily; some clubs to 2am Friday and Saturday.

Businesses Open 8:30am to 4:30pm Monday to Friday; some post offices open 9am to noon Saturday.

Restaurants Breakfast 6am to 10am; lunch 11:30am to 2pm; dinner 5pm to 9:30pm.

Shops Open 9am to 5pm Monday to Saturday; some also open noon to 5pm Sunday; major shopping areas and malls keep extended hours.

CHILDREN

Kaua'i is perfect for kids, with shallow protected lagoons, colorful gardens, sweet treats and an informal atmosphere. Driving distances are short, minimizing road-trip crankiness. The large hotels often offer cross-cultural opportunities through day camps and workshops on Hawaiian arts and crafts. Still, successful travel with young *keiki* (children) requires planning and effort. Try not to overdo things; even for adults, packing too much into the time available only means exhaustion and overload. Include children in the trip planning; if they've helped to choose where you'll go and what you'll do, they'll more likely be gung ho when you're there. Consult Lonely Planet's *Travel with Children*, which has lots of valuable tips and interesting anecdotes. When the going gets tough, stop for shave ice.

If you're traveling with infants and come up short, **Baby's Away** (☎ 800-996-9030; www.babysaway.com) rents cribs, strollers, playpens, high chairs and more.

For day camp and babysitting options, see p176.

DIRECTORY

Practicalities

Best for families are condos or vacation homes, as they include eat-in kitchens. Also ideal are places with both pool and beach nearby; tiny tots occasionally fear the ocean (even the sound of waves might spook them). Kids are welcome most everywhere, except at a few B&Bs. Children under 17 or 18 often stay free when sharing a room with their parents and using existing bedding, but always confirm. Cots and rollaway beds are usually available (for an additional fee) at hotels and resorts.

Many restaurants have children's menus with significantly lower prices. High chairs are usually available, but it pays to inquire ahead of time. Likewise, sights and activities are often discounted for kids, but applicable age ranges can vary, so inquire beforehand. Ziplining, horseback riding, all-terrain vehicle (ATV) tours and other potentially 'risky' adventures enforce age or height minimums.

Most car-rental companies (see p236) lease child-safety seats (cost per day $8, per week $40 to $45), but they're not always on hand; reserve in advance.

CLIMATE CHARTS

Especially in winter, rain is a given, particularly on the Eastside and the North Shore. Mt Wai'ale'ale (5148ft), almost smack in the middle of the island, is considered the wettest place on earth, averaging 460in of rain annually. The upside is that showers are usually balmy and short-lived (and produce rainbows). Summer is generally drier than winter, but downpours in summer and brilliant sunshine in winter are not uncommon.

Kaua'i's geological and tradewind patterns produce climactic variances across the island: The Westside and South Shore tend to be dry and sunny, while the North Shore and Eastside see regular showers. Of course, the biggest factor is elevation, and you'll notice an increase in precipitation as you head *mauka* (inland).

Since the island is only 33 miles wide and 25 miles from north to south, it's easy to escape to your preferred climate. Temperatures drop at higher elevations (eg at Koke'e State Park) but never to any extremes.

The National Weather Service provides recorded **local weather information** (☎ 245-6001) and **marine forecasts** (☎ 245-3564).

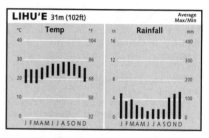

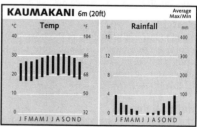

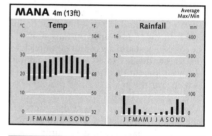

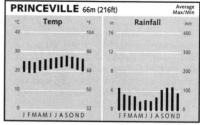

CUSTOMS

Each visitor can bring 1L of liquor and 200 cigarettes duty-free into the US, but you must be at least 21 years old to possess the former and 18 years old to possess the latter. In addition, each traveler is permitted to bring up to $100 worth of gift merchandise into the US without incurring any duty.

Most fresh fruits and plants are restricted from entry into Hawaii, and customs officials are militant. To help prevent the pestilent spread of invasive alien species, it's also important to clean shoes and outdoor gear brought to the island. Because Hawaii is a rabies-free state, the pet quarantine laws are draconian and require a 120-day quarantine, but you can slice the time (and reduce the $1000-plus cost) to five days ($224) if your pet meets specific requirements (see www.hawaiiag.org/aqs/aqsbrochure.pdf). For complete details, contact the **Hawaiian Department of Agriculture** (☎ 808-483-7151; www.hawaiiag.org).

Upon departure at the airport your luggage must pass a pre-flight check for any fruits or plants not inspected for fruit flies. Note that you can leave with agricultural products but they must be properly certified. For details call the **US Department of Agriculture** (☎ 245-2831) at Lihu'e Airport. Commercially packaged items are often precertified.

DANGERS & ANNOYANCES

Tourism is the state's biggest industry by far, thus officials want to ensure that visitors are safe and happy. Concern about visitors' negative experiences in Hawaii has led state officials to establish the **Visitor Aloha Society of Hawaii** (VASH; ☎ 808-926-8274; www.visitoralohasocietyofhawaii.org), an organization providing aid to island visitors who become the victims of accidents or crimes.

Drugs

Since the 1990s the entire state has been coping with a rampant 'ice' (crystal methamphetamine) epidemic and its ensuing crime and social problems. Be on guard for addicts, especially in rural areas. Kaua'i's thriving *pakalolo* (marijuana) industry remains highly profitable, despite years of government crackdowns through Operation Green Harvest, a statewide helicopter-surveillance program launched in the 1980s to eradicate island-grown pot.

Flooding

During heavy rains, rivers overflow and can threaten safety if you are hiking. Never try to ford a river that is high. Cars are also affected by flooding as North Shore bridges are closed if they are flooded during storms. If you are stuck on one side, you will have no choice but to wait it out.

Scams

The main scams directed towards visitors involve the sale of 'Hawaiian' souvenirs actually made in China, Korea, the Philippines and so forth. Such items are commonly seen in tourist-trap shops and small souvenir booths at outdoor bazaars and farmers markets. Don't waste your money on cheap fakes.

Timeshare sales booths are another scam, often disguised as tourist-information centers. Salespeople will offer enticing deals, from free luau shows to sunset cruises, if you'll just hear their 'no obligation' pitch.

Theft & Violence

In relative terms, Kaua'i is very safe. In 2005 there was only one murder (victim and perpetrator were both residents). But like all the Hawaiian Islands, Kaua'i is notorious for break-ins into parked rental cars, whether at a secluded parking area at a trailhead or in a crowded parking lot. Never leave anything valuable in your car. Other than break-ins, most hassles are from addicts and alcoholics. Be tuned in to the vibes at beaches after dark and in places where folks hang out to drink, such as public campgrounds.

Bear in mind, due to the influx of outsiders, there are pockets of resentment against tourists and transplants (people who moved to the island as adults). Remote beaches might be deemed 'locals-only' territory, where you'll see groups picnicking under tarps or a crowd of local surfers; don't horn in without a proper introduction. Also be wary about crossing private property, especially when 'Kapu' (No Trespassing) signs are posted.

Although theft and violence have decreased, campers should be conscious of their surroundings. People traveling alone, especially women, should be particularly cautious (see p228). The less you look like a tourist, the less likely you'll be a target. Choose your park carefully; some are deserted roadside pit stops frequented mostly by troublemakers. Generally, the farther you go from population centers, the less likely you'll be hassled.

Tsunami

Tsunami are generated by earthquakes, typhoons or volcanic eruptions. As evidenced by the Sumatra earthquake and massive

DIRECTORY

tsunami in December 2004, they can be catastrophic. The largest tsunami ever to hit Kaua'i occurred in 1957. At Ha'ena the sea rose 32ft above normal and only four of 29 homes survived, and between 75 and 80 homes were damaged or destroyed along Hanalei Bay and Hanalei River. Today, new homes built in tsunami-prone areas (flood zones) must be built high off the ground.

Hawaii has had a tsunami every 10 years or so over the past century, killing more people statewide than all other natural disasters combined and causing millions of dollars in property damage. If you're in a low-lying coastal area when one occurs, immediately head for higher ground. The front section of the telephone books show maps of areas susceptible to tsunami and safety evacuation zones.

For more on ocean safety, see p55.

DISABLED TRAVELERS

Kaua'i is eager to accommodate all travelers, with hotels offering wheelchair-accessible rooms, elevators and TTD-capable phones, which typically must be requested in advance. But since the island's main attractions are found in nature – from backcountry trails to secluded beaches down rocky paths – disabled travelers will find it hard to navigate beyond the developed areas. Also, Kaua'i is a rural place, so roads are tight and sidewalks rare; many attractions sit alongside highways and thus negotiating the way in a wheelchair can be tricky.

Seeing-eye and guide dogs are not subject to the general quarantine rules for pets, provided they meet the Department of Agriculture's minimum requirements; see www.hawaiiag.org/hdoa/ai_aqs_guidedog.htm for details. All animals must enter the state at Honolulu International Airport.

The **Disability & Communication Access Board** (☎ 586-8121; www.hawaii.gov/health/dcab; 919 Ala Moana Blvd, Rm 101, Honolulu, HI 96814) offers a three-part *Aloha Guide to Accessibility*. Part I contains general information and is obtainable free by mail. Parts II and III ($15) detail beach, park, shopping-center and visitor-attraction accessibility and list hotels with wheelchair access or specially adapted facilities.

Travelers should also pack their disabled parking placard or apply for a new one upon arrival. Online applications are

available at www.hawaii.gov/health/dcab/resources/parking/applications/application.pdf. But the Kaua'i County website strongly recommends bringing one with you (probably because turnaround time here could take the length of your trip).

Wheelchair-accessible transportation must be planned in advance. On Kauai there are no car rental agencies with lift-equipped vehicles. **Gammie HomeCare** (☎ 632-2333; www.gammie.com; 3215 Kuhio Hwy, Lihu'e, HI 96766; ☯ 8:30am-5pm) rents portable ramps, as well as wheelchairs, hospital beds, walking aids and more.

Wheelchair Getaways (☎ 800-638-1912; www.wheelchairgetaways.com; per day/week $110/665) is a nationwide company that rents wheelchair-accessible vans.

On mainland US, the **Society for the Advancement of Travel for the Handicapped** (SATH; ☎ 212-447-7284; www.sath.org; 347 Fifth Ave, Suite 610, New York, NY 10016) publishes a quarterly magazine and has various information sheets on travel for the disabled.

Kaua'i County provides a Landeez all-terrain wheelchair at lifeguard stations at Po'ipu Beach Park (p170), Lydgate Beach Park (p95) and Salt Pond Beach Park (p189). The Landeez chair can traverse sand and navigate close to the water's edge. These parks also offer accessible parking, paths, pavilions, rest rooms and showers. Most hiking trails aren't wheelchair-accessible, but the short path to Kilauea Lighthouse (p128) is paved.

DISCOUNTS

Since Kaua'i is a popular destination for retirees and families, you'll find many discounts for seniors and kids. The applicable senior age is constantly creeping lower so inquire about who's covered. The **American Association of Retired Persons** (AARP; ☎ 888-687-2277; www.aarp.org; Membership Center, 3200 E Carson St, Lakewood, CA 90712), an advocacy group for Americans 50 years of age and older, is a good source for travel bargains.

Students with valid identification often receive discounts for sights and activities. For all travelers, the freebie tourist guides widely distributed around town are full of discount coupons. Some outfits, especially the smaller ones, are flexible with cutting prices; if they like you, you'll receive favorable treatment. But never be pushy and demand a discount – it's not the local way.

EMBASSIES & CONSULATES
US Embassies & Consulates
Australia (☎ 02-6214 5600; 21 Moonah Pl, Yarralumla, Canberra, ACT 2600)
Canada (☎ 613-238 5335; 490 Sussex Dr, Ottawa, Ontario K1N 1G8)
France (☎ 33 1 43 12 22 22; 2 Av Gabriel, 75008 Paris)
Germany (☎ 030-8305 0; Neustädtische Kirchstrasse 4-5, 10117 Berlin)
Ireland (☎ 353 1 668 8777; 42 Elgin Rd, Ballsbridge, Dublin 4)
Italy (☎ 39 06 46741; Via Veneto 119/A, 00187 Rome)
Japan (☎ 03-3224 5000; 10-5, Akasaka 1-chome, Minato-ku, Tokyo)
Netherlands (☎ 070-310 9209; Lange Voorhout 102, 2514 EJ The Hague)
New Zealand (☎ 04-462 6000; 29 Fitzherbert Tce, PO Box 1190, Thorndon, Wellington)
UK (☎ 020-7499 9000; 24/31 Grosvenor Sq, London W1A 1AE)

Embassies & Consulates in Hawaii
All consulates in the state, including those listed below, are located in Honolulu:
Australia (☎ 524-5050; 1000 Bishop St)
Germany (☎ 946-3819; 252 Paoa Pl)
Italy (☎ 531-1277; Suite 201, 735 Bishop St)
Japan (☎ 543-3111; 1742 Nu'uanu Ave)
Netherlands (☎ 531-6897; Suite 702, 745 Fort St Mall)
New Zealand (☎ 547-5117; Suite 414, 900 Richards St)
Philippines (☎ 595-6316; 2433 Pali Hwy)

FESTIVALS & EVENTS
For more information on Kaua'i festivals and events, see www.kauaifestivals.com, and the Festivals & Events sections in regional chapters.

January
New Year New Year's Eve means massive fireworks, from backyard firecrackers and sparklers to extravagant resort displays; many businesses are closed on New Year's Day. For fireworks, head to Po'ipu Beach Park (p173).
Kaua'ian Days (www.kauaiandays.org) Islandwide celebration during mid- to late January highlighting King Kaumuali'i and Kauaian culture, with parade and *ho'olaule'a* celebration (p84), sports events, workshops and more. Most events held in Lihu'e.
E Pili Kakou I Ho'okahi Lahui (Lihu'e; p84)

February
Humpback Whale Awareness Month (www.hawaii humpbackwhale.noaa.gov) All are invited to bring binoculars and learn to spot whales from prime locations. Events, including whale counting and expert lectures, are offered year-round.
Waimea Town Celebration (Waimea; p195)

March
Prince Kuhio Celebration of the Arts (Po'ipu; p173)

April
Spring Gourmet Gala (Lihu'e; p84)

May
Kaua'i Polynesian Festival (Lihu'e; p84)

June
Annual Taste of Hawaii (Wailua; p106)

July
Obon Celebration Islandwide summertime Japanese celebration held in July and August to remember the dead. Includes traditional drumming, group bon dance and delicious food. It's held on different nights (at 8pm) at temples islandwide. Check the *Garden Island* newspaper for a schedule.
Fourth of July Concert in the Sky (Lihu'e; p85)
Koloa Plantation Days Celebration (Koloa; p164)

August
Heiva I Kaua'i Iaorana Tahiti (Kapa'a; p118)
Kaua'i Products Council Craft Fair (Po'ipu; p173)
Kaua'i County Farm Bureau Fair (Lihu'e; p85)
Aloha Festival (☎ in Honolulu 589-1771; www .alohafestivals.com) Originally established in 1946, this Hawaiian cultural celebration now spans two months, from late August to early October, statewide; on Kaua'i, the festival kicks off in late August with presentation of the royal court (p106) in Wailua and continues with a parade and *ho'olaule'a* celebration in Lihu'e (p85), and a rodeo (p173) in Po'ipu. See the website for the full event list and contact phone numbers.

September
Kaua'i Mokihana Festival (☎ 822-2166; www .mokihana.kauai.net) One of Kaua'i's signature festivals, the annual Mokihana Festival in mid- to late September highlights Native Hawaiian culture through a week of events, including a music-composition contest (p85) and hula competition (p173). The festival, which started from a music-composition contest in 1984, is named after the violet *mokihana* flower and green berry grown only on Kaua'i. Venues can vary from year to year, so check the website for details.

October
Coconut Festival (Kapa'a; p118)
Annual Eo e Emalani I Alaka'i (Koke'e State Park; p212)

Hawaii International Film Festival (☎ in Honolulu 528-3456; www.hiff.org; admission $4-6) Established in 1981, this statewide film festival in late October features films from Asia, North America and the Pacific islands. It's an ideal venue to see locally made films that present Hawaii in a culturally accurate way. Typically, screenings take place at the Kukui Grove Cinemas (p89) and Waimea Theatre (p197).

NOVEMBER
'Kaua'i Style' Hawaiian Slack Key Guitar Festival (Lihu'e; p85)
PGA Grand Slam of Golf (Po'ipu; p173)

DECEMBER
Lights on Rice Parade (Lihu'e; p85)

FOOD
Reviews in the Eating section for each destination are broken down into three price categories: budget (for those meals costing $10 or less), midrange (where most main dishes cost $10 to $20) and top-end (where most dinner mains cost more than $20). These price estimates do not include taxes, tips or beverages. In this book, reviews are listed by price, from lowest to highest within each category.

Opening hours for restaurants are specified for each listing, but typical restaurant meal times are as follows: breakfast 6am to 10am, lunch 11:30am to 2pm, dinner 5pm to 9:30pm.

For details about local cuisine, see p66.

GAY & LESBIAN TRAVELERS
Gay Hawaii in general is not an in-your-face kind of place; public hand-holding and other outward signs of affection between gays is not commonplace. Without question, the main gay scene is in Waikiki on O'ahu. Kaua'i's gay community is spread over the island, but concentrated more on the Eastside and North Shore. Donkey Beach (p122), between Kapa'a and Anahola, is well-known as a gay-friendly, clothing-optional, alternative beach (despite the official ban against nudity).

An excellent Internet resource is **Gay Kaua'i Online** (www.aloha.net/~lambda), the website of Lambda Aloha. Included are tips on gay-friendly businesses, plus amusing (and spot-on) general advice on local customs (which apply to gays and straights, too). Also see the website for **Out in Hawaii** (www.outinhawaii.com), a statewide gay community network that has a Kaua'i-specific bulletin board, personals, classifieds, calendar, accommodations list and more.

HOLIDAYS
The following are state holidays. See p223 for other important dates.
New Year's Day January 1
Martin Luther King Jr Day Third Monday in January
Presidents Day Third Monday in February
Kuhio Day March 26
Good Friday Friday before Easter Sunday
Memorial Day Last Monday in May
King Kamehameha Day June 11
Independence Day July 4
Statehood Day Third Friday in August
Labor Day First Monday in September
Election Day Second Tuesday in November
Veterans Day November 11
Thanksgiving Fourth Thursday in November
Christmas Day December 25

INSURANCE
It's expensive to get sick, crash a car or have things stolen from you in the US. For auto insurance see p235 and for health insurance see p239). To protect yourself from car theft, consult your homeowner's (or renter's) insurance policy before leaving home.

INTERNET ACCESS
In most towns, you'll find at least a couple Internet cafés or business centers offering computer and Internet access at the going rate (per 10 minutes $2). If you absolutely need to stay connected, bring your own computer (in a pinch you can at least use a phone modem). Don't expect the ubiquitous wireless Internet access you'd find in a big city or college campus.

A small number of accommodation options provide free Internet and computer access for travelers without laptops; their reviews are noted with the 🖳 symbol. If B&B hosts allow you to use their computer, handle with care (and monitor kids), as some have reported damage. Top-end accommodations are more likely to provide wireless or high-speed Internet access, often for a fee. Other options are to use your cell phone (and a cable or Bluetooth connection) to go online or to dial up using a phone line.

If you bring a laptop from outside the US, invest in a universal AC and plug adapter. Also, your PC card modem may not work once you leave your home country – but you won't know until you try. The safest option? Buy a reputable 'global' modem before leaving home. Ensure that you have at least a US RJ-11 telephone adapter that works with your modem. For more technical help, visit www.teleadapt.com.

LEGAL MATTERS

You have the right to an attorney from the very first moment you are arrested. If you can't afford one, the state must provide one for free. The **Hawaii State Bar Association** (☎ 537-9140, 800-808-4722) makes attorney referrals, but foreign visitors may want to call their consulate for advice.

In Hawaii, anyone driving with a blood alcohol level of 0.08% or higher is guilty of driving 'under the influence,' which carries severe penalties. As with most places, the possession of marijuana and narcotics is illegal. Under the state medical marijuana law, certified users can have up to three mature marijuana plants, four immature plants and an ounce of usable pot per mature plant.

Hawaii's **Department of Commerce & Consumer Affairs** (☎ 587-1234) offers information on your rights regarding refunds and exchanges, time-share contracts, car rental and similar topics.

Hitchhiking is illegal but commonly practiced statewide. See p238.

MAPS

All drivers should use the **Ready Mapbook of Kauai** ($11), a 65-page road atlas that covers virtually every dirt, 4WD and paved road, plus beaches and their access points. Minor errors occasionally pop up, but overall it's accurate. Updated frequently, it's sold online at www.geckofarms.com and at island bookstores.

LEGAL AGE

The legal age in Hawaii varies by activity:

- Drinking: 21
- Driving: 16
- Sex: 16
- Voting: 18

For hikers, the detailed topographical map ($5) available from Na Ala Hele, the trails unit of the Division of Forestry & Wildlife (p51), shows the island's network of trails. You can request a copy to be mailed to you by sending a check or money order for $6 (for foreign addresses add $1).

The following fold-up maps, each serving a different purpose, are also highly recommended: **Franko's Dive Map of Kaua'i** ($7) is a well-drawn, colorful fold-up map on waterproof paper, which lists all the top sites for scuba diving, snorkeling, kayaking and surfing, plus major trails and roads. The illustrated directory of tropical fish is worth the price by itself.

Kaua'i Visitors Atlas ($7) is a comprehensive set of maps, covering climate, geology, archaeology, Hawaiian name translations, places and activities. Visually rewarding, this map is akin to a mini book on Kaua'i. It even maps each hole of major golf courses. One caveat: the Hawaiian pronunciations are not always correct.

Map of Kaua'i ($4) by James A Bier, University of Hawai'i Press, is a classic, but it might be too detailed for the average tourist. This topographic map lists every geographic item imaginable, including bays, points, valleys, rivers, streams, reservoirs and mountains. An index on the back helps you search for specific items.

MONEY

ATMs are great for quick cash and can negate the need for traveler's checks, but beware of ATM surcharges. Most banks charge around US$1.50 per withdrawal.

American Savings Bank (www.asbhawaii.com), **Bank of Hawaii** (www.boh.com) and **First Hawaiian Bank** (www.fhb.com) have branches in major towns plus ATM networks that give cash advances on major credit cards and allow cash withdrawals with affiliated ATM cards. Most ATMs in Hawaii accept bank cards from the Plus and Cirrus systems. Look for ATMs outside banks and in supermarkets, shopping centers, convenience stores and gas stations.

Cash

If you're carrying foreign currency, it can be exchanged for US dollars at Honolulu International Airport and at main bank branches on Kaua'i.

DIRECTORY

Credit Cards

Major credit cards are widely accepted at retailers and restaurants islandwide, but not by most B&Bs and inns.

Tipping

In restaurants, tip at least 15% for good service and 10% if it's mediocre. Leaving no tip is rare and requires real cause. Taxi drivers and hairstylists are typically tipped 10% and hotel bellhops $1 per bag.

Traveler's Checks

Traveler's checks provide protection from theft and loss. Keep a record of all check numbers separate from the checks themselves. For refunds on lost or stolen traveler's checks, call **American Express** (☎ 800-992-3404) or **Thomas Cook** (☎ 800-287-7362). Foreign visitors carrying traveler's checks will find things infinitely easier if the checks are drawn in US dollars. Note that personal checks not drawn from a Hawaiian bank are generally not accepted.

PHOTOGRAPHY

Photography is well into the digital age, but if you're still carrying print and slide film, consider developing your film here if your trip is long, as the high temperature and humidity accelerate the deterioration of exposed film. Don't pack unprocessed film (including the roll inside your camera) into checked luggage because exposure to high-powered x-ray equipment will cause it to fog. X-ray scanners used for carry-on baggage are less powerful and generally won't cause visible damage; to be safe, carry your film separately and submit it to airport security officials for a 'hand check.'

POST

Mail delivery to and from Hawaii via the **US postal service** (USPS; ☎ 800-275-8777; www.usps.gov) is reliable but takes a little longer than similar services across the US mainland (about 10 days for air mail and four to six weeks for parcel post).

First-class mail between Hawaii and the mainland goes by air and usually takes three to four days. For 1st-class mail sent and delivered within the US, postage rates are 39¢ for letters up to 1oz (24¢ for each additional ounce) and 24¢ for standard-size postcards.

International airmail rates for letters up to 1oz are 63¢ to Canada or Mexico and 84¢ to other countries. Postcards cost 55¢ to Canada and Mexico and 75¢ to other countries.

You can receive mail c/o General Delivery at Kaua'i post offices but, according to the official rule, you must first complete an application in person. Bring two forms of ID and your temporary local address. The accepted application is valid for 30 days; mail is held for a maximum of 15 days. But exceptions are made, so ask. Hotels and other accommodations might hold mail for incoming guests.

Note the numerical prefix in street addresses along Kaua'i's highways, eg 3-4567 Kuhio Hwy. There are five prefixes that cover Kaua'i's five districts. One refers to Waimea and vicinity, including Ni'ihau; 2 is Koloa and Po'ipu; 3 is Lihu'e to the Wailua River; 4 is Kapa'a and Anahola; and 5 is the North Shore.

SHOPPING

The best way to remember Kaua'i is to buy Kaua'i-made items. Many are edible, from taro chips to tropical granola; see p66 for recommendations. While Kaua'i coffee lacks the world-class reputation of Kona coffee, it's quite good; try beans from major producer Kaua'i Coffee Company (p185) or boutique Blair Estate Organic Coffee Farm (p117).

While Kaua'i's red dirt probably accompanies all visitors home (under their shoes), take back the iconic souvenir, a red-dirt T-shirt (p91). Top-quality T-shirts featuring unique Kaua'i designs are sold at Pohaku T's (p166) and Nite Owl T-Shirts (p188).

Locally made arts and crafts abound in galleries across the island, particularly in Hanapepe (p190). Look for paintings, koa bowls and Ni'ihau shell jewelry. For less than $20 you can buy a hand-painted 're-move your shoes' tile (ubiquitous in Hawaii) from Banana Patch, the originator. Another place to find Kaua'i-made souvenirs is the C&H Kaua'i Products Store in Lihu'e. Remember, genuine items are meticulously created and never cheap. See p44 for more on Hawaiian arts and crafts.

Aloha shirts might seem a cliché but they're still the official male uniform. The classiest, worn by local professionals, use lightweight cotton and subdued colors, often reverse-fabric prints. See p90 for a list of the top five shops that stock them.

In early 2006 the Kaua'i County Office of Economic Development launched a 'Kaua'i Made' label for vendors who sell products either made on the island or with Kaua'i materials. Look for it!

Note that bargaining is not the norm among locals, except at farmers markets.

SOLO TRAVELERS

Kaua'i's compact size and small-town atmosphere make solo travel easy. Group tours and lessons give singles the option to meet others. That said, accommodations will always cost more for singles, especially because few places differentiate between single and double rates. Hiking and swimming alone is never wise, and solo travelers, particularly females, should try to find a trusted companion or group when venturing to isolated areas.

TELEPHONE

Always dial '1' before toll-free (☎ 800, 888 etc), domestic long-distance numbers and interisland calls. While the area code ☎ 808 applies to all islands, it must be dialed for interisland calls (from one island to another); for calls within Kaua'i, just dial the number.

Pay phones are readily found in shopping centers, beach parks and other public places. Calls within Kaua'i are considered local and cost 25¢ or 50¢. Interisland calls are always long distance and more expensive. Hotels often add a hefty service charge of $1 for calls made from room phones.

Private prepaid phone cards are available from convenience stores, supermarkets and pharmacies.

Cell Phones

The US uses a variety of cell-phone systems, 99% of which are incompatible with the GSM 900/1800 standard used throughout Europe and Asia. Check with your cellular service provider before departure about using your phone in Hawaii. On Kaua'i only Verizon and Cingular provide decent coverage islandwide; other providers' coverage is limited to main towns; none provide service in remote locations; eg around Waimea Canyon.

Long-Distance & International Calls

To make international calls direct from Hawaii, dial ☎ 011 + country code + area code + number. (An exception is to Canada, where you dial ☎ 1 + area code + number, but international rates still apply.)

For international operator assistance, dial ☎ 0. The operator can provide specific rate information and tell you which time periods are the cheapest for calling.

If you're calling Hawaii from abroad, the international country code for the US is ☎ 1. All calls to Hawaii are followed by the area code ☎ 808 and the seven-digit local number. As mentioned earlier, dial the area code when calling from one island to another.

TIME

Hawaii does not observe daylight saving time, thus the time difference is one hour greater during those months when other countries *are* observing daylight saving time (eg the first Sunday in April to the last Sunday in October in North America).

Hawaii has 11 hours of daylight in midwinter (December) and 13½ hours in midsummer (June). In midwinter, the sun rises at around 7am and sets at around 6pm. In midsummer, it rises before 6am and sets after 7pm.

And then there's 'Hawaiian time,' a slowdown-the-clock pace or a euphemism for being late.

TOURIST INFORMATION

The **Kaua'i Visitors Bureau** (Map p78; ☎ 245-3971, 800-262-1400; www.kauaidiscovery.com; 4334 Rice St, Suite 101) website is a good first-stop resource; request its 'vacation planning kit.' Its statewide parent organization is the **Hawaii Visitors & Convention Bureau** (☎ 800-464-2924; www.gohawaii .com; Suite 801, 2270 Kalakaua Ave, Waikiki, HI 96815), which also provides online information.

You'll find scads of tourist magazines in racks at the airport and at shopping centers. The best are *101 Things To Do* and *This Week*, which are handy for current entertainment listings, simple maps and discount coupons.

TOURS

Active tours, such as hiking, kayaking and snorkeling, are listed under Activities in the destination chapters and are also featured in the Outdoors chapter (p54). Listed under Tours in destination chapters are those focused on culture, history or basic sightseeing, including helicopter rides (p62).

Boat

Sightseeing cruises and boat tours depart mainly from Port Allen (p185). In winter, the main attraction is whale watching.

Bus & Van

Bus tour operators offer full- and half-day whirlwind van tours, passing major towns and stopping at a few sights: Waimea Canyon (only to the Waimea Canyon Lookout at 3400ft) and Spouting Horn to the south and west; the Fern Grotto and Opaeka'a Falls to the east. Conventional buses cannot go past Princeville due to the one-lane bridges so the North Shore is inaccessible to such tours. Make no mistake, such mad dashes allow a ridiculously unsatisfying glimpse and you might be better off watching a PBS documentary about Kaua'i instead.

Tour prices depend on your departure point: Lihu'e and Wailua are the cheapest; Po'ipu and Princeville cost at least $5 and $12 more, respectively. Full-day tours start at adult/child $64/44, half-day tours at $44/32. While such bus tours are not recommended, here are three longstanding companies:

Kaua'i Paradise Tours (☎ 246-3999; kauaiaufdeut sch@msn.com; 6/8hr tour $66/88) Specializes in tours narrated in German.

Polynesian Adventure Tours (☎ 246-0122, 800-622-3011; www.polyad.com)

Roberts Hawaii (☎ 539-9400; www.robertshawaii.com)

More adventurous are the 4WD tours by **Aloha Kaua'i Tours** (☎ 245-6400, 800-452-8113; www.alohakauaitours.com; 1702 Haleukana St, Lihu'e), which offers a full-day Koke'e Park–Waimea Canyon circuit (adult/child $125/90) that visits harder-to-reach places like the Kilohana Crater, and a 5½-hour mountain bike/hike tour (adult/child aged five to eight/aged nine to 12 $100/50/75) on the Eastside, ending in a remote beach beyond Maha'ulepu.

Tour Groups

Elderhostel (☎ 617-426-7788, 877-426-8056; www.elderhostel.org; 1-/2-week programs $650/1300) offers stimulating educational programs on Hawaiian culture or natural environment for those aged 55 or older and includes accommodations, meals and classes. Kaua'i offerings include a birding tour and a combination Big Island–Kaua'i tour.

See p232 for package tours and p233 for cruises to the Hawaiian Islands.

VISAS

Entering the US can often be a bureaucratic nightmare, depending on your country of origin. To make matters worse, rules change rapidly. For up-to-date information about visas and immigration, check with the **US State Department** (www.unitedstatesvisas .gov/visiting.html).

Note that the Visa Waiver Program allows citizens of 27 specified countries to enter the US for stays of 90 days or less without first obtaining a US visa. See www.travel .state.gov/visa/temp/without/without_1990 .html. Under this program you must have a machine-readable passport or a US visa, plus a return ticket (or onward ticket to any foreign destination) that is nonrefundable in the US. Your passport should be valid for at least six months longer than your stay.

For additional information, see the website of the **Bureau of Citizenship & Immigration Service** (BCIS; www.bcis.gov).

VOLUNTEERING

The **Koke'e Resource Conservation Program** (☎ 335-9975; www.krcp.org) accepts short-term volunteers and eight-week interns to help in weed-control projects in and around Koke'e, Waimea Canyon and Na Pali Coast State Parks. The work involves strenuous hiking, and herbicide use. In exchange for work, bunk-bed housing is provided at the Civilian Conservation Corps Camp, a remote site suited to folks who would welcome solitude. Volunteers and interns must provide their own health insurance.

Hawaiian Islands Humpback Whale National Marine Sanctuary (☎ 246-2860; www.hawaiihump backwhale.noaa.gov), a statewide organization, has formal programs only on Maui, but volunteer opportunities do exist on Kaua'i. Contact Jean Souza, the **Kaua'i Programs Coordinator** (jean.souza@noaa.gov).

WOMEN TRAVELERS

Kaua'i presents few problems specific to women travelers, and may be more relaxed and comfortable than many mainland destinations. Of course women, especially solo travelers, should be wary of isolated beaches, campsites and hiking trails. County parks and secluded picnic sites, eg Keahua Arboretum, are notorious for late-night partying.

WORK

US citizens can work in Hawaii – the problem is finding a decent job. Foreign visitors in Hawaii on tourist visas, however, cannot legally be employed.

Finding serious 'professional' employment is difficult in the state's already-tight labor market. The biggest exceptions to this rule are for teachers and nurses. Also, residential construction is booming, and there's a shortage of licensed carpenters, plumbers, painters, electricians and roofers. Waiting on tables or front-desk reception is probably what you can expect. Folks with language, scuba, fishing or other outdoor skills can investigate employment at resorts and activity outfits.

Check the classifieds of newspapers to get an idea of employment opportunities. An excellent general resource is Kaua'i's branch of the **State Workforce Development Division** (☎ 274-3056; www.hawaii.gov/labor/wdd; 3100 Kuhio Hwy, Suite C-10, Lihu'e, HI 96766). Also check the website of the **State Department of Labor & Industrial Relations** (☎ 586-8700; www.dlir.state .hi.us; 830 Punchbowl St, Honolulu, HI 96813).

Transportation

CONTENTS

TRANSPORTATION (side tab)

GETTING THERE & AWAY

No surprise: the majority of all visitors to Hawaii arrive by air because Hawaii is smack in the middle of the Pacific Ocean. All international and most domestic flights arrive at Honolulu International Airport. If you are flying to Kaua'i through Honolulu, make sure the ticket agent marks your baggage with Lihu'e as the final destination. Flights and tours can be booked online at www.lonelyplanet.com/travel_services.

ENTERING THE COUNTRY

A passport is required for all foreign citizens, except Canadians who need to show only proof of residence. Residents of most other countries need a tourist visa (see p228). It's always advisable to confirm this information since it changes rapidly.

AIR

US domestic and international airfares vary tremendously depending on the season, general tourism trends to the islands, and how much flexibility the ticket allows for flight changes and refunds. Since nothing determines fares more than demand, when things are slow, airlines lower their fares to fill empty seats. Competition is fierce, and at any given time, any one of the airlines could have the cheapest fare.

> **THINGS CHANGE...**
>
> The information in this chapter is particularly vulnerable to change. Check directly with the airline or a travel agent to make sure you understand how a fare (and ticket you may buy) works and be aware of the security requirements for international travel. Shop carefully. The details given in this chapter should be regarded as pointers and are not a substitute for your own careful, up-to-date research.

Airports & Airlines

All commercial flights land in Lihu'e: most likely you'll stop in Honolulu first – flight time from Honolulu to Lihu'e is 25 minutes. Kaua'i also has two small airports – Burns Field (p190) in Hanapepe and Princeville Airport (p137) – that serve helicopter tours.
Lihu'e Airport (LIH; ☎ 246-1448; www.hawaii.gov/dot/airports/kauai/lih; ☼ visitor hotline 6:30am-9pm) See p91.
Honolulu International Airport (HNL; ☎ 836-6413; www.honoluluairport.com)

Outside of Hawaii, the gateway airports for flights to Honolulu include the following:
Atlanta International Airport (ATL; ☎ 800-897-1910; www.atlanta-airport.com)
Chicago O'Hare International Airport (ORD; ☎ 773-686-2200; www.ohare.com)
Denver International Airport (DEN; ☎ 303-342-2000; www.flydenver.com)
Las Vegas McCarran International Airport (LAS; ☎ 702-261-5211; www.mccarran.com)
Los Angeles International Airport (LAX; ☎ 310-646-5252; www.los-angeles-lax.com)
New York JFK International Airport (JFK; ☎ 718-244-4444; www.panynj.gov)
Phoenix Sky Harbor International Airport (PHX; ☎ 602-273-3300; www.phoenix-phx.com)
San Francisco International Airport (SFO; ☎ 650-876-2222; www.flysfo.com)
Seattle-Tacoma International Airport (SEA; ☎ 206-433-5388; www.portseattle.org)
Washington Dulles International Airport (IAD; ☎ 703-572-2700; www.metwashairports.com)

If you are among the vast majority of visitors from overseas and the US mainland

who arrive at Honolulu International Airport, you must then catch an interisland flight. But three airlines (plus those that do chartered vacation tours) do fly directly from the US mainland to Lihu'e Airport, as well as to Honolulu International Airport:
American Airlines (☎ 800-223-5436; www.aa.com)
United Airlines (☎ 800-241-6522; www.ual.com)
US Airways (☎ 800-428-4322; www.usairways.com)

Airlines flying into Honolulu (but not directly to Kaua'i) include the following:
Air Canada (☎ 888-247-2262; www.aircanada.ca)
All Nippon Airways (ANA; www.anaskyweb.com, www.ana.co.jp in Japanese)
Aloha Airlines (☎ 800-367-5250; www.alohaairlines.com)
Air New Zealand (☎ 800-262-1234; www.airnz.co.nz)
Air Pacific (☎ 800-227-4446; www.airpacific.com)
Alaska Airlines (☎ 800-252-7522; www.alaskaair.com)
American Trans Air (☎ 800-435-9282; www.ata.com)
British Airways (☎ 800-247-9297; www.britishairways.com)
China Airlines (☎ 800-227-5118; www.china-airlines.com)
Continental (☎ 800-523-3273; www.continental.com)
Delta (☎ 800-221-1212; www.delta.com)
Hawaiian Airlines (☎ 800-367-5320; www.hawaiianair.com)
Japan Airlines (☎ 800-525-3663; www.japanair.com)
Korean Airlines (☎ 800-438-5000; www.koreanair.com)
Northwest-KLM (☎ 800-225-2525; www.nwa.com)
Philippine Airlines (☎ 800-435-9725; www.philippineair.com)
Qantas Airways (☎ 800-227-4500; www.qantasusa.com)
US Airways (☎ 800-428-4322; www.usairways.com)

For interisland flights, there are currently four carriers. Aloha and Hawaiian also fly domestic and international flights.
Aloha Airlines (☎ 800-367-5250; www.alohaairlines.com)
go! (☎ 888-435-9462; www.iflygo.com)
Hawaiian Airlines (☎ 800-367-5320; www.hawaiianair.com)
Island Air (☎ US mainland 800-323-3345, Neighbor Islands 800-652-6541; www.islandair.com)

Tickets

There's no guaranteed formula for finding the cheapest fares, but the best deals are usually found online. Recommended travel websites include the following:

- www.kayak.com
- www.mobissimo.com
- www.sidestep.com
- www.travelocity.com
- www.expedia.com
- www.orbitz.com
- www.cheaptickets.com
- www.lowestfare.com
- www.sta.com (for travelers under 26)

Round-the-world (RTW) tickets allow you to fly on the combined routes of two or more airlines and can be a good deal if you're coming from a great distance and want to visit other parts of the world in addition to Hawaii. British Airways and Qantas Airways offer the best plans through programs called Oneworld Explorer and Global Explorer, respectively.

Circle Pacific tickets are essentially a takeoff on RTW tickets, but instead of requiring you to continue moving in one general direction, they allow you to keep traveling in the same circular direction. Because you start and end at a city that borders the Pacific, these tickets are most practical for travelers who live in or near the Pacific region. Contact Air New Zealand or Continental, whose program is called 'Circle Micronesia.' Continental's flights originate in Los Angeles, San Francisco and Honolulu.

Australia

Hawaiian Airlines flies nonstop between Sydney and Honolulu. Qantas flies to Honolulu from Sydney and Melbourne (via Sydney, but without changing planes). Return fares range seasonally from A$900 to A$1400.

Canada

Air Canada offers direct flights to Honolulu from Vancouver and also other Canadian cities via Vancouver. The cheapest return fares to Honolulu are about C$800 from Vancouver, C$1100 from Calgary or Edmonton, and C$1400 from Toronto.

Hawaiian Airlines also flies from Vancouver, Calgary, Edmonton and Toronto, with stopovers in Phoenix and Honolulu.

Japan

Japan Airlines flies directly between Honolulu and Tokyo, Osaka, Nagoya or Fukuoka. Return fares vary according to departure

TRANSPORTATION

TRANSPORTATION

city and season but, with the exception of busier holiday periods (particularly Golden Week in May, Obon in August and around the New Year), they're around ¥40,000 for a ticket valid for three months.

Fares to Honolulu on All Nippon Airways (ANA), which also depart from Sapporo and Kumamoto, are sometimes discounted to around ¥70,000. Continental and Northwest-KLM have several flights to Honolulu from Tokyo and Osaka; ticket prices are comparable to those offered by Japan Airlines.

Micronesia & New Zealand
Continental offers nonstop flights from Guam to Honolulu with return fares at about US$1100. Air New Zealand flies from Auckland to Honolulu at about NZ$1650 return.

South Pacific Islands
Hawaiian Airlines flies to Honolulu from Tahiti and American Samoa. From American Samoa return fares are about US$600; from Tahiti they're about US$700.

Air New Zealand offers return tickets from Fiji to Honolulu via Auckland for about NZ$1370. It also flies to Honolulu from Tonga, the Cook Islands and Western Samoa for around NZ$870 (from Western Samoa) or NZ$1080 (from Tonga and the Cook Islands) return.

UK & Continental Europe
The most common route to Hawaii from Europe is west via New York, Chicago or Los Angeles. If you're interested in heading east with stops in Asia, it may be cheaper to get a RTW ticket instead of returning the same way.

The lowest return fares with American Airlines from London, Paris and Frankfurt to Honolulu are usually around €790. United, Delta and Continental have a similarly priced service to Honolulu from some European cities.

London is arguably the world's headquarters for bucket shops specializing in discount tickets. Two good, reliable agents for cheap tickets in the UK:

STA Travel (☎ 020-7240 9821; www.statravel.co.uk; 33 Bedford St, Covent Garden, London)

Trailfinders (☎ 020-7628 7628; www.trailfinders.co.uk; 1 Threadneedle St, London)

US Mainland
Competition is high among airlines flying to Honolulu from major mainland cities. Typically, the lowest round-trip fares from the US mainland to Hawaii are approximately $600 from the east coast and $400 from the west coast.

The vast majority of mainland flights fly only into Honolulu, but there are three airlines with direct flights from the mainland: United Airlines and American Airlines fly directly to Lihu'e from Los Angeles; and United also flies directly to Lihu'e from San Francisco. US Airways flies one direct flight daily between Phoenix and Lihu'e.

If you live in mainland cities served by Aloha Airlines (eg Oakland and Orange County) or Hawaiian Airlines (eg Seattle, Portland, Las Vegas, Phoenix and all major California cities), they're ideal options because these carriers serves both the mainland and interisland links and the overall fare is quite reduced.

For those with limited time, package tours can sometimes be the cheapest way to go. Basic tours usually cover airfare and accommodations, while deluxe packages can include car rental, island hopping and all sorts of activities. If you're planning to visit Hawaii on a short getaway, you may find that packages cost little more than what the airfare alone would cost. Although costs vary, one-week tours with airfare and no-frills hotel accommodations usually start at around $500 from the US west coast, and $800 from the US east coast, based on double occupancy. **Pleasant Hawaiian Holidays** (☎ 800-742-9244; www.pleasantholidays .com) has departures from various US mainland points. **SunTrips** (☎ 800-786-8747; www .suntrips.com) offers packages from Oakland, California.

If you're a flexible, last-minute traveler, try Air Tech's Space-Available FlightPass, which can be the cheapest way to fly between the west coast and Hawaii. **Air Tech** (☎ 212-219-7000; www.airtech.com) goes as low as $159 one way, within a four-day travel window – but flights to Kaua'i are available only during summer months. West coast departure cities are San Francisco and Los Angeles.

The flight time to Hawaii is approximately 5½ hours nonstop from the west coast or 11 hours from the east coast.

Within Hawaii

Hawaiian Airlines and Aloha Airlines are the two biggie interisland airlines. Both schedule 14 daily flights between Honolulu and Lihu'e. Internet fares start at around $75 to $80 one way, but prices can drop to $39 during special offers. Flights booked by phone start at $105 one way. Fares max out at around $158 one way. Both companies offer mileage bonuses for frequent travelers.

Another option is Island Air, which flies small 18- and 37-seat planes to Lihu'e from Honolulu and Maui. Flights are limited to one daily from Honolulu and three from Kahului, Maui. Fares range from about $60 to $200 one way, depending on when you book your flight.

In June 2006, Mesa Air Group's new discount carrier, go!, started offering interisland flights starting at $39 one way. Hawaiian and Aloha cut their summer rates to match that price – and only time will tell whether go! is here to stay.

SEA
Outside Hawaii

In recent years, a handful of cruise ships has begun offering tours that include Hawaii. Most cruises last 10 to 12 days and have fares that start at around US$150 a day per person, based on double occupancy – though discounts and promotions can bring that price down to under US$100 a day. Airfare to and from the departure point costs extra.

Most Hawaiian cruises include stopovers in Honolulu, Maui, Kaua'i and the Big Island. Cruise lines include the following:

Holland America Cruise Line (☎ 877-724-5425; www.hollandamerica.com) Typically departs for Honolulu from San Diego, Seattle or Vancouver.

Princess Cruises (☎ 800-568-3262; www.princess .com) Offers the most cruises; operates between Honolulu and Tahiti.

You can also get to Hawaii by private yacht. If you don't have one of your own, and you're hoping to get on a crew, start poking around the Honolulu ports in early spring. Experienced crew should try www .boatcrew.net, a well-organized site with a database of boats leaving from various mainland ports. Membership is US$10 per month (or US$100 per year).

Within Hawaii

In response to the increasing costs of interisland flights, a new ferry service will be launched in spring 2007. **Hawaii Superferry** (www.hawaiisuperferry.com) will sail two state-of-the-art catamarans, each carrying up to 900 passengers and almost 300 cars, from O'ahu to Kaua'i, Maui and the Big Island. The trip from Honolulu Harbor (O'ahu) to Nawiliwili Harbor (Kaua'i) will take three hours, and one-way fares will cost $42 to $60, depending on advance purchase and peak or off-peak hours. Transporting your car will cost $55 to $65.

Environmental groups filed a lawsuit against Hawaii Superferry, seeking lengthy environmental studies regarding effects on migrating whales, transmission of invasive species and conflicts with other harbor users; but in September 2005, a US district judge dismissed the suit.

Norwegian Cruise Line (NCL; ☎ 800-327-7030; www.ncl.com) is the only company that operates cruises between the Hawaiian Islands that start and end in Hawaii, launching either in Honolulu or Maui. Since 2004, NCL America has sailed US-flagged cruise ships, including the *Pride of Aloha*, the *Pride of America* and the *Pride of Hawaii*; so you need not travel all the way to Fanning Island in the Republic of Kiribati (foreign-registered ships must make such an international stop during their tours). But NCL does offer longer 10- or 11-day cruises (on the *Norwegian Star* and *Norwegian Wind*) that do include Fanning Island (and a much longer time aboard ship).

Seven-day trips (starting in Honolulu and stopping in Maui, Kaua'i, Hilo and Kona) are offered. On Kaua'i, ships dock at Nawiliwili Harbor for one night: the *Pride of Aloha* on Monday and the *Pride of America* on Thursday.

Onboard there are six restaurants, 13 lounges and bars, full spa, conference rooms, a wedding chapel, golf shop and a cultural center. While customer service on the early runs of the *Pride of Aloha* was sometimes problematic, currently everything seems to be shipshape.

Prices vary depending on season (rates are approximately 50% higher in summer and winter than in spring and fall) and on type of cabin. For the seven-day cruise, an interior cabin, double occupancy, starts around US$1000 per person, while an ocean-view cabin starts around US$1700 per person.

GETTING AROUND

BICYCLE

It's possible to cycle around much of Kaua'i, but you'll encounter the gamut of terrain and weather. Note that you must backtrack because the belt road does not connect. Winter months are particularly wet, but showers are common year-round. The main challenges, however, are the lack of bicycle lanes and the narrow, winding roads, which are heavily trafficked. Riding along the North Shore, full of zigzags overlooking sea cliffs, is not recommended; the two-lane highway is narrow even for two cars to pass.

An 18-mile coastal bicycle path is slated to run from Lihu'e all the way to Anahola by 2008, and the path is partly completed. Thus perhaps selective bike transportation might work well. But in general cycling is not especially popular and is better suited for recreation than real transportation.

Bicycle-rental shops are mainly in Kapa'a (p117), Hanalei (p150), Po'ipu (p180). If you bring your own bike to Hawaii, which costs upwards of US$100 on flights from the mainland, it will cost an additional US$25 to transport it on interisland flights. The bicycle can be checked in at the counter, the same as any baggage, but you'll need to prepare the bike first, either by wrapping the handlebars and pedals in foam or by fixing the handlebars to the side and removing the pedals.

In general, bicycles are required to follow the same state laws and rules of the road as cars.

BUS

Let's face it, Kaua'i is not a bus-riding type of place. It's far too rural, with too many destinations inaccessible by conventional buses (and often difficult even for standard cars).

Kaua'i Bus (☎ 241-6410; www.kauai.gov; 3220 Ho'olako St, Lihu'e; per trip adult/senior & youth 7-18 $1.50/75¢; ⏱ 7:45am-4:30pm Mon-Fri), the county public bus, offers bare-bones islandwide service Monday to Friday, with further-limited service on Saturday. There is no service on Sunday and county holidays. Schedules are available at the **Kaua'i Visitors Bureau** (Map p78; ☎ 245-3971, 800-262-1400; www.kauaidiscovery.com; 4334 Rice St, Suite 101, Lihu'e). Check the website for current information. All buses stop in Lihu'e. The number of trips per route varies; for example, for intra-Lihu'e travel, there is an average of eight departures on weekdays, but for longer routes, such as Lihu'e to Po'ipu, you are stuck with one daily departure from each end.

A few caveats: drivers accept only the exact fare; a monthly pass costs $15; you can transport a boogie board (but not a surfboard), folding baby stroller or bicycle; stops are marked but might be hard to spot, and the schedule does not include a map.

KAUA'I BUS ROUTES

Route	Route No	Main stops	Frequency
Lihu'e-Kekaha	100 (eastbound) & 200 (westbound)	Lihu'e Big Save; Kukui Grove Shopping Center; Lawa'i; Kalaheo; Hanapepe; Waimea; Kekaha Neighborhood Center	8 Mon-Fri, 4 Sat
Lihu'e-Po'ipu	100E (eastbound) & 200E (westbound)	Koloa; Po'ipu Rd; all stops on Lihu'e-Kekaha route	1 Mon-Fri, 1 Sat
Lihu'e-Hanalei	400 (eastbound) & 500 (westbound)	Kukui Grove Shopping Center; Lihu'e Big Save; Wilcox Memorial Hospital; Kapa'a Big Save; Kealia Beach; Kilauea Food Mart; Princeville Shopping Center; Hanalei Center	12 Mon-Fri, 4 Sat
Lihu'e Extension	700	Kukui Grove Shopping Center; Garden Island Inn (Nawiliwili Harbor); Lihu'e Big Save; Wilcox Memorial Hospital; Rice Shopping Center	8 Mon-Fri

TRANSPORTATION

Buses are air-conditioned and equipped with bicycle racks and wheelchair ramps.

CAR & MOTORCYCLE

Statistically speaking, 75% of all visitors to Hawaii's Neighbor Islands rent their own vehicles – so chances are you'll be driving on Kaua'i. Indeed, driving is virtually an imperative here, as bus service is limited and riders can be sketchy characters.

The minimum age for driving a car in Hawaii is 16 years, though most major car-rental companies enforce a minimum age of 25. Thrifty Car Rental is one of the few renting to drivers 21 and above. If you're under age 25, you should call the car-rental agencies in advance to check their policies regarding restrictions and surcharges.

Kaua'i has one belt road running three-quarters of the way around the island, from Ke'e Beach in the north, to Polihale in the west; the Na Pali Coast is only accessible by boat or on foot, and even then only partway. Congestion is rampant, especially between Lihu'e and Kapa'a where rush-hour traffic is a given. To combat traffic, a 'contra-flow' lane is created weekdays from 5am to 10:30am on Kuhio Hwy (Hwy 56) in the Wailua area; this turns a northbound lane into a southbound lane by reversing the flow of traffic, so that commuters to Lihu'e have an extra lane open.

Gas prices are steep across the state and especially high on Kaua'i. Prices vary greatly on the island, with the Eastside generally the cheapest and Princeville the reigning high charger. Check www.kauai world.com/gasprices for the current highs and lows.

Motorcycle rental is not common in Hawaii. The minimum age to rent one at most places is 21 and you'll need to show a valid motorcycle license. The minimum age for renting a scooter or moped (the former can go highway speeds while the latter is only for around town) is 16 years.

There are no helmet laws in Hawaii and even typically cautious riders will be tempted to let loose helmet-free as they lean into curves down scenic stretches. Squelch that temptation. Remember that rental agencies often provide free helmets.

Riding anywhere on Kaua'i, particularly in upland areas, requires hard-core rain gear, which some rental shops also supply.

Snug cuffs and waterproof seams are essential, and a stash of double-sided Velcro and seam sealer will work wonders for your disposition.

State law requires mopeds to be ridden by one person only and prohibits their use on sidewalks and freeways. Mopeds must always be driven in single file and may not be driven at speeds in excess of 30mph. Bizarrely, mopeds can be more expensive to rent than cars.

Automobile Associations

The **American Automobile Association** (AAA; ☎ 800-736-2886; www.aaa-hawaii.com), which has its only Hawaii office in Honolulu, provides members with maps and other information. Members get discounts on car rental, air tickets, some hotels, some sightseeing attractions, as well as emergency road service and towing (☎ 800-222-4357). For information on joining, call ☎ 800-564-6222. AAA has reciprocal agreements with automobile associations in other countries, so bring your membership card from home.

Driver's License

An international driving license, obtained before you leave home, is necessary only if your country of origin is a non-English-speaking one.

Fuel & Towing

Fuel is readily available everywhere except in remote areas such as Waimea Canyon and the North Shore beyond Princeville. Expect to pay at least 50¢ more per US gallon than on the mainland. Still, for Europeans and Canadians, it will be less expensive than at home.

If you get into trouble with your car, towing is mighty expensive and therefore to be avoided at all costs. Figure the fees at about $65 to start, plus $6.50 for every mile you have to be towed. The best way to avoid it? Don't drive on the island's worst dirt roads, especially when they are muddy, in anything but a 4WD.

Insurance

Liability insurance covers people and property if you hit them. For damage to the actual rental vehicle, a collision damage waiver (CDW) is available for about $15 a day. If you have collision coverage on your vehicle

TRANSPORTATION

ROAD DISTANCES (miles)

	Anahola	Hanalei	Hanapepe	Kapa'a	Ke'e Beach	Kilauea Lighthouse	Lihu'e	Po'ipu	Port Allen	Princeville	Waimea
Hanalei	16										
Hanapepe	31	47									
Kapa'a	5	22	25								
Ke'e Beach	23	7	54	28							
Kilauea Lighthouse	11	9	43	17	17						
Lihu'e	14	31	16	8	40	25					
Po'ipu	28	44	12	23	51	40	10				
Port Allen	29	47	1	24	53	42	15	11			
Princeville	15	3	45	20	10	6	28	42	44		
Waimea	36	54	6	31	60	49	23	18	7	51	
Waimea Canyon	45	62	15	40	69	58	42	27	16	60	9

at home, it might cover damages to rental cars; inquire before departing. Additionally, some credit cards offer reimbursement coverage for collision damages if you rent the car with that credit card; again, check before departing. Most credit-card coverage isn't valid for rentals of more than 15 days or for exotic models, vans and 4WDs. For recorded information on your legal rights, call the state **Department of Commerce & Consumer Affairs** (☎ 808-587-1234 ext 7222).

Rental

Rental cars are readily available, but advance reservations are highly recommended. The daily rate for a compact car ranges from $30 to $50 and the typical weekly rate is $160 to $250, excluding taxes and other fees that total roughly 18% of the base estimate. Rates for 4WD vehicles average $75 to $85 per day and $400 per week. Rental rates generally include unlimited mileage.

Ask for the *total* price when shopping around. Also remember that rates depend on season and availability and are volatile, changing by the day or even by the hour.

The best way to snag a deal is to repeatedly check online – and to reserve (and lock in) the lowest rate you find. If you belong to an auto club or a frequent-flyer program, inquire about discounts. It always pays to shop around; Dollar tends to run the cheapest. Booking in advance ensures better selection (especially if you want a 4WD).

Having a major credit card greatly simplifies the car rental process. Without one, some agents simply will not rent vehicles, while others require prepayment, a deposit of $200 per week, pay stubs, proof of return airfare and more.

The following major agencies are your best bets:

Alamo (☎ 800-327-9633, Lihu'e 246-0645; www.alamo.com)

Avis (☎ 800-831-2847, Lihu'e 245-7995; www.avis.com)

Budget (☎ 800-527-0700, Lihu'e 245-9031; www.budget.com)

Dollar (☎ 800-800-4000, Lihu'e 742-8351; www.dollarcar.com)

Hertz (☎ 800-654-3011, Lihu'e 245-3356; www.hertz.com)

National (☎ 888-868-6207, Lihu'e 245-5636; www
.nationalcar.com)
Thrifty (☎ 800-847-4389, Lihu'e 866-450-5101; www
.thrifty.com)

Local car-rental agencies are also generally reliable, economical and keep more of
your tourist dollars in Kaua'i. The following offer airport pick-ups and may rent to
travelers under 25 and/or those without a
credit card:

Hawaiian Riders (Map pp168-9; ☎ 742-9888; www
.hawaiianriders.com; 2320 Po'ipu Rd, Po'ipu) Rents Jeeps.
Island Cars (Map p76; ☎ 246-6000; www.islandcars
.net; 2983 Aukele St, Lihu'e) Daily/weekly rates start at
$24/129.
Rent-A-Wreck (Map p76; ☎ 632-0741; www
.rentawreck.com; Harbor Mall, 3501 Rice St, Lihu'e) Not
local exactly, but still cheaper than the big boys at $33/175
per day/week.

No helmet laws and the wide, open roads
make motorcycle rentals, particularly Harley Davidsons, popular. You must have a
motorcycle license or endorsement; you
might need previous Harley experience to
rent one. Rates hover around $100/170 for
10/24 hours:

Hawaiian Riders (Map pp168-9; ☎ 742-9888; www
.hawaiianriders.com; 2320 Po'ipu Rd, Po'ipu) Also rents
mopeds (per day $50).
Street Eagle (Map p76; ☎ 241-7020, 877-212-9253;
www.streeteagle.com; 3-1866 Kaumuali'i Hwy, Lihu'e)
Two Wheels (Map p76; ☎ 246-9457; www.2wheels
.com; 3486 Rice St, Lihu'e)

Road Conditions & Hazards
While a two-lane highway is much sim-
pler to navigate than the multilane network
on the US mainland, Kaua'i driving can
nevertheless be hazardous. Highways are
rarely wide and straight, and speeding is a
growing problem. Kaua'i sees about 10 fatal
car crashes per year, most due to speeding.
Nighttime driving is tricky, with few street
lamps and winding, narrow roads. Drivers
under the influence of alcohol, marijuana
or 'ice' (crystal methamphetamine) are a
hazard, no matter if it's 11am or 11pm. The
crime of driving while intoxicated (DWI)
is legally defined as having a blood alcohol
level greater than 0.08%.

Sections of roads and bridges can be
washed out during heavy downpours. Particularly prone areas include the North
Shore bridges and anywhere near rivers
and streams. In rain or shine, stay alert for
one-lane-bridge crossings; heed the advice
on p141. Whenever there's no sign on one-
lane stretches, downhill traffic must yield
to uphill traffic.

Driving on rough, often-muddy, remote
4WD-only roads is not for the timid. Conditions are hazardous and you'll probably
be miles from any help or even cell phone
access. If you have never driven a 4WD
vehicle, don't do your trial run here.

Locals typically call highways by common nicknames rather than by number.
Memorize them:

Hwy 50 Kaumuali'i Hwy.
Hwy 51 Kapule Hwy.
Hwy 56 Kuhio Hwy.
Hwy 58 Nawiliwili Rd.
Hwy 560 Kuhio Hwy.
Hwy 520 Maluhia Rd (Tree Tunnel) and Po'ipu Rd.
Hwy 530 Koloa Rd.
Hwy 540 Halewili Rd.
Hwy 550 Waimea Canyon Dr.
Hwy 552 Koke'e Rd.
Hwy 570 Ahukini Rd.
Hwy 580 Kuamo'o Rd.
Hwy 581 Kamalu Rd and Olohena Rd.
Hwy 583 Ma'alo Rd.

Road Rules
As in mainland US, drivers keep to the
right-hand side of the road. On unpaved
or poorly paved roads, however, locals tend
to hog the middle stripe until an oncoming
car approaches.

Drivers at a red light can turn right after
coming to a full stop and yielding to oncoming traffic, unless there is a sign at the
intersection prohibiting the turn. Island
drivers will usually just wait for the next
green light.

Locals will tell you there are three golden
rules for driving on the islands: don't honk
your horn, don't follow too closely and let
faster drivers pass whenever it's safe to do
so. Play by the rules and drivers express
their *mahalo* (thanks) by waving the *shaka*
(local hand greeting) sign. Horn honking is
considered rude unless absolutely necessary
for safety.

Hawaii requires the use of seat belts for
drivers and front-seat passengers. Heed
this, as the penalty is stiff. State law also
strictly requires the use of child-safety seats

TRANSPORTATION

TRANSPORTATION

for children aged three and under, while four-year-olds must either be in a safety seat or secured by a seat belt. Most car-rental companies lease child-safety seats for around $5 a day, but they don't always have them on hand; reserve one in advance if you can.

Speed limits are posted *and* enforced. If you're stopped for speeding, expect a ticket, as the police rarely give only warnings. Most accidents are caused by excessive speed.

HITCHHIKING

Hitchhiking, though technically illegal state-wide, is not unusual (and cops have more important matters at hand). It can be an efficient, cheap way to get around, espe-cially along well-trafficked highways, such as Kuhio Hwy from Lihu'e to the North Shore. Riders often reach their destination in stages, snagging a ride from Lihu'e to Kapa'a, another from Kapa'a to Kilauea and so on. The Princeville Center is a popular hitchhiking spot, and it's relatively easy to find rides to the end of the road.

That said, hitchhiking is risky anywhere in the world. Hitchhikers should size up each situation carefully before getting in cars, and women should be especially wary of hitching alone. If you do hitchhike, travel in pairs and let someone know where you plan to go.

TAXI

Locals rarely use taxicabs so you'll find only a dozen companies. Fares are based on mileage regardless of the number of passengers. Since cabs are often station wagons or minivans, they're good value for groups (and strongly recommended if the designated driver joins in the partying). The bonus: cab drivers are typically locals who are familiar with the island and often act as tour guides. It's easy to find a cab at the airport during normal business hours, but cabs don't run all night or cruise for passengers; in town (and at most hotels) you'll need to call ahead. Pick-ups from remote locations (eg after long through-hikes) can be arranged by calling, and pos-sibly paying, in advance.

Taxis charge $2 at flag fall and $2 per sub-sequent mile, metered in 25¢ increments.

Taxi companies include **Akiko's Taxi** (☎ 822-7588), in the Lihu'e-Kapa'a area; **North Shore Cab** (☎ 826-4118; www.northshorecab.com), based in Princeville; and **Southshore Cab** (☎ 742-1525), in Po'ipu.

Health Dr David Goldberg

Kaua'i encompasses a wide range of climates and terrains, but none is especially severe or requires special gear. The greatest threats are drowning and car accidents, both of which can be avoided by prudence. The high level of hygiene here means that infectious diseases are not a significant concern for most travelers.

BEFORE YOU GO

INSURANCE

The US offers possibly the finest health care in the world. The problem is that, unless you have good insurance, it can be prohibitively expensive. It's essential to purchase travel health insurance if your regular policy doesn't cover you when you're abroad.

Bring any medications you may need in their original containers, clearly labeled. A signed, dated letter from your physician that describes all medical conditions and medications, including generic names, is also a good idea.

If your health insurance does not cover you for medical expenses abroad, consider supplemental insurance. Find out in advance if your insurance plan will make payments directly to providers or reimburse you later for overseas health expenditures.

RECOMMENDED VACCINATIONS

No special vaccines are required or recommended for travel to the US. All travelers should be up-to-date on routine immunizations, listed below.

INTERNET RESOURCES

There is a wealth of travel health advice on the Internet. The World Health Organization publishes a superb book, called *International Travel and Health,* which is revised annually and is available online at no cost at www.who.int/ith. Another website of general interest is MD Travel Health at www.mdtravelhealth.com, which provides complete travel health recommendations for every country, updated daily, also at no cost.

It's usually a good idea to consult your government's travel-health website before departure, if one is available:

Australia (www.smartraveller.gov.au)
Canada (www.hc-sc.gc.ca/english/index.html)
UK (www.dh.gov.uk/PolicyAndGuidance/HealthAdvice ForTravellers/fs/en)
US (www.cdc.gov/travel)

RECOMMENDED VACCINATIONS

Vaccine	Recommended for	Dosage	Side effects
tetanus-diphtheria	all travelers who haven't had booster within 10 years	one dose lasts 10 years	soreness at injection site
measles	travelers born after 1956 who've had only one measles vaccination	one dose	fever; rash; joint pains; allergic reactions
chicken pox	travelers who've never had chicken pox	two doses a month apart	fever; mild case of chicken pox
influenza	all travelers during flu season (Nov–Mar)	one dose	soreness at injection site; fever

---

MEDICAL CHECKLIST

- acetaminophen (eg Tylenol) or aspirin
- anti-inflammatory drugs (eg ibuprofen)
- antihistamines (for hay fever and allergic reactions)
- antibacterial ointment (eg Neosporin) for cuts and abrasions
- steroid cream or cortisone (for poison ivy and other allergic rashes)
- bandages, gauze, gauze rolls
- adhesive or paper tape
- scissors, safety pins, tweezers
- thermometer
- pocket knife
- DEET-containing insect repellent for the skin
- permethrin-containing insect spray for clothing, tents and bed nets
- sunblock

ON KAUA'I

AVAILABILITY & COST OF HEALTH CARE

For immediate medical assistance, call ☎ 911. In general, if you have a medical emergency, the best bet is to find the nearest hospital and go to its emergency room. If the problem isn't urgent, you can call a nearby hospital and ask for a referral to a local physician, which is usually much cheaper than a trip to the emergency room. Keep in mind that medical helicopter evacuation may not always be possible from remote areas. The only major hospital, the **Wilcox Memorial Hospital** (Map p76; ☎ 245-1010, TTY 245-1133; 3420 Kuhio Hwy, Lihu'e), is located in Lihu'e.

Pharmacies in Hawaii are abundantly supplied, but you may find that some medications that are available over-the-counter in your home country require a prescription in the USA. And, as always, if you don't have insurance to cover the cost of prescriptions, they can often be shockingly expensive.

INFECTIOUS DISEASES

In addition to the more common ailments, there are several infectious diseases that are unknown or uncommon outside of the mainland. Most are acquired by mosquito or tick bites, or environmental exposure. Currently Hawaii is rabies-free.

Dengue Fever

Dengue is transmitted by aedes mosquitoes, which bite mostly during the daytime and are usually found close to human habitations, often indoors. They breed primarily in artificial water containers such as jars, barrels, cans, cisterns, metal drums, plastic containers and discarded tires. Thus, dengue is especially common in densely populated, urban areas. In Hawaii the last outbreak was in 2002; Kaua'i's last cases occurred in 2001. For updates, check the website of the **Hawaii State Department of Health** (www.state.hi.us/doh).

Dengue usually causes flulike symptoms, including fever, muscle aches, joint pains, headaches, nausea and vomiting, often followed by a rash. There is no treatment for dengue except taking analgesics such as acetaminophen/paracetamol (eg Tylenol) – don't take aspirin as it increases the likelihood of hemorrhaging – and drink plenty of fluids. See a doctor to be diagnosed and monitored. Severe cases may require hospitalization for intravenous fluids and care. There is no vaccine. The key to prevention is insect-protection measures (see p242).

Giardiasis

This parasitic infection of the small intestine occurs throughout the world. Symptoms may include nausea, bloating, cramps and diarrhea, and may last for weeks. To protect yourself, you should avoid drinking directly from waterfalls, ponds, streams and rivers, which may be contaminated by animal or human feces. The infection can also be transmitted from person to person if proper hand washing is not done. Giardiasis is easily diagnosed by a stool test and readily treated with antibiotics.

Leptospirosis

Leptospirosis is acquired by exposure to water contaminated by the urine of infected animals such as rats, mongooses and feral pigs. Outbreaks often occur at times of flooding, when sudden overflow may contaminate water sources downstream from animal habitats. Even an idyllic waterfall may, in fact, be infected with leptospirosis. The initial symptoms, which resemble a mild flu, usually subside in a few days, but a minority of cases are complicated by jaundice or meningitis. It can also cause hepatitis and renal failure, which might be fatal. Diagnosis is through blood tests and the disease is easily treated with doxycycline. There is no vaccine. You can minimize your risk by staying out of bodies of fresh water (eg waterfalls, pools, streams) that may be contaminated, especially if you have any open cuts or sores. Because hikers account for many of the cases of leptospirosis in Hawaii, the state posts warning signs at trailheads. If you're camping, water purification is essential.

West Nile Virus

These infections were unknown in the US until a few years ago, but have now been reported in almost every state. Humans in Hawaii have not been affected so far, but the rising number of reported cases in California is cause for concern. The virus is transmitted by culex mosquitoes, which are active in late summer and early fall and generally bite after dusk. Most infections are mild or asymptomatic, but the virus may infect the central nervous system causing fever, headache, confusion, lethargy, coma and sometimes death. There is no treatment.

For the latest update on the areas affected by West Nile, go to the **US Geological Survey website** (http://westnilemaps.usgs.gov).

For protection measures against mosquito bites see p242.

ENVIRONMENTAL HAZARDS
Bites & Stings

There is no established wild snake population on Kaua'i.

Leeches are found in humid rain-forest areas. They do not transmit any disease but their bites are often intensely itchy for weeks afterwards and can easily become infected. Apply an iodine-based antiseptic to any leech bite to help prevent infection.

Bee and wasp stings mainly cause problems for people who are allergic to them. Anyone with a serious bee or wasp allergy should carry an injection of adrenaline for

emergency treatment. For others pain is the main problem – apply ice to the sting and take painkillers.

Commonsense approaches to these concerns are the most effective: wear long sleeves and pants, hats and shoes (rather than sandals) to protect yourself.

MAMMAL BITES

Do not attempt to pet, handle or feed any animal, with the exception of domestic animals known to be free of any infectious disease. Most animal injuries are directly related to a person's attempt to touch or feed the animal.

Any bite or scratch by a mammal, including bats or feral pigs, goats etc, should be promptly and thoroughly cleansed with large amounts of soap and water, followed by application of an antiseptic such as iodine or alcohol. It may also be advisable to start an antibiotic, since wounds caused by animal bites and scratches frequently become infected.

MARINE ANIMALS

Marine spikes, such as those found on sea urchins, scorpion fish and Hawaiian lionfish, can cause severe local pain. If this occurs, immediately immerse the affected area in hot water (as high a temperature as can be tolerated). Keep topping up with hot water until the pain subsides and medical care can be reached. The same advice applies if you are stung by a cone shell.

Marine stings from jellyfish and Portuguese man-of-war (aka 'bluebottles,' which have translucent, bluish, bladder-like floats) also occur. Even touching a bluebottle a few hours after it's washed up onshore can result in burning stings. Jellyfish are often seen eight to 10 days after a full moon when they float into shallow waters; the influx usually lasts for three days. If you are stung, first aid consists of washing the skin with vinegar to prevent further discharge of remaining stinging cells, followed by rapid transfer to a hospital; antivenoms are widely available.

Despite extensive media coverage, the risk of shark attack in Hawaiian waters is no greater than in other countries with extensive coastlines. Avoid swimming in waters with runoff after heavy rainfall (eg around river mouths) and those areas frequented by commercial fishing operators. Do not swim if you

HEALTH

are actively bleeding, as this attracts sharks. Check with lifeguards about local risks. Keep in mind that your chances of being hit by a falling coconut on the beach are greater than those of a shark attack, though!

MOSQUITO BITES

When traveling in areas where mosquito-borne illnesses have been reported, keep yourself covered and apply a good insect repellent, preferably one containing DEET, to exposed skin and clothing. In general, adults and children over 12 should use preparations containing 25% to 35% DEET, which usually lasts about six hours. Children between two and 12 years of age should use preparations containing no more than 10% DEET, applied sparingly, which will usually last about three hours. Neurologic toxicity has been reported from DEET, especially in children, but appears to be extremely uncommon and generally related to overuse. DEET-containing compounds should not be used on children under the age of two.

Insect repellents containing certain botanical products, including oil of eucalyptus and soybean oil, are effective but last only 1½ to two hours. Products based on citronella are not effective.

Visit the website of the **Center for Disease Control** (CDC; www.cdc.gov/ncidod/dvbid/westnile/qa/prevention.htm) for prevention information.

SPIDER BITES

Although there are many species of spiders in the US, the only ones that cause significant human illness are the black widow, brown recluse and hobo spiders. It is a matter of debate which of these species are conclusively found in Hawaii. The black widow is black or brown in color, measuring about 15mm in body length, with a shiny top, fat body, and distinctive red or orange hourglass figure on its underside. It's found usually in woodpiles, sheds, harvested crops and bowls of outdoor toilets. The brown recluse spider is brown in color, usually 10mm in body length, with a dark violin-shaped mark on the top of the upper section of the body. It is active mostly at night, lives in dark sheltered areas such as under porches and in woodpiles, and typically bites when trapped. The symptoms of a hobo-spider bite are similar to those of a brown recluse, but milder.

If bitten by a black widow, you should apply ice or cold packs and go immediately to the nearest emergency room. Complications of a black widow bite may include muscle spasms, breathing difficulties and high blood pressure. The bite of a brown recluse or hobo spider typically causes a large, inflamed wound, sometimes associated with fever and chills. If bitten, apply ice and see a physician.

Diving & Snorkeling Hazards

Divers, snorkelers and surfers should seek specialized advice before travel to ensure their medical kit contains treatment for coral cuts and tropical ear infections, as well as the standard problems. Divers should ensure their insurance covers them for decompression illness – get specialized dive insurance through an organization such as **Divers Alert Network** (DAN; www.diversalertnetwork.org). Have a dive medical before you leave your home country – there are certain medical conditions that are incompatible with diving that your dive operator may not ask you about.

See p55 for advice on ocean safety.

Heat

Travelers should drink plenty of fluids and avoid strenuous exercise when the temperature is high.

Dehydration is the main contributor to heat exhaustion. Symptoms include feeling weak, headaches, irritability, nausea or vomiting, sweaty skin, a fast, weak pulse and a normal or slightly elevated body temperature. Treatment involves getting out of the heat and/or sun, fanning the victim and applying cool wet cloths to the skin, laying the victim flat with their legs raised and rehydrating with water containing one-quarter of a teaspoon of salt per liter. Recovery is usually rapid and it is common to feel weak for some days afterwards.

Heatstroke is a serious medical emergency. Symptoms come on suddenly and include weakness, nausea, a hot, dry body with a body temperature of over 106°F, dizziness, confusion, loss of coordination, fits and eventually collapse and loss of consciousness. Seek medical help and commence cooling by getting the person out of the heat, removing their clothes, fanning them and applying cool, wet cloths or ice to their body, especially to the groin and armpits.

Language

Hawaii has two official state languages: English and Hawaiian. Although English has long replaced Hawaiian as the dominant language, many Hawaiian words and phrases are commonly used in speech and in print.

Prior to the arrival of Christian missionaries in 1820, the Hawaiians had no written language. Knowledge was passed on through complex oral genealogies, stories, chants, songs and descriptive place names. The missionaries rendered the spoken language into the Roman alphabet and established the first presses in the islands, which were used to print the Bible and other religious instructional materials in Hawaiian.

Throughout the 19th century, as more and more foreigners (particularly the Americans and the British) settled in the islands, the everyday use of Hawaiian declined. In the 1890s, English was made the official language of government and education.

The push for statehood, from 1900 to 1959, added to the decline of the Hawaiian language. Speaking Hawaiian was seen as a deterrent to American assimilation, thus adult native speakers were strongly discouraged from teaching their children Hawaiian as the primary language in the home.

This attitude remained until the early 1970s when the Hawaiian community began to experience a cultural renaissance. A handful of young Hawaiians lobbied to establish Hawaiian language classes at the University of Hawai'i, and Hawaiian language immersion preschools followed in the 1980s. These preschools are modeled after Maori *kohanga reo* (language nests), where the primary method of language perpetuation is through speaking and hearing the language on a daily basis. In Hawaii's 'Aha Punana Leo preschools, all learning and communication takes place in the mother tongue – *ka 'olelo makuahine.*

Hawaiian has now been revived from the point of extinction and is growing throughout the community. Record numbers of students enroll in Hawaiian language classes in high schools and colleges, and immersion school graduates are raising a new generation of native speakers.

If you'd like to discover more about the Hawaiian language, get a copy of Lonely Planet's *South Pacific Phrasebook.*

PRONUNCIATION

Written Hawaiian has just 13 letters: five vowels (**a, e, i, o, u**) and seven consonants (**h, k, l, m, n, p, w**). The letters **h, l, m** and **n** are pronounced much the same as in English. Usually every letter in Hawaiian words is pronounced. Each vowel has a different pronunciation depending on whether it is stressed or unstressed.

Consonants

p/k	similar to English, but with less aspiration; **k** may be replaced with **t**
w	after **i** and **e**, usually a soft English 'v;' thus the town of Hale'iwa is pronounced 'Haleiva,' After **u** or **o** it's often like English 'w,' thus Olowalu is pronounced as written. After **a** or at the beginning of a word it can be as English 'w' or 'v,' thus you'll hear both Hawai'i and Havai'i (The Big Island).

Unstressed vowels (without macron)

a	as in 'ago'
e	as in 'bet'
i	as the 'y' in 'city'
o	as in 'sole'
u	as in 'rude'

Glottal Stops & Macrons

Written Hawaiian uses both glottal stops ('), called *'okina*, and macrons (a straight bar above a vowel, eg **ā**), called *kahako*. In modern print both the glottal stop and the macron are often omitted. In this guidebook, the macrons have been omitted, but glottal stops have been included, as they can be helpful in striving to pronounce common place names and words correctly.

The glottal stop indicates a break between two vowels, producing an effect similar to saying 'oh-oh' in English. For example, *'a'a*, a type of lava, is pronounced 'ah-ah,' and Ho'okena, a place name, is pronounced 'Ho-oh-kena.' A macron inidicates that the vowel is stressed and has a long pronunciation.

Glottal stops and macrons not only affect pronunciation, but can give a word a completely different meaning. For example, *ai* (with no glottal) means 'sexual intercourse,' but *'ai* (with the glottal) means 'food.' Similarly, the word *ka'a* (with no macron over the second **a**) means 'to roll, turn or twist,' but *ka'ā* (with a macron over the second **a**) is a thread or line, used in fishing.

Compound Words

In the written form, many Hawaiian words are compound words made up of several different words. For example, the word *humuhumunukunukuapua'a* can be broken down as follows: *humuhumu-nukunuku-a-pua'a* (literally, trigger fish with a snout like a pig,' meaning 'the fish with a snout like a pig.' The place name Waikiki is also a compound word: *wai-kiki* (literally, freshwater sprouting), referring to the freshwater swamps once found in the area. Some words are doubled to emphasize their meaning, much like in English. For example, *wiki* means 'quick,' while *wikiwiki* means 'very quick.'

Common Hawaiian Words

For more Hawaiian words, see the Glossary on p245.

aloha – love, hello, welcome, goodbye
hale – house
heiau – religious temple
kane – man
kapu – taboo, restricted
luau – traditional Hawaiian feast
mahalo – thank you
mahimahi – dolphin fish, popular in restaurants
mauka – a directional, toward the mountains
makai – a directional, toward the sea
'ono – delicious, tasty
pau – finished, completed
poi – staple food made from taro
ukulele – four-stringed musical instrument, used in modern Hawaiian music (literally, 'leaping flea,' because of the action of the fingers when playing)
wahine – woman

PIDGIN

Hawaii pidgin is a distinct language, spoken by over 500,000 people. It developed on sugar plantations where the *luna* (foreman) had to communicate with field laborers from many foreign countries. Early plantation pidgin used a very minimal and condensed form of English as the root language, to which elements from Cantonese, Hawaiian and Portuguese were added. It became the second language of first-generation immigrants and many Hawaiians.

As this English-based pidgin evolved, it took on its own grammatical structure and syntax. Many words were pronounced differently and combined in ways not found in English. Rather than a careless or broken form of English, it evolved into a separate language, called Hawaii Creole by linguists.

Today, there is ongoing controversy about the validity of pidgin, with opponents saying that it erodes standard English and becomes a barrier to social and educational advancement. Proponents argue that pidgin is a rich and vibrant language that should not be looked down upon or banned from schools, and that pidgin speakers are often unjustly seen as less intelligent.

In recent years much poetry and many award-winning plays and books have been written in pidgin by local authors who are passionate in their determination to keep pidgin alive in the community. See the Culture chapter (p44) for more on pidgin and Hawaii literature.

Common Pidgin Words & Phrases

brah – shortened form of *bradah* (brother); also used as 'hey you'
broke da mout – delicious, as in 'My auntie make *broke da mout kine* fish!'
buggahs – guys, as in 'Da buggahs went to without me!'
bumbye – later on, as in 'We go movies *bumbye den* (then)'
bummahs – bummer; an expression of disappointment or regret
chicken skin – goose bumps
cockaroach – to steal, as in 'Who went *cockaroach* my *slippahs*?'
da kine – whatchamacallit; used whenever you can't think of the word you want
Fo' real? – Really? Are you kidding me?
funny kine – strange or different, as in 'He stay *acking* (acting) all *funny kine*.'
geev 'um – Go for it! Give it all you got!
Howzit? – Hi, how's it going? As in 'Eh, *howzit brah*?'
How you stay? – How are you doing these days?
kay den – 'OK then,' as in '*Kay den*, we go beach'
laydahs – Later on. I'll see you later, as in, '*Kay den, laydahs.*'
no ack – (Literally, 'no act.') Stop showing off, cool it.
rubbah slippahs – (rubber) thongs, flip-flops
talk story – any kind of casual conversation
to da max – a suffix that adds emphasis to something, as in '*Da waves* was big *to da max*!'

Glossary

For food and drink terms, see p72.

'a'a – type of lava that is rough and jagged, and flows slowly
'ahinahina – silversword plant with pointed silver leaves
ahu – stone cairns used to mark a trail; or an altar or shrine
ahupua'a – traditional land division, usually in a wedge shape that extends from the mountains to the sea
aikane – friend; also refers to homosexuality
'aina – land
'akala – Hawaiian raspberry; also called a thimbleberry
akamai – clever
'akepa – endangered honeycreeper
akua – god, spirit, idol
'alae ke'oke'o – endangered Hawaiian coot
alaia – shorter, stand-up surfboard
'alala – Hawaiian crow
ali'i – chief, royalty
aloha – the traditional greeting meaning love, welcome, good-bye
aloha 'aina – love of the land
'amakihi – small, yellow-green bird; one of the more common native birds
anchialine pool – contains a mixture of seawater and fresh water
'a'o – Newell's shearwater (a seabird)
'apapane – bright-red native Hawaiian honeycreeper
'aumakua – protective deity; deified ancestor

'elepaio – a brownish native bird with a white rump, found in the understory of native forests

goza – roll-up straw mat used at beaches and parks

hala – pandanus tree; the *lau* (leaves) are used in weaving mats and baskets
hale – house
hana – work; a bay, when used as a compound in place names
haole – Caucasian; literally, 'without breath'
hapa – portion or fragment; person of mixed blood
hau – indigenous lowland hibiscus tree whose wood is often used for making canoe outriggers (stabilizing arms that jut out from the hull)
Hawai'i nei – all the Hawaiian Islands taken as a group; indicates affection (ie 'beloved' or 'cherished' Hawai'i)
he'e nalu – surfing (literally, 'wave sliding')
heiau – ancient stone temple, a place of worship in Hawaii

Hina – Polynesian goddess (wife of Ku, one of the four main gods)
hoaloha – friend
holoholo – to walk, drive or ramble around for pleasure
holua – sled or sled course
honu – turtle
honu'ea – hawksbill sea turtle
ho'olaule'a – celebration, party
ho'onanea – to pass the time in ease, peace and pleasure
huhu – angry
hui – group, organization
hukilau – fishing with a seine (a large net), involving a group of people who pull in the net
hula – Hawaiian dance form, either traditional or modern
hula 'auana, hula 'auwana – modern hula, developed after the introduction of Western music
hula halau – hula school or troupe
hula kahiko – traditional (ancient) hula
hula ohelo – hula style in which some of the dancers' motions imitate sexual intercourse

'i'iwi – a bright-orange Hawaiian honeycreeper with a curved, salmon-colored beak
'iliahi – Hawaiian sandalwood
'ili'ili – smooth pebbles
'ilima – native coastal plant, a ground cover with delicate yellow-orange flowers
'io – Hawaiian hawk
issei – first-generation Japanese immigrants

kahili – a feathered standard, used as a symbol of royalty
kahuna – knowledgeable person in any field; commonly a priest, healer or sorcerer
kahuna nui – high priest
kaku – barracuda
kama'aina – person born and raised in Hawaii; literally, 'child of the land'
kanaka – man, human being, person
kanaka maoli – pure-blooded Native Hawaiian person
Kanaloa – god of the underworld
kane/Kane – man; also the name of one of four main Hawaiian gods
kapa – cloth made by pounding the inner bark of the paper mulberry tree, used for early Hawaiian clothing (*tapa* in Tahitian)
kapu – taboo, part of strict ancient Hawaiian social and religious system
kaukau wagon – lunch wagon
kauna'oa – a parasitic groundcover vine with yellow-orange tendrils; used to make lei

kava – see *'awa*

keiki – child, offspring

ki – see *ti*

kiawe – Algoraba tree, a relative of the mesquite tree introduced to Hawaii in the 1820s, now very common; its branches are covered with sharp thorns

ki'i – see *tiki*

kiko'o – longer, stand-up surfboard

kilau – a stiff, weedy fern

kioe – small surfboard, belly board (2ft to 4ft long)

kipuka – an area of land spared when lava flows around it; an oasis

ko – sugarcane

koa – native hardwood tree often used in making furniture, bowls and canoes

ko'a – fishing shrine

kohola – whale

koi – brightly colored, ornamental Japanese carp

koki'o ke'oke'o – native Hawaiian white hibiscus tree

kokua – help, cooperation

kona – leeward side; a leeward wind

konane – a strategy game similar to checkers

ko'olau – windward side

Ku – Polynesian god of many manifestations, including god of war, farming and fishing (husband of Hina)

kukui – candlenut tree and the official state tree; its oily nuts were once burned in lamps

kupuna – grandparent, elder

ku'ula – a stone idol placed at fishing shrines, believed to attract fish

Laka – goddess of the *hula*

lama – native plant in the persimmon family

lanai – porch or veranda

lau – leaf

lauhala – leaves of the *hala* plant used in weaving

lei – garland, usually of flowers, but also of leaves or shells

limu – seaweed (*ogo* in Japanese)

lo'i – irrigated terrace, usually for *kalo* (taro)

loko i'a – fish pond

lolo – feeble-minded, crazy

lomi – to rub, soften, press or squeeze; *lomilomi* salmon is a dish of minced, salted salmon, diced tomatoes and green onion

Lono – Polynesian god of harvest, agriculture, fertility and peace

loulu – all species of native fan palms

luakini – a type of *heiau* (temple) dedicated to the war god Ku and used for human sacrifices

luau – traditional Hawaiian feast; modern term, formerly called *'aha'aina*

mahalo – thank you

mahele – to divide; usually refers to the Western-influenced land divisions of 1848

ma'i ho'oka'awale – leprosy; literally, 'the separating sickness'

maile – native plant with twining habit and fragrant sap; often used to make lei

maka'ainana – commoners; literally, 'people who tend the land'

makaha – a sluice gate, used to regulate the level of water in a fish pond

makahiki – traditional annual wet-season winter festival dedicated to the agricultural god Lono

makai – toward the sea

malama 'aina – to take care of the islands' natural resources

malihini – newcomer, visitor

malo – loincloth

mamane – a native tree with bright-yellow flowers; used to make lei

mana – spiritual power

manini – convict tang (a reef fish); also used to refer to something small or insignificant, or someone who is stingy

mano – shark

mauka – toward the mountains; inland

mele – song, chant

menehune – the 'little people' who built many of Hawaii's fishponds, *heiau* and other stonework, according to legend

milo – a native shade tree with beautiful hardwood

moa pahe'e – a game, similar to *'ulu maika*, using wooden darts and spears

mokihana – an endemic tree or shrub, with scented green berries used to make lei

mo'o – serpent, dragon, lizard, reptile

mu – a 'body catcher' who secured sacrificial victims for the *heiau* altar

mu'umu'u – a long, loose-fitting dress introduced by the missionaries

naupaka – a native shrub with delicate white flowers

Neighbor Islands – the term used to refer to the main Hawaiian Islands other than O'ahu

nene – a native goose; Hawaii's state bird

nisei – second-generation Japanese immigrants

niu – coconut palm

nui – large, great, many, much; *aloha nui loa* means very much aloha

nuku pu'u – a native honeycreeper with a bright yellow-green underbelly

'ohana – family, extended family

'ohi'a lehua – native Hawaiian tree with tufted, feathery, pom-pom-like flowers

'okole – buttocks

olo – traditional longer, wooden surfboard

one hanau – birthplace, homeland

pahoehoe – type of lava that is smooth and undulating, and flows quickly

pakalolo – marijuana; literally, 'crazy tobacco'

palaka – Hawaiian-style plaid shirt made from sturdy cotton

pali – cliff

palila – endemic honeycreeper

paniolo – cowboy

pau – finished, no more

Pele – goddess of volcanoes; her home is Halema'uma'u Crater in Kilauea Caldera

piko – navel, umbilical cord

pili – a bunchgrass, commonly used for thatching houses

pilo – native shrub in the coffee family

pohaku – rock

pohuehue – morning glory

Poliahu – goddess of snow

po'ouli – endangered endemic honeycreeper

pua aloalo – a hibiscus flower

pueo – Hawaiian owl

puhi – eel

pu'ili – bamboo sticks used in hula performances

puka – any kind of hole or opening; small shells that are made into necklaces

pukiawe – native plant with red and white berries and evergreen leaves; used to make lei

pulu – golden, silky 'hair' found at the base of *hapu'u* (tree fern) fiddlehead stems

pupu – snack food, hors d'oeuvres; also Hawaiian word for shell

pu'u – hill, cinder cone

pu'uhonua – place of refuge

raku – a style of Japanese pottery characterized by a rough, handmade appearance

sansei – third-generation Japanese immigrants

shaka – hand gesture used in Hawaii as a greeting or sign of local pride

tabi – Japanese reef-walking shoes

talk story – to strike up a conversation, make small talk

tapa – see *kapa*

ti – common native plant; its long shiny leaves are used for wrapping food and making hula skirts;

tiki – image, statue (often of a deity)

tutu – grandmother or grandfather; also term of respect for any member of that generation

'ua'u – dark-rumped petrel, an endangered sea bird

ukulele – a stringed musical instrument derived from the *braguinha,* which was introduced to Hawaii in the late 19th century by Portuguese immigrants

'ulu maika – ancient Hawaiian bowling game using stones

wahine – woman

wikiwiki – hurry, quick

wiliwili – the lightest of the native woods, balsa-like

zazen – Zen meditation

zendo – communal Zen meditation hall

Behind the Scenes

THIS BOOK

This first edition of *Kaua'i* was written by Luci Yamamoto. It was commissioned in Lonely Planet's Oakland office, and produced in Melbourne by the following:

Commissioning Editor Emily K Wolman
Coordinating Editor Brooke Lyons
Coordinating Cartographer Owen Eszeki
Coordinating Layout Designer Carol Jackson
Managing Editor Brigitte Ellemor
Managing Cartographers Alison Lyall, Emma McNicol, Andrew Smith
Assisting Editors Helen Christinis, Andrea Dobbin, Emma Gilmour, Katie Lynch, Kate McLeod, Alan Murphy, Maryanne Netto, Kate Whitfield
Assisting Layout Designers Yvonne Bischofberger, Jim Hsu, Wibowo Rusli, Christine Wieser
Cover Designer James Hardy
Color Designer Jacqui Saunders
Project Manager Sarah Sloane
Language Content Coordinator Quentin Frayne

Thanks to Raphael Richards, Sally Darmody, Celia Wood, Mark Germanchis, Glenn van der Kniff, Suzannah Shwer, Helen Christinis, Katie Lynch, Kate McDonald

THANKS
LUCI YAMAMOTO

Mahalo nui loa to Lonely Planet commissioning editor Emily Wolman for guiding my initiatory first-edition book with patience and enthusiasm; and to my fellow LP authors Sam Benson, Conner Gorry, Ned Friary and Glenda Bendure, whose prior work on Kaua'i was invaluable. This book owes much to Na Ala Hele's Craig Koga, a Kaua'i native who is the best example of *kama'aina* that I know. I am grateful to Jon Letman for his sharp insights and humor; to Richard Sugiyama, my Kapa'a expert (I owe you a shave ice); to Dennis Fujimoto, my informative source at *The Garden Island*; to Michael Locey for generously sharing his Hawaiian culture; to specialist authors Nanette Napoleon *(hana hou!)* and David Boynton; and to Karen Christensen at UC Berkeley for accommodating my life as a writer. To the locals and tourists whom I accosted and interviewed on the road, this one's for you. As always, thanks to my parents and Junko for standing by me through it all. To MJP – words fail me. *Aloha nui loa.*

OUR READERS

Many thanks to the travelers who used the last edition of *Hawaii* and wrote to us with helpful hints, useful advice and interesting anecdotes about Kaua'i:

Pierpaola Conte, Sara Elida Mills, Dario Frigo Walter Rask, Sara Rosier, Antonio Scarica, Ueli Schläpfer, Heidi Smith, Catherine Ulrich

ACKNOWLEDGEMENTS

Many thanks to the following for the use of their content:

Image of the Blair Estate Organic Farm – Les, Gigi and Jessica Drent

THE LONELY PLANET STORY

The story begins with a classic travel adventure: Tony and Maureen Wheeler's 1972 journey across Europe and Asia to Australia. There was no useful information about the overland trail then, so Tony and Maureen published the first Lonely Planet guidebook to meet a growing need.

From a kitchen table, Lonely Planet has grown to become the largest independent travel publisher in the world, with offices in Melbourne (Australia), Oakland (USA) and London (UK). Today Lonely Planet guidebooks cover the globe. There is an ever-growing list of books and information in a variety of media. Some things haven't changed. The main aim is still to make it possible for adventurous travelers to get out there – to explore and better understand the world.

At Lonely Planet we believe travelers can make a positive contribution to the countries they visit – if they respect their host communities and spend their money wisely. Every year 5% of company profit is donated to charities around the world.

SEND US YOUR FEEDBACK

We love to hear from travelers – your comments keep us on our toes and help make our books better. Our well-traveled team reads every word on what you loved or loathed about this book. Although we cannot reply individually to postal submissions, we always guarantee that your feedback goes straight to the appropriate authors, in time for the next edition. Each person who sends us information is thanked in the next edition – and the most useful submissions are rewarded with a free book.

To send us your updates – and find out about Lonely Planet events, newsletters and travel news – visit our award-winning website: **www.lonelyplanet.com/feedback**.

Note: We may edit, reproduce and incorporate your comments in Lonely Planet products such as guidebooks, websites and digital products, so let us know if you don't want your comments reproduced or your name acknowledged. For a copy of our privacy policy visit www.lonelyplanet.com/privacy.

Index

12am	1am	2am	3am	4am	5am	6am	7am	8am	9am	10am	11am	12pm

ARCTIC OCEAN

Mon / Sun

International Date Line

CHUKCHI SEA

Queen Elizabeth Is (Can)

Ellesmere Is (Can)

BAFFIN BAY

GREENLAND SEA

Russia

BEAUFORT SEA

Banks Is (Can)

Victoria Is (Can)

Greenland (Denmark) 9am

NORWEGIAN SEA

Alaska (US)

5am

Baffin Is (Can)

11am

Iceland

NORTH SEA

3am

4am

HUDSON BAY

United Kingdom

BERING SEA

GULF OF ALASKA

Canada

LABRADOR SEA

Ireland

2am

6am

8am

NORTH ATLANTIC OCEAN

7am

8.30am

1am

Midway Is (US)

NORTH PACIFIC OCEAN

United States

Bermuda (UK)

Azores (Port)

Portugal Spain

Hawaii (US)

Morocco

Mexico

GULF OF MEXICO

The Bahamas

Canary Is (Sp)

Cuba

Mauritania Mali

Guatemala

Haiti

Cape Verde

12pm

Nicaragua

CARIBBEAN SEA

Eastern Caribbean Islands

Senegal Burkina Guinea Faso

Panama

Venezuela Guyana

Liberia Ghana

EQUATOR

Kiribati

Galapagos Is (Ecuador)

Colombia Suriname

GULF OF GUINEA

Ecuador

Samoa

Ascension (UK)

2.30am

8am

Peru

Brazil 9am

Tonga

12am

Cook Is (NZ)

Tahiti French Polynesia (Fr)

7am

Bolivia

SOUTH ATLANTIC OCEAN

2am

Pitcairn Is (UK) 3.30am

Easter Is (Chile)

Paraguay

1am

Chile

Uruguay

New Zealand

Argentina

Tristan da Cunha (UK)

12.45am

Chatham Is (NZ)

SOUTH PACIFIC OCEAN

Gough Is (UK)

Falkland Is (UK)

South Georgia & South Sandwich Is (UK)

Bouvet Is (Norway)

12am	1am	2am	3am	4am	5am	6am	7am	8am	9am	10am	11am	12pm

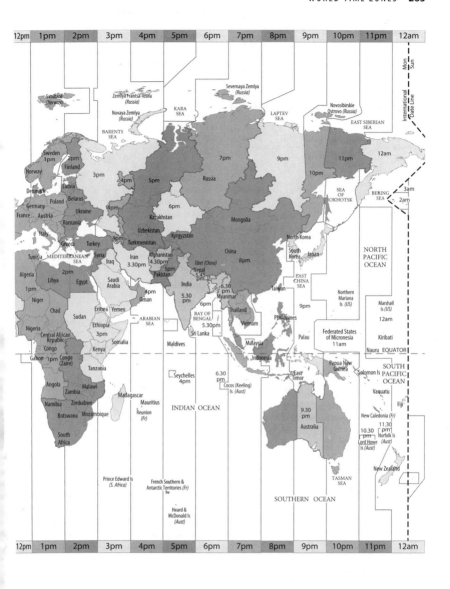

12pm	1pm	2pm	3pm	4pm	5pm	6pm	7pm	8pm	9pm	10pm	11pm	12am

Mon
Sun

International Date Line

Svalbard (Norway)

Zemlya Frantsa-Iosifa (Russia)

Severnaya Zemlya (Russia)

Novaya Zemlya (Russia)

KARA SEA

LAPTEV SEA

Novosibirskie Ostrovo (Russia)

EAST SIBERIAN SEA

BARENTS SEA

Sweden 1pm
2pm
Finland
Norway
Latvia
Denmark
Germany Poland Belarus
France Austria Ukraine
Italy Romania
Greece Turkey
Tunisia MEDITERRANEAN SEA Syria
Algeria Libya Egypt
Niger
Chad Sudan
Nigeria
Central African Republic
Congo Gabon 1pm Congo (Zaire)
Angola
Namibia Zambia Malawi Mozambique
Botswana Zimbabwe
South Africa

3pm
4pm
4pm
4pm
2pm
1pm
Saudi Arabia
Eritrea Yemen
Ethiopia 3pm
Somalia
Kenya
Tanzania
Madagascar
Mauritius
Réunion (Fr)

5pm
6pm
Kazakhstan
Uzbekistan
Turkmenistan
Iran 3.30pm
Iraq
Afghanistan 4.30pm
5pm
Pakistan

7pm
Russia
Mongolia
China 8pm
Tibet (China)
Nepal 5.45
pm
India 5.30pm
6.30 pm Myanmar
Thailand
Vietnam
Maldives
Sri Lanka 5.30pm

9pm
North Korea
South Korea Japan
SEA OF OKHOTSK

10pm
11pm
12am

BERING SEA 3am
2am

NORTH PACIFIC OCEAN

EAST CHINA SEA

Taiwan
Philippines 9pm
Palau
Northern Mariana Is (US)
Marshall Is (US) 12am
Federated States of Micronesia 11am
Kiribati
Nauru EQUATOR

ARABIAN SEA

BAY OF BENGAL

Oman 4pm

Seychelles 4pm
Cocos (Keeling) Is (Aust) 6.30 pm

Malaysia
Indonesia
East Timor
Papua New Guinea
Solomon Is
SOUTH PACIFIC OCEAN
Vanuatu
Fiji
New Caledonia (Fr)
11.30 pm
10.30 pm Norfolk Is (Aust)
Lord Howe Is (Aust)

INDIAN OCEAN

Australia 9.30 pm

New Zealand

Prince Edward Is (S. Africa)
French Southern & Antarctic Territories (Fr)
Heard & McDonald Is (Aust)

TASMAN SEA

SOUTHERN OCEAN

12pm	1pm	2pm	3pm	4pm	5pm	6pm	7pm	8pm	9pm	10pm	11pm	12am

264

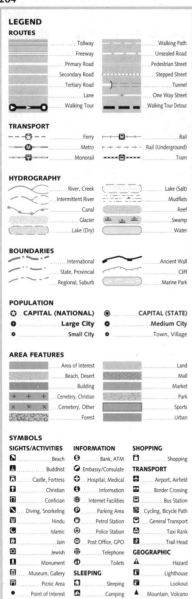